Muslim Minorities in Europe and India

Politics of Accommodation of Islamic Identities

Muslim Minorities in Europe and India

Politics of Accommodation of Islamic Identities

Edited by

Anwar Alam

Department of International Relations,
Zirve University, Gaziantep (Turkey)

and

Konrad Pędziwiatr

Department of European Studies,
Cracow University of Economics (Poland)

New Century Publications
New Delhi, India

NEW CENTURY PUBLICATIONS
4800/24, Bharat Ram Road,
Ansari Road, Daryaganj,
New Delhi - 110 002 (India)

Tel.: 011-2324 7798, 4358 7398, 6539 6605
Fax: 011-4101 7798
E-mail: indiatax@vsnl.com • info@newcenturypublications.com
www.newcenturypublications.com

Editorial office:
LG–7, Aakarshan Bhawan,
4754-57/23, Ansari Road, Daryaganj,
New Delhi – 110 002

Tel.: 011-4356 0919

First Published: **July 2016**

ISBN: **978-81-7708-430-6**

Published by New Century Publications and printed at Salasar Imaging Systems, New Delhi.

Designs: Patch Creative Unit, New Delhi.

PRINTED IN INDIA

About the Book

The issue of accommodation of religious minorities within the structure of nation-states has been a subject of intense discussions among scholars and policy makers across the world since the late 20th century. Most societies and nation-states in the world are either experiencing strains in accommodating the social, economic and political concerns of minority communities or facing difficulties in managing majority-minority relationship.

More than any other community, it is the integration of minority Muslim communities that has been the subject of global debates and deliberations, particularly in the western hemisphere. The emergence of political radicalism within some sections of Muslim communities in the West and a series of terrorist attacks has further compounded this problem. These developments have reinforced the pervasive thinking among a large section of non-Muslim host societies that Islam suffers from structural deficiencies for a meaningful integration in the host societies.

The edited volume is a collection of 14 scholarly articles including introduction, which deals with the problem of accommodation of Muslim minority communities in the European and Indian contexts. It interrogates the notion of modernity, Muslim modernity, secularism, pluralism and multiculturalism in both European and Indian settings. Linkages of religion, ethnicity and politics for the integration of Muslim minorities within the structure of nation-state are also explored in a cross-cultural comparative framework.

About the Editors

Anwar Alam teaches at the Department of International Relations, Zirve University, Gaziantep (Turkey). Earlier he was associated with Aligarh Muslim University, Jawaharlal Nehru University and Jamia Millia Islamia, New Delhi (India). Among others, he has been a recipient of the Alexander Von Humboldt Fellowship (Germany).

Konrad Pędziwiatr teaches at the Department of European Studies, Cracow University of Economics (Poland). He has been researching various aspects of Islam and migrations in Europe, Middle-East and North Africa in close collaboration with the Södertörn University (Sweden), Tischner European University and University of Warsaw (Poland).

Contents

Contributors

Hilal Ahmed is an Assistant Professor at Centre for the Study of Developing Societies, which is one of India's leading institutes for research in social sciences and humanities. Ahmed works on political Islam, Muslim modernities/representation, and politics of symbols in South Asia. His latest book *Muslim Political Discourse in Post-colonial India: Monuments, Memory, Contestation* (Routledge, 2014), looks at these thematic concerns to make sense of the nature of contemporary Muslim political discourse. As a Rajya Sabha Fellow (2015-16), Ahmed is currently working on the politics of Muslim political representation in post-colonial India and edits a *Hindi Reader* of Sudipta Kaviraj's writings. Ahmed was a Visiting Fellow, at Victoria University, Wellington (2013-14), Visiting Asia Fellow, University of Dhaka (2011) and Visiting Professor at University of Pune (2011). He has thought courses on political sociology (Victoria University, Wellington), History, Memory and Identity, and Research Methods and Identities: Issues and Debates in Post-colonial India (CSDS Teaching programme) and political science at the University of Delhi. He writes for journals, newspapers, and websites in English and Hindi and has produced two documentaries *Encountering the Political Jama Masjid* (2006) and *Images of Qutub Minar* (2015).

Anwar Alam is Professor at the Department of International Relations, Zirve University, Gaziantep, Turkey. Prior to this, he served as Professor and Director at the Centre for West Asian Studies, Jamia Millia Islamia (JMI) and Associate Professor, School of International Studies, Jawaharlal Nehru University (JNU), New Delhi. He has been awarded a number of long-term and short-term fellowships including Alexandor Von Humboldt Post-doctoral Fellowship, Germany (2004-2006). He was a visiting professor at Fatih University, Istanbul, Turkey (September 2010-August 2011). His latest publications include: *Arab Spring: Reflections on Political Changes in the Arab World* *and its Future* (ed., 2014), *India, Global Powers and West Asia: Political and Economic Dynamics* (ed., 2011) and *India and Iran: An Assessment of Contemporary Relations* (ed., 2011). Besides, he has contributed several articles in national and international referred journals and chapters in edited books. His recent articles include, "Emergence of Muslim Middle Class in Post-Independence India and its Political Orientations" in *Journal of Muslim Minority Affairs* (Volume 35/1, 2015), "The Arab Spring: A View From India" in *Routledge Handbook of the Arab Spring: Rethinking Democratisation* (2014) and "Islam and Violence" in *GITAM Journal of Gandhian Studies* (Volume 3/1, 2014). His area of research interests includes international politics, political theory, religion and politics, political Islam, globalisation and Muslim society.

Katayoun Alidadi is a research fellow at the Max Planck Institute for Social Anthropology, Halle, Germany. Her research focuses on human rights, non-discrimination law, labour law, private international law and comparative law. She obtained her law degree from the KULeuven and holds an LL.M. in International Legal Studies from Harvard Law School. In her Ph.D. thesis, *Faith, Identity and Participation in the Workplace: A Comparative Legal Study on the Role of Religion and Belief in Individual Labour Relations and Unemployment Benefits Litigation* (2015, KULeuven), she analysed the legal protection of the freedom of religion or belief and non-discrimination on the grounds of religion or belief in the private workplace and in the frame of unemployment disputes in Europe and North America. From 2010 to 2013, she was a leading project researcher in the inter-disciplinary EU-funded FP7 Programme RELIGARE (*Religious Diversity and Secular Models in Europe: Innovative Approaches to Law and Policy*). She is the co-editor of '*A Test of Faith: Religious Diversity and Accommodation in the European Workplace*' (Ashgate, 2012, along with M.C. Foblets and J. Vrielink) and '*Belief, Law and Politics: What Future for a Secular Europe?*' (Ashgate, 2014, along with M.C. Foblets, J. Nielsen and Z. Yanasmayan).

Michael Dusche studied philosophy, German literature and linguistics at the University of Tübingen, Germany, where he obtained his Magister Artium in both subjects in 1993. He worked towards his Doctor of Philosophy as a fellow of the German Research Foundation at the Centre for Ethics in Sciences and Humanities. He completed his Ph.D. under the guidance of Axel Honneth, Frankfurt, where he defended his dissertation on John Rawls and Global Justice in December 1999. In 2000, he joined the Centre for German Studies at the Jawaharlal Nehru University, New Delhi, where he worked for five years as an Assistant Professor and DAAD Lecturer. Since then, he has been back to India on various month-long research assignments (in 2006 and 2007). During the academic year 2009-10, he was a Fellow at the Jawaharlal Nehru Institute for Advanced Studies and during 2013-14 he worked as a Senior Fellow at the Centre for the Study of Developing Societies in Delhi. In July 2014, he joined the Manipal Centre for Philosophy and Humanities as an Associate Professor for Sociology. He has published two monographs, one in German (*Rawls and Global Justice*) and one in English (*Identity Politics in India and Europe*). He also co-edited a special issue of the *Indian Journal of Medical Ethics* and a volume on *Justice (Political, Social, Juridical)* together with Rajeev Bhargava. He is currently working on the non-state legal practices in India and on the *ethopoiesis* of Indian lifeworlds.

Anne Fornerod holds Ph.D. in public law from University of Paris XI. She is a researcher at the Centre of Research DRES (Law, Religion, Business and Society), University of Strasbourg/National Centre for Scientific Research. Her main research interests are law and religion, religious heritage, principle of laïcité, public funding for religious groups and religious pluralism. She edited a book on chaplaincies in 2012 (Presses de l'Université de Strasbourg), a book on the funding of religious heritage (Ashgate, 2015) and published another book and several papers on cultural and religious heritage.

Kumar Suresh is currently Professor at the National University of Educational Planning and Administration, New Delhi. Earlier, he was with the Centre for Federal Studies, Jamia Hamdard, New Delhi. Spanning nearly two decades of his academic career, he has extensively worked in the areas of pluralism, multiculturalism and federalism; issue of identity and accommodation of minorities and disadvantaged groups; and public policy and multicultural governance. Besides over 20 research papers published in journals and edited volumes, he has co-authored and co-edited two books and published three monographs on the theme of pluralism, multiculturalism, federalism with added emphasis on the mode of negotiating differences in multicultural societies. His publications are widely reviewed in international and national journals and periodicals. He was awarded Suma cum Laud (Distinction) at the Institute of Federalism, University of Fribourg, Switzerland, 2005 in a competence development programme on federalism and conflict transformation. He has also been associated with a number of international programmes and projects including the Bergoff Foundation of Germany to its Sri Lanka office, and Forum of Federation, Canada as a resource person besides a collective project on Citizenship, Canada. He is member of different professional bodies including International Sociological Association and its Research Committees: RC-05 Race and Ethnic Relations; and RC-28 Social Stratification and Mobility.

Bruce B. Lawrence is a 1962 magna-cum-laude graduate of Princeton in History and Middle East Studies. After a tour of duty with the US Navy, he earned a Masters of Divinity from Episcopal Divinity School (Cambridge) in 1967, and then in 1972 received his Ph.D. from Yale, specializing in History of Religions, with emphasis on Islam and Hinduism. He joined the Duke faculty in 1971 and continues to teach at Duke, though he has also taught abroad (first at Aligarh Muslim University and later Oxford), while also enjoying brief stints at Dartmouth and also the University of Chicago. Since 2000, he has been the

Marcus Family Professor of the Humanities at Duke University, and since 2006, Inaugural Director of the Duke Islamic Studies Centre. He has authored, co-authored, edited and co-edited 15 books, many of which have won prizes. His research focuses on Islam in all phases and all disciplines, with special attention to institutional Islam in South Asia, Indo-Persian Sufism, the religious masks of violence, and contemporary Islam as both Abrahamic faith and religious ideology. In 2008, he was awarded a Carnegie Scholarship on Islam, in order to pursue his current project on minority citizenship in Africa as well as Asia. He is currently Professor Emeritus, Duke University.

T.K. Oommen holds a Ph.D. from University of Pune. He taught at University of Delhi from 1964-71 and joined Jawaharlal Nehru University as an associate professor in 1971 and retired in 2002 after being a professor for 26 years, where he is Professor Emeritus at present. Professor Oommen has served as President of the International Sociological Association as well as the President of the Indian Sociological Society. He has been a visiting Professor at the University of California, Berkeley; the Maison des Sciences de l'Homme, Paris; the Wissenshaftszentrum, Berlin; and Senior Fellow at the Australian National University, Canberra; the Institute of Advanced Studies in Budapest and the Institute of Advanced Studies, Uppsala. He is the recipient of the V.K.R.V. Rao Prize in Sociology (1981), the G.S. Ghurye Prize in Sociology and Anthropology (1985), and the Swami Pranavananda Award in Sociology (1997). Professor Oommen is the author/co-author of 20 and editor/co-editor of 8 books and numerous articles. Books authored by him include: "Citizenship, Nationality and Ethnicity: Reconciling Competing Identities" (Polity Press, 1997), "Pluralism, Equality and Identity: Comparative Studies" (Oxford University Press, 2002), "Crisis and Contention in Indian Society" (Sage Publications, 2005), "Understanding Security: A New Perspective" (Macmillan, 2006), "Knowledge and Society: Situating Sociology and Social Anthropology" (Oxford University Press, 2007) and

"Reconciliation in Post-Godhra Gujarat: Role of Civil Society" (Pearson Education, 2008). Professor Oommen was a member of the Prime Minister's High Level Committee (2004-06) for the study of Social, Economic and Educational Status of the Muslim Community in India. He was conferred the Padma Bhushan award by the Government of India in 2008, for his contribution to the field of higher education.

Z. Fareen Parvez is Assistant Professor of Sociology at the University of Massachusetts-Amherst. She holds a Ph.D. (2011) and M.A. (2004) in Sociology from the University of California, Berkley and MPP (Public Policy) from University of Michigan, Ann Arbor. Her research focuses on Islamic revival and politics in India and France, where she has conducted extensive ethnographic research in Hyderabad and Lyon. Her book *Politicizing Islam* is forthcoming from Oxford University Press.

Konrad Pędziwiatr holds a Ph.D. in Social Sciences from the Katholieke Universiteit Leuven (Belgium) and M.A. in European Studies from the University of Exeter (UK) and in Sociology from the Jagiellonian University (Poland). He is author of two monographs, *The New Muslim Elites in European Cities: Religion and Active Social Citizenship amongst Young Organized Muslims in Brussels and London* (2010) and *From Islam of Immigrants to Islam of Citizens: Muslims in the Countries of Western Europe* (2005, 2007), co-author of *Polish Migration Politics* (2015) and author of numerous other scientific publications on Islam and Muslims in Europe, religions, migrations, minorities and social movements in Europe and Middle East and North Africa. He was a Research Fellow at Institute of Social and Cultural Anthropology, University of Oxford, Marie Curie Research Fellow at the University of Bradford and Open Society Institute's Civic Education Project Fellow. He is currently Assistant Professor at the Cracow University of Economics (Poland) and researcher collaborating closely with the Södertörn University (Sweden), as well as, with

Tischner European University (Poland) and the Centre for Migration Research at University of Warsaw (Poland).

Husain Qutbuddin received his Ph.D. in Qur'anic Studies from University of Cambridge, UK in 2009. In 2008-2009, he was a EUME-fellow at Wissenschaftskolleg, Berlin. He is currently a Research Fellow at the Academy of Advanced Studies in South-Asian Islam and Arabic (AASSIA), Mumbai. He has taught Islam, Arabic, and Computer Science at various institutions including the American University in Cairo, University of Cambridge, as well as Free University, Berlin. His research interests include Fatimid-Ismaili exegesis of the Qur'an, modern interpretation of the Qur'an, development of *tafsir* databases, and the pragmatic analysis of Qur'anic quotations in Arabic texts. Some of his publications include: "Fatimid Legal Exegesis of the Qur'an" in *Journal of Qur'anic Studies*, 12 (2010); "Introduction", in *Reflections on Knowledge and Language in Middle Eastern Societies*, (eds.) Bruno De Nicola, Husain Qutbuddin and Yoni Mendel (Cambridge Scholars Publishing, 2010). He is currently working on his monograph on the interpretation of the Qur'an by the Fatimid-Ismailis.

Kyriaki Topidi obtained her Maîtrise en Droit from the Robert Schuman Faculty of Law in Strasbourg, in 1999. She then completed a Masters programme in international studies at the University of Birmingham. In that context, her dissertation on Minority Rights in Europe was awarded the classification of 'Distinction'. In 2001, she commenced her scholarship-funded doctoral research (Ph.D.) at the Institute of European Studies of Queen's University Belfast (N. Ireland) in the area of EU law and minority rights within the framework of enlargement to Central and Eastern Europe. Her thesis was completed in 2006. Her previous work experience includes positions held at the European Parliament in Brussels, at research centres and NGOs in Germany and Greece as well as at the American University of Athens, as ILEX course leader.

Her teaching experience covers primarily public law areas of the English legal system as well as European law.

Markha Valenta is an inter-disciplinary scholar whose work focuses on the politics of religion, (in)equality, and pluralist democracy in India, the Netherlands and the United States. A current project entails a comparative study of iconic religious building in three world cities—Mumbai, Amsterdam and New York—examining the ways in which intensified global mobilities (of people, capital, imaginaries, violence and moral communities) engender the interpenetration of political structures, sensibilities, and relations formerly kept separate under imperial modernity. A second project addresses the contested place of Muslims as global minorities in secular democracies since the launch of the War on Terror. Valenta currently teaches on US democracy, global engagements and religion in the Department of American Studies at Radboud University (The Netherlands).

Introduction: Accommodating Muslim Minorities: Political Experiences of Europe and India

Anwar Alam and Konrad Pędziwiatr

Introduction

The issue of accommodation of religious minorities within the structure of nation-state has been subject of intense discussions among scholars and policy makers across the globe since late 20th century. These debates have been taking place both, in societies where one may observe dynamic processes of secularization (e.g. Western European countries), [1] as well as, in the places where religion has been still playing very important role in private and public sphere (e.g. US, Poland). [2] Most societies and nation-states in the world are either experiencing strains in accommodating the social, economic and political concerns of minority communities or facing difficulties in managing majority-minority relationship. More than any other community, it is the *problematic* integration of minority Muslim community, unlike the integration of other immigrant groups that has been the subject of global debates and discussions, particularly in the western hemisphere. The emergence of political radicalism within some sections of Muslim communities in the West [3] and a series of terrorist attacks (especially those carried out by European-born or socialized Muslims e.g. in London in 2005, in Paris in 2015 and Brussels in 2016) has further compounded this problem. These developments have further reinforced the pervasive thinking among a large section of non-Muslim host societies, particularly in the western hemisphere where Muslims live as minority, that Islam suffers from structural deficiencies for a meaningful integration in the host societies.

The collection of articles in this edited volume, for which

the initial incentive came from a seminar organized at Jamia Millia Islamia (New Delhi) in 2010, deals with the issue of nature of problem of accommodation of Muslim minority communities in the European and Indian contexts. There has been numerous studies regarding issues of integration, discrimination, inclusion or exclusion of Muslims living within a specific country of Europe [4] and in India. [5] Further, there exists a good number of comparative studies of public policies of European countries (particularly Germany, United Kingdom, France, Belgium and Netherlands) [6] or comparison with the United States of America [7] vis-à-vis Muslim immigrants. However, a cross-cultural comparative work in this field is rare. To the best of our knowledge, so far there has not been any volume published that would comparatively look at the accommodation of Muslims in Europe and India.

At the same time, the development of post-modernism that jolted the foundation of Enlightenment philosophy as 'the universal framework of progress', rise of multiculturalism and growing socio-religious diversity [8] and the relative failure of liberal legal universalism to assimilate the Muslim immigrant communities along with relatively negligible participation of Indian Muslims in the 'politics of Jihadi Islam', [9] made the scholars in the West to look at other models of accommodation of Muslim communities, [10] including the Indian multicultural model of integration. [11]

The increasing recognition of India both from the point of view of its accelerated development for the past last two decades and its multicultural mode of governance led to a few scholarly productions involving some comparison of India and Europe, if not an in-depth comparison. [12] Besides, there are a fairly large number of publications authored by both Indian and Western scholars in the related field of secularism and multiculturalism that touches upon a comparative account of political traditions of India and Europe with reference to religious minorities. [13] However, there has not been much work that has dealt with 'Muslim question' in India and in Europe in a comparative framework, though a small contribution in this regard has been made by one of the authors of this edited book. [14]

Thus, from this point of view, this volume makes a modest contribution to the ongoing debates and discussions on the issue of accommodation of Muslim communities in Europe and India. Within Europe, the primary focus of the book is on the political experiences of West European nations with accommodation of concerns of their Muslim citizens and residents. Particular attention is paid to the countries with the largest and most organised Muslim populations in this part of Europe that is: France, Germany, United Kingdom, Netherlands and Belgium.

Europe and India: Grounds for Comparisons

1. Both Europe and India share two common features: a secular, liberal-democratic polity and Muslims as the most dominant religious minority. According to the 2011 Census, Muslim population in India stood at 172 million accounting for 14.2 percent of the entire Indian population. Though there is no consensus on the actual figure of Muslims residing in Western Europe, it is estimated that their numbers vary between 15 million and 20 million, measuring around 6 percent of the entire population of the region. [15] There is hardly any other part of world where Muslims live as a minority in such great numbers within the liberal polity. Moreover, the development of discourse of multiculturalism throughout 1980s and 1990s in Western Europe was, to a large extent, aimed at addressing the religious concerns and issues of Muslim immigrant communities. Within India, the minority rights, particularly with reference to Muslim community, is the focal point of any public debate related to secularism, democracy and multiculturalism.

2. In both the geographical spaces, Muslims are internally diverse communities in terms of region, language, ethnicity, culture, social practices, sectarian orientations and class

differences. Notwithstanding this internal diversity of Muslim communities, there is a tendency in mainstream media, both electronic and print, among general intelligentsia excluding a small section of academia and among a large spectrum of political class to confuse Muslims as a sociological category and Islam as a religious tradition. Thus, the focus on Muslims as people who live in various social, political and economic contexts in any society has been mostly ignored.

As a result, any feature of the Muslim groups becomes 'Islamic', irrespective of groups' regional, social, economic, ideological or political background. This has seriously implications in terms of formulations of public policies towards minority Muslim communities, which are often centred on the understanding of Muslim subject and Islam as 'monolithic entity', despite their inherent pluralities.

Thus, while such perspectives have contributed to the development of 'discourse of Islamophobia' and 'securitisation of Islam' in Europe, in India this has led to an increase in governmental surveillance over the community, process of ghettoization and negative perception about Islam and Muslim communities in public at large but without producing the 'discourse of Islamophobia' and 'securitisation of Islam'. Moreover, the political understanding of Muslim communities as 'undifferentiated socio-religious group' in India is also the result of 'system of competing electoral democracy' wherein political parties, whether national or regional, cutting across ideological spectrums treats the community as 'undifferentiated' for the purpose of ensuring the 'en-block Muslim votes', contrary to differentiated political understanding of majority Hindu communities in terms of caste.

3. Western Europe had an early and in some places prolonged (e.g. in Iberian Peninsula from 711 till 1492) encounter with Islam that was virtually displaced as a result of the Reconquista and forced conversions and did not play an important role in the demographic making of modern Europe. However, Islam remained a factor in shaping the European

identity. As Delanty has vividly shown, Islam has played significant role as the key 'European other' that assisted Europe, or more precisely the political elites, in its identity formation. Orient was in fact not only a determining factor in the shaping of the idea of Europe but also in the creation of Europe as the 'West'. [16] Islam has started refiguring itself demographically in the context of colonial encounter and waves of migrations that became particularly significant in the context of post-Second World War reconstruction of Europe. In India, in contrast, Islam has had a more or less continuous presence from as early as 7th century AD and has substantially contributed to the making of Indian culture and civilization. Thus, both India and West European nations have rich, though very diverse historical legacy of encounter with Islam.

4. Equal opportunity for different communities placed group equality on the agenda of late 20th century liberalism. This equality is supposed to include not only certain social rights but also cultural ones. The issue missing in the Marshallian model of citizenship, [17] that is of a relationship between cultural pluralism and citizenship was addressed, inter alia, by Pakulski [18] and Delanty, [19] who have forcefully argued that a fourth dimension of citizenship (apart from civil, political and social rights) should be culture. They have pointed out that today there are other kinds of exclusion which cannot be accommodated by a model of social rights. The recognition of these forms of exclusion has committed many people to the view that policies of universal equality would not be adequate and that therefore some kind of radical difference is necessary in the recognition of the group rights.

The 2004 edition of the Human Development Report makes a bold attempt to expand the idea of human development by incorporating respect for cultural diversity. With these changes in liberal sensibilities, the Indian constitution does not appear to be alien or hostile to the Western liberal agenda. Once liberalism makes space for the concepts of equal opportunity and group equality, the idea that all religious and cultural communities must be equal in public domain appears reasonably compatible with concerns of liberalism. Indeed, the system of minority rights in India appears to reflect the concern of minorities within liberalism and western democracies.

5. Irrespective of legal positions of religious minority—whether citizen or immigrant status—the loyalty of religious minority is always suspected in the eyes of a section of religious majority, which in part flows from majoritarian locale of nation-state. Nation-state, to a large extent, remained a majoritarian entity, at least at the level of praxis. Thus, Muslims in India are 'historical communities' with legitimate claim to 'shared history and culture' as reflected in what is called 'composite', 'fuzzy', 'syncretic' or 'liminal' notion of Indian traditions. Despite this shared historical background, Muslims are frequently accused of maintaining separate, distinct identity at the cost of 'majoritarian' conception of national identity in contemporary India. The 'Partition' created the overarching, "single Muslim identity" for all Muslim generations to come against the plural identities—regional, sectarian, linguistic, social—with which Muslims were referred in the past and recognized [20] and are now permanently juxtaposed against the constructed notion of 'Hindu' nation. [21] To this extent, Muslims will continue to suffer from the charge of 'non-integration', 'disloyalty', 'stubborn' and 'non-conformist' to national (read majoritarian) tradition and culture and laws and values of the state.

In contrast, Muslims from the *longe duree* perspective are a relatively recent transplant in the Western European countries and are struggling for the recognition of citizenship and other rights. As such they are not historically developed communities but faced the similar charge of "non-integration" 'isolationism' and 'ghettoissation'. [22] This description of Muslim minority communities in two different political, social and national contexts only reinforces the recognition of a general political tendency that the minority community, irrespective of its legal status—citizen or immigrant—in the context of modern nation-state will suffer from the burden of proving their loyalty to the nation or joining what is called the 'national mainstream' in the Indian public political vocabulary.

6. Last but not the least, the variation in accommodation of Muslims in Europe and in India depends upon the place of religion in the public sphere and religion-state relations. In India, religion or rather religions are very much a part of the public sphere. They are not perceived as a threat to the State at least as long as they do not enter electoral process as the basis of political contestation. Citizenship remains secular but religious identification plays a major role in the everyday life of an Indian. In Europe, where by and large the processes of secularization have been quite dynamic over the last half a century, the public sphere is not a privileged domain of religion, and especially so, if it is a religion of a relatively newly established minority group. [23] Religious practices and beliefs are highly welcomed (since without the idea of religion the concept of the secular cannot do) but mainly in the private sphere. To use the words of Talal Asad, "religions in Europe are welcomed in the space where they cannot threaten political stability and the liberties of a 'free-thinking' citizen". [24]

When it comes to official relation between the State and Muslim communities in India, the governmental institutions hardly have any problem in engaging with wide range of Muslim organizations and dealing with different Muslim groups, like any other religious groups. There is no issue of Muslims' representative body or dilemma of 'who is speaking in the name of Islam'. In Europe, in contrast, the state makes great effort to find or, if this is not feasible, to set up an organization that would speak on behalf of all the Muslims in the country.

Many European states have asked the Muslim communities in the last two decades for a single voice to act as an interlocutor in order to deal with Muslim demands and needs. While from the Church-State relations perspective, this seems like a reasonable request, given that it would be very confusing to attempt to address a multitude of requests and opinions from perspectives as diverse as the Muslim community can have, a closer examination shows that it is often an unrealistic demand on the part of European states. Almost all West European states, save France, recognize and deal with multitude of denominational Christian sects and Churches without asking them to come under one umbrella organisation. One of the researchers analysing the organizational, ethnic, sectarian diversity of the Muslim communities have even called it a form of a 'search for the Holy Grail'. [25]

The present volume is thematically divided into four parts. The first part deals with the significance of minorities in the present globalized world and implications of the linkage between ethnicity, religion, state and nation for the integration of religious minorities within the structure of nation-state in a cross-cultural comparative framework. The second part critically interrogates the notion of modernity, particularly its idea of secularism and pluralism in cross-cultural setting of India, Netherlands, Turkey, Germany and United Kingdom, along with the notion of Muslim modernity and highlights its implications for integration of Muslim minority community. The third part broadly reflects upon pattern of negotiating the social, political and economic rights with reference to India, France, Belgium, United Kingdom and the European Union.

The last part deals with the emerging nature of debates and public policies surrounding the concept of multiculturalism and explores the textual Islamic and nature of Muslim responses to the discourses of multiculturalism in India and in Europe. It further provides a comparative understanding of 'class politics of Islam' and its variation in religious expression and identity among Muslims in Hyderabad city of India and Lyon city of France.

Nation-State and Minorities

The opening piece of the book, *Minority Matters: Perspectives from the Indian Ocean* by Bruce B. Lawrence deals with some of these aspects associated with minorities while highlighting the role of religious minorities such as Copts in Egypt, Muslims in Ethiopia, Kristens and Catholics in Indonesia, and Moros in the Philippines in shaping the contours of public space or what he calls 'public square'. He further points out that the effectiveness of role of minorities in influencing the public discourses or sharing the public spaces depends upon the nature of process of transforming itself from a community into a minority within the evolving structure of nation-state, its rural or urban location, its relationship with power structure at a given time and place and nature of secular and democratic tradition of nation-state in any country.

But who is a minority? How one becomes a minority? How minority is constructed? Here, the term minority is used in two specific connotations: as a socio-religious collective having far less numbers vis-à-vis socio-religious majority and in a sense of dispossession, marginalization and exclusion. Prior to modern formation of nation-state and territorial nationalism, there were only communities—in both religious and secular sense—without being labelled as 'minority' and 'majority'. The transformation of communities into 'minority' and 'majority' is one of the functions of process of formation of modern nation-state. This, in turn, is related to two inter-linked questions of formation of a nation: '*what is a nation*' and '*who is a nation*'. [26] The former is open-ended inclusive democratic process informed by the liberal-democratic tradition of the country that formally invites everyone, irrespective of his/her what is called 'primordial identities', to participate and constitute a political union called 'nation' through the mediatory agency of citizenship. The constitutional edifice of liberal democracy prescribes such understanding of nation and accordingly offers model of citizenship to its people and outsiders, based on the principle of birth, naturalisation and also through invitation.

The latter is closed, informal and exclusive and prescribes an ethnic understanding of nation in which a dominant, numerically large ethnic/religious group considers itself as *constitutive* or *natural guardian* of a nation and considers those who do not share their ethnicity as 'other' of nation. The 'nation' and 'majority' becomes conterminous in the eyes of a section of majority religious community. The principle of majoritarianism, homogeneity and uniformity has, by and large, guided the nation building process in much of the European continent despite the variation in conceptions of 'imagined nationhood' such as *multicultural*, *ethnic-assimilationist*, *republican-assimilationist* and *pillarization-separationist* in case of Great Britain, Germany, France and Netherlands respectively.

Similarly, as India moves towards achieving the goal of nation-state, it increasingly identifies itself with majoritarian Hindu ethos, identity and aspirations. Thus, the formation of religious minority as 'other' is inherently a part of modern nation building process itself. How the 'religious other' will transform into an 'enemy other' leading to ethnic cleansing, pogrom, communal riots etc., depends on a number of factors including the relationship between, ethnicity, religion and nation-state and a particular tradition of minority-majority relationship.

T.K. Oommen's *State and Religious Minorities in India and Europe: The Rupture between Vision and Reality,* Anne Fornerod's *Muslims and Naturalization Process in France,* Kyriaki Topidi's *Religion and the Constitutional Order in the Orbit of the European Union: De-Constructing State Neutrality in Germany and Turkey* and Katayoun Alidadi's *Protecting Muslim Minorities in the Work Place: Europe and India* in this volume have broadly dealt with the issue of implication for religious minorities arising out the complexity of linkage between 'what is a nation' and 'who is a nation'.

It is the dialectics of these two questions and their strength in shaping each other that determines the social, political and economic location of a religious minority in a given country. A country with strong secular and democratic constitution and state tradition of secular governance offers a greater degree of protection to the religious minority community despite majoritarian conception of nation and nationalism. Thus, the strong democratic and secular tradition of Europe provides adequate protection to members of minority religious communities within the framework of individualized citizenship, human rights and anti-racism laws and even managed to prevent the violent backlash from section of right wing majoritarian community against the minority community in view of growing incidents of terrorism such as bombings in Spain (2004), UK (2005), France (2015)and Belgium (2016) conducted by members of the minority community.

On the contrary, despite the Constitutional protection of collective rights including minority rights (Article 28-29), existence of Minority Commission bodies at national and at various state levels and favourable political culture of accommodating the religious and cultural demands of minority community, the Indian state has a poor record of preventing violent majoritarian backlash against the member of minority community, particularly Muslims, on account of its relatively weak secular and democratic tradition. However, in both geographical spaces, the Muslim minority suffers from a varying degree of discrimination in the labour market.

Katayoun Alidadi's paper, *Protecting Muslim Minorities in the Work Place: Europe and India*, has explored the various forms of discriminations from which Muslims suffer in the labour market of both the territories. In this regard, she demonstrates how despite much of anti-discriminatory laws by EU and respective states in European countries, which has been enunciated from time to time, sections of Muslim immigrant communities continue to suffer from varying degree of discrimination in the field of formal and informal sectors of employment. In respect of India, she points out how the Muslim community in the country, despite its proven social and educational backwardness and low participation in public employment opportunity structure as testified by various governmental commissions, [27] has been continuously excluded from the government affirmative policies of reservation on the ground that Constitutional provisions do not grant the benefit of reservation system on the basis of religion. [28]

Citizenship and Neutrality Debate: Is Neutrality of Nation-State Possible?

T.K. Oommen's *State and Religious Minorities in India and Europe: The Rupture between Vision and Reality* amply demonstrates the adverse consequence of linkage between religion, territory, nationality and state for the minority communities irrespective of religious traditions (Islam, Christianity, Judaism, Hinduism) and strongly recommends the decoupling of religion and state on the one hand and citizenship and nationality on the other hand. However, the decoupling of state and religion on the one hand and citizenship and nationality on the other hand is premised on the idea of absolute neutrality of nation-state. In the European landscape, it is the secular mode of governance that qualifies for the neutrality of the state, an essential condition for establishing harmony and tolerance among different faiths, communities and individuals of different orientations. The principle of neutrality of state is secured through the idea of secularity of state that does not favour or discriminate, at least in theory, against any religion or religious community. But is a secular state, a neutral state? Is absolute neutrality of state possible? Or can the decoupling of religion and state and citizenship and nationality ensure the neutrality of nation-state?

If secularism is a world view of value and orientation then no government can claim to ensure a neutral governance as such governance only privileges secular conception of governance as against religious conception of governance in the name of non-discrimination and equality. [29] Moreover, political experiences of post-colonial states, particularly in Turkey, indicates how the notion of secularity of state or secularism has been used as a discourse of power and an instrument of domination by minority secular elites in the past to discriminate against the majority religious masses. Moreover, multiculturalism has exposed the myth of neutrality of secular state by showing how secular nation-state carries and expresses values of 'national' majoritarian community, though often masked under the liberal doctrine of private-public dichotomy. [30] As Charles Taylor points out, "*liberalism that cannot, should not claim complete cultural neutrality*". [31]

Kyriaki Topidi's *Religion and the Constitutional Order in the Orbit of the European Union: De-Constructing State Neutrality in Germany and Turkey* examined this question of neutrality of state with reference to secular practice of state in Germany and Turkey and found how in both the countries, the state regulates, controls, favours, discriminates and even defines the forms for religious practices in varying degrees. As the myth of secular neutrality of state is increasingly being exposed both in terms of everyday state practices in the midst of growing religious and cultural diversity of West European nations, there is a growing voice towards acceptance of relative neutrality of the state. [32]

The Indian model of secularism underscores the relative neutrality of state in which state keeps what Rajeev Bhargava calls 'principled distance' [33] with all religious traditions and with favourable political attitude towards them. This relational neutrality of Indian state has been maintained by way of avoiding any constitutional definition of secularism and the adoption of the *kind* of operative definition of secularism *(Sarva Dharam Sambhav)* that neither endorses the American model of secularism in terms of complete separation of religion and politics (constitutionally speaking, if not in political practice), nor the European model of secularism, save France, that recognizes and maintains the varying forms of institutional linkages between religion and state. Second, it not only underlines the principle of *non-discrimination* but proclaimed equal treatment *of* religions in the public realm.

Third, it provides a degree of associational religious freedom and communal autonomy that is required in particular for religious minorities if only to protect them from "intrusive interference" by states and majority religions.

Anne Fornerod's *Muslims and Naturalization Process in France* also highlights the paradox of 'what is a nation and who is a nation' in the French political life. The author shows how the political consideration has led the French Court to deny the rights of citizenship to many Muslim immigrants on the ground of 'behavioural non-conformity' to the principle of laicism. France is not alone in restricting the grant of citizenship to some Muslim immigrants. A large number of European countries have resurrected 19th century liberal assimilationist model of integration by prescribing the language, history and behaviour-cultural test for the immigrants that has made the prospects of acquiring citizenship in concerned European country more difficult. [34] In this context, a large number of scholars have noted the setback to multicultural policies that was considered to prevail during the 1980s and 1990s. [35]

Multiculturalism, Secularism and Question of Collective Identity

It must be noted that the much hailed multicultural policies in West European countries were confined to largely cosmetic concessions to the Muslim immigrants: provision of halal food, burial rights, etc. and rarely addressed the core issues of collective rights of Muslim immigrant community ranging from demands to construct mosques with minarets, provision for Islamic religious instruction in public funded schools, recognition of *Eid* as a national holiday, right to wear hijab for women at work places, right to call five times azan etc. In other words, multiculturalism in terms of public recognition of 'equality of cultures' in national public sphere has been rarely a state practice in the Western hemisphere. The emerging idea of 'post-national age' in Europe in the context of post-modernism, as reflected in some academic works [36] though does indicate a subtle shift in European national identity from 'once exclusive, ethnic, ideological nationalism', to 'non-ethnic, non-ideological idea of a nation' but without being translated into public policies.

To this extent, there remains a disjunction between the pluralist claim of liberal-democratic nation-state and its construction of exclusive conception of nation and nationalism as derived from a common descent, religion, culture, language or history. [37] The operative laws concerning grant of rights related to citizenship and immigration flows, to a large extent, from the 'imagined exclusive political conception of nation and nationalism'. In this construction of nation and nationalism, outsiders are either excluded in principle or they have to be completely assimilated. This makes the task difficult for the western policy makers to accommodate the religious and cultural demands of Muslim immigrant communities at national political level.

A second reason for contradiction between the claim of multicultural public policies and its inherent bias towards assimilationist model of integration is partly on account of historical tradition of secularism and formation of secular state or pattern of Church-State relationship in the European context, which is characterized by state's regulation, control and domination over the Church in varying degree, irrespective of its denominations. In other words, *territorialisation* or *nationalization* of Church has been the dominant trajectory of discourse of secularism and formation of secular state in the European context in order to contain, rather eliminate, the trans-national political loyalty of Church. The functional autonomy to the Church was only restored in the mid-20th century on account of the fact that owing to hegemonic discourse of 'privatization of religion' and 'secularization of Church' itself', the Church has lost the political influence to pose a threat to the secular state in any effective manner. [38]

Thus, one is not surprised to find that the European states, to a large extent, have displayed a similar political outlook towards Islam as reflected in a number of academic publications in this regard. [39] However, the European government's attempt to 'singularize/nationalize' Islam as evident from government's attempt to forge a representative institutions of Muslim immigrant communities from above (e.g. French Council of the Muslim Faith, Islamic Commission of Spain, Central Council of Muslims in Germany, Muslim Executive of Belgium) or to favour one Islamic group/organization over others (e.g. British Muslim Council till 2007, [40] or Muslim Religious Union in the Republic of Poland) [41] has proved to be problematic and not very successful.

The legitimacy of such political exercise is deeply suspected in the eyes of majority of Muslim communities. Part of the failure of Western policies emanates from its 'post-reformation Church understanding of religion including Islam', which treats religion a privatized, specific faith activity. Islam, being essentially a diversified, decentralised entity without a single centre of authority has historically resisted such centralizing and homogenising trends across Muslim and non-Muslim majority contexts.

However, notwithstanding the shift in approach of the West European government from multicultural to time tested liberal assimilated model of integration partly in order to tame the tide of rising wave of Far Right Parties in Europe, as well as, to counter the threat of Islamic terrorism, there a growing recognition among the critical scholars and policy makers about the inherent limitation of liberal assimilationist model of integration vis-à-vis Muslim immigrant communities. While Europe found the solution of 'Jewish Question' in the form of coercive assimilation, oppression and extermination, the same cannot be applied to the Muslim immigrants for several reasons. First, Europe has learnt the lesson of Holocaust and the Second World War atrocities and knows well how the mechanism of scapegoating works. In order to prevent its recurrence on European soil, it introduced over the last decades, numerous institutional and non-institutional checks and barriers.

Second, multiculturalism has exposed the neutrality of the state and public culture and has succeeded in shifting the debate from recognition of cultural equality in the private realm to the recognition of equality of cultures in the public sphere.

Third, the right to group equality has become a legitimate part of late 20th century liberal discourse. The UN has incorporated right to culture as a part of fundamental rights and human rights. Fourth, the development of minority rights discourse with its emphasis upon the preservation of cultural rights of minorities has eroded the legitimacy of assimilationist model of integration. Fifth, the development of global public scrutiny of state actions has eroded the capacity of nation-state to enforce assimilation on its minority population. Finally, the development of cultural ethnic infrastructure sustained by the ever-revolutionizing technology of communication and information has negated the possibility of full cultural assimilation.

Negotiating Citizenship and Indian Political Experience

Many scholars [42] in the West in recent years have demanded a revision of the Marshallian theory of citizenship in order to accommodate the principle of difference and recognition of group rights [43] within the universal notion of equality and citizenship. According to them, the issue missing in the Marshallian model of citizenship is of a relationship between cultural pluralism and citizenship and argues that a fourth dimension of citizenship is culture. In other words, this equality is supposed to include not only certain civil, political and social rights but also cultural ones. In recent times, a good number of European scholars including Jocelyne Cesari and Tariq Ramadhan have strongly advocated the need for symbolic recognition of Islamic cultural and religious identity in public sphere in addition to accessibility to opportunity structure as a necessary step to integrate the Muslim community in the western societies. [44]

Konrad Pędziwiatr's *New Muslim Brokers in European Cities and Politics of Muslim Citizenship* follows the similar line of inquiry and argues for revisiting and expanding the scope of the Marshallian theory of citizenship from its traditional focus on class dimension of citizenship (political, social and economic equality) to the recognition of cultural factors in the notion of citizenship. Based on his research on some Muslim organisations in Britain and Belgium, he found out how the new generation of Muslim leadership in Europe is venting this understanding of citizenship that combines the recognition of their equal rights to participate in national opportunity structure as well as recognition of their cultural and religious identity in the public sphere. According to him, these new Muslim generations, who are born in the host European societies, do not recognize any contradiction between their religious (Muslim/Islam) and national identity (Belgian, French, German, British etc.) and use the narrative of citizenship to redefine their place in European societies and to demand certain rights from equal footing as other European citizens.

As Europe continues to debate over the merit and demerit of public recognition of collective cultural and religious identity of Muslim immigrant community, Indian Constitution (Part Third, Articles 29-30) provides Constitutional recognition of a set of group rights including the minority rights as a part of justiciable fundamental rights. The Constitution attempts to strike a balance between what is called legal universalism (universal citizenship rights) and legal pluralism (group rights/personal laws) and offers a governing model in managing the religious and cultural diversity and carving a sense of national unity out of localised diversities of caste, ethnicity, religion, region, language, tribes etc. The framing of liberal discourse of 'unity in diversity' and 'diversity in unity' has guided the Indian nation-building process since its inception and has been relatively successfully in maintaining its national cohesion and territorial integrity. Kumar Suresh's *Citizenship and Affirmation of Group Difference: Constitutional Mode of Negotiating Religious Identities in India* outlines the various Constitutional articles and state practices of secularism that gives effect to this balance between legal universalism and legal pluralism.

Along with this article of Kumar Suresh, there are numerous other academic works [45] that have explored the Indian Constitutional mandate of establishing a balance between legal universalism and legal pluralism in great detail. But how does this balancing act is achieved or played out in everyday political process of Indian society? A tentative answer to this question lies, in part, in adoption of principle of relative neutrality of state as indicated earlier in the preceding pages and partly lies in understanding the particular *manner* in which the Indian state system functions and relates itself with the various social groups including the Muslim communities in the society. The noticeable features about this particular manner within which the Indian state system has, till very recently, been functioning are its flexibility about norms, doctrines and principles, its being non-definitional, its fuzziness about the things 'political' and decision-making process, its capacity to live with uncertain situations, its tendency to look for context-specific solutions and developing a political grammar that recognizes the public-private, formal-informal distinctions but without making it official.

Thus, while the Indian Constitution and state practices attach due importance to multiculturalism in matters of governance, no attempt has ever been made to declare multiculturalism as a fundamental aspect of Constitution or state practice officially. Similarly, while the Constitution and law of the land speaks both about the rights of the individual and the groups, no specific procedure or guidelines were laid down in the Constitution; neither any attempt was ever made by the Supreme Court nor by the Indian Parliament to realize the same so as to determine why the state should support one or the other in case of conflict between the two. In the same manner, while the concern for equal right of all communities led to the recognition, even legitimisation, of collective religious worship as well as observances of religious practices in the public-political realm, the modern sensibility of constructing a liberal-secular state, which demands the separation of religion from political, led to the incorporation of the provision in the Representation of Peoples Act, 1952 (further amended in 1961), that prevents the misuse of religion for corrupt practices.

One of the positive implications of the above narrated ambiguous, flexible, vague and non-doctrinal nature of secularism and national identity in particular and the larger political process in general is that Indian government—whether at national, state or local level—have demonstrated a high degree of flexibility in negotiating the cultural or religious demands of socio-religious groups including the Muslim communities, irrespective of sects and orientations, and without raising the issue of representative character of Muslim organizations as demanded in the West. Thus, minorities', particularly the Muslims, religious and cultural symbols continue to enjoy the due recognition in the public realm as a part of the evolved political culture, if not as an outright constitutional right. Thus, out of 14 declared national religious holidays, 10 belong to minority communities (four Muslim, two Christian, two Sikh, one Buddhist, and one Jain).

In the Indian context, this balance is not merely confined to the realm of recognition of collective minority rights and grant of personal laws, which is predominantly understood in relation to Muslim community but otherwise guaranteed to all religious groups. It also operates at a wider level that includes federal mode of governance as well as pronouncement of affirmative public policies from time to time in favour of disadvantaged social groups in the public opportunity structure. This process has also helped a section of Muslim community in securing the upward mobility [46] in addition to the fact that the regime of minority rights along with Indian notion of secularism that accommodates religious and cultural demands of Muslim community in public sphere goes a long way in arresting the growth of Islamic militancy and preventing the development of 'enemy perception' about Indian state and society among Indian Muslims despite the pervasive discourse of discrimination and alienation that thrives among a major section of Indian Muslims. [47]

Modernity, Muslim Modernity and Accommodation of Islam

The thesis of incompatibility of Islam and modernity continues to find favourable reception among a section of citizens and intelligentsia, mostly belonging to the Right, in Europe as well as in India. To what extent the self-perception of Islam mitigates the values of modernity such as secularism, nationalism, gender justice, tolerance, human rights, pluralism and individualism?—there is no easy answer to such questions as the answer itself depends upon the approach one takes towards Islam. A liberal-moderate interpretation of Islam would show greater reception towards these modern values, while a literalist-fundamentalist vision of Islam would outrightly reject such values as un-Islamic. T.K. Oommen and Michael Dusche bring about into the Islamic notion of *Ummah* that rejects territorial nationalism.

However, it is worth noting that there are several credible works that have demonstrated the co-habitation of Islam with nation-state in various forms. [48] In fact, there is no single Islamic position on the notion of *Ummah*. As several authors point out, it may range from a vision of political mobilisation of Muslim community all over the world under one Caliphal rule to universal spiritual association of fraternal Muslim brotherhood while living under different nation-states. [49] Husain Qutbuddin's *Islamic Responses to Multiculturalism:*

An Analysis of Qur'anic Citations is instructive in this regard. He takes a position that there cannot be a single *objective* Islamic position and one has to contend with plurality of interpretation of Islam. Anwar Alam's *Muslim Responses to Multiculturalism in India and Europe* demonstrates plurality of Muslim responses to the question of multiculturalism.

It is not Islam, but Islamism—a modern political construct, of various shades that finds it sometimes difficult to co-exist with modern values. Islam with its universal, moral and ethical principles, with its rituals and localised diversified value systems, can live under any political dispensation but Islamism as modern ideological construct has inherent limitation to cohabit with modern values of liberalism, pluralism, democracy and secularism. Part of the reason for this lies in the fact that both modernism and Islamism, if not modernity and Islam, are essentializing and homogenizing political forces/projects. Michael Dusche in his paper *Modernity, Nation-State and Islamic Identity Politics* has explored the reasons as to why Islamism as an expression of Islamic identity politics militates against western modernity. Z. Fareen Parvez's *Role of Muslim Class Relations in the Politics of Islam in France and India* has situated the discourse of Islamism, without referring the term, within the class politics and relations of Muslim communities.

Thus, she demonstrates how the trend of Salafism, and politics of Islamic identity and recognition is more prevalent among the poor and middle class segments of Muslim populations living in Hyderabad, India and in Lyon, France respectively, which also depends upon the nature of relationship between state and Muslim communities in these countries.

Islam is certainly a factor in the various policy pronouncements of the European governments in managing the emerging religious diversity of European nations. To a large extent, it has shaped the discourse of multiculturalism in Europe, whereas in India, Islam is constitutive of Indian nationhood. The governments in Europe and in India have historically been concerned with the political assertion of Islam, however it is Europe where Islam has come to signify as a threat to the European national identity. Orientalism (Islamic, Middle-Eastern) versus Occidentalism (Christianized Europe) continues to shape the discourse over European identity. Hence, a brief recall of pattern of historical interaction with Islam that has shaped the western understanding of Islam will not be out of place here.

There are four historical moments in this encounter. The first moment is period of Reconquista of Iberian Peninsula and crusades. The second moment is the rise of Ottomans, from the conquest of Constantinople (present day Istanbul, 1453) to the Second Siege of Vienna (1683). The third is the European domination of Muslim lands during the major part of 19th and first half of 20th centuries. The fourth and the last is the recent arrival of a significant number of Muslim immigrants and then refugees since the end of Second World War. In all these encounters, the European powers mostly confronted the political mobilisation of Muslims in the name of Islam which continues till date as reflected in the Honeyford affair and the Bradford riots in early 1980s and the Rushdie affair (1989) in UK. [50]

These incidents coupled with the Iranian Revolution in 1979 and the rise of Islamic fundamentalism with anti-western tone in the Muslim world made the Western governments more sensitive to the need of regulating Islam in European hemisphere. The governments in Europe were alarmed by the fact that demand for recognition of Islam in public sphere came from second and third generation Muslims who were expected to get assimilated into the dominant European culture. Controlling the Islamic fundamentalism became government's overall concern in dealing with Muslim immigrant communities. This was also necessitated with the slow realization that Muslim immigrants were no more guest-workers but a permanent reality—a part of European landscape. In the backdrop of 9/11, the West/Europe produced the discourse of 'Islamophobia' and 'securitisation of Islam' with focus on ever increasing police surveillance, control and regulation over the Muslim immigrant communities.

However, notwithstanding the political role of Islam that has shaped the public perception of Europeans, it is also the self-perception of European modernity and along with its gradual transformation from essentially a discourse to an identity of European states and society that has made conditions difficult for accommodating Islam in the European public sphere. Europe resurrected the 'ideal' discourse of modernity to exclude Islam, whereas the really existing modernity in Europe provides enough space to accommodate some aspects of Islamic symbolism. Thus, most of the collective religious and cultural demands of Muslim immigrant communities (such as *halal* provision of meat, Islamic religious instruction in government funded public schools, Islam to be covered under blasphemy law, recognition of Muslim communities as faith communities, provision of wearing headscarf—if not burqa—in public spaces, construction of mosques with minarets, right to five time public azan, etc.) would be fitting as per the existing modern practices in Europe.

After all, the dominant European practice of secularism and democracy provides various forms of engagement and interactions between religion and the state and a modest space for recognition of group identity in public sphere, as it has been demonstrated in ample number of academic works including those in this volume (e.g. Markha and Topidi), rather than separation of religion of state or privatisation of religion. Casanova's 'theory of de-privatisation' [51] nailed this modernist myth of separation of religion and state and privatisation of religion. What concerns the European government is not the public role of religion—which the religion is already performing in the form of social work—but the political role of religion in the public sphere. Historically, the European nation-state conscripted the political role of Church, if not its public role in the societies. Given these existing modern realities in European landscape, what makes the European governments to refuse the similar religious concessions to the Muslim communities on the ground of being compromising to 'fundamental, ideal type values of modernity'?

Markha Valenta's *Beyond the East-West Binary: Pluralist Secularism and the Muslim Problem in India and the Netherlands* has looked into this emerging political dualism of European Governments vis-à-vis Muslim communities in Europe. She argues that Europe's universal discourse of modernity is being deeply ruptured by Europe's decreasing role in shaping the world—at the very moment when the world is increasingly shaping Europe—the process of which is partly accelerated by the forces of globalisation. As a result, European modernity as such is no more coherent, no more rational, and no more secure in its identity and achievements than the modernity to be found outside Europe. In other words, what she is arguing is that the discrepancy between the universal, ideal type of modernity and really existing modernity one confronts vis-à-vis Muslim question in Europe is a product of transformation of Europe from a site of universal modernity into a site of one of local multiple modernity, which in turn produces a profound sense of identity crisis.

Dipesh Chakrabarty [52] has succinctly captured this internal transformation of reason from universal to local that is taking place within Europe. In this regard, Hilal Ahmed's *Exploring Muslim Modernities: Public Presence of Mosques in Delhi and London* has explored the meaning of Muslim modernity as a form of multiple modernity through the narratives of mosques in Delhi and London, which finds its acceptance within the Indian trajectory of modernity but suffers from non-recognition in the public sphere of London despite the fact that UK is no more a site of universal modernity but increasingly becoming a site of multiple modernity.

In sum, the collection of articles in this edited volume offers multiple perspectives and thus contributes to the ongoing debates on the question of accommodation and integration of minority communities within the structure of nation-state. The term 'integration' is a slippery slope in which a member of minority continues to suffer from the charge of 'non-integration' unless he or she or the community in question arrives at the centre of power structure with a high degree of assimilation into national-majoritarian value system, often shaped by dominant minority group within the majoritarian community. [53] This has been the trajectory so far for a member of a minority community to be qualified as 'integrated' in the host societies.

However, as the process of globalization deepens and affects the unitary form of nation-state and brings out multicultural face, as well as, democratic deficit of every society, and nation-state including in Europe, it is hoped that sooner or later the secular idea of citizenship would further strengthen the democratic governance on the one hand and come to include cultural entitlements of all social groups and its recognition in public sphere on the other. This would in turn mitigate some concerns of minority communities, if not all visible and invisible forms of class-based discriminations and exclusions.

Finally, we take this opportunity to thank all the contributors to make this book a reality. Thanks also to Mr. Sandeep Sury, CEO of New Century Publications, to bring out this manuscript in the public domain for wider debates and discussions. All omissions and errors related to this work rest with the editors of this book.

End Notes

1. P. Berger (2008), "Religious America, Secular Europe? A Theme and Variations", Ashgate; G. Davie (2002), "Europe, the Exceptional Case: Parameters of Faith in the Modern World".

2. P.L. Berger (ed.) (1999), "The Desecularization of the World: Resurgent Religion and World Politics, Wm. B. Eerdmans Publishing; J. Casanova (1994), "Public Religions in the Modern World", Chicago University Press, Chicago; P. Norris and R. Inglehart (2011), "Sacred and Secular: Religion and Politics Worldwide", Cambridge University Press, Cambridge.
3. S. Taj-Farouki, "Islamists and the Threat of Jihad: Hizb ut-Tahrir and al-Muhajiroun on Israel and the Jews", in B.S. Turner (ed.) (2003), "Islam: Critical Concepts in Sociology", Routledge, London; Q. Wiktorowicz (2005), "Radical Islam Rising: Muslim Extremism in the West", Rowman and Littlefield Publishers, Oxford.
4. For example, J. Cesari (1994), "Être musulman en France: Associations, militants et mosquées", IREMAM, Aix-en-Provence; F. Dassetto (1997), "Facettes de l'Islam belge", Bruylant-Academia., Louvain-la-Neuve; P. Lewis (2002), "Islamic Britain", I.B. Tauris & Co. Ltd., London; W. Schiffauer (2000), "Die Gottesmänner: Türkische Islamisten in Deutschland", Eine Studie zur Herstellung religiöser Evidenz, Suhrkamp, Frankfurt am Main.
5. Some of the important works are: Zafar Imam (ed.) (1975), "Muslims in India", New Delhi: Orient Longman; Mohammad Mujeeb (1985), "Indian Muslims", New Delhi: Munshiram Manoharlal Publishers Pvt. Ltd.; Mushirul Hasan (1997), "Legacy of Divided Nation: India's Muslims Since Independence", Boulder, CO: Westview Press; Lauren Gayer and Christopher Jafferlot (2012), "Muslims in Indian Cities: Trajectories of Marginalisation", New Delhi: Harper Collins.
6. F. Dassetto (1996), "La construction de l'Islam européen: Approche socio-anthropologique", Harmattan, Paris; J.L. Fetzer (2005), "Muslims and the State in Britain, France, and Germany", Cambridge University Press, Cambridge; J.S. Nielsen (1979), "Forms and Problems of Legal Recognition for Muslims in Europe", Centre for the Study of Islam and Christian-Muslim Relations, Birmingham, Research Paper 2; J.S. Nielsen (2004), "Muslims in Western Europe", Edinburgh University Press.
7. J. Cesari (2004), "When Islam and Democracy Meet: Muslims in Europe and in the United States", Palgrave, New York; P. Mandaville (2004), "Transnational Muslim Politics: Reimaging

the Umma", Routledge, New York; D. Westerlund (ed.) (2014), "Sufism in Europe and North America", Routledge.

8. T. Modood (2006), "Multiculturalism, Muslims and Citizenship: A European Approach", Routledge, London; T. Modood (2007), "Multiculturalism: A Civic Idea", Polity, London; S. Vertovec (2007), "Super-diversity and its Implications", *Ethnic and Racial Studies*, Vol. 30, No. 6, pp. 1024-1054.
9. Here, most commonly is mentioned a fact that while out of 172 million Indian Muslims, only 18 were found joining ISIS, whereas from France, which is home to around 5 million Muslims, there is an estimated 2000 ISIS fighters. M. Mishra, "What European Muslims Can Learn from Indian Muslims", 2015, available at: http://blogs.timesofindia.indiatimes.com/mind-the-gap/what-european-muslims-can-learn-from-indian-muslims.
10. W. Kymlicka and E. Pfostl (2014), "Multiculturalism and Minority Rights in the Arab World", Oxford University Press, New York, NY.
11. W. Kymlicka and B. He (eds.) (2005), "Multiculturalism in Asia", Oxford University Press, Oxford; Richard A. Sheweder, Martha Minow, and Hazel Rose Markus (ed.) (2002), "Engaging Cultural Differences: The Multicultural Challenges in Liberal Democarcies", Rusesell Sage Foundation, New York.
12. Imtiaz Ahmad and Helmut Reifeld (2007), "Middle Class Values in India and Western Europe", Social Science Press, Delhi; Michael Dusche (2010), "Identity Politics in India and Europe", Sage Publications, Delhi; Rajendra K. Jain (ed.) (2014), "Multiculturalism in India and Europe", Aakar Books, Delhi.
13. Gurpeet Mahajan (1998), "Identities and Rights: Aspects of Liberal Democracy in India", Delhi: Oxford University Press; Rajeev Bhargḥav (ed.) (1998), "Secularism and Its Critics", Delhi: Oxford University Press; Rajendra K. Jain (ed.) (2014), "Multiculturalism in India and Europe", Delhi: Aakar Books; J. Tripathy and S. Padmanabhan (ed.) (2014), "Becoming Minority: How Discources and Policies Produce Minorities in Europe and India", Sage Publications, Los Angles.
14. See, Anwar Alam, "Scholarly Islam and Everyday Islam: Reflections on the Debate over Integration of the Muslim Minority in India and Western Europe", *Journal of Muslim*

Minority Affairs, 27:2, pp. 241-260, also, "Liberal States and Muslim Minorities", *Seminar,* 621, May 2011, pp. 2-6; Anwar Alam: Interview in Michael Dusche, "Identity Politics in India and Europe", Sage Publications, New Delhi, 2010, pp. 162-168.

15. Almost a similar number of Muslims live in Central and Eastern part of the continent. However, the character of these communities is different hence the volume focuses mainly on the Western communities. For detailed statistics, see PEW, "The Future of the Global Muslim Population", PEW, New York 2011.
16. G. Delanty (1995), "Inventing Europe: Idea, Identity, Reality", Palgrave Macmillan, London.
17. T.H. Marshal (1950), "Citizenship and Social Class and Other Essays", CUP, Cambridge.
18. J. Pakulski (1997), "Cultural Citizenship", *Citizenship Studies,* Vol. 1(1), pp. 73-86.
19. G. Delanty (2002), "Two Conceptions of Cultural Citizenship: A Review of Recent Literature on Culture and Citizenship", *The Global Review of Ethnopolitics,* Vol. 1, No. 1, pp. 60-66.
20. See Gyanendra Pandey (1999), "Can a Muslim be an Indian", *Comparative Studies in Society and History,* Vol. 4, pp. 608-699. Also, Shibani Roy and S.H.M. Rizvi (2005), "The Hindi Musalman: A Retrospection", *Islam and Muslim Societies: A Social Science Journal,* Vol. 1, No. 1, pp. 93-121.
21. For some of the academic works on construction of Hindu nationalism, See, Gyan Pandey (1991), "The Construction of Communalism in Colonial North India", New Delhi: Oxford University Press; Vasudha Dalmia (1995), "Representing Hinduism: The Construction of Religious Tradition and National Identity", New Delhi: Sage Publications.
22. M. Seddon (2003), "British Muslims: Loyalty and Belonging", The Islamic Foundation and Citizen Organising Foundation, Leicester; S. Seddon (2004), "British Muslims Between Assimilation and Segregation", The Islamic Foundation, Leicester.
23. It is not without importance which religious group strives for more room in the public sphere. Some newly set up Christian evangelical communities find it much easier to claim such a space than, for example, Muslim groups. The former ones are, in fact, re-claiming it, while the latter ones claiming it for the first

time in the history of the analyzed countries.

24. T. Asad (2003), "Formations of the Secular: Christianity, Islam, Modernity: Cultural Memory in the Present", Stanford University Press, California.
25. D. Hussain (2003), "The Holy Grail of Muslims in Western Europe: Representation and their Relationship with the State", in J. Esposito (ed.) (2003), "Modernizing Islam: Religion in the Public Sphere in the Middle East and in Europe", Rutgers University Press, Hurst and Company, London.
26. Fort the implications of these questions on majority-minority relationships, See, Imtiaz Ahmed (2014), "The Multicultural Discourse in India", in Rajendra K. Jain (ed.), "Multiculturalism in India and Europe", Aakar Books, Delhi, pp. 99-121.
27. Prime Minister's High Level Committee (2006), "Social, Economic and Educational Status of the Muslim Community of India: A Report", Cabinet Secretariat, Government of India, New Delhi, November; Ranganath Mishra Commission Report; Gopal Singh Commission Report, 1982.
28. In this regard, it may be noted that while SCs within the Hindu Community enjoy this privilege, the same has been denied to similar caste groups within the Muslim community. Similarly, recently, the Supreme Court has struck down the preceding Congress government's policy of reserving 4 percent quota within the 29 percent Quota for OBCs in centrally sanctioned public employment schemes on the ground that religion cannot be a basis for affirmation of public policies. Earlier, the Maharashtra government withdrew the benefit of reservation in employment to those SC communities who converted to Buddhism under the leadership of Ambedkar, but later restored the benefit in view of growing criticism and political mobilization of neo-Buddhists.
29. T. Asad (1993), "Formations of the Secular: Christianity, Islam, Modernity: Cultural Memory in the Present", op. cit.; T. Asad (1993), "Genealogies of Religion", John Hopkins University Press, Baltimore; T. Modood, "Multiculturalism, Muslims and Citizenship: a European Approach"...op. cit.
30. W. Kymlicka (2001), "Politics in the Vernacular: Nationalism, Multiculturalism, and Citizenship", Oxford University Press, Oxford, UK, New York; W. Kymlicka (1995), "Multicultural Citizenship: A Liberal Theory of Minority Rights", Clarendon

Press.

31. C. Taylor (1992), "Multiculturalism and the "Politics of Recognition", Princeton University Press, p. 95.
32. See Veit Bader (2003), "Religious Diversity and Democratic Institutional Pluralism", Political Theory, Vol. 31, No. 2, pp. 265-294.
33. Rajeev Bhargava (2016), "The Distinctiveness of Indian Secularism", available at: http://www.chereum.umontreal.ca/activites_pdf/session%202/Barghava_Distinctiveness%20of%20Indian.pdf, accessed on May 5, 2016.
34. The various policy pronouncements that limits the prospect of grant of citizenship to immigrants range from Law on Civic Integration on New Comers (1998) in Netherlands which obliges non-European new comers to take 600 hours of languages and civic lessons to the adoption of Cantle Report (2001) in Britain that emphasised that 'the greater sense of citizenship', 'common elements of nationhood' and 'the use of English language' that had to be strengthened in the minority communities, and overall the immigrants had to develop a greater acceptance of, and engagement with the principle national institutions. Similar programmes are being introduced by various other European governments both left and right wing—including Scandinavian countries, Belgium, Austria and Germany.
35. T. Modood (2004), "Muslims and Politics of Difference", *The Political Quarterly*, Vol. 74, No. 1, pp. 100-115; Joppke Christian (2004), "The Retreat of Multiculturalism in the Liberal State: Theory and Policy", *The British Journal of Sociology*, Vol. 55, Issue 2, pp. 237-257.
36. Y.N. Soysal (1994), "Limits of Citizenship: Migrants and Post-national Membership in Europe", Chicago University Press, Chicago; R. Falk (1994), "The Making of Global Citizenship", in B. Steenbergen van (ed.) (1994), "The Conditions of Citizenship", Sage, London; S. Strange (2000), "The Declining Authority of States", in D. Held (ed.), "The Global Transfornations Reader", Polity, Cambridge, pp. 148-155.
37. A.D. Smith (1986), "The Ethnic Origins of Nations", Oxford University Press, Oxford.
38. See, Gurpreet Mahajhan, "Aspects of Liberal State", op. cit., p. 45.

39. L. Panafit (1999), "Quand le droit écrit l'Islam. L'intégration juridique de l'Islam en Belgique", Bruylant, Bruxelles; S. Ferrari (2000), "Islam and European Legal Systems", Ashgate, Darthmouth; D. Hussain, "The Holy Grail of Muslims in Western Europe: Representation and their Relationship with the State", op. cit.; D. Hussain (2006), "Brytyjscy muzulmanie 9/11 i 7/7", in K. Pędziwiatr, K. Górak-Sosnowska and P. Kubicki (eds.), "Islam i obywatelskosc w Europie".
40. K. Pędziwiatr (2007), "Creating New Discursive Arenas and Influencing the Policies of the State: The Case of the Muslim Council of Britain", *Social Compass*, t. 54, no. 2, pp. 267-280.
41. K. Pędziwiatr (2011), "The Established and Newcomers in Islam in Poland or the Inter-Group Relations within the Polish Muslim Community", in K. Górak-Sosnowska (ed.) (2011), "Muslims in Poland and Eastern Europe: Widening the European Discourse on Islam", Warszawa.
42. See, J. Pakulski (1997), "Cultural Citizenship", *Citizenship Studies*, Vol. 1(1), pp. 73-86; G. Delanty (1995), "Inventing Europe: Idea, Identity, Reality", Palgrave Macmillan, London; Delanty, Gerard (2002), "Models of European Identity: Reconciling Universalism and Particularism", *European Politics and Society,* 3(3), pp. 345-359; Will Kmlicka (1995), "Multicultural Citizenship: A Liberal Theory of Minority Rights", New York: Oxford University Press; Engin F. Isin and Patricia K. Wood (1999), "Citizenship and Identity", Sage Publications.
43. It refers to rights specific to particular group of people (e.g. women, ethnic and religious minorities) which protects and enables realisation of the particular needs, interests and priorities of these groups. These are the rights, which Isaac Berlin saw as an embodiment of the third form of freedom.
44. See Cesari (2015), "The Lack of Symbolic Integration of Islam in Europe", available at: http://councilforeuropeanstudies.org/critcom/the-lack-of-symbolic-integration-of-islam-in-europe-as-illustrated-by-the-charlie-hebdo-attacks-2, accessed on November 27, 2015; T. Ramdhan (2004), "Western Muslims and the Future of Islam", Oxford; New York: Oxford University Press.
45. See Gurpreet Mahajan (2015), "Negotiating Cultural Diversity and Minority Rights in India", available at:

http://www.idea.int/publications/dchs/upload/dchs_vol2_sec3_4.pdf , accessed on November 29, 2015; Gurpreet Mahajan, "Identities and Rights: Aspects of Liberal Democracy in India", op.cit., also, Lloyld I. Rudolph and Sussanne Hoeber Rudolph, "Living with Multiculturalism: Universalism and Particularlism in an Indian Historical Context", in Richard A. Sheweder, Martha Minow and Hazel Rose Markus (ed.), "Engaging Cultural Differences: The Multicultural Challenges in Liberal Democracies, Rusesell Sage Foundation, New York, 2002, pp. 43-62, Subrata K. Mitr, "Constitutional Design, Democratic Vote Counting, and India's Fortuitious Multiculturalism", Heidelberg Papers in South Asian and Comparative Politics, Working Paper No.4: 1-3, 2001, available at: http://archiv.ub.uni-heidelberg.de/volltextserver/4009.

46. Muslims groups now receive the benefit of reservation in states of Kerala, Tamil Nadu, Karnataka, Andhra Pradesh, Bihar and West Bengal. In Kerala, 12 percent of jobs are currently reserved for Muslims. Karnataka and Andhra Pradesh brought in 4 percent and 5 percent reservation for Muslims in 1994 and 2005 respectively. In Tamil Nadu and Bihar, Muslims are entitled to reservation under the 30 percent and 17 percent category earmarked for other backward classes (OBCs). In 2010, the government of West Bengal has also made provision of 10 percent reservation for Muslims in state educational institutions and public services. In addition to this, some 80 lower caste Muslim groups enjoy the benefit of 27 percent reservation in Central government services and educational institutions as per the Mandal Commission Recommendations.
47. Anwar Alam (2007), "Political Management of Islamic Fundamentalism: A View from India", *Ethnicities,* Vol. 7(1): 30-60.
48. See, James P. Piscatori (1983), "Islam in a World of Nation State", Cambridge University Press, Cambridge; also, "Islam in the Political Process", Cambridge University Press, Cambridge.
49. M. Cooke (2005), "Muslim Networks from Hajj to Hip Hop", University of North Carolina Press; P. Mandaville, "Transnational Muslim Politics: Reimaging the Umma...", op. cit.; P. Mandaville, "Reimagining Islam in Diaspora: The Politics of Mediated Community", *International Communication Gazette*, 2001, t. 63, no. 2-3, pp. 169-186; P. Mandaville,

"Global Political Islam", Routledge, New York, 2007.

50. C. Husband, "The Political Context of Muslim Communities", in, B. Lewis (ed.), "Muslims in Europe", Pinter, London 1994; P. Lewis, "Islamic Britain... ", op. cit.
51. Jose Casonova (1994), "Public Religion in the Modern World", University of Chicago Press.
52. D. Chakrabarty (2007), "Provincializing Europe: Post-Colonial Thought and Historical Differences", Princeton University Press.
53. See, Bruce B. Lawrence, "New Faiths, Old Fears: Muslims and Other Asian Immigrants in American Religious Life", Columbia University Press, New York.

Part I: Nation-States and Religious Minorities: General Overview

1

Minority Matters: Perspectives from the Indian Ocean

Bruce B. Lawrence

In Spring 2009, I was traveling back to Singapore from Manila, where I had just done fieldwork on Muslim minorities in the Southern Philippines. At the airport I bought the latest issue of *Newsweek*. Buried away in "Letters to the Editor", Islam appeared. The subject was the loyalty of Israeli Arabs to the State of Israel. The writer attacked those Israeli Arabs who had supported Hamas during the Gaza conflict of December 2008-January 2009. Though it had been an asymmetrical conflict, one that resulted in over 1,400 Palestinian casualties and another 4,500 injuries, while the Israelis suffered 13 dead, and another 326 wounded, the letter to the editor focused on those Israeli Arabs who had sided with Hamas during that conflict. Not only were these Israeli Arabs guilty of treason, alleged the writer, but, he went on to claim, "Muslims who live in a country where they are a minority—whether they are citizens or not—are often not loyal to that country". [1]

To restate his claim: "Muslim minorities are more often than not disloyal to the countries where they reside. It doesn't matter whether they are mere subjects or full-fledged citizens; they remain disaffected and so disloyal to their country of residence". I was stunned. Who was the writer? He was not a stakeholder in the Arab-Israeli conflict; he appeared to be an Indian. "Gautaum Se" was the signature or pseudonym for this person who had published a broadside attack on Muslim minorities via the Internet. Perhaps he had used the Arab-Israeli conflict as a surrogate for the religious conflict in which he was a stakeholder, Pakistan-India. After all, Hindu India is flanked by two majority Muslim neighbors, Pakistan and Bangladesh. While Bangladesh is largely ignored in the media, Muslim Pakistan is frequently pitted against Hindu India, with Indian Muslims depicted by Hindu extremists (and their relentless media) as a troubling fifth column within the Republic of India.

Whatever the writer's location or identity, one must revisit his presumption that Muslim minorities, wherever they are and whatever the provocation, do not act as loyal citizens: though they may be pious, critics claim, they are seldom patriotic. I want to make the counter claim, to wit, that religious minorities, whether Muslim or Christian, can be—indeed, often are—loyal citizens; they are pious patriots. While that claim might be challenged, the rebuttal would have to account for evidence from countries where minorities are not just immigrants, or recent arrivals, but rather long-standing members of age-old communities. Moreover, these same minorities do not practice their religion quietly in mosques or churches. They also assert their beliefs, and validate their practices, in the public domain. In all the cases I examine, Islam enters the public square; Muslim perspectives infuse the debate about religion, no matter what proportion of the population is actually Muslim. India is no exception but there are other cases in the Indian Ocean that also merit attention at a conference committed to comparing Indian Muslims with Muslim minorities in Europe. Looking east as well as looking west can have its advantages.

I have chosen four polities, two each from North-east Africa or the Horn of Africa, and two others from South-East Asia, or the Phil-Indo Archipelago. There are many other minorities whom I could've chosen—Christians in Sudan and Nigeria, Buddhists and Muslims in China—but in what follows I will look at lessons to be gleaned from four minorities that have persisted over time in coastal Africa and maritime Asia: Copts in Egypt, Muslims in Ethiopia, Kristens and Katolics in Indonesia, and Moros in the Philippines. I will try to demonstrate how the internal dynamics, as also the overseas relations, of these four major polities—Egypt and Ethiopia, Indonesia and the Philippines—depend on the public square. Without examining the public square we cannot understand why minorities matter in the 21st century.

Minorities proliferate in the vast Indian Ocean. Long-standing patterns of trade and interaction from East Africa to Southeast Asia have produced numerous minority communities, often marked by religion. Muslim Egypt borders the Red Sea, and through the Gulf of Aden, accesses the Indian Ocean. It has a large Coptic minority. Christian Ethiopia, though it has no direct access to the Indian Ocean, relying on Somali ports, does share not only the Nile River but also a significant Muslim population with its northern neighbors: Sudan and Egypt. On the other side of the Indian Ocean, Islamic communities emerged in Southeast Asia through trade, and then were displaced in part of Indonesia, as also the Philippines, by Iberian Catholic powers, first Portugal, then Spain. But the Dutch later brought a further religious marking, Protestantism, to Java and surrounding islands. The result today is several minority communities—Muslims in the southern part of Catholic Philippines, with Protestants, Catholics, as also Hindus and 'Chinese' in neighboring Muslim Indonesia.

Overview

If it is water that links these countries, it is water that also separates them. Egypt (via the Red Sea) and Ethiopia (via Somalia) border on the Indian Ocean, yet their survival depends on Nile water. A major head of the Nile begins in Ethiopia, flows through the Sudan and into Egypt. Both Egypt and Ethiopia are riverine, linked by a single river and reliant on the resources, as well as open to the hazards, of a massive internal waterway. By contrast, both Indonesia and the Philippines are maritime nations. They have much more water than land, and the water is oceanic, surrounding and so defining their basic economic and cultural options. Indonesia has over 17,000 islands, the Philippines over 7,000 islands. Not all are inhabited, yet collectively the ethos of maritime history defines them even more than the riverine frame defines Egypt and Ethiopia.

While minority populations proliferate through the Afro-Eurasian *oikumene*, they share minority identities that often seem to put them at risk. Though most are pious patriots, all are secondary citizens: they relate to central power—the capital city with its elites—through asymmetric mechanisms of control. It does not seem to matter whether the minorities are heavily urban, as in the Philippines, or mostly rural, as in Ethiopia. Yet it does matter that Ethiopia, like the Philippines (and also Indonesia), faces attrition through permeable borders. While Egypt and Ethiopia would seem to be well defined through history, Ethiopia has been challenged first by Eritrea and now by Somali claims outside their borders, as well as Oromo nationalists within. [2]

On the other side of the Indian Ocean, the borders for both the Philippines and Indonesia are not only permeable but also malleable: secessionists succeeded in mid-1990s East Timor, and still threaten in 21st Aceh and Papua. To the north, in the present day Philippines, the Muslim minority has been defined by the Moro movement in Mindanao: while it is a low level conflict in military terms, it continues to simmer, and so threatens the internal coherence as well as the external legitimacy of the Filipino government. The Moros are no doubt the least satisfied of all the minority groups considered below, and yet even most of them strive to be pious patriots, to function as both loyal citizens and devout believers, in 21st century Philippines.

If the Moros resemble the Kristens and Katolics of Indonesia, they also share much with the Muslims of Ethiopia and the Copts of Egypt. All four communities are defined as minorities because they are located literally or metaphorically on the margins of what is declared to be the core, central, dominant group of the polity within which they exist. Their actual numbers are less important than how those numbers are managed/manipulated for the interests of others who are not deemed to be 'minorities'. At the same time, one must constantly try to see them as they see themselves. To do so, one must look at minorities not just through top down analysis but also through local vignettes, that is, ethnographies. [3]

My thesis accents citizenship, at once religious and secular. It poses a seeming paradox: Muslim and Christian minorities survive—and occasionally thrive—as secondary citizens in secular polities. If this is true for Egypt, is it also true for Ethiopia? Can it happen in Indonesia but not next door in the Philippines? How do different local histories, diasporic networks, and global patterns shape ground level realities? Are there lessons from Northeast Africa for the rest of Africa, from Southeast Asia for the rest of Asia? And how might Afro-Asian lessons apply to minority citizenship in Western Europe and the Republic of India? Questions abound. Not all can be answered, but the first effort to address them begins with Egypt.

Egypt

Of the four sites, Egypt is the best known globally. Boasting an ancient, Pharaonic culture, Egypt has now become the foremost Mediterranean nation-state, along with Lebanon, which has a majority Muslim population with minority Christian communities. Cultural politics frames, even as it complicates, the issue of religious relationships. The central question asked again and again is: how do people define themselves in relation to compatriots who are not co-religionists? Coupled with this question is the related, equally compelling question: what role does the state play in setting the parameters for the interaction of Muslims and Christians?

While the state is crucial for Egypt, its role in protecting religious freedom has been fiercely debated. Islam came to Egypt overland through Arab armies and conquests dating back to the 7th century. Egyptians were Copts before they were Muslims, but not all Copts became Muslims. A Christian minority has persisted for more than 1200 years. Coptic Orthodox Christianity indeed is the indigenous Christianity of Egypt that, according to tradition, the apostle Mark established in the middle of the first century, ca. 42 AD. The Church belongs to what is known as Oriental Orthodoxy, and Coptic Orthodox Christianity has existed as a distinct church body since the Council of Chalcedon in 451. The head of the church is known as the Pope of Alexandria and the Patriarch of all Africa on the Holy See of Saint Mark.

Hence, the 11 million Copts of Egypt count them as their co-religionists Copts from the south, specifically, the 38 million Copts of Ethiopia and another 2.5 million of Eritrea. The history of Egyptian Christianity thus crosses national borders, though the orientation of most Egyptian Copts has been increasingly shaped by colonialism, nationalism and now the end of the Cold War. [4]

Indeed, one cannot grasp the outlook of Copts today without discerning their role in the emergence of modern Egypt. Here, the picture is not one of Christian-Muslim relations so much as the relation of Western Christians to Eastern Christians as well as to their Muslim compatriots. It is crucial to take some historical snapshots. From the mid-19th century onwards, Egypt was ruled by Britain, and British elites serving in Cairo, like their compatriots back in London, had a very mixed view of Copts. On the one hand, mass literacy had expanded the book reading public. Imaginative travel writers took up the topic of the exotic Orient. They painted Egypt in pictures of luxuriant antiquity along with, and often rivaling, India.

Yet at the same time, there was the pervasive notion that the Copts would somehow degenerate Christians. Some Anglicans saw the need to reform the elaborate Eastern rites that Copts practiced; they advocated exposing their co-religionists to God's unmediated world. But not all Anglicans adopted this hard edged approach towards the Copts. The Society for the Propagation of Christian Knowledge (SPCK), for instance, was content to influence indigenous ecclesial hierarchies, while evangelicals of the Church Missionary Society (CSM) took the opposite tack, often resorting to direct confrontation and outright proselytization. Especially after 1857, with the opening of the Suez Canal, Egypt became an even more important nodal point in the British imperium. Though a presence among the Copts was deemed critical to all Anglican missionaries, no single overriding policy emerged.

Ironically, during the same period when higher criticism of the Bible was drawing more scholarly attention to 'pure' Coptic biblical texts, Copts themselves were regarded either as unworthy carriers of this scriptural treasure or else as outright heretics. Even those from the SPCK who tolerated the Copts were not willing to invest the time, as well as the money and prestige, which American Presbyterians, for instance, invested in trying to provide educational venues for motivated, upwardly mobile, urban Copts. American University of Cairo, like its sister institutions in Beirut and Istanbul, was the product of Presbyterian, not Anglican, commitment to the well being of 'Easterners' as modern subjects and potential citizens.

As Hannah Arendt made clear, minorities emerged in the aftermath of World War I, largely to cement newly configured nation-states. [5] Minority issues then became a fixture of internal as well as external political arrangements. Within British controlled Egypt, the Copts came to be seen as the Christian minority within a dominant Muslim majoritarian state, much as did the Muslim minority within a dominant Hindu majoritarian state in colonial South Asia. Till today, the recurrent question has been: how do Coptic citizens respond to the increasing efforts to Islamize Egyptian society, with parallel efforts by international agencies to protect them as vulnerable and in need of 'outside' protection? The storyline goes back more than one hundred years.

In 1882, Britain occupied Egypt, allegedly for a limited

time but in fact, for an extended period that did not end till 1936 when the British signed an Anglo-Egyptian treaty, even though British dominance continued till the Free Officers' Revolution of 1952, and arguably did not end till the Suez Crisis of 1956. 1882 marked the beginning of a pattern of government-church relations that endured well beyond 1952, when Egypt celebrated independence from indirect British control. What evolved was an effort by rival groups within the state and within the Church to project their image as the correct, and dominant one in public space. During the last decade of the 19th century, Coptic priests and patriarchs were engaged in an internal struggle for reform, and into that fray Coptic elites, especially landowners and rich shopkeepers in Alexandria and Cairo, tried to influence the outcome.

The British public became more and more aware of a 'Coptic problem'. The accent increasingly came to focus on race. The Copts were deemed to be a separate race, at once weak and sickly, compared with the stolid Egyptian Muslim peasant or fellah. The British governor, Lord Cromer, once remarked famously that the Copts were just Egyptians who went to church, but then as the fires of nationalism began to warm around the Nile, Cromer, along with his successors, changed their view. They adopted a pro-Coptic policy which maintained them as a race separate from their Muslim compatriots and because the older, also the superior race. [6]

Egyptian Muslims reacted to the racial accent on Coptic difference by lauding themselves as the true liberators of Egypt, first from the Turks and now from the oppressive British. They stigmatized the Copts as a dead weight from the past, mere 'sons of Pharaoh'. Yet to Coptic elites, the stigma became a badge of pride. Indeed, they were the sons of Pharaoh, the only true descendants of the ancient Egyptians. And were they not only the most ancient and authentic Christian community on earth but also the originators of Western civilization, having passed on their wisdom to the ancient Greeks? Not all Copts followed their elites in channelling Pharaonic ideology to religious or sectarian ends. Some used it as the basis for an appeal to their Egyptian compatriots. They tried to make common cause at once against the British and against Pan-Islamists, those who advocated Islam as the single, unifying principle for a post-colonial future marked by national independence.

All these arguments and counter arguments were advanced in public space, a new and widening public space made possible by rapid use of the press, pamphlet and telegram after the 1880s. Foreigners as well as Egyptians engaged each other in this space. [7] But it was the Egyptian Muslims who availed themselves of the new media by putting the debate into the starkest racialist terms. They maintained their own identity as true Egyptians while depicting European and others as outside manipulators of indigenous groups, including the Copts. Even as Coptic separatists tried to argue that the genuine Egyptians are the Christian Copts who alone trace an unadulterated descent from the race to whom the civilization and the culture of the ancients was largely due, Lutfi as-Sayyid, leader of the Egyptian national movement, countered that Coptic separate electorates derived not from racial origins but from Islamic law. The Copts were a sect (*ta'ifah*), not a nation (*ummah*). Though they could be marked off as different, they never had been, nor should they ever be, recognized as a wholly separate community.

It was not, however, local arguments or ground level events that determined the future of Copt-Muslim relations. 20th century Egypt was shaped, above all, by events before and after World War I. Before the War, the British found themselves struggling to combat German diplomatic advances, for instance, with Turkey, and they could not afford to alienate Muslim opinion. Coptic claims to be given preferential treatment as an aggrieved Christian minority were subordinated to the larger goal of co-opting Muslim leaders to form an Egyptian front against the Kaiser. In the aftermath of the Great War, the world congresses of European powers, overseeing the formation of new Arab states, strove to make them consensual unities based on the greatest majority. The case for Coptic separatism was lost.

Gradually, Copts assimilated more and more to their Muslim neighbors. Often they lived in adjacent or mixed neighborhoods. Many Copts learned classical Arabic and were taught the Qur'an. During World War I and its aftermath, there were sporadic anti-Copt outbreaks, yet more often mullahs and Coptic priests were projected in the popular press as demonstrating side by side for a common cause: to oppose British presence on Egyptian soil.

From 1874, a consultative council, the Majlis al-Milli, which was composed of lay Copt members, helped to govern the affairs and activities of the Coptic Church. The Majlis al-Milli was established as a parallel institution to the Coptic Orthodox Church with a mandate to oversee Coptic endowments (*awqāf*), Coptic schools and institutions, and Copts' personal status courts, but under Nasser, the government made policies to deliberately curb the powers of the Majlis al-Milli. The 1957 presidential decree regarding laws for electing the patriarch reflected the will of conservative clerics and dismissed all the concerns and propositions of the Majlis al-Milli. Yet the weakening of the Majlis al-Milli was not accompanied by the strengthening of any other institution that pressed the church for greater accountability, transparency, and reform.

Till today, the leadership and the laity of the Coptic Church are conflicted about what they can, or should, derive from participation in the Egyptian public sphere. In the past decade, many Egyptian Copts demanded more equality between Copts and Muslims in Egypt. They have been asking for full citizenship rights, especially for protection against discrimination in the Egyptian legal and social spheres. During the 2006 debates regarding Constitutional Amendments, some public Coptic figures went so far as to request the abolition of Sharia law as the basis of legislation for the Egyptian Constitution. They argued that for them to be an equal and integral part of the Egyptian society, the Egyptian Constitution should be derived from secular rather than Islamic legal basis.

Yet, it could be argued, "their public discontents and their interest in reform have only been heralded at improving their own legal and social status in the Egyptian pubic sphere. The Coptic Orthodox Church's reform agenda is narrowly focused on Copts' own survival as a religious minority in Egypt, rather than supporting democratization. Coptic civil society organizations are more concerned with empowering the poor and marginalized sections of the society than with supporting civic and political rights causes. Moreover, many Egyptian Copts support the existing status quo and do not want the country to democratize. They feel that the Egyptian ruling elite, including the Coptic hierarchy, over-emphasize the Islamic fundamentalist threat". [8]

At the same time, however, "there are now too many important players on both sides with diverse and changing agendas beyond the 'will' of the Pope, among them the plural and active Coptic diaspora. Some Copts now openly contest the Pope's authority to speak on behalf of all Copts and are using their own power bases to mediate requests that radically challenge the way in which the Egyptian state chooses (or prefers) to handle the "Coptic question" in Egypt...At the same time, the state security apparatus (which can, and does, operate as a parallel authority to the political establishment, i.e., the President, cabinet ministers, etc.) does not always comply with government policy, and since there is little evidence of a deep personal entente between President Mubarak and Pope Shenouda, it is increasingly difficult for both sides to secure their part of the bargain". [9]

As bleak as these perspectives are, suggesting a constricted space for the Coptic minority within contemporary Cairene socio-political circles, there is a countervailing view from the street. Some interviewees argue that they have become stronger because they have to be aware of their minority status. Though they dislike discrimination—in the media, in movies, on identification cards—they still feel that the current government protects them and even that they are living in a relatively good era. They have an incentive to be creative. While some do fear that the Muslim Brotherhood will continue to target Copts, many more feel that the Muslim Brotherhood is not representative of Egyptian Muslims at large. What they truly fear is the 'protection' shown towards them by Copts abroad; the intervention of these long distance nationalists worries them more than do the designs of Islamists to impose Sharia laws, and so curtail all pluralist options in the Cairene public square. [10]

Ethiopia

When one travels south from Egypt to Ethiopia, one finds the passage up the Nile clogged at the level of public discourse. The same expansion of the public square to include religious issues, and above all, discussion of religious identity, has not occurred in 21st century Ethiopia. There is no public square in Addis Ababa that begins to be measured next to, much less competitive with, the actors and agents that abound, even as they contest each other, in Cairo.

The very notion of Islam in Ethiopia or Ethiopian Muslims is unfamiliar outside a small circle of academic aficionados. That inattention has deep historical roots. Ethiopian Muslims are, in fact, blighted by their nation's history—distant, medieval and modern. Ethiopia is defined more by its storied past than by its uncertain present. The majority of books, whether scholarly or popular, relate to ancient Ethiopia. They project the glories of Aksum, medieval dynasties engaged by Ottomans, Portuguese, then Italian and British interlopers, and finally the emergence of Haile Selassie and his Derg successors in the 20th century. There is, of course, a nasty contemporary codicil, the Eritrean-Ethiopian War that smouldered during the 1970s, then produced an independent, if still contested, Eritrea in northern Ethiopia during the 1990s. Eritrea remains an independent, if far from self-sufficient, Red Sea nation, at the same time that a post-Derg, constitutionally redefined Ethiopia has emerged under Meles Zinawi, the Tigray head of the TGE (Transitional Government of Ethiopia), who came to power in 1991 and now as Prime Minister of the FDRE (Federal Democratic Republic of Ethiopia) continues to win elections, albeit disputed, and to govern from Addis Ababa.

In part, it is rampant regionalism that has characterized post-1991 Ethiopia and makes any Muslim identity difficult to project, much less sustain. The history of internal conflict is protracted, complex and volatile. The 1991 Addis Ababa Conference established 12 provinces, based on ethnicities as defined by dominant mother tongues. Oromia emerged as the largest province, but had to include several pockets of non-Oromo speakers, and its neighbour, which also is its closest competitor for national dominance, Amhara, included groups with varied histories and dialectical preferences, the Gurage, Kembata and Hadiya, now merged into a single province with Amharic as its language. [11]

It is no surprise then that post-1991 Ethiopia stresses ethnic federalism rather than religion: with more than 82 ethnic minorities, the Federal Democratic Republic of Ethiopia is still experimenting with a project of national integration that is far from complete. The most celebrated national day occurs in early December. Labelled Nations and Nationalities Day in Ethiopia, it brings representatives from all 82 ethnic/regional groups to Addis Ababa where they celebrate their distinctive contributions to the Federal Democratic Republic that Ethiopia strives to be. It is this “museum of nations” approach to collective identity and nation-building that has prevailed since 1991, and shows every sign of continuation.

The impact of this history and practice on the status of Ethiopian Muslims is determinative. It fosters continuous debate about complex relationship between language, ethnicity and religion in contemporary Ethiopia. Since 1991 and even more since 1994, Ethiopia has reconstituted itself in multi-ethnic terms [12] with the result that at the local level there has been a shift away from Amharic, not least due to "a regionalization policy that meant change to a curriculum (for education) in local languages". In the past fifteen years, Amhara has become no more than "a constituent identity within a larger polyglot state". [13]

The most durable, as also regrettable, consequence is for knowledge production about Islam. Under Haile Selassie, Muslims were marginalized and excluded. [14] His successors, the Derg (1974-1991), [15] were deemed to be even handed: they were opposed to all religious groups and so depressed the dominant Amharic speaking Ethiopian Orthodox more than others. The result, however, is that the current generation of devout Muslims, who are also loyal Ethiopians, have to wrestle with a double identity, at once national and religious. They confront regional disparities as well as ethnic/linguistic discriminations. Yet all 82 ethnicities have at least some Muslim members, and so Islam is the most trans-regional of Ethiopia's dominant religions. (The Orthodox Christians, by contrast, have majorities only in Amhara and Tigray, though they have a sizable presence—1/3rd of the population—in Oromia). But a key challenge that pervades all these processes comes from the 'other' Christian group or groups: evangelical Protestant missionaries.

One of the outcomes of the 1991 accords in Addis Ababa was not only the opening of Ethiopian public space to outside groups, NGO support groups and regional peace keepers, but also missionaries. They have especially focused in the Southern Nations, Nationalities, and Peoples Region (SNNPR). There, the Protestant missionaries, but especially Pentecostals, project a progressive, inclusive Ethiopian polity—at once secular and pluralist—committed to public square discussion, debate, and decision-making. [16]

A major consequence of the Protestant presence is their

aggravation of Muslim-Orthodox relations. On the one hand, they irritate the Orthodox since the major converts are not from Muslim but Orthodox or pagan groups, but at the same time, it is Ethiopian Orthodox converts to Protestantism who are more virulently anti-Muslim than their co-religionists, inflaming sectarian sensibilities not just regionally but nationally as well. [17]

The generation shift among Ethiopian Muslims may yet be decisive: pre-Derg there was not much knowledge production among Oromo or Shawa urban elites who were Muslims. [18] Most of the G-7 global leadership and the Euro-Am public at large imagined—and continues to imagine—Ethiopia as above all a Christian island in a Muslim sea. Ethiopia is seen to have always been, and still to be, marked forever as an Orthodox Christian, Amharic speaking nation.

The large scale problem is knowledge production from within Ethiopia. Knowledge that indigenous Ethiopian Muslims have produced about their own past, distant and recent, remains minimal. It is foreign scholars, to wit, Spencer Trimingham, Donald Levine, and Haggai Erlich, who are most often quoted in illustrating the nature of Ethiopian collective experience. [19]

Since the texture of Ethiopian Muslim life must be gleaned from other sources, the asymmetry between the issues highlighting terror and other long-term structural and social relations remains as notable as it is regrettable. When it bleeds, it leads, in modern media, and the sub-surface changes that portend future tectonic shifts are often missed.

We noted a wealth of sites that provide information about Copts and Muslims in the Cairene public square, yet the opposite is true for Ethiopian Muslims. One must search out evidence from myriad, microelements, and piece together a tapestry of information, mostly from local parties and also from the younger generation of university students who are becoming familiar with a Muslim identity that is not solely regional but also not foreign directed, or Salafi dominated.

Too often the accents are on heroes—or villains—of the Ethiopian Muslim Diaspora, reflecting the larger Ethiopian Diaspora, abetted by both economics and politics, yet the most important developments for Ethiopian comity may be internal: the shifting relationship between regional entities, the rising accent on religious identity, and, above all, the process of generational change. Especially the last may be decisive. A new generation of urban Ethiopian elites (those who have come from rural or regional locations to Addis Ababa, where they account for a large number of the 16 percent of all Ethiopians who are urban) now live in a new era. While still marked by conflict, children of the new post-1991 era do not accept, or relive, the horrors of past divisions. There are signs that Ethiopian Muslims, together with their Christian compatriots, may be reaching for a calmer, more integrative future.

That future will depend partly on outside forces and their impact on developments within Ethiopia, but they may be more electronic than dogmatic in nature. The Internet has expanded, with an increasing number of websites coming online that engage Ethiopia specific concerns, options and audiences. NGOs, too, are attracted to Addis Ababa, in part because it is the center for UN peacekeeping operations throughout the Horn of Africa, in part because of missionary activities that spur foreign interest, but also because many groups want to see Ethiopia as 'the model for integration'. Meles Zinawi and the FDRE are, of course, at the center of this re-definitional project, but there are also notable foreign groups who participate in Ethiopian initiatives and reinforce this image. [20]

Finally, there is the question of measurement. It relates back to the issue of scope and scale, to wit, which minorities are being described and how large, or small, are the communities they are alleged to represent. In the first instance, the question has yet to be resolved about the importance of religious minorities from Africa and Asia generally, and

Muslim-Christian, Christian-Muslim minorities in particular. Religious identity never stands apart from other identity markers. How does it compete against, or elide with, other identities? The question has been raised acutely in Egypt where all are presumed to share a common national heritage and historical context, but in Ethiopia such convergences do not rest on either a collective memory or a public will that is consensual, much less unanimous.

On the most basic issue of scale, one must revisit ground level realities and disparities. How many Muslims are there in Ethiopia? The question has been complicated by a December 2008 census that indicates that the Muslim 'minority' population remains at 32.8 percent of the total Ethiopian population of ca. 80 million. Yet, beneath that statistics lies a firestorm of controversy. Not just indigenous Muslim sources but also the CIA Factbook claims that Muslims represent 45-50 percent of the total population, and since Ethiopia is a country of four religions—Muslim, Orthodox, Protestant and animist—that would make Ethiopia a predominantly Muslim country. [21]

One could use this statistical stand-off either to confirm that Ethiopia is, in the words of one Ethiopian Orthodox author, "a model nation of minorities" [22] or the opposite: that there is systematic discrimination against Muslims, denying them their role, and also their privilege, as the 'true' majority population of modern day Ethiopia.

Whatever the outcome of these queries, there persists the need to identify the local profiles of a religiously subaltern community (whether majority or minority, whether Oromo or Amharic or other) within a broad yet far from seamless national profile. Who are the leaders and opinion shapers of the Ethiopian Muslim community? Will there emerge a more vibrant public square? How can one assess the fears and hopes, the limits and options that Ethiopian Muslims face in the 21st century? At the very least, we need to measure the scope and scale of overseas, immigrant networks, and ask: what is the impact of these networks on perceptions of nationhood and citizenship for Muslims committed to the Ethiopian nation-state? Few of these questions can be answered from analytical sources, but some clues do appear from recent, in depth interviews. [23]

The Moros of Mindanao

When we travel across the Indian Ocean, from the Horn of Africa to Southeast Asia, the very first move has to be a move to restore balance, not just between South and North, as equally important on a global canvas but also towards a research agenda that links theoretical reflection to empirical reality. The issues of community definition, tension between prescriptive norms and individual choices, between minority rights and majority needs—all deserve sustained attention, but not at the expense of omitting local issues and also ignoring local disparities.

And the most major initial decision is how to talk about the common geo-political but also cultural-religious environment that links Philippines to Indonesia. A standard account of the Philippines invokes this 7,000 island maritime region as "a melting pot of nations and different influences". We are told that: "it has been the meeting point of numerous migrations. The Philippines started being colonized by foreign traders from the 10th century onwards: Moslems settled in the southern regions and the Chinese settled in Luzon. Philippines was a country without cities; its urban development coincides with the arrival of Western culture in the 16th century. Philippines only began to widen its trading horizons after the arrival of the Spaniards, by means of an extensive trading network that united all continents. The Philippines remained under the Spanish Crown until 1898, while many of its neighbour territories fell successively under the influence of different European powers: Portugal, France, Holland and Great Britain". [24]

End of story, or is it? For what this blinkered view of

history ignores is the internal narrative of historical separation between Northern and Southern sectors of the Philippine archipelago. [25] The key word is "Sulu". It was signalled in stark, graphic terms by the Australian historian James F. Warren, and more recently by the Japanese scholar, Sinzo Hayase. [26] Warren provided the first comprehensive study of Sulu.

He demonstrated the pivotal role of the Sulu islands as also western Mindanao, especially Maguindanao, in developing an extensive, profitable but also fragile maritime network, apart from the Visayas and Luzon. Hayase then charted in detail what he terms East Maritime Southeast Asia. In this East-West, instead of North-South, construction of the Philippines, Mindanao plays a central role (rather than its current, peripheral role). Hayase does not argue for the prioritization of Islam or Islamic identity.

Instead, he observes, "by emphasizing Islam, we tend to miss what was there before the area became Islamized". What is preferred instead is the quotidian context needed for a background to discuss current problems and today's social/political issues, and so Hayase portrays "the relationship between Muslims and non-Muslims, including Christians, in the setting of peaceful everyday life". [27] From his study emerges a profile of the maritime world as above all an open society, one where networks crisscross almost all prescribed boundaries. It is a social space where amiable behaviour is the norm rather than periodic warfare.

From there it is a long leap into the artifice of the contemporary nation-state. As American historian Michael Hawkins has observed, "There is no historical pre-colonial basis for the Philippines current territorial boundaries". (Hawkins, 2008:24) In other words, the boundaries were imposed. They did not evolve. Under the Treaty of 1898, Spain ceded Philippines to the US, and Philippines remained under the US control till 1946. The aftermath was an artificial state, GRP (Government of the Republic of the Philippines).

Equally problematic was the Moro Declaration of 1976, which laid claim to another, equally fictive entity, an 'eternal' Bangsamoro homeland. In both the cases of GPR and Bangsamoro, it was the long arm of European colonial rule that defined the most basic geo-political frame of reference. In protest against this state above nation or statist approach, we now have a fresh corrective from an old time SE Asian hand, Theodore (Dorie) Friend. Former president of Swarthmore College, Friend has spent years in both Philippines and Indonesia, and he has continued to light the fires of debate about this vast archipelago through his writings. One is an edited volume, titled: *Religion and Religiosity in the Philippines and Indonesia—Essays on State, Society and Public Creeds* (SAIS, 2006).

Friend treats the entire archipelago as water connected islands and not a contiguous landmass, so much so that the initial map in his timely book highlights only that part of SE Asia, from the Indian Ocean to the Pacific Ocean, which is marked by islands. And so it excludes Malaysia, Singapore, as also East Timor and Australia. In effect, Friend invites us to think not of separate nations but of one archipelago: the "Phil-Indo Archipelago". The accompanying map gives Philippines and Indonesian islands, one color. This visual ploy, for Friend, as also for his contributors, makes the case that there is geographically but one archipelago. It may also be considered to contain one basic ethnicity and one common language family, with a population exceeding 330 million. If this were one nation, it would be the third largest in the world, after China and, of course India. It would be bigger than the US.

While this is an interesting—some would say, flighty—exercise in "re-imagining" brute facts, on the ground, we have carved Phil-Indo into two nations, each with a different majority religion. Yet, Friend's sweeping description is instructive: "majority politics evoke minority resentments, with incomplete assimilations. Unitary visions and definitions produce systematic contradictions, unsuccessful secession movements, and random bloody divisiveness". [28]

The first systematic contradiction to observe is the very naming of the two broad entities discussed. According to Pramoedya Ananta Toer, arguably Indonesia's foremost modern novelist and also social commentator, Indonesia was not the first choice of its inhabitants. It refers to 'Indian islands', the dream destiny of the expansionist Spanish, while in fact, a preferred, pre-Spanish name is Nusantara (the islands between, that is, between major seas) (or sometimes, Dipantara, the fortress or chain of islands, between major seas). Similarly, Philippines did not emerge naturally as the name of first choice for the islands to the north of Nusantara/Dipantara. They could be, and briefly were, named Islas de Poniente, the Islands of the West (by Lopez de Villabolos, who preceded by three years (1541-1544) the renaming of these same islands as Las Islas Filipinas, after Philip II of Spain).

Imagine how different would be the image of this vast maritime region if one talked about its northern part as Islas de Poniente (Islands of the West) and its southern part as Nusantara (the westerly islands between the Indian Ocean and the Pacific). It is worth noting that at least one group, the founders of AMAN, an advocacy group for Indigenous Persons or IPs in Jakarta, have extracted more symbolic capital for their movement from Nusantara than the familiar 'colonial' name for their nation-state. As in many acronyms, AMAN stands for words that can be more easily recalled than parsed: Aliansi Masyarakat Adat Nusantara, that is, alliance of the community (bound together by) customary law in the archipelago. [29]

Even though the past is seldom re-inscribed without the European traces that have shaped both parts of the Phil-Indo Archipelago, we can still project a new imaginary about the social meaning of Phil-Indo in the 21st century. In what follows I will accent the public sphere. I am not arguing that the public sphere supplants the need for political reforms, economic change and social justice. But I do assert that in part due to the new information age, as described by Manuel Castells, but also due in even larger part to the renewed accent on civil society and public intellectuals as agents challenging status quo politics, the public sphere now in 2009 has become a site of information, discussion, contestation, political struggle, and organization that includes the broadcasting media and new cyberspaces as well as the face-to-face interactions of everyday life.

In terms of both parts of the Phil-Indo Archipelago, the public sphere has become a place where arguments about local identity and nation formation should, can and do take place.

But first one must note of some characteristics of the modern constructs of the Philippines, and also Indonesia. Both are top-down, region-directed, centrist-ruled, elite privileged nation-state polities.

(a) Top-down: Each has its political—as also economic, social and cultural—options determined from a major metropole, Manila in the Philippines and Jakarta in Indonesia. Statistics in both cases are conjectural, but widely cited are estimates that of a total Filipino population of 90 million in 2009, 2 million live in Metro Manila, while 15-20 million live in Greater Metro Manila, that is between 1/6 to 2/9 of the total populace is directly and daily linked to the capital city. In Jakarta, the numbers and proportions are also striking. Of an estimated 230 million Indonesians in 2009, 130 million or 55 percent live on the single island of Java, with 8.5 million living in Jakarta City and 29 million living in Greater Jakarta. That is, 1 out of every 4 Javanese, and 1 out of every 8 Indonesians reside in the orbit of Jakarta.

(b) The demographic dominance of the metropole is enhanced by other regional factors. The island of Quezon is but one of three major island groupings (in a constellation of 7,100) in GRP, yet it sets the tone for the others, just as Java, one of the 3-4 major islands of the Indo-part of the Phil-Indo archipelago, dominates the others.

(c) Political developments under colonial rule—Americans in Quezon, the Dutch in Java—not only favoured the capital city/metropole but also cultivated certain groups to prevail over others in major sectors of economic, political and social life. [30] Elites in both countries have masked their privileged status through stratagems of populist rhetoric and broad patronage networks. [31]

(d) Even more compelling as a parallel of monolithic, class-directed national politics between both ends of the Phil-Indo archipelago is the role of mass demonstrations as a lever for political change. Friend not only makes the argument that the entire archipelago should be seen as a continuous cultural space but also that the major events defining the Philippines were EDSA I, II, III and maybe IV. Filipino scholars do not even define EDSA; it is so pervasive in the literature and so well known in discourse, both academic and popular. [32] They are popular uprisings that brought about a change in government but not in society at large, in 1986, 2001 (twice). These mass demonstrations of people power are hailed as evidence of the strength of civil society, but they also show the greater power of elites to manipulate evident dissent, and apparent revolt, to their own advantage. "The main beneficiaries of EDSA I and II, those who dominate Philippine society and politics today", writes US-based historian Vicente Rafael, himself a student of Ben Anderson, "find themselves in a bind. For they are at once the inheritors and the targets of ghostly calls for justice (from the masses), embodying while seeking to exorcise the spectrality of a nation colonized by the state". [33]

The spectrality of a nation colonized by the state—it is a sinister, terrifying image, but it is one also conjured in Indonesia since 1997: the masses seemed to rise up, there was a change in government, but the power structures in both society and politics remained, and still, unchanged. [34]

And so in 2010, Moros in Mindanao as well as Katolics and Kristens in Indonesia find themselves situated as marginal minorities, defined by location as much as by ethnicity or religion, and relegated to second-class citizenship in nation-states that never lose their hyphenation. In Vicente Rafael's dictum when applied to the Philippines but also relevant to Indonesia, "it is this historical conundrum, of the nation colonized by the state, which the hyphen in 'nation-state' at once evokes and obscures". [35] Both Moros and Kristens share membership in a nation-state where boundaries between state and nation are uncomfortably elided.

Yet, even prior to considering that datum, one must recognize the gap of public instruments in each polity. For Philippines, it is the deceptive artifice of a democratic republic that conceals the reality of a moniker monolith, relying on structural asymmetry to project a Manila centered, Catholic ethos as the sole, exclusive brand of contemporary Filipino national identity. In addition to inadequate resources, there are also informal censorship policies, and above all, lack of a vibrant, sustainable and easily accessible public square. Multiple institutions represent, project and also contest each other, but they do so at the local level for local constituencies. [36] Collectively, they offer more a cacophony than a panacea for the ills of Moro Filipinos.

To the extent that there is any instrument from civil society struggling to make the case that Filipino identity transcends, and in time can reform, the ills of the current GRP, it comes not from the left but from the right. It is articulated, above all, by academics from UP-Diliman who are trained linguists yet argue that the project of indigenization involves rethinking the central unity of *kabuuang bayan* (the national whole). [37] What is highlighted is a double need: (i) to promote *tagalog* over English as the medium of instruction and also public square debate, and (ii) to locate all such debates in the Philippines, not abroad, whether in W. Europe or N. America. [38] In the name of transcending politics, especially elite nationalist politics, the *kabuuang bayan* movement has reclaimed the nation from nation-state. It privileges '*bayan*' as the desired cultural nation, in opposition to '*bansa*', the official/elite nation [39] and it has formulated ADHIKA, yet another moniker framed as an acronym, that means "Aspiration/Vision for the Philippines", with the express goal of getting elementary school teachers and local community leaders to transform the social sciences in general and history in particular for multiple constituents". [40]

On the face of it this could be an integrative, dialogic initiative benefiting Muslims and Lumads as well as Christian Filipinos. But the actual deployment of ADHIKA suggests that its vision accents history as teleological, producing a single, coherent Filipino ethos, race and nationality, [41] and so to redefine Moros as but one more minority at par with others. Mendoza, in theorizing the growth and vision of the indigenization project, dismisses the Moro struggle as merely the outcome of an American divide-and-rule policy. [42] Not once does Mendoza acknowledge the settler policy, a draconian policy emanating from Manila that has changed the face of Mindanao during the past 100 years. From 76 percent of the population, Moros are now 20 percent "as a result of internal Christian migration, corporate expansion, land grabbing and seizures, and family displacements from the armed conflict". [43]

What the indigenization movement and its several social/educational instruments do is to allow GRP to claim that it is maintaining its openness to Moro participation in the Manila-based, Quezon-oriented, Catholic-dominant, elite controlled Filipino public square. The arbiter, as also the beneficiary of Filipino culture wars is the moniker state, i.e. a state that reinvents itself through new modifiers, acronyms that refer to projects of national interest that seem to signify novelty while in fact retaining a century-old purpose: to have the ruling elite from Manila benefit from all the trafficking in new ideas and names, meetings and treaties that allure the listener/reader/observer but do not change facts on the ground.

Much more could and should be said about the dense,

often complex twists and turns of diplomatic/military manoeuvres in Filipino politics but the above leads to one inescapable conclusion: while there are multiple, often contradictory, ways of thinking about Moro-state relations in contemporary Philippines, the only wisp of hope for the Moro masses is not unlike what Max Lane traces for post-Suharto Indonesia: *pergerakan*, or a national revolution of social norms, with change from the bottom up (through civil society, including inter-religious dialogue initiatives) instead of the top down (due to political stalemate, at least through May 2010, with majority/minority relations defined as zero-sum and no political will to buck the anti-Moro sentiment from Catholics and Protestants but also from some Lumad and other IP segments of Mindanawon society. [44]

Civil society initiatives have multiplied in Mindanao, especially since the end of the Marcos era via the EDSA I revolution (1986). Carolyn Arguillas, arguably the leading independent reporter on the Southern Philippines, has charted their emergence, and also their impact. [45] Yet her conclusion is far from roseate. "Despite the best efforts of civil society actors", she warns, "the powers to decide rests in Metro Manila with people who have not, and will not feel, the consequences of their decisions".

What she observed in 2003 remains even more forcefully and painfully true in 2010. To begin to feel just how much more precarious the so-called peace process has become since August 1, 2008, here is the lament of Father Jun, aka Father Eliseo Mercado, former President of NDU in Cotabato, and also Director of Institute for Autonomy and Governance at NDU. Writing in his own periodical, [46] he observed that "at the end of August 2008, the peace talks between GPR and MILF (Moro Islamic Liberation Front) had collapsed. The peace process was on the brink of making history through signing of a MoA AD between GPR and MILF negotiators in KL on August 5, 2008, only to be enjoined by a restraining order from the Philippine Supreme Court on petition by

Christian political leaders who claimed that they were not consulted about the contents of the agreement.

Since the restraining order has been issued, GPR has backtracked from its earlier commitment to sign the agreement and declared that it will not forge any ancestral domain agreement in any form with MILF at this time.

GPR also unveiled its new policy in the peace negotiations. They must be community-based and anchored on willingness of MILF and other armed groups to agree on inclusion of a provision for DDR (demobilization, disarmament and reintegration) in future peace agreements. AFP also has waged armed offensives against particular base commanders of MILF that GPR officials claim were responsible for attacking communities in Maguindanao and Lanao provinces".

And these same GPR claims only became louder when in the aftermath of the 41st anniversary of Bangsamoro Day (March 18, 2009)—which commemorates the infamous Jabidah massacre on the Island of Corregidor that remains unsolved till today—there was a bomb attack on a power transmission tower in Kabacan, North Catabato that resulted in power shortages throughout Southern Mindanao for most of the following week. [47] And, of course, in late November 2009, there was the massacre of 57 members of a rival candidate's entourage, also in Southern Mindanao. [48]

As a final commentary, one has to echo the cynic's lament, to wit, that the public square, like civil society, like human rights, can be co-opted by those who use its form to laud their 'democratic credentials but whose tactics empty it of all meaning. Could GRP really have been surprised that Christian groups would protest MoA AD? Were they not in fact counting on this riposte even as they inked the treaty in KL? [49]

The end result is a classic Catch 22 for Filipino Muslims, one etched by Eder and McKenna even before the Supreme Court of the Philippines listened to the brief of opponents to

MoA AD and ruled that the agreement was "unconstitutional" in August 2008. Leaders of the Bangsamoro movement are caught between two extreme positions, but it is the first position which dictates the second. "The first is the extreme reluctance on the part of the Philippine government to transfer any real power to the autonomous region it has authorized". Their reluctance fuels the cause of extremists, producing the second position, "a new risk that the mainstream movement for Muslim autonomy may be high jacked or derailed by international Islamic extremists following the model of Osama bin Laden". [50]

And of course, every time that the radicals attack, the government claims new justification for retaliation by AFP, at the same time that it curtails further peace talks or introduces still more outlandishly self-serving conditions that the MILF has no choice except to reject.

"For the MILF, lasting peace is impossible as long as there exist nine major issues which constitute what they call the "Bangsamoro problem". The right of ancestral domain tops the list, followed by concern for displaced and landless Bangsamoro...The Philippine government, by contrast, makes the first element in the Six Paths to Peace: "the values and principles of the Filipino as one community". This strikes a discordant note among Muslims in the southern Philippines, who feel that to identify themselves as Filipinos is to accept core Christian-based values they do not share. Even Muslims themselves come from 13 different ethno-linguistic groups, though they are members of the community of believers in Islam (*ummah*).

"(One is left with) two diametrically opposed realities: the central Philippine government will never allow a dismemberment of the Philippine state, while the MILF refuses to engage in the Philippine government system, even through the constitutionally created ARMM (Autonomous Region of Muslim Mindanao)". [51]

There is clearly a zero-sum mentality, a no-win strategy in Metro Manila for the ARMM and its MILF advocates. The prospects for a near term achievement of citizenship rights are bleak for all who self-identify, or are identified by others, as Muslim Filipinos.

Indonesia

Indonesia is the most populous and also the most complex Afro-Asian nation when considering religious citizenship and minority rights. One must begin with the central island of Java. Even though Java is but one of the 17,000 Indonesian islands, it is impossible to understand the contemporary profile of Indonesia without visiting Java and especially its capital city, Jakarta. Back in the 1920s, Jakarta was not Jakarta but Batavia. It was the capital of a Dutch empire that extended from the Malay straits to Borneo. It was a rich jewel in the maritime overseas commerce that Holland had enjoyed since the early 17th century, when the Dutch bested the Portuguese, and made truce with the British and became the European power controlling most of SE Asia.

Today, Batavia is Jakarta, the capital of an independent nation, Indonesia. Indonesia is majority Muslim. With close to 250 million people, it is the fourth most populous country in the world. Only China, India and the United States have more persons within their borders than Indonesia. But, unlike China, India or the US, most Indonesians are Muslims. Exceeding 85 percent of the total population, the 200 million Muslims of Indonesia account for almost 1/5th of all Muslims in the world. While Indonesia is the most populous Muslim country, Java is by far the most populous of Indonesia's 17,000 islands. Home to 110 million, a fuil 10 percent or ca. 11 million Javanese live or work in the capital city of Jakarta.

Though Christians are a minority, they are the second largest religious group in Indonesia. Divided into Protestant and Catholic, there may be as many as 16 million Protestants, together with another 5 million Catholics, through the archipelago. They are dispersed throughout the main cities of Java and adjacent islands, with significant internal differences.

So Islam and Christianity share public space in a moderate, pluralist, openly secular polity: the Republic of Indonesia. Law and tradition protect minorities. Christians and Muslims, along with Hindus, Buddhists, Confucians and animists, are guaranteed freedom of religion in the 21st century Indonesia. But hovering over this picture of serene convivencia is a cloud, a very dark cloud. It comes from public Islam, the violent face of public Islam. In spring 2006, everyone in Jakarta, it seemed, was talking about the cartoon controversy. The controversy had begun when a Danish newspaper published cartoons of Muhammad, the Prophet of Islam. The cartoons showed him to be a terrorist and a wife abuser. Riots erupted in many capitals of the Muslim world. In Jakarta protestors burned flags in front of the Danish embassy at the same time as they accused the West in general of having flamed this fire.

The protests continued for much of February. Late in February 2006, I was speaking in Yogyakarta, the cultural capital of Indonesia. I was speaking at a huge public event attended by more than 2,000 people, and carried live on the most popular local TV station. The person speaking with me was Amien Rais, leader of the second largest Muslim organization, known as Muhammadiya. When asked about the cartoon furore, Rais replied: "Protest once—yes. Protest twice—no. Firmly but calmly, Muslims can, and should, protest against any insult to our Prophet. But they should not protest twice, and never should they protest with violence. Those who do not share the sense of insult will only be further aggrieved at prolonged public outcries".

These wise words came from a former candidate for the presidency of Indonesia, a man educated at Notre Dame and the University of Chicago. Afterwards I joked with him that he had perhaps become too much of a mainstream American due to all his time in the Midwest of the US. "No", he quipped, with a smile, "I just learned from Catholic educators that most Americans and most Indonesians share the same values: you must believe but you also must allow others to disbelieve at the same time!"

At its core what Amien Rais demonstrated is the ability to stand outside oneself, not as a sceptic but as a believer. Not just a believer but one who actually affirms the right of others to disbelieve. It is as if he was enacting the Muslim version of Wallace Stevens' splendid verse: "We believe beyond belief without belief". This is the opposite of the profile of public Islam that extremist Muslims—or extremist Christians—project. It calls on a different sense of self and religion. Even though Islam remains the bedrock of Javanese, and by extension, Indonesian sense of self, it is not Arab Islam. To be sure, the Qur'an in Arabic continues to occupy a special place in Indonesia as it does elsewhere in the Muslim world, but is a special place qualified by the Malay culture of SE Asia. Yet it is not Malay Islam, since it does not prize racial or ethnic identity as the first preference for Islam, as do Muslims next door in Malaysia. Indonesian Islam is, above all, Island Islam, because what connects Indonesians to one another is a sense of multiple, crisscrossing networks. In public discourse, the vast archipelago of Indonesia is known as 'land water' (*tanah a-ir*) or 'outer, westerly islands' *(nusantara)*. Not a single landmass or an interior territory, Indonesia is island after island connected by shipping, trade and travel.

Had it not been for spices, the islands might have remained separate entities; they might never have acquired an overarching political or economic structure. It was the fall of Constantinople in 1453 that propelled the Portuguese and Spanish to seek new sea routes for cloves and nutmeg, the much prized spices of SE Asia. Their Catholic empires were succeeded by Protestant empires, as Dutch and English traders sought to share the lucrative spice trade. Traces of each empire linger till today, the British in Singapore and Malaysia, the Spanish in the Philippines, the Dutch in Indonesia, but the means of transport that brought them to SE Asia also lingers. Not till the late 20th century did air travel become a substitute for water travel, and in much of the archipelago, it is still boats not planes that connect Indonesians to one another and to the outside world.

It is crucial to remember the maritime nature, the islandness of Indonesia when thinking about Muslim-Christian relations, whether in Java or its neighbours. In February 2006, at the same time that the international media was focusing on the cartoon controversy, there was a huge national debate about religious space. A Bill was introduced in mid-March to regulate worship space for all Indonesians, whatever their religious outlook. Some evangelical Christians decried the bill as "a clear danger to religious freedom", while the rector or president of UIN-JKT, the largest Islamic university in Indonesia, embraced the opposite stance. He was a Muslim inclusivist, like Amien Rais, quoted earlier. Azra Azyumardi deemed the new measure a modest improvement over its predecessor, a regulation dating back to 1969. He asked people of all faiths to try to abide by its guidelines during a trial period. It was not a top down regulation but one openly debated and then modified to meet objections. Debate continued: the Indonesian Churches Association (PGI), [52] representing Protestants, along with the Indonesian Bishops Conference (KWI), representing Catholics, protested the initial provisions and so, by late April, a key provision in the bill was changed, reducing the local support needed in order to construct a new worship edifice.

As minor as this matter may seem to non-Indonesians, it is a telltale feature of religious pluralism Indonesian-style that warrants sustained scrutiny. What is most interesting in the debate among contemporary Muslim and Christian Indonesians over the joint ministerial decree [53] is that it exists at all. Indonesia is after all a majority Muslim country, and one would be hard pressed to find another majority Muslim country where such a national debate, or such a government measure, would even be contemplated. Not Saudi Arabia or Iran, not Nigeria or Sudan, not Pakistan or

Bangladesh. Possibly in Jordan or Morocco or Algeria but the populations of these countries are far smaller and less varied than is Indonesia's 250 million island citizens.

If lively public debate distinguishes Indonesia, so does the zest for pursuing pluralism through educational structures, especially metropolitan universities. When in Indonesia as a senior Fulbright scholar during spring 2006, my task was to teach in a new interdisciplinary unit within the leading Islamic University of Indonesia. UIN-JKT is unlike any other Islamic university. Set in the teeming capital city of the world's most populous majority Muslim country, it is dedicated to training religious professionals who are alert to other religions but also to other than fideist approaches to the study of religion. [54] Not that the fideist approach is unrepresented. In the same faculty where I taught a course on religion and conflict to 18 students, half male, half female, with all the females wearing the modified headgear known as *jilbab*, there were also faculties of:

- Islamic thought.
- *Shari'ah.*
- Islamic education.
- Islamic history and civilization.
- *Tafsir* and *hadith* (scriptural commentary).
- Arabic language and literature.
- *Da'wah* (proselytization).
- Islamic economy.

Even before my course had begun, one local newspaper had published a critique of the program in which I was to teach. It was not Islam being taught, claimed the writer, but Western/Christian imports disguised as 'objective' study. The real purpose of the IIS unit of UIN-JKT, alleged the writer, was to convert Muslims to a Western/Christian way of thinking and perhaps in time to actually convert them from Islam to Christianity.

The fear of Christianization versus Islamization has been highlighted again and again. In a recent book provocatively titled *Feeling Threatened*, Mujiburrahman of Sulawesi explores how Christian and Muslim groups embraced public discourse in order to influence and find their place in the emerging Indonesian society of the New Order. This discourse was complex, involving a variety of Muslim approaches for relating Islam to Indonesian political development at the same time that Christians voiced the key concerns of a religious minority trying to negotiate its space in a dominantly Muslim state.

Feeling threatened [55] underscores that the context of Christian and Muslim discourse from Indonesian Independence until the end of the New Order period is, above all, defined by fear. There were twin fears, or fears that mirrored each other. Muslim fears of Christianization were matched, and mirrored, by Christian fears of the Islamization of Indonesian society and in particular the formation of an Islamic state. Muslim fears were actually two-fold: a fear of Christian evangelization of the Muslim population and a fear of Christian opposition to Muslim efforts to implement Islamic law and values within the Indonesian society. These fears arose in a complex context that included Muslim perceptions that in the post-colonial period, Christians would continue the perceived colonialist agenda of making Indonesia a Christian nation. Such fears were exacerbated by a Muslim discourse that asserted that all calls for religious freedom and participation of Christian missions in economic development were a smokescreen for Christian evangelism and the continued presence of foreign missionaries.

By contrast, Christian discourse was driven by fear of an Islamic state and thus supported the New Order government's resistance to implementing Muslim demands for the same. The government of Suharto played an unhelpful role in this discourse of fear, since, as I already noted, it did not seek religious welfare so much as its own continuation in power. The New Order sought primarily to insure its own power by creating ambiguous laws whose implementation was deferred to the distant future or left to local authorities to interpret for themselves.

One should not be surprised that efforts by New Order officials to sponsor inter-religious dialogue rarely reached beyond superficial speechmaking. In effect, Indonesian religious discourse was beset by a zero-sum or war game mentality in which every gain for one religious group was seen as a loss for another. The Suharto Government either could not, or would not, advance a social framework in which both Christians and Muslims might achieve their goals. Instead they preferred that all groups remain dissatisfied and dependent on it as a broker (a tactic very similar to that pursued by the Mubarak regime in Egypt) and also by Arroyo in the years since she succeeded Estrada as the 'elected' President of the GRP.

And so it would seem impossible to escape an unceasing tug of war between inclusivists and exclusivists. There are voices clamouring on both sides in the (largely urban) public square of Jakarta, Indonesia. As Isaiah Berlin astutely observed, "Toleration is historically the product of the realization of the irreconcilability of two equally dogmatic faiths, and the practical improbability of complete victory of one over the other". [56] Martin van Bruinessen would agree. He has shown how likely it is that the center of tolerance, long remarked as a sustained achievement of Javanese/Indonesian island cosmopolitanism, will hold due to the Muslim parties not despite them. "Islamist groups, many of them organized as *jama`ah,* function as another type of civil society organizations. The large mass organizations Muhammadiyah and NU constitute the stable centre of Indonesia's Muslim community and important props of civil society. Many members of these associations are also active in other, non-religious networks and organizations, investing in bridging social capital. Moderation and tolerance have long been characteristic of the mainstream members of these associations. Both have resolutely opposed issues that could lead to the further polarization of society (such as the Jakarta Charter)". [57]

Just three years later, in March 2006, a government decree was opposed by Christian groups and the Ahmadiyya because they contended that the decree would: (a) make it even more difficult for them to worship and (b) the state had no right to regulate the basic right to practice one's faith. [58] The issue of equal protection for places of worship and equal rights to worship will continue to dog all future Muslim-Christian conversations. By the very nature of local autonomy, this issue will continue to resurface, but it will likely remain the basis for low level conflict and not the ratcheted up violence that occurred in the past and—one can dare hope—will be deferred, contained or eliminated in the future. [59]

Conclusion, for North-East Africa and for Southeast Asia

Critical is the scale of religious identity. Since religious identity never stands apart from other identity markers, how does it compete against, or elide with, other identities? What are its limits? This question may be raised acutely in the Philippines, where the fictive notion of a long atavistic past, invoked as Sultanate sovereignty, presumes that all Moros share a common national heritage and historical context, but that is no more secure than its counterpart to the south of this vast archipelago. In Indonesia, the convergences invoked, draw on neither a collective memory nor a public will that is consensual, despite the touted strength of *pancasila* as a robust integrating slogan for an island nation with a myriad of languages, ethnic groups, and local identities. [60]

Even the question of scope for religious minorities remains unanswered. How many Moros are there in the Philippines, how many Kristens and Katoliks in Indonesia? Neither question has a satisfactory answer. [61] For both countries, whatever the answer, the symbolic as well as numerical power of a majority—Catholic to the north, Muslim to the South—will continue to demand for itself, rights reflecting its 'superior' status. The chimera of "a model nation of minorities", which Talal Asad projects to be ideal in a pluralist society, is unattainable, at least for the near future. Discourse and channels of majority/minority identity will persist, with the majority as well as the minority retaining a toxic level of religious illiteracy and so projecting in the public square a zero sum game that finally provides neither success for the nation nor hope for the next generation of its citizens.

Whether we look at Indonesia or Philippines, Ethiopia or even Egypt, nation formation is still an ongoing process. Indonesians need far more stability and continuity than just the brief 10-11 years that have elapsed since the *reformasi* era. In the words of one seasoned observer, Max Lane, Indonesia remains a dream deferred, "a nation unfinished". [62]

For Southeast Asia, even more than for the Horn of Africa, the future is as varied and fluid as the Nusantara/Islas de Poniente. There remains the need to identify the specific local profiles of a religiously subaltern community (whether majority or minority, whether Moros or NGOs supporting Moro rights in Manila, whether Kristens or Katolics in dialogue with Muslim partners on TV and on the Internet in Java). Apart from a vibrant public square, where faces can be seen, voices heard, and views debated and disseminated, how can one gauge the future for Moros in the Islands of the West, and Kristens in the Space between the Seas?

Paramount, though difficult to measure, is the scope and scale of overseas, immigrant networks, as also externally funded NGOs. 'Helping hands from abroad' continue to shape the outlook of pious patriots: 'long distance nationalism' impacts not just perceptions of nationhood but also mechanisms for citizenship in both maritime island states, home to many nations all vying for recognition and respect. The stakes are no less high, for consolidating citizenship rights across the Indian Ocean, in the Horn of Africa, especially for the populous, riverine polities of Egypt and Ethiopia. Their Muslim minorities, like their Christian counterparts, want to be both pious and patriotic, daily confronting multiple forces—internal and external, local and foreign—which strain, without (so far) breaking, that twin allegiance.

Religious minorities remain pious patriots at risk. They survive, but seldom thrive. Their challenges will always exceed their comforts, and yet their well-being—above all, the options they have as compatriots with the religious majority—defines democracy at the local, regional, national and transnational level. Indeed, there is no better measure of the health of democracy than the health of its minorities.

Endnotes

1. Newsweek (March 30, 2009), In the analysis that follows, I pre-suppose, and draw on, research from a number of countries, all of which I was privileged to visit, and to engage with local stakeholders, thanks to the Carnegie Corporation of America. I was honoured to be a Carnegie Scholar of Islam (2008-2010), and used that opportunity to travel to Southeast Asia as well as the Horn of Africa. I acknowledge with gratitude the support I received from the Carnegie Corporation, at the same time that they are not responsible from the views expressed below, all of which are my own.
2. The relationship of Somalis from Ogaden, the Southeastern province of Ethiopia, to their ethnic/religious cohort in Somalia is complex. During the Derg era (1974-91) these ties were exploited by the Soviets who initially supported their Somali client claims against the Mengistu regime, before trying to restore balance and protect the Derg, also a Soviet client state. Only when the Somali war ended could the Mengitsu regime try to bolster its forces against the separatist Eritreans, but it was too late: the latter ultimately succeeded in forming an independent, if fragile, state in 1992. [Harold G. Marcus, *A History of Ethiopia*, Berkeley: University of California Press, 1994-2002: 196-198, 236-245] Overemphasis on the conflict in Ethiopia's North has detracted from the continuing importance of its ties to the South; both frontiers deserve media attention, and sustained analysis.
3. No one has ever before attempted to do actual ethnographies for these four minority communities, connecting riverine Africa to

maritime Asia via the Indian Ocean. The analysis that follows must remain partial because of its novelty and also because of the disparities that it, like other studies, cannot avoid. Disparities exist within as well as between the different minority communities. Such disparities are both empirical and practical. Empirical disparity derives from the fact that some are 'well known', others scarcely recognized. The practical disparity is even more immediate. All these are local studies. They rely on indigenous or native researchers who are now at different stages—of their life experience and also their training as professionals (and therefore aptitude for this kind of fine grained observation, recording, and analysis of diffused data).

4. There continues to be debate about how many Copts there actually are. The MB claims that there are but 6 percent of the total Egyptian population, which would make them about 5 million, but Bishop Marcos, spokesperson for the Coptic Church, announced in mid-2007 that the number of Copts ranges between ten to twelve million, about 15 percent of the Egyptian population (*Nahdat Misr,* July 12-13, 2007). The Egyptian government has long avoided any public announcements regarding the percentage of Copts (Tadros, 2009:284, n. 8).
5. Hannah Arendt, *The Origins of Totalitarianism,* New York: Harcourt Brace & Company, 1948-1973: 269-290.
6. C.A. Bayly, "Representing Copts and Muhammadans" in Fawaz and Bayly, *Modernity and Culture–From the Mediterranean to the Indian Ocean,* New York: Columbia University Press, 2002: 170. Much of the analysis that follows is dependent on Bayly's astute and detailed essay about perceptions of, and attitudes, toward Copts, from Egyptian Muslims as well as British occupiers. While the Arab Spring, that occurred after this paper was given, has changed much in Cairo and elsewhere in Egypt, the range of issues facing Copts and Muslims has remained constant, the challenge of meeting them unchanged.
7. Bayly: 174.
8. Nadine Sika, "Egyptian Copts and the Persistence of Authoritarianism in Egypt", paper given at July 2009 Leipzig Conference on African Studies, Panel 1: Contested Public Spaces: Politics and Religious Movements in Contemporary Northeast Africa, organized by Jon Abbink and Alexandra M. Dias.

9. Abbreviated from Mariz Tadros "Vicissitudes in the Entente between the Coptic Orthodox Church and the State in Egypt (1952-2007), *IJMES,* 41, 2009: 282-284.
10. There are 30 interviews of a variety of Cairene, mostly Coptic interlocutors, provided by a Duke undergraduate Andrew Simon, working with an AUC graduate Reem Abbas, during July-August 2009. Due to lack of time and space, their rich content, and multiple perspectives, have not been included in this draft. They need to be—and will be—included in future iterations of this project. I am indebted to Andrew, to Reem and also to Professor Mbaye Lo, who facilitated arrangements with them in Cairo during summer 2009.
11. Harold G. Marcus, *A History of Ethiopia*, Berkeley: University of California, 2002: 233-234.
12. Ulrich Braukamper, *Islamic History and Culture in Southern Ethiopia: Collected Essays* , Hamburg: Lit Verlag, 2002:27.
13. Ibid., 145, 292.
14. See. e.g., the account of the pseudonymous, Abu Ahmad Al-Ithyobi, as described in *JIS*, 1992:40.
15. Derg Amharic for 'committee', projecting the ideal but far from the actual structure of political rule under the Communist junta.
16. This advocacy is reminiscent of feminism in parts of the Arab/Muslim world. A worthy ideal in itself, it was linked to colonial influence, and so apart from its 'universal' appeal, it acquired a local, ideological tone that undercut, and so reduced, its 'universality'.
17. This view is often expressed in the interviews conducted by Jonathan Cross, a Duke undergraduate, who worked with Sofiya Ali, an Ethiopian graduate student, in order to produce 28 verbatim reports from Addis Ababa during May-July 2009. I am grateful to both Jonathan and Sofiya for their labour, even though this draft was too restricted to include more than a fragment of their far ranging, insightful commentary on the next generation of Ethiopian Muslims.
18. For a notable exception, see Shaykh Said Muhammad Sadiq, as depicted in 2007 M.A. thesis by Endri Mohammed.
19. More recently, some other foreign scholars with interests in ground level social relations and cultural exchanges have begun to appear. Two notable ones are Germans Patrick Desplat (see especially, "The Articulation of Religious Identities and their

Boundaries in Ethiopia: Labelling Different Processes of Contextualization in Islam", *Journal of Religion in Africa,* 2005, and Ulrich Braukamper (see Islamic History and Culture in Southern Ethiopia: Collected Essays, 2002). Another is the prolific Dutch social anthropologist, Jon Abbink, "A Historical-Anthropological Approach to Islam in Ethiopia: Issues of Identity and Practice" in *Journal of African Cultural Studies,* 11/2 (December 1998). And Dereje Feyissa, though EOC in background, is now emerging as a scholar not just of Gambela but of Muslim Ethiopians in diaspora. On the former, see Dereje Feyissa, 'Ethnic Federalism in Ethiopia: The Experience of the Gambella Regional State', in D. Turton (ed.), *Ethnic Federalism in Ethiopia: Prospects and Challenges,* James Currey (2006): 208-230, and also Guenther Schlee in 'The Mbororo Migration into Southern Sudan and Western Ethiopia' in G. Schlee and E. Watson (eds.), *Changing Identifications and Alliances in North-east Africa,* Oxford: Berghahn Publishers, 2009. And for the latter, see "Setting a Social Reform Agenda at Home: The Identity Politics of Ethiopian Muslims in the Diaspora", paper presented at the European Conference on African Studies, Leipzig, June 4-7, 2009.

20. See for instance the December 6-9, 2007 conference in Vienna, The Culture of Accommodation and Tolerance: Islam and Christianity in Ethiopia. Its two organizers were Teshome Wondwosen and Jeruslaem Negash. Their sanguine conclusions are reinforced by a provocative and eloquent set of papers/articles on peace/reconciliation in the new millennium (post-September 2007) for Ethiopia.

    See http://www.einesps.org/forum, especially Donald Levine, "The Promise of Ethiopia", but also less sanguine reflections from Gnamow, Abbas Haji, "Islam, The Orthodox Church and Oromo Nationalism (Ethiopia)" in *Cahiers d'etudes africaines,* 165 (2002):99-120, and also Hussein Ahmed, "Coexistence and/or Confrontation?: Towards a Reappraisal of Christian-Muslim Encounter in Contemporary Ethiopia", [4-22] in *The Journal of Religion in Africa,* Vol. 36, No. 1, 2006.

21. See Hussein Ahmed (1992):17, fn. 9 where he cites a British 1990 source giving 45 percent as Muslims, 40 percent Christians, with the remainder animists, but then later Hussein Ahmed (2001):188, fn.1 provides multiple statistical variations,

the last of which, provided by the FDRE in 1994, gives 32.8 percent as the percentage of Ethiopian Muslims in the overall population.

22. Berhanu Abegaz, "Ethiopia: A Model of Nations" posted on http://www.ethiomedia.com/newpress/census_portrait.pdf, June 1, 2005. This is also the form of polity favored by Talal Asad. It is an ideal type of political arrangement, at once secular and religious, where heterogeneous time prevails, that is to say, "embodied practices (can exist) in multiple traditions; (they can encode) differences between horizons of expectation and spaces of experience—differences that continually dislocate the present from the past, the world experienced from the world anticipated, and (at the same time) call for their revision and reconnection", Talal Asad, *Formations of the Secular–Christianity, Islam, Modernity,* Stanford: Stanford University Press, 2003: 179.
23. For lack of space here, the 28 interviews from Addis Ababa Summer 2009, made available by Jonathan Cross and Sofiya Ali, will be explored and interpreted in a later paper. See footnote 14 above.
24. http://www.aenet.org/manila-expo/page10.htm, accessed on March 28, 2009.
25. http://www.aenet.org/manila-expo/page10.htm, accessed on March 28, 2009.
26. James Francis Warren, "The Sulu Zone, 1768-1898: The Dynamics of External Trace, Slavery, and Ethnicity in the Transformation of a Southeast Asian Maritime State", Singapore: Singapore University Press, 1981. Shinzo Hayase, "Mindanao Ethno-history beyond Nations: Maguindanao, Sangir and Bagobo Societies in East Maritime Southeast Asia", Manila: Ateno de Manila University Press, 2007.
27. Hayase, *op. cit.*, 214.
28. Friend, *op. cit.*, 3
29. See Duncan (2008):107-108, but for a fuller exposition of this group, as also the complexity of their key term, adapt, see Jamie S. Davidson and David Henley (eds.), "The Revival of Tradition in Indonesian Politics: The Deployment of Adat from Colonialism to Indigenism", London: Routledge, 2007.
30. The compelling story of the ilustrato elites has been recounted in Abinales and Ambroso (eds.), "State and Society in the Philippines", Manila: 2005.

31. Exclusionary politics in the Philippines have been noted, though only in broad strokes, in Benedict Anderson, "The Spectre of Comparisons: Nationalism, Southeast Asia and the World", London: Verso, 1998, while the protracted nature of ideological conflict, always controlled by elites and ultimately serving their interests, has been charted for Post-Soharto Indonesia in Max Lane, "The Unfinished Nation: Indonesia Before and After Soharto", London: Verso, 2008.
32. See several essays (Cruz, Rafael and Rocamora) in Friend, op. cit., as also the accompanying vivid pictures (illustrations at pp. 19-23, 31-38).
33. Friend (2006): 58.
34. See Max Lane, op.cit., pp. 260-291, on what he terms the paramount need for "a break out of the conjunctural straitjacket" (284), that is, the rigorous, sustained intervention of a new generation of Javanists to fill the ideological vacuum of the past 45 years (since 1965-66 massacres) that has fostered neo-liberal dependency on IMF, World Bank, and external corporations, authoritarian centralism redeployed as decentralized democracy, and also pervasive fragmentation—of regions and religions—throughout the archipelago.
35. Friend (2006): 62, fn. 4.
36. There are almost too many NGOs and CSOs vying for attention in Mindanao; a brief sampling of their efforts, often convergent but also competitive, is provided in Miriam C. Ferrer, "The Philippine Peace Process", in Teresa S. Encarnacion Tadem and Noel M. Morada (eds.), *Philippine Politics and Governance: Challenges to Democratization and Governance* (Diliman, Quezon City, Department of Political Science, University of the Philippines, 2006: 123-159.
37. S. Lily Mendoza (2006), "Between the Homeland and the Diaspora: The Politics of Theorizing Filipino and Filipino American Identity", Routledge, Manila, p. 216.
38. As Andrew Simon has observed, this Filipino irredentist tactic resonates with a parallel tactic favoured by Copts in Egypt. The Copts too want to control the debate on Copt-Muslim relations and "solve the problem from within".
39. Mendoza, op.cit., 125, 216.
40. Ibid,, 107-108.

41. See, e.g., the several blogs on *Wikipilipinas*, the hip 'n' free Philippine Encyclopaedia, like its Anglo-Wikipedia precursor, but dedicated to a new generation of Filipino intellectuals. And also the annual conference papers of major speakers like Rowena Reyes-Boquiren, Professor of History, College of Social Sciences, University of the Philippines Baguio, who does invoke Moors and/or Muslims in lectures such as "Peoples' Concept of Mission: A Historical Perspective" but only to subsume them under the category IP (Indigenous Peoples).
42. Mendoza citing Azurin (1996) on 82: n39; Azurin is the anthropologist who also wrote on minoritization of Muslims in Thailand and Malaysia.
43. Moro Reader: 33.
44. On the complications of the Lumad and other Indigenous Peoples, see the class study by Rudy Rodil, *The Minoritization of the Indigenous Communities of Mindanao and the Sulu Archipleago* (Davao: Alternative Forum for Research in Mindanao, Inc., 1994). And now that the Bangsamoro AD or ancestral domain has evolved into the Bangsamoro Juridical Entity (BJE), the issue is still more contentious. It has been adroitly, and humorously, presented in 'straight talk' on the following website: http://adayinthelifeofrj.com/2008/08/beginners-guide-to-understanding-bangsa-moro-judirical-entity-bje-moa-ad/cold water on any and all efforts to seek MOA-AD-BJE peace has been provided in Lualhati M. Abreu, "Ancestral Domain: The Core Issue", in *The Moro Reader,* pp. 47-58.
45. See her online essay, "Enlarging Spaces and Strengthening Voices for Peace: Civil Society Initiatives in Mindanao", http://www.c-r.org/our-work/accord/philippines-mindanao/enlarging-spaces.php.
46. Cited from *Autonomy & Peace Review*, 4/3, July-September 2008.
47. I experienced those shortages first hand as I was staying in motel, Azaleas, where we had no power for three nights running, from March 21-24, 2009.
48. See my essay on this brutal, and collusionary attack on women as well as men in "Religion Dispatches", available at:

http://www.religiondispatches.org/archive/humanrights/2076/massacre_in_mindanao%3A_the_irresistible_urge_to_blame_religion

49. For confirmation, one can retrace the sinister history of government manipulations of the language and process of AD, as outlined with admirable clarity by Erasga in, "Ancestral Domain Claim: The Case of the Indigenous People in Muslim Mindanao (ARMM)", *Asia-Pacific Social Science Review*, 8:1, (2008):33-44.
50. Eder/McKenna in Duncan (2008):80.
51. Cited from an online essay on Conciliation Resources, one of the best virtual portals for accessing and reviewing the complex, and still desperate, process of finding peace for Moros in Mindanao. See final section available at: http://www.c-r.org/our-work/accord/philippines-mindanao/negotiations-detours.php.
52. PGI intersects with MADIA (Society for Inter-Religious Dialogue), the second oldest Indonesian organization involved in inter-religious dialogue. Established in 1996 in Jakarta, MADIA started several multilateral and bilateral (Muslim-Christian) dialogue projects. These projects are aimed at Indonesian religious leaders and youth. MADIA operates on an issue basis. Started in 2002, their most recent project is concentrated on the cultural and political question concerning the implementation of the Sharia law, with an emphasis on its gender dimensions.
53. It is a 'joint' ministerial decree because it involves both the Ministry of Religious Affairs and the Ministry of Home Affairs.
54. I am using fideism here in the sense that it proposes faith to the exclusion of all other instruments of knowing or believing but especially pluralism. Competing dogmas characterize fideist worldviews. The existence of other religions puts a fundamental question to fideists—if faith is the only way to know the truth of God, how are we to know which God to have faith in? For fideists there is but one way, and they alone know it.
55. Mujibburrahman (2006), "Feeling Threatened: Muslim-Christian Relations in Indonesia's New Order", Amsterdam: Amsterdam University Press. See also Martin van Bruinessen, "Post-Suharto Muslims Engagements with Civil Society and Democratization", August 2003 workshop, available at:

http://www.let.uu.nl/~martin.vanbruinessen/personal/publications/Post_Suharto_Islam_and_civil_society.html)
and now Alexander R. Arifianto (2009), "Explaining the Cause of Muslim-Christian Conflicts in Indonesia and Tracing the Origins of Kristeniasi (Christianization) and Islamisasi (Islamization)", *Islam and Christian-Muslim Relations*, 20/1, January, 73-89.

56. Isaiah Berlin (1998), "The Originality of Machiavelli in The Proper Study of Mankind", New York: Farrar, Strauss, Giroux, 269-325.
57. Martin van Bruinessen (2003), "Post-Suharto Muslims Engagements with Civil Society and Democratization", August workshop, available at:
http://www.let.uu.nl/~martin.vanbruinessen/personal/publications/Post_Suharto_Islam_and_civil_society.html.
58. See several articles including the *Jakarta Post* front page of March 25, 2006, "Faiths Take Joint Stand against New Decree".
59. This judgment is confirmed in the latest issue of *The Economist* to address Indonesia. See the special section from September 14, 2009.
60. So diverse is Indonesia ethnically that while the official number of ethnic groups is said to be 300, a major human rights advocate, Habib Chirzin stated that the actual number is 1,173 at a seminar in Le Meridien for Religion-Society Dialogue, March 13, 2009.
61. In Spring 2009, I heard a prominent Roman Catholic priest from Jakarta assert that Catholics were 5 percent of the population, with all Protestant groups another 5 percent, but that same evening his statistics were challenged by a major Muslim intellectual, who gave the statistics as 3-4 percent Roman Catholic, with 6-8 percent Protestant! (The official figures provided in the initial map are, of course, still different!) And in the Philippines, a major Moro scholar/activist, Edilwassif Baddiri, as also one of the prominent MILF leaders, Salamat Hashim, both cite the figure of 7-8 million while other, non-Moro scholars give the figure from the official Philippine Yearbook 2002 as 4-4.5 percent of the total population, which is less than 4 million in a population of 98 million. Even one of the most respected US scholars on Moro history, Thomas McKenna, states without source citation in a recent publication that "there

are an estimated 3.5 million Muslims in the Philippines, the only predominantly Christian country in Southeast Asia".

62. For Lane, the notion of agency or change on the part of the masses remains a utopian ideal bereft of a vanguard organization to implement its goals. PAPERNAS (acronym for United Party for National Liberation) "is too small to break through the many bureaucratic obstacles put in the way of its electoral registration by the parliament (that is, by all the elite-controlled parties)". Lane (2008):290.

2

State and Religious Minorities in India and Europe: The Rupture between Vision and Reality

T.K. Oommen

This article intends to provide a comparative understanding of state behaviour towards religious minorities, with special reference to Muslims in India and Europe. To accomplish this task, we need to situate comparatively the relevant religions in terms of their conceptions of the relationship between religion, nation and territory. The differing orientations of proselytizing religions and non-proselytizing religions are crucial in this context. Further, even when the constitution of a democratic state is 'secular', its behaviour vis-à-vis religious minorities may be substantially conditioned by the conceptions the religious majority of the state holds with regard to the relationship between nation, religion and territory.

To explicate this argument I propose to attempt a brief analysis of: (a) the conceptions the four religions—Judaism, Hinduism, Islam and Christianity—hold about a nation and (b) the conceptualizations regarding citizenship endorsed by those states, which declare themselves to be secular. (It is axiomatic that the theocratic state's concept of 'citizenship' privileges the relevant religious group). To provide empirical content to the analysis, I shall compare two situations: one, those in which the Muslims constitute a majority and those in which they are, in a minority; two, where the Muslims are 'nationals' (i.e. legal and cultural insiders), and/or 'ethnies' (where they are legal insiders but perceived as cultural outsiders by the majority community/civil society) and sojourners (where they are legal and cultural outsiders, i.e. immigrants).

Section I

Let me first consider the link between religion and territory of the two non-proselytizing religions, namely Judaism and Hinduism [1] because co-terminality between territory and religion is logically sustainable in their cases. [2] The Jews are a territorially dispersed community and yet they claim Israel as their exclusive homeland. It is necessary to allude briefly to the historical background of the Jewish state of Israel. The 1917 Balfour Declaration promised a Jewish homeland, that is a nation, but not a state. The King-Crane Commission sent by President Wilson in 1919 found that 90 percent of the population in the territory identified for the Jewish homeland was non-Jewish, that is, Muslims and Christians. However, after the establishment of Israel, the population of religious minorities was reduced to 10 percent.

Jews, Christians and Muslims had a legitimate moral claim to the territory of Israel, which was their common ancestral homeland. But the moment religion was invoked to define nation and create a mono-religious state, genocide and culturocide [3] followed, unleashing insecurity to non-Jewish people. As Emerson observed:

"The conception of creating a Jewish national home in Palestine could not possibly be squared with the principle of self-determination…on the basis of any generally accepted criteria…Palestine has been the ancient Jewish homeland many centuries ago; but to accept the legitimacy of claims to self-determination whose basis is possession broken off by two thousand five hundred years earlier would be to stir up such a host of conflicting and unrealizable demands as totally to discredit the principle". [4] Emerson's evaluation stands vindicated and yet the Jewish state of Israel is a reality today.

The legitimacy for the creation of the Jewish state of Israel is located in Jewish history and in the values of Judaism. For example, Grosby [5] argued that ancient Israel was a 'nation', the common homeland of 12 tribes with clear territorial boundaries. He suggests that the trans-tribal national sentiment of Israel was that of a broader kinship which characterizes modern nations. He further stated that the nation of Israel consists of the putative descendants of Abraham, Isaac and Jacob, the Jewish ancestors who worshipped a common God: 'The ancient Israelites at some point during their history became a nation when they believed that the territory of Israel in its entirety belonged to them...and only to them because Yaweh their God and the only God to be worshipped in the land (and thus, whose law was the only law to be obeyed in that land) had promised it to them'. [6]

As a general characterization of ancient Israel this is probably admissible, but it does not fit a contemporary democratic polity. First, de-territorialization of religious communities is an acknowledged fact. Therefore, no religion can claim the entire territory of a nation as its exclusive territory. Second, to the extent that the people inhabiting the national territory follow different religions and they have different godheads. Third, if there are different gods they are likely to promulgate different legal systems. Fourth, if each of these Gods promises the entire land of the nation to its respective followers and commands them to obey only the laws prescribed by their God, conflict and insecurity will prevail in such a nation.

There are other difficulties if one endorses Grosby's position. Israel gave birth not only to Judaism but also to Christianity and Islam. Christians and Muslims, too, claim that they are descendants of Abraham, Issac and Jacob; that Israel is their ancestral homeland and their ancestors are Israelites; and they too, have to obey divine laws. The inevitable consequence of linking religion, territory and laws is the creation of a mono-religious nation. But empirical reality is at variance with this logic, which necessitates the externalization (that is, perceiving and treating them as outsiders) of some of these religions, usually the minority religions, leading to the crystallization of an acute identity crisis among the followers of these minority religions.

Political Hinduism or Hindutva is very similar in its enunciation of the relationship between religion and territory. First, Hindus are defined as the original and obvious inhabitants of Hindustan, that is India. According to Golwalkar: 'Hindu society living in this country since times immemorial is the national...society here....The same Hindu people have built the life values, ideals and culture of this country and, therefore, their nationhood is self-evident'. [7] Further, '...we, the Hindus, have been in undisputed and undisturbed possession of this land for eight or even ten thousand years before the land was invaded by any foreign race'. [8] Therefore, Golwalkar prescribed:

"The non-Hindu people in Hindustan must learn to either adopt the Hindu culture and language, must learn to respect and hold in reverence Hindu religion, must entertain no idea but those of glorification of the Hindu race and culture...may stay in the country, wholly subordinated to the Hindu nation, claiming nothing, deserving no privileges not even citizen rights. In this country, Hindus alone are national and Muslims and others, (read Christians, author) if not actually anti-national, are at least outside the body of the nation". [9]

This position would, admittedly, inculcate a deep sense of alienation in the non-Hindu people of India. But Savarkar, another Hindutva ideologue, took an expansive view of Hinduism: 'Hinduism must necessarily mean the religion or religions that are peculiar or native to this land...It should be applied to all the religious beliefs that the different communities of the Hindu people hold'.[10] In this rendition, Hinduism includes all the Indic religions, which undermines the identity of Buddhism, Jainism and Sikhism. If Golwalkar's exclusionary perspective, is a recipe for the alienation of all religious minorities of alien origin, Savarkar's expansionism denies identity to all the minority religions of Indic origin.

Section II

In contradistinction to Hinduism and Judaism, Islam rejects the idea of territorial nationalism and upholds the notion of universal community of faith; the Ummah. But the community of faith excludes Muslims of some denominations. Ahmadis, the 'renegade sect', for example, are outside the pale of universal community. The dhimmis, the other people of the Book such as Jews and Christians, are also discriminated against although treated often better than Ahmadis. This prompted an analyst to conclude that a '...multi-cultural society in which ethnies of different beliefs are treated as equals is essentially incompatible with Islam. The often cited status of dhimmis in the Islamic empires provides the example. Members of dhimmis were treated as second-class citizens who seldom could hold public office or build new churches and temples'. [11]

The formation of Turkey as a nation-state illustrates this. The Armenian homeland lay between the Black, Caspian and Mediterranean Seas on both sides of the Soviet-Turkish frontier. By the end of the fourteenth century, the last Armenian Kingdom had collapsed and it became a stateless nation. Under the Ottoman Empire, which expanded to its zenith by the seventeenth century, the Armenians constituted the only prosperous Christian community. While they enjoyed freedom of worship, they could not use their language for purposes other than domestic conversation and recitation of prayers. Of the various subjects, people of the Ottoman Empire, the Armenians were the most dispersed and by the middle of the nineteenth century they no longer constituted a majority in much of their historic homelands. [12]

The multi-cultural Ottoman Empire gave a certain amount of freedom and autonomy to the religious minorities under the millet system. But the decline of the empire and the simultaneous spread of the idea of the nation-state from Western Europe prompted cultural homogenization. In Turkey, this led to the genocide of the Armenians, expulsion of the

Greeks, impoverishment of the Jews and Turkification that is, cultural assimilation of the rest. [13] Members of minorities could become members of the majority by adopting its language, culture and religion, which few did voluntarily. Even the progressive elements such as Young Turks were pursuing the goal of transforming the heterogeneous empire into a homogeneous state based on the concept of 'one nation, one people'. [14]

The Armenians formed a formidable obstacle in achieving this goal, as they were the only non-Muslim group whose ancient homeland lay in the very heart of Turkey. To give up this land would inevitably lead to the dissolution of the Turkish state. The fact that Armenian and Turkish villages co-existed peacefully side by side for centuries did not in any way dissuade the nationalists from their homogenization project. World War I provided an opportune moment for the Turkish state to strike at the Armenian nation. But the Armenians, understandably, did not want to part with their ancient homeland. The conflict between the two groups was 'a struggle between two nations for the possession of a single homeland that ended with the terrible holocaust of 1915, when a million and a half Armenians perished'. [15]

The genocide of the Armenians eloquently unfolds the disastrous consequences of the effort to create a nation-state, perhaps more than the genocide of the Jews in Germany, because the Armenians were in their ancient homeland whereas the Jews were immigrants. It also shows the untenability of defining a nation based on religion as the Turks and Armenians shared a common homeland. Further, the Armenians did not seek to establish their own state, they only wanted to preserve their cultural identity, which was indeed deeply rooted in religion. They did not pose a threat to the Turkish state, particularly after 1908 when the regime of Abdul Hamid ended. In fact, a section of the Armenian leadership was in league with the Young Turks. [16] Finally, the Armenians were reckoned as the 'people of the Book' in the traditional Muslim view, and they were the most loyal millet of the Ottoman Empire. And yet, the integral nationalism of Ziya Gokalp ignored it all.

The Armenians did seek greater autonomy in internal matters and governmental protection against Kurdish designs. But they did not confront the Turks in any way, nor did they want to secede or join Russia. The Armenian 'programme was essentially one of reform within the Ottoman empire'. In fact, they believed that 'a complete separation of Armenia from Turkey was ethnographically and geographically impossible'. [17]

What then was the reason behind the ethnification [18] and physical liquidation of the Armenians? Ottomanism hoped to sustain the empire by providing for cultural autonomy to all, regardless of religion and national origin. But the disintegration of the empire and the consequent secession of the Christian Balkans led to the crystallization of two competing orientations: pan-Islamism and Turkish nationalism. However, it was not possible to sustain pan-Islamism because first Albania and Macedonia, both predominantly populated by Muslims, revolted, followed by the Muslim Arabs. Consequently, Ottomanism and pan-Islamism were abandoned by 1914, and the Young Turks turned to Turkish nationalism and building the Turkish nation-state.

In the first phase, Turkish nationalism assumed a pan-Turkish orientation called Turanism, according to which all the Turkic-speaking people shared a common culture and should be unified into one political entity. This meant constituting a new state spread far and wide—over the Russian Caucasus, Central Asia, Kazakhstan and the Crimea—and comparable in size to the Ottoman Empire, but without the unwanted non-Muslim minorities. Although the project did not take off, it did intensify Turkish nationalism among Ottoman Turks. Conversely, it eroded the confidence of the minorities such as the Armenians to live as culturally distinct groups within the projected Turkish nation-state.

The ideologue of Turkish nationalism was Ziya Gokalp who conceptualized integral nationalism, while the architect of the Turkish nation-state was Mustafa Kamal who tried to create a homogeneous nation-state. The Greeks and Turks were exchanged, and the bulk of the Armenians left Turkey gradually. [19] To Gokalp, a nation was a society consisting of people who speak the same language, have had the same education and are unified in their religious, moral and aesthetic ideals—in short, those who have common culture and religion. Non-Turkish people such as 'Greeks, Armenians and Jews who lived in Turkey were Turks only in respect of citizenship but not of nationality…they would remain a foreign body in the national Turkish state'. [20] Even those whose ancestral homeland was in Turkey were cultural outsiders because they were not Muslims; that is, the nationals were defined as ethnies. Thus, the ultimate rationale of the genocide perpetrated on the Armenians was the homogenization of the population living in the Turkish nation-state. Indeed, Turainism and Hindutva are precariously proximate in spite of the utterly divergent orientations of Islam and Hinduism to territory based nation.

Like Islam, Christianity is also a proselytizing religion. [21] And, the notion of universal church in Catholic Christianity is similar to that of the concept of Ummah in Islam. However, scholarly opinions are diametrically opposed in the West. Hans Kohn propounded what he called the 'universal sociological law', namely, 'religious groupings lose power when confronted with the consciousness of a common nationality and speech'. [22] On the other hand, W.C. Smith holds: 'The driving force of nationalism has become more and more religious, the more the movement has penetrated the masses'. [23] He lists religion as a defining feature of nation. [24] The problem it seems to me partly arises from the empirical referents the authors had. Those who had Catholic

Christianity in mind are right in delinking religion and nationality. On the other hand those authors who had either Orthodox Christianity or Protestant Christianity in mind had seen a firm link between religion and nationality. [25]

Let me discuss two authors, both of whom consider religion to be an important ingredient of a nation. Ernest Barker, having conceded that the secular trend was fast becoming visible, remarked: 'nations long dreamt for their national unity in some common fund of religious ideas'. [26] And he insisted: 'the connection between religion and national life is obviously close. In some cases we may even say that religion is the nation and the nation is, what it is in virtue of its religion'. [27] Barker points out that the Greek nation survived largely because of the Greek Orthodox Church, that Scotch national unity is sustained due to the Scottish Church and he elaborates the role that the Anglican Church played in consolidating the English nation. Other examples cited are Holland and Switzerland, where Calvinism played a prominent role. In all these cases the idea of a national church came to be deeply institutionalized following Reformation in the sixteenth century.

However, the idea of a national church is patently antagonistic to the notion of a universal church proffered by Catholicism. In those nations where two or more Christian denominations (as in Germany) or two or more religious communities (as in Lebanon or India) co-exist, nationality based on religion becomes untenable if one takes this view to its logical end. Even in the case of uni-denominational nations, those who refused to belong to the official church, or rationalists, secularists, atheists and agnostics—in one word 'the deviants'—will have to face serious negative consequences. In fact, this is precisely what happened in England. The non-conformists established their own congregations which ignored the Established Church, but had to pay a heavy price: 'They could not hold office, municipal or national and by various statutes they were deprived even of the social right of maintaining schools and giving instruction'. [28] This means that the idea of fusing citizenship and churchmanship as a goal is not a viable one even in uni-denominational nations, as the first is common to all and the second applies only to a section of the national population. In the contemporary world, most nations (I am not referring to states) are multi-religious and multi-denominational, and hence religion cannot be the basis of nation formation. And if religion is invoked as the basis of state formation, violence inevitably follows irrespective of the conceptions held by religions with regard to the relationship between nation, religion and territory. [29]

Section III

I have argued that both empirical reality (heterogeneity of contemporary state populations) and the prevailing value orientations (commitment to democracy and secularism) militate against the linkage between religion and nationality and derivatively between nationality and citizenship. This suggestion, however, is not as startling as it appears. Habermas puts it succinctly: 'Citizenship was never conceptually tied to national identity'. [30] Greenfeld and Chirot [31] identify three initial conceptualizations regarding the linkage between citizenship and nationality, while delineating the relationship between nationalism and aggression, which is an extension of Greenfeld's earlier attempt. [32] It seems to me that these linkages were attempted to meet the specific requirements of state-building. The empirical reality has changed substantially due to the emergence of the New World (The Americas, Australia etc.), dislocation of populations wrought by socialist states, the failure of the homogenization project initiated by nation-states and the ongoing turbulence of inter-state migration accelerated by modernization and abetted by globalization.

The English 'nation' was initially conceptualized as a collective of sovereign individuals; this later gave birth to the individualistic libertarian concept of the state. If individuals constitute the units of a nation, citizenship and nationality could be conceptually bifurcated. Great Britain was thus conceived as a collectivity of citizens drawn from different nations—England, Scotland, Wales and part of Ireland. This conception was functional to its state-building given the persisting ambivalence in characterizing both Great Britain and its constituting units as 'nations' even among scholars, while in reality the former is a multi-national state and the latter are nations. [33] Other examples of this type are Switzerland, the Indian Union and the European Union. In contrast to this is the conceptualization that views nation as a distinct people, the collectivistic-ethnic nation. In this mode of conceptualization, citizenship and nationality are fused, giving birth to the collectivistic-authoritarian state. The typical examples of this concept of nation are the German and Italian nation-states.

These two types of conceptualizations have given birth to two different criteria of membership in the nation. Where nationality and citizenship are bifurcated, the former, at least in principle, is civic, that is, open and voluntaristic; it can be acquired. In contrast, where the two are fused, membership in the nation is inherent, that is, nationality has nothing to do with an individual's will and citizenship is inherited. One implies the other. The collectivistic nation and the multi-national state are patently contradictory to each other.

The third mode of conceptualization is a mutation of the two and is exemplified by the French case. In France, an individual can acquire nationality, that is, citizenship, through a process of 'Frenchification'—learning the French language, receiving French education and internalizing French culture, irrespective of race and religion. This, in principle, gives birth to a civic-collectivistic state fostering a community of citizens. However, there is a hierarchy of citizens and nationals even here; the white, Catholic French-speaking citizens of France at the top, the black Muslim 'immigrant' non-citizens at the bottom and the 'Frenchified' black Muslims, say from Algeria, who are ethnic-citizens, in the middle.

It is clear from the above analysis that de-linking nationality based on religion and language and citizenship is imperative if the society is to be rendered open and if the polity is to remain democratic. This should not endanger the integrity of the polity because it is possible to construct a political culture dissociated from national and ethnic origins, but anchored to the principle of multi-culturalism as noted by Habermas. [34] The British model, in principle, fits the bill. But in practice, a variety of collectivities feel deprived—both nationals and ethnies. Thus Ireland, Wales and Scotland are characterized as 'internal colonies' of the dominant English nation, although the nationals of these 'colonies' are full-fledged citizens of the British state. The lower classes from these colonies may feel that they are 'second-class' citizens. [35] If so, the predicament of the non-national citizens, particularly the coloured immigrants, who are also largely of the underclass, can well be visualized. Granting citizenship will not necessarily lead to their being accepted as co-nationals, but citizenship entitlements will at least partially erode the stigma associated with them as ethnies.

The three conceptualizations of citizenship—individualistic libertarian (British), collectivistic authoritarian (German) and civic collectivistic (French) are not rooted in theological conceptions or even moulded by the religious compositions of these polities. Great Britain is a multi-national state and its constituent units—England, Scotland, Wales and Northern Ireland—are all predominantly populated by Protestants. Two of them have their national churches—the Church of England (Anglican) and the Scottish Church (Presbyterian). The Welsh Christians (Methodist, Baptist and Independents) and the non-Catholics of Northern Ireland also identify with their respective homelands. Given this empirical reality, fusing citizenship and nationality and linking nationality and religion are untenable. De-coupling nationality and citizenship and dissociating nationality and religion are pre-requisites for the survival of Great Britain, paradoxically designated as United Kingdom! In spite of this, there is great revulsion against immigrants in general and Muslims in particular as evident from the statement made by one of the MPs on June 20, 1990, in the British House of Commons: 'One in three children born in London today is of ethnic origin...That is a frightening concept for the country to come to terms with. We have already seen the problems of massive Muslim immigration'. [36]

In contrast to UK, Germany although have both Protestants and Catholics, its predominant religious ethos is that of Protestantism. The fact is that Martin Luther, who rebelled against the notion of papal infallibility led to the dominant presence of the Lutheran Church in Germany. This facilitated the process of fusing citizenship and nationality anchored to Protestant Christianity. All the elements perceived as non-nationals—Jews, Gypsies and Slavs—were marginalized, stigmatized and persecuted. Slavs were viewed as sub-human, Gypsies were imprisoned and enslaved. But the Jews were perceived as non-human and liquidated. [37] The attitude to Muslims in Germany is but an extension of the same treatment to all aliens, that is, non-nationals, who cannot be granted citizenship. It is well-known that the Turks constitute a substantial immigrant community in Germany (320,000 in West Germany in 1990) and some of them lived there for generations. And yet they are patented as others in Germany as the following passage illustrates: 'When a Turk stupidly looks at me, my hands tend to hit him. They show archaic behaviour, they are illiterates from a completely alien, 'cultural' context and have Islam as their religion...The best policy for these Turks is: Kick in the ass and out'. [38]

Similarly, in spite of the theoretical possibility of a person or collectivity acquiring French citizenship given France's civic-collectivistic orientation in the conceptualization of citizenship, there is a hierarchy of citizens and immigrants as noted above. This is clearly articulated by Le Pen, the leader of Front National, the rightist national party of France: 'I like my daughters better than my neighbours, my neighbours better than strangers and strangers better than enemies'. [39] But the imagery does not quite fit the reality. The neighbours are acceptable only if spatial proximity coincides with racial, religious and cultural proximity. Thus, the Muslims of Bosnia and Turkey, although are neighbours, that is, Europeans, are worse than strangers, sometimes instant enemies. But the mental distance increases cumulatively even between French citizens if one belongs to a different race and religion.

Thus, the Algerian Muslim who is a French citizen is often a stranger and even an enemy. But the Portuguese, the Spaniard or the Italian who is Catholic and white but not a French citizen may succeed in establishing an elective affinity with the white Catholic French citizen. Thus, in spite of the conceptual possibility of non-whites and non-Catholics acquiring citizenship in France, citizenship and nationality are disengaged in the empirical context. This means both 'modern' Europe and 'traditional' India indulge in the process of constructing/inventing the Other'. [40]

Section IV

I have tried to compare different conceptualizations of the relationship between nation and territory in non-proselytizing (Judaism and Hinduism) and proselytizing (Christianity and Islam) religions. These conceptions do vary in that non-proselytizing religions give birth to territorial nationalism, which produces instant intolerance towards religious minorities as exemplified by the conservative Jews of Israel. But even as a section of the majority religious community professes territorial nationalism, if the state is 'secular' and refuses to endorse that view it is theoretically possible to create a polity in which the religious minority communities are accommodated. Such a possibility is illustrated by the Indian case.

A comparison of the countries in which two proselytizing religions, Catholic Christianity and Islam, which uphold the notions of universal church and universal brotherhood respectively, of co-religionists are in majority, demonstrate that their religious conceptions do not necessarily block the possibility of polities in which they are in majority emerging as nation-states. Thus, both Turkey a Muslim majority country and France a predominantly Catholic country have emerged as strong nation-states. However, while in Turkey non-Muslims are not tolerated, in France a hierarchy of citizens who have differing religious affiliations have emerged.

The two protestant countries which endorse the notion of national churches, United Kingdom and Germany, also have produced differing empirical situations. Germany fusing citizenship and nationality (with a strong content of religion) produced Nazism, an extremist version of nationalism. But such a causal link *via* religion seems to be unsustainable because Italy, which is almost exclusively Catholic, also gave birth to fascism, another extremist version of nationalism. That is to say, religion, be it Protestantism with a strong orientation towards national church or Catholicism which endorses universal church, seems to be a neutral element. The same logic can be extended to Islam which also conceives of a universal brotherhood of co-religionists irrespective of national identities have also produced an extreme version of territorial nationalism, as in the case of Turkey.

It is clear from our analysis that there are several possible permutations and combinations which constrict or facilitate the participation of religious minorities in the public sphere. I shall list five of them.

1. Majority religious community with the vision of territorial nationalism, which is endorsed and nurtured by the state. In such a polity, the minority religious communities will only have very limited possibility of being participants in the public arena. The examples are Israel today and Turkey in the past. It is important to underline here that the

religious vision of nation becomes irrelevant if a nation-state is sought to be built.

2. Even as the majority religious community professes territorial nationalism and if the state is democratic and secular the members of minority religious communities will enjoy full citizenship entitlements and hence can be participants in the public sphere. However, the majority religious community may stigmatize the religious minorities as cultural outsiders. This will partly restrict their full participation in the public arena. This situation is exemplified by the Indian case.
3. Territorially anchored secular nationalism, which decouples citizenship and nationality, accommodates national religious/denominational minorities as cultural insiders if the latter accepts a language, which is common to the entire country. But in such a polity ethnic minorities, particularly immigrants, will be discriminated and marginalized. The United Kingdom affords an example of this type.
4. Territorially anchored secular nationalism, which fuses citizenship and nationality, is extremely intolerant towards religious minorities, which are of alien origin. While both Germany and Italy fits this description the former has predominantly Protestantism, which endorses the notion of national church and the latter has Catholicism, which pursues the idea of universal church. This means the vision the majority religion/denomination holds with regard to the nature of church is irrelevant.
5. De-territorialised secular nationalism, which fuses citizenship and nationality accommodates minorities drawn from even outside the racial and religious groups through a process of cultural assimilation. However, the possibility is that a hierarchy of citizens is likely to emerge as in the case of France.

My crunch conclusions are two. One, the conception of nationalism that the majority religious community of a country holds is not critical in constricting the participation of religious minorities in the public space if the state is democratic and secular. Two, to nurture a democratic secular polity de-coupling of nationality based on religion and citizenship is a pre-requisite.

Endnotes

1. That there is considerable de-territorialization of Judaism and Hinduism, through Diaspora and immigration respectively, is well-known. Even the claim of these religions as non-proselytizing is not necessarily sustainable. For evidence with regard to Hinduism see, Rowena Robinson, and Clarke Sathianathan, (eds.), "Religious Conversion in India: Modes, Motivations, and Meanings", Delhi, Oxford University Press, 2003, pp. 98-118 and 222-284.
2. For evidence with regard to Judaism, see E.A. Speiser, "People and Nation of Israel", *Journal of Biblical Literature,* 79, 1960, pp. 157-163.
3. By culturocide I mean the systematic destruction/stigmatization of the cultures/lifestyles of weak and minority groups by the state and/or the 'cultural mainstream'. See, T.K. Oommen, "Insiders and Outsiders in India: Primordial Collectivism and Cultural Pluralism in Nation Building", *International Sociology*, 1(i), 1986, pp. 53-74 (reproduced in T.K. Oommen, 'State and Society in India', Sage Publications, 1990, pp. 43-66.
4. Rupert Emerson (1962), "From Empire to Nation: The Rise and Self-Assertion of Asian and African People", Boston, Beacon Press, p. 313.
5. Steven Grosby, "Religion and Nationality in Antiquity: The Worship of Yahweh and Ancient Israel", *European Journal of Sociology*, 32, 1991, pp. 229-265.
6. Ibid., p. 242.
7. Cited in D.R. Goyal (1979), "Rashtriya Swayam Sewak Sangh", Delhi: Radhakrishna, p. 40.
8. See, M.S. Golwalkar (1939), "We or Our Nationhood Defined", Nagpur: Bharat Prakashan, p. 49.
9. Ibid., pp. 55-56.
10. V.D. Savarkar (1949), "Hindutva", Bharat Sahitya Sadan, New Delhi, pp. 104-105.

11. However, there is contrary evidence. For example, the Jews in Spain did enjoy a bloom under the Muslim rule. But when the Catholics re-conquered Spain, the Muslims and Jews were given three options: to convert to Christianity, to bc massacred or to leave the country! See, Barbara Harff (1993), "Minorities, Rebellion and Repression in North Africa and the Middle East", in Ted Gurr (ed.), 'Minorities at Risk', Washington, US Institute of Peace Studies, 1993, p. 250.
12. Frank Chalk and Kurt Jonassohn (1990), "The History and Sociology of Genocide", New Haven, Yale University Press.
13. Werner J. Cahnman (1994), "Religion and Nationality", *American Journal of Sociology*, 49(4), pp. 524-529.
14. Chalk and Jonassohn, op. cit., pp. 249, 259.
15. Bernad Lewis (1961), "The Emergence of Modern Turkey", Oxford, Oxford University Press, p. 356.
16. Ibid., pp. 210-211.
17. R.H. Davidson (1948), "The Armenian Crisis: 1912-14", *American Historical Review*, 53, pp. 483-505.
18. For an explication of the notion of ethnification, see T.K. Oommen, "Citizenship, Nationality and Ethnicity: Reconciling Competing Identities", Cambridge: Polity Press, 1997, pp. 13-20.
19. Uriel Heyd (1950), "Foundations of Turkish Nationalism: The Life and Teachings of Ziya Gokalp", London: Luzae, p. 132.
20. Cited in Ibid., pp. 63, 132.
21. The first proselytizing religion of the world however is Buddhism, a fact which is not known widely or recognized by those who stigmatise Christianity and Islam as proselytizing religions. There are several cases of Buddhist majority countries (example Sri Lanka) which endeavour to establish as nation-states.
22. Hans Kohn (1932), "Nationalism and Imperialism in the Hither East", London: Routledge, p. 229.
23. W.C. Smith (1957), "Islam in Modern History", Princeton: Princeton University Press, p. 75.
24. W.C. Smith, (1981):64.
25. It is of interest to note here that Orthodox Christianity was/is dominant in Finland, Greece, Bulgaria, Romania, Serbia, Hungary and Russia; while in the former two countries democracy and the national church co-existed, the latter five

countries in spite of becoming socialist and endorsing proletarian internationalism, did not dilute the nationalist orientation of their churches. This varying empirical reality once again points to the possibility of different permutations and combinations of the political and religious institutions and orientations.

26. Ernest Barker (1948), "National Character and the Factors in its Formation", London: Methuen and Co., p. 14.
27. Ibid., p. 151.
28. Barker, op. cit., p. 171.
29. See T.K. Oommen (2001), "Religion as a Source of Violence: A Sociological Perspective", *The Ecumenical Review*, 53(2), pp. 168-179.
30. Jurgen Habermas (1992), "Citizenship and National Identity: Some Reflections on the Future of Europe", *Praxis International*, 12, p. 11.
31. Liah Greenfeld and Daniel Chirot (1994), "Nationalism and Aggression", *Theory and Society*, 23(1), pp. 79-130.
32. Liah Greenfeld (1992), "Nationalism: Five Roads to Modernity", Cambridge: Harvard University Press, p. 11.
33. Oommen (1997), op. cit.
34. Habermass (1992), op. cit., p. 7.
35. Hechter (1975), op. cit.
36. Quoted in Teun Van Dijk (1993), "Principles of Critical Discourse Analysis", *Discourse and Society*, 4(2), pp. 249-284.
37. See Yehuda Bauer (1982), "A History of Holocaust", New York, Franklin Watts.
38. Cited in Teun Van Dijk (1987), "Communicating Racism", Newsbury Park: Sage Publications, p. 233.
39. Quoted in Van Dijk (1993), op. cit., p. 266.
40. See T.K. Oommen (2000), "The Changing Trajectory of Constructing the Other: West Europe and South Asia", in T.K. Oommen, 'Pluralism, Equality and Identity: Comparative Studies', Delhi: Oxford University Press, pp. 111-126.

Part II: Modernity, Secularism and Muslim Minorities

3

Modernity, Nation-State and Islamic Identity Politics [1]

Michael Dusche

Any resurgence of religion in the age of globalisation takes place against the backdrop of a world society that is guided by the ideas and values of modernity. [2] While pre-modern or non-modern cultural reference frames tend to take social structure as basic, which ascribes roles to each individual according to age, gender, family, profession, cast, estate, tribe, or religion, the modern cultural reference frame takes an individual as basic. All other institutions like marriage, family, association or state are construed as based on the free consent of individuals engaged in them. It is by reference to the individual that the roles of these collective institutions are defined and not the other way round. No longer the collective defines the role of an individual but every collective is gauged by reference to the benefit that it gives to its members.

These advantages, Meyer reminds us, are expressed in terms of justice and progress in the modern cultural reference frame. If a collective does not stand the test of justice, it needs to prove at least that it progresses in the way justice prescribes. If it proves to be stagnating or even regressing, it looses its legitimacy. Progress in the way of justice is normally translated into expansion of equal liberties for all individuals. Accordingly, politics is construed as the result of individual citizens' decisions in elections and party memberships. Religion and culture are framed as based on individual choices regarding beliefs and values.

For those like Habermas, [3] who believe that modernity

remains an incomplete project, these constructions play the role of regulative ideas. For those like Fukuyama, [4] who believe in the end of history, these constructions could only be myths, for their implementation in actuality is thwarted by what Meyer [5] calls "decoupling". In many ways, the present world order reflects the global cultural reference frame and its universalist values of progressive expansion of equal liberties for all individuals. [6] The Universal Declaration of Human Rights of 1948, the creation of the United Nations system with its aim to ban any unilateral use of force in the international arena, the attempts to strengthen the international law regime by creating international tribunals, the attempts to create an international court of justice etc. all point in that direction.

In other ways, however, the current world order is also marred by contradictions that prove the incompleteness of the implementation of modernity's universalist values. These contradictions centre on the status of collective actors like ethnic groups, nations and individual states vis-à-vis their individual members. Can collective rights override individual rights? Can aspirations for national independence override the sovereignty of the states to which these 'nations' belong? Can national sovereignty override the human rights of individual citizens? Can 'national interest' override the ban on the unilateral use of force in the international arena?

While certain state actors benefit from the inconsistencies of the present order, others suffer the consequences of these indeterminacies. They are given a voice, however, by international human rights organisations who advocate strict adherence to international human rights standards by all collective actors including the most powerful states. Whence the call for their institutionalisation in the form of an international court of justice, which is consistently torpedoed, like all other attempts at consolidating an international order based on independent institutions, by states who base their foreign policy predominantly on what they perceive as their 'national' interest.

Other challenges to this self-conflicting global order stem from churches or religious movements. The Catholic Church as well as Islamist political movements question the importance given to the so called 'nation-state'. To the Catholic Church, for example, the idea of absolute sovereignty of individual states has always been doubtful. It has, however unsuccessfully, advocated the idea of a religio-political order limiting the idea of absolute sovereignty for individual states. Until very recently and unlike the cosmopolitan order promoted by advocates of an independent global judiciary, this alternative was not based on modern normative individualism. Only after Vatican II (1965), did the Catholic Church formally embraced normative individualism in the form of human rights and democracy.

The struggle of Islamic thinkers with the emerging paradigm of the 'nation-state' and modern precepts such as secular law, human rights and popular sovereignty is as old as nationalism itself, possibly beginning with Rifa'a Rafi' al-Tahtawi (1834) in Egypt. [7] While some oppose the introduction of the concept of nationhood on grounds that it would be divisive for the *ummahi*, others interpret the *ummah* itself as a nation. Some realise that modern politics needs a material base and thus a defined territory. Others remain silent on where the *ummah*, understood as a nation, should materialise. The need for a material basis for his 'Muslim nation' led Jinnah to demand the partition of the Indian sub-continent while other Indian Muslims like Iqbal would have been happy with an *ummah* in the air and a religiously neutral polity on sub-continental ground.

Besides this, there is also a long tradition of liberal Islamic thought to demonstrate that Islamic principles of law can be brought into congruence with the nation state, human rights and democracy. [8] Until now, however, such liberal-Islamic thinking remains the mainstay of a mostly silent part of the *ummah*. Whether the majority of Muslims think that way or not, in any case, liberal Islamic thinking has not sparked any social movement.

The present paper is not concerned with this literature. It is not concerned with the question whether Islam is ('essentially'), or could be, democratic and human rights abiding. This has been the subject of another paper. [9] Instead what this paper is looking at are those brands of Islamic thinking that form the ideological basis for effective Islamist movements. The paper reviews the current survey literature on how Islamist movements and their ideologues relate to ideas of democracy and nationalism.

By 'Islamism', the paper understands a political ideology that would like to base the polity on an Islamic foundation. [10] This does not necessarily mean that those adhering to such an ideology would like to advance it by violent means. Thus, Islamism does not in itself amount to Islamic radicalism or 'jihadism'. From a perspective of liberal democratic theory, however, to base a polity on any religion is in itself problematic for it is precisely the task of the liberal democratic state not to grant privileges based on race, religion, caste, class, or gender to any of its citizens. Thus, trivially, Islamism, as any other ideology that would like to found the polity on religion, cannot be liberal-democratic. The same holds true of any ideology that would like to base any given polity on cultural or ethnic identity. I have labelled such ideologies and their corresponding practices as "Identity Politics". [11]

The Islamist ideas examined here have some features in common with the phenomenon of identity politics. Firstly, they are an expression of a lack of democratic political culture. Furthermore, they are prone to conflict in specific ways that will become apparent when we analyse Islamism in relation to the larger phenomenon of identity politics. In the following section, the phenomenon of identity politics shall be briefly reviewed.

Identity Politics

This paper rests on the observation that identity politics

dominates political culture in formative stages of new polities or in transitory periods of existing ones, often in the guise of ethno-religious nationalism. It features prominently during the birth of new states since the 1800s and it remains an indicator for the democratic quality of political culture in any established polity. This thesis was derived from explorative studies into various contexts, past and present, in which identity politics led to the creation of new states. From these explorations, it appears that identity politics is largely serving the ends of activist elites. Identity politics does not necessarily translate into an increase in democratic participation for those it purports to represent. On the contrary, participation remains largely symbolic.

The individual in totality tends to be seen as part of an organic whole and not as a party to a social contract, which would limit the ends that may be pursued through politics. Moreover, the organiscist image of society derived from European, particularly German, romanticist political thought, renders identity politics inapt to handle inner conflict in a rational, non-coercive manner. Instead of managing differing interests non-violently, it attempts to create a unity, based on fear. Those articulating differences are threatened with the stigma of heresy or treason. The paper attempts to show that similar propositions hold true of identity politics based on religion. [12] Islamist political thought is used as an example here but of course identity politics based on other religions run into similar problems.

Ethnic Nationalism and Religious Fundamentalism

Nationalism, especially in its integral form, has often been described as a religion of modern times or the substitute of religion. [13] This makes ethnic nationalism and religious fundamentalism comparable. Both ideologies entail a higher readiness to use force in order to reach their goal, which has contributed to an increase in atrocities and civilian victims during the 'new wars' of the last decades in comparison to conventional state warfare. The asymmetry of combatants has lifted the limits of violence and blurred the line between times of war and times of peace. [14] So-called ethnic conflicts have claimed millions of civilian lives after the end of the Cold War and the number of victims of terrorism motivated by religious fanaticism tends to be higher than the number claimed by terrorism of other ideologies. [15] Gagnon [16], exhorts in an analysis of the Balkan wars of the 1990s: "The greatest threats to peace in this century have come from those regions in which partitions along ethnic or religious lines have taken place. Examples include Greece-Turkey (1922), Ireland (1921), the Sudetenland (1938), India-Pakistan (1947), South African apartheid (1948), Palestine (1948) and Cyprus (1974)". [17]

From a normative perspective, identity politics in general and ethnic nationalism in particular are ambiguous. On one hand, they have the potential to liberate groups of people from foreign rule (or from home-grown authoritative government). Modern mass politics, on which nationalism is based, has the potential of including former subjects as citizens in processes of political deliberation. On the other hand, identity politics has the tendency to pitch one group of people against another, which frequently leads to violent conflict or even outright war. The basic idea underlying ethnic nationalism is that 'peoples' exist prior to, or independently of, any state and that ideally each 'people' should inhabit its own sovereign state. This idea is rooted in the romantic notion of peoplehood following Herder. Later, due to developments in bio-philosophy in the 1860s, 'peoples' were increasingly defined in racial terms. Social Darwinism following Herbert Spencer (1857) declared Darwin's 'survival of the fittest' as a natural law among racially defined nations. This school of thought helped the European powers to justify their dominance over non-European 'peoples' and their hegemony vis-à-vis each other. Ultimately, the competition among the 'fitter' ones among the European 'nations' culminated in the First World War.

With identity politics focussing on religion instead of the

ethnie, the postulated members of the religious group become the carriers and the resource of an ideology. The religious ascription of each individual develops into a political asset for the mobilising elites. A conversion into the other camp amounts to desertion. When religion and its followers become a political asset, conflicts are sparked off by religious symbols and conversions. Temples, mosques and churches, religious symbols and processions suddenly gain immense significance. [18]

Often religionists resist such misuse of their beliefs. As Wieland points out, in the case of Bosnia, the majority of Muslims did not want a Muslim state. Similarly, in the case of the Indian subcontinent, most Muslims did not support the idea of an independent Muslim state. The movement towards an independent state of Pakistan was spearheaded by the Muslim salaried class of North India [19]—"a class that was the product of the colonial transformation of Indian social structure in the nineteenth century and...comprised those who had received an education that would equip them for employment in the expanding colonial state apparatus as scribes and functionaries". [20]

This class "did not represent the interests of the majority of the Muslim peasants in rural India or those of the Muslims in south India". [21] Consequently, the majority of the Muslims of the continent stayed back in India after partition where they still outnumber the Muslim inhabitants of Pakistan. Ahmad Khan's Aligharh Movement was against an independent Muslim state, as well as—for opposite reasons—Maududi's Islamist movement Jama'at-i-Islami.

Frequently, the contents of the conflicts have little to do with the people's descent, faith, language or habits. These features serve only as "docking stations" (Wieland) for an accelerated political mobilization. Neither in India nor in the Balkans did ethnic groups fight each other as such. [22] Wieland points to the fact that the idea of an ethnically or religiously homogeneous state is self-defeating, because, as the example of Pakistan shows, once ethnic homogeneity is achieved, the category of 'ethnicity' becomes redundant. Since primordial cleavages *per se* do not exist, 'ethnic groups' must be politicized to achieve political ends on the basis of ethnic or religious mobilisation. Once each 'ethnic group' has 'its' state, this logic leads to the creation of ever new and smaller entities. [23] Thus, predictably, Jinnah abandoned ethno-religious nationalism as soon as he received his 'Muslim' state. Pakistan, however, is still struggling to get the *djinni* of identity politics back into the lamp. Whenever moderately Islamic or secular parties gain an upper hand, the military plays with the Islamist identity politics to further prevent the democratisation of Pakistan. [24]

These are examples of ethno-religious identity politics that remain within the framework of nationalism. There is however a different kind of identity politics which resorts to religion as a means to mass mobilisation but does not follow the paradigm of nationalism. Islamism is an example of this kind.

Islamism as a Form of Identity Politics

El-Solh [25] divides Islamist schools of thought into three groups with regard to their attitude towards democracy and human rights. [26] Group one rejects democracy outright (i.e. the Lebanese 'Movement of Islamic Unification' or the Algerian 'Islamic Salvation Front'). There is not even a pretence to claim legitimacy from dominant patterns of normative order available from the global cultural reference frame. These groups thus represent a counter culture in opposition to modernity but also part of it. [27]

Group two maintains that Islam is inherently democratic, without necessarily implying that representative forms of government conform to Western standards. [28] This school of thought does not take into account the inner plurality of legal and political views among Muslims. The evocation of an harmonious Muslim identity leaves no room for legitimate disagreement. It therein resembles ethnic forms of identity politics.

Group three, according to El-Solh, places more emphasis on democracy in its representative forms (i.e. Muhammad' Amara, Egyptian public intellectual, and Muhammad al-Ghazali, co-founder of the Egyptian 'Muslim Brotherhood'). According to El-Solh, this school of thought insists on the ruler being subjected to the rule of law and some form of consultation (*shurah*). They also advocate an adaptation of Western democracy to Islamic principles by some form of public reasoning (*ijtihad*).

However 'democratic' any of these groups may appear to Muslims themselves, none of their proponents take into account the equal right of non-Muslims living in the same polity to own the state and to be co-authors of its laws. This is not in congruence with democratic principles where state and law are owned in equal parts by each citizen no matter which religion s/he belongs to.

Democracy requires that traditional doctrines transform themselves into reasonable comprehensive doctrines [29] that take into account that "the fact of reasonable pluralism is a permanent feature of democratic culture". [30] This pluralism, even in the Muslim world, includes non-orthodox Muslims as well as non-Muslims and apostates. Religious comprehensive doctrines are compatible with principles of democracy, as understood by John Rawls and Jürgen Habermas, only if out of their own free choice they refrain from imposing by force their religious wisdom on others.

According to Habermas, religious communities have to consider a reflection in three steps: "The religious mind has to first handle the encounter with other confessions or religions. Second, it has to brace for the authority of the sciences that maintain the monopoly on world knowledge. And finally it has to get involved with the prerequisites of a democratic constitutional state that is founded on profane morality". [31] None of the Islamist thinkers that we have encountered so far meet these requirements of a democratic political culture.

A second important surveyor of Islamist literature, Gudrun Krämer [32] bases her assessment of Islamist notions of democracy on what she considers "voices of the Sunni Arabic mainstream" (i.e. the Egyptian and the Jordanian Muslim Brotherhoods, the Tunisian al-Ghanushi movement and voices of the so-called Islamic awakening). [33] Among these voices of the male urban elite and middle classes, Krämer notes, there is general agreement on the rejection of secularism and the applicability of *Sharia*. Islam, in their mind, is religion and state (*din wa_dawla*) but the precise form of government is left to human reason alone.

This does not rule out the adoption of democracy. Certain Islamic values are in congruence with ideas of democracy, i.e. that all people are born equal, that government is ac- countable to the people etc. Forough Jahanbakhsh [34], hints at the fact that al-Farabi and Ibn Rushd used the Arabic word *jama'iya* in the same sense that the Greek of the time used 'democracy'. Thus, a clearly defined model of democracy existed for the Muslim world as early as in the 9th to 12th centuries CE.

Other ideas however do not seem to combine well with democratic political culture. There are ideas that sovereignty rests with God alone and that laws are not authored by the citizens of the state but by God, for example. However, the application of law admittedly rests with the people. This leaves room for an interpretation of Islamic law that conforms to human rights and democratic standards. The Islamist mainstream, however, does not take such a stand. Wolfgang Merkel [35], shows that it is the combination of Arabic and Islamic culture that is accountable for the reluctance in those parts of the world to accept the globally dominant normative scripts of pluralism, liberalism and democracy. Quoting Clague et al. [36], Merkel infers that it must be the Arab-Islamic cultural impregnation, way above any socio-economical variable, that explains the lack of democratic progress in the Muslim world. [37]

Most Islamist authors have difficulties, Krämer notes, "in

envisaging consultation and participation as a genuinely political process involving interest representation, competition and contestation. It reflects the continued prevalence of a moral rather than a political discourse, strictly speaking. The ideals of unity (*wahda*), consensus (*ijma*) and a balanced harmony of groups and interests (*tawazun*), often associated with the theological concept of *tawhid* (the oneness of God), are still paramount. In the debate about pluralism, there is general recognition that God created people to be different, and that therefore differences of opinion (*ikhtilaf*) are natural, legitimate and even beneficial to humankind and the Muslim community—provided they remain within the confines of the faith and common decency. There is great reluctance to allow for unlimited freedom of speech and organization of those different opinions...As long as there is no certainty as to who defines the 'framework of Islam', and where exactly power and interest come into play, pluralism and democracy remain in jeopardy". [38]

Krämer concludes, thereby reconfirming our earlier finding, that the denial of plurality is indicative of the lack of democratic culture among Islamist movements. The utopian vision of a harmonious body politic with no room for the articulation of disagreement and for the democratic organisation of competing interests is a feature that Islamism has in common with ethno-religious identity politics. In both instances, an inability to deal with inner conflict leads to an upholding of a forced unity. To legitimise this use of force, an outward enemy, real or imagined, needs to be projected. This can lead to external conflicts. Thus, the inability to deal with internal disagreement, the lack of institutional means of resolving internal conflict democratically (i.e. non-violently) explains the propensity of identity politics.

Differences between Ethnic and Religious Identity Politics

As we have noted earlier, a main feature defining an *ethnie* can be religion. Thus, Hindu ethnic nationalism and Hindu religious fundamentalism are essentially the same. But this is not true of all religious identity politics. Islamic fundamentalism often stands orthogonal to the divide between civic and ethnic nationalism. Islamism does not accept the basic idea entailed in both that mankind has to be divided along territorial or ethnic lines and polities can only function within the confines of such entities. Islamism transcends such territorial or ethnic restrictions and bases the polity on the community of all believers. The Muslim *ummah* is neither territorially nor ethnically exclusive. Every human being and every country is welcome provided they embrace Islam. The vision is of a global polity embracing all mankind turned Muslims. This humanist and global outlook is only paralleled by cosmopolitan visions of world polity or world state.

Despite many Islamists who identify the *ummah* with the 'Muslim nation' (Usama bin Laden for instance speaks of the *ummah* as the Islamic nation, [39] the question arises as to how much Islamism falls into the same category as nationalism when compared on the level of identity politics. In a way it seems that Islamism overcomes the aporiae of nationalism in a similar way as liberal-democratic cosmopolitanism. The true controversy, thus, does not seem to be between nationalism and Islamism, i.e. between ethnic versus religious identity politics, but between liberal and Islamic cosmopolitanism. This line of argument has been taken up by a number of authors including Talal Asad, [40] Saba Mahmood [41] and William T. Cavanaugh. [42] Their criticism of liberal democracy is summarised by Goldstone. [43] Goldstone argues that liberal democracy is founded on a mythical account of how religion as a foundation for politics engenders conflict and how liberal democracy is the way to prevent such conflict from escalating into violence. According to him,

"[S]ecular liberalism...far from eliminating extreme forms of violence (as it purports to do), instead tries to redefine the manner in which, and, most importantly, the *reasons* for which one should be willing to defend and offend, suffer and inflict suffering, and even to kill and die". [44]

Goldstone suggests that in actuality it is the other way round. While religion, according to him, once provided a foundation for politics that was less prone to violent conflict, it is instead the modern nation-state based on secular liberal-democratic principles that is the cause of much violent conflict and oppression. Here, "one's sense of *political* belonging (emphasis in the original)", Goldstone writes, "*no longer* derives primarily from one's religious community...but is instead founded in the nation-state and its values". [45] This suggests that Goldstone views the pre-modern religious world as a rather peaceful one. In his writing nothing suggests that the Latin-Christian world was forged into unity by the crusaders' swords and through the pyres of the inquisition and, similarly, the integration of the Muslim world was the result of military conquest and much destruction and violence against non-believers and their temples. While Goldstone is certainly right in pointing to the violence accompanying the unfolding of the modern world, his depiction of earlier periods seems rather idyllic.

Sure enough, the post-Westphalian system of sovereign states, has emerged out of thirty years of rampant war. It was the cause of much violence and continues to generate violence. Goldstone, however, seems to conflate the notions of unlimited sovereignty and nationalism with liberalism and democracy. The former may be questionable accompaniments of processes of modernity. However, liberalism and democracy are notions independent of these. Already in the late enlightenment period and well before the emergence of nationalism, liberal cosmopolitan thinkers like Immanuel Kant in his Perpetual Peace [46] transcended the notion of unlimited sovereignty.

Goldstone, citing Cavanaugh, [47] correctly indicates that the post-Westphalian order emerged from decades of conflict where the emerging sovereigns of the newly independent states used religion as a means of mobilisation for wars that were primarily designed to wrest their autonomy from imperial and papal tutelage. To speak of 'religious wars' in this context, would be misleading. Instead both sides, the defendants of the old religio-political order as well as the proponents of the nascent order of independent states used religion as a resource for political and military mobilisation. Goldstone, however, suggests that only the latter used religion in that way.

Notions of the political have changed dramatically over the centuries. Goldstone's idea of 'political belonging' equally carries very different meanings when referring to the 13th, the 17th or the 21st century. He takes no count of this. Instead he projects modern notions of 'civil society' back into a time when such concepts had no, or very different, meanings. [48] Thus, it remains in question what he has in mind when he refers to a pre-liberal, pre-secular 'political' order that, as he alleges, would have been less violent-prone—or at least not worse—than the present secular and liberal-democratic normative order.

Goldstone seems to believe that present day democratic liberalism as a paradigm for normative order is ethically not better than the religio-political order of past days. For liberalism to function, it has to assume that everybody is liberal or otherwise be forced to obey its principles. Equally the older religio-political order rested on the assumption that everybody is Christian or else would have to be forced to accept Christianity. Today, non-liberals are under suspicion of being fundamentalists. In the bygone age, non-Christians were suspected to be siding with the anti-Christ. Thus, where is the difference in terms of the use of force to maintain order? This seems to be the question that Goldstone and his paragons are asking.

Can one answer this question without already presupposing major tenets of liberal-democratic thinking? A liberal would answer that it does make a difference whether somebody is disciplined by violent means only when he/she in his or her outward behaviour does not obey the law or whether somebody is disciplined when his or her inner allegiance to the established order is in question. According to liberal precepts, all that matters is that a person abides by the law in his or her outer behaviour. But if the credentials of a believer are disputed in a Christian or Muslim society, life might become a little difficult. At certain times there may be provisions for certain minorities. But these are always limited in scope and do not warrant an equal standing at par with the subjects of the established religion.

To take this line of defence, liberalism presupposes that freedom of conscience and equality before the law would mean something to the opponent. If they don't, the dialogue has to begin with these matters. Why are human beings equal in value irrespective of their status, race, gender or creed and should therefore enjoy equal rights in any polity? Why should there be no coercion in matters of conscience? Why should political matters be limited to certain sphere and should not be all-embracing? These are the disputes of the enlightenment epoch. If these arguments fail to convince the opponent, the prospects for this dispute to take a non-violent form are slight.

Goldstone admonishes that even a secular, liberal-democratic order sanctions certain kinds of violence and is therefore, according to him, no better off than the religio-political order that it castigates as oppressive and worth overcoming. The only force, however, that can be justified within a liberal-democratic order would be directed against those who infringe on the liberties of others, i.e. as a defensive means against those who use force in the first place. The use of force in the case of self-defence is not normally put on the same level as the aggressive use of force that grows out of the intolerance towards religious dissenters. Goldstone does not seem to agree. Instead he romanticises the Middle Ages as an age of a peaceful "religious consensus of civil society". [49] A Christian reverie, it would seem, paralleling the Islamist myth of the age of the four rightly guided caliphs.

Endnotes

1. Different versions of this paper were presented at two

conferences, first at the conference on "Islamic Resurgence in the Age of Globalization" at the University of Trondheim, Norway, September 4-6, 2009, and secondly at the conference on "Negotiating and Accommodating Religious Identity in Public Arena" at Jamia Millia Islamia University, Delhi, India, February 10-12, 2010. Great thanks to the respective organisers for inviting me and to the participants for their helpful comments. All remaining shortcomings are the sole responsibility of this author. It was previously published in *International Journal on Humanistic Ideology*, Vol. 2, 2009, No. 2, pp. 63-80.

2. John W. Meyer (2009), "World Society: The Writings of John W. Meyer", Oxford: Oxford University Press; Shmual Noah Eisenstadt Theorie und Moderne (2006), "Soziologische Essays", Wiesbaden: Verlag für Sozialwissenschaften.
3. See Jürgen Habermas (1985), "Der Philosophische Diskurs der Moderne", Frankfurt am Main: Suhrkamp.
4. Francis Fukuyama (1992), "The End of History and the Last Man", New York: Free Press.
5. See John W. Meyer (2005), "Weltkultur Wie die Westlichen Prinzipien die Welt durchdringen", World Culture: How Western Principles Permeate the World, Frankfurt am Main: Suhrkamp, p. 149.
6. Meyer (2009), p. 290.
7. Azzam S. Tamimi (1997), "Democracy in Islamic Political Thought", lecture given in Belfast Mosque, available at: http://www.iol.ie/~afifi/Articles/democracy.htm, accessed on August 12, 2009.
8. See An-Na'im, Abdullahi Ahmed An-Na'im (ed.) (1992), "Human Rights in Cross Cultural Perspectives: A Quest for Consensus", Philadelphia: University of Pennsylvania Press; "Towards an Islamic Reformation: Civil Liberties, Human Rights and International Law", Syracuse: Syracuse University Press, 1996, "Human Rights in the Muslim World" in Henry Steiner and Philipp Alston (eds.), "International Human Rights in Context", Oxford: Clarendon, 1996; Mashood A. Baderin (2003), "International Human Rights and Islamic Law", Oxford: Oxford University Press.
9. Michael Dusche (2008), "Die 'wahre' Religion und ihre politische Instrumentalisier-ung", in Claudia Bickmann et al.,

"Religion und Philosophie im Widerstreit?" *Internationaler Kongress an der Universität zu Köln*, Juli 13-16, 2006, Nordhausen: Bautz, 2008: 427-446.

10. See Ibrahim M. Abu-Rabi (2006), "Contemporary Islamic Intellectual History: A Theoretical Perspective", in Singapore Islamic Religious Council (MUIS) Occasional Paper Series 2: 1-24. For a history of Islamic political thought, See Tamimi, 1997, op. cit.
11. Michael Dusche (2009), "Identity Politics in India and Europe", Thousand Oaks, London, New Delhi: Sage Publications.
12. For details, see Michael Dusche, "Identity Politics in Israel, Palestine and Turkey", Thousand Oaks, London, New Delhi: Sage Publications (forthcoming); and "Wissenschaftliche Eliten und vorherrschende Ordnungsvorstellungen unter dem Eindruck wahrgenommener Bedrohungen in Europa und der islamischen Welt: Indien, Israel, Palästina, Türkei", in Jamal Malik (ed.), "Mobilisierung von Religion in Europa", Frankfurt am Main: Peter Lang.
13. Meyer (2009), 57 ff.
14. Herfried Münkler (2002), "Die neuen Kriege", Reinbeck: Rowohlt, 57 ff.; also, Ernst-Otto Czempiel (2000), "Weltpolitik im Umbruch", München: Beck.
15. Carsten Wieland (2006), "Nation-State by Accident: The Politicisation of Ethnic Groups and the Ethnicization of Politics. Bosnia, India, Pakistan. New Delhi: Manohar, 2006,14f.; Hoffman, Bruce Hoffman, *Terrorismus – der unerklärte Krieg. Neue Gefahren politischer Gewalt.* Frankfurt am Main: Fischer, 2001
16. V.P. Gagnon Jr. (1994), "Ethnic Nationalism and International Conflict: The Case of Serbia", in *International Security*, 19(3): 130-166, also, "The Myth of Ethnic War: Serbia and Croatia in the 1990s", Ithaka: Cornell University Press, 2006.
17. Ibid., p. 330 and fn. 3.
18. Wieland (2006), p. 370.
19. Abu-Rabi (2006), op. cit., p. 15.
20. Allavi (1998), p. 68.
21. Abu-Rabi, ibid.
22. Wieland (2006), p. 382.
23. Ibid., 387.
24. Vali Nasr (2004), "Military Rule, Islamism and Democracy in

Pakistan", *Middle East Journal*, 58(2): 195-209.

25. Raghid El-Solh (1993), "Islamist Attitudes towards Democracy: A Review of the Ideas of al-Ghasali, al-Turabi and Amara", in *British Journal of Middle Eastern Studies*, 20(1): 57-63.
26. See also Baderin (2003), op. cit.
27. Meyer (2005), op. cit., 110.
28. I.G. Hasan al-Turabi, leader of the Sudanese 'Islamic National Front'. For a detailed account of his thought see Moussalli 1994. According to Turabi, "all the people believe in the principles and details of *Sharia* law, and apply them wholeheartedly as an expression of their free will. Thus, there is no need for force (after El-Solh 1993: 60). Turabi thereby denies the fact of plurality within the Muslim community itself, not to speak of non-Muslim minorities who by democratic standards should have an equal share in the authorship of the law by which they are governed. Muslims themselves may follow different schools of Islamic law and even within these schools there are divergent opinions regarding its applications to present concerns. In its denial of plurality, this brand of Islamism parallels ethnic identity politics. The evocation of a harmonious unity among Muslims leaves no room for legitimate disagreement and thus no peaceful way of resolving conflicts among Muslims themselves and among Muslims and non-Muslims. Where no space exists to resolve conflicts by democratic means the outcome is oppression and violence. Al-Turabi will therefore have to resort to force to bring about the unity that he evokes. Denial of plurality is a feature of identity politics common to all the instances of ethnic nationalism surveyed so far. In this second group, religious Identity Politics resembles ethnic Identity Politics. As such it is indicative of a lack of democratic culture in the political movements that aim at the creation of new polities and states.
29. John Rawls (1993), "Political Liberalism", New York: Columbia University Press.
30. Ibid., xviii, 36.
31. Jürgen Habermas (2001), "Glaube, Wissen–Öffnung", in *Süddeutsche Zeitung*, October 15, p. 17.
32. Gudrun Krämer (1993), "Islamist Notions of Democracy", in *Middle East Report*, 138 (July-August): 2-8.
33. Ibid., p. 4.
34. Forough Jahanbakhsh (2001), "Islam, Democracy and Religious

Movements in Iran (1953-2000) from Bazargan to Soroush", Leiden: Brill.

35. Wolfgang Merkel (2005), "Islam, Islamismus, der Westen und die Demokratie", in André Kaiser and Wolfgang Leidhold (eds.), Demokratie Chancen und Herausforder-ungen im 21, Jahrhundert, Münster: LIT Verlag, pp. 41-69.
36. Christopher Clague, Gleason Suzanne, and Knack Stephen (1997), "Determinants of Lasting Democracy in Poor Countries", College Park: University of Maryland Centre for Institutional Reform and the Informal Sector, Working Paper 209.
37. Merkel, op. cit., p. 52.
38. Kramer, op. cit., 7f.
39. Hillel Fradkin and Husain Haqqani (2005), "Introduction", in Hillel Fradkin, Husain Haqqani and Eric Brown (eds.), Current Trends in Islamist Ideology, Washington D.C.: Hudson Institute.
40. Talal Asad (2003), "Formations of the Secular: Christianity, Islam, Modernity", Stanford: University Press.
41. Saba Mahmood (2005), "Politics of Piety: The Islamic Revival and the Feminist Subject", Princeton: Princeton University Press.
42. William T. Cavanaugh (2002), "Theopolitical Imagination: Discovering the Liturgy as a Political Act in an Age of Global Consumerism", New York: T&T Clark.
43. Brian Goldstone (2007), "Violence and the Profane: Islamism, Liberal Democracy and the Limits of the Secular Discipline", in *Anthropological Quarterly*, 80(1): 207-235.
44. Ibid., 208, parenthesis and emphasis in the original
45. Ibid., emphasis mine.
46. Immanuel Kant (2006), "Towards Perpetual Peace and Other Writings on Politics, Peace and History", New Haven: Yale University Press, 2006.
47. Cavanaugh (2002), op. cit.
48. Goldstone, op. cit., 221.
49. Ibid., 221.

4

Beyond the East-West Binary: Pluralist Secularism and the Muslim Problem in India and the Netherlands

Markha Valenta

It has become common to argue that the European narrative of modernization neither fits nor accommodates developments in other regions of the world. From conceiving of modernity as universal, there has been a shift to multiple modernities. [1] This approach opens rich new possibilities for understanding global divergences not as failures but as productive difference. At the same time, it largely leaves untouched the narrative of Europe, against which others continue to be explicitly and implicitly compared. And this in turn obscures a critical fact: the extent to which the classic European account of modernity fails to explain contemporary Europe itself.

Central to the politics of secularism in Europe today is the narrative of modernity. The assumptions founding this narrative are being deeply ruptured by Europe's decreasing role in shaping the world at the very moment when the world is increasingly shaping Europe. Responses to this condition are deeply divided. Some call for a renewed commitment to European modernity as self-consciously European, while others strive to realize pluralist, globalist alternatives. Both the political rhetoric and actual practices are quickly shifting fields, even as the gap between the most strident public rhetoric and actual local practices is vast. Indeed, a vital component of this whole dynamic is precisely that liberalization of traditional media, economics and politics and the rise of new media is utterly transforming the relation between debate, ideology and democratic praxis. [2]

"Secularism" and its conjunct "the Islam problem" have become one of the prime sites at which these transformations are engaged. While in this paper, most of these dynamics cannot be considered, it is useful to keep them in mind. One aspect for which I do want to take more time, however, is the question of Europe's modernity. Highly slippery and shifting as a concept, it is one of the key players in the debate on how to govern Western Europe's shifting pluralism. Most often presented as simply given, it is precisely the fact that Europe's modernity—as much in its economic as in its cultural form—is neither given nor coherent that sustains much of the anxiety underlying European Islamophobia. With this in view, it is essential to trace a number of paradoxes of that modernity in order to understand the politics of religion it foments. This then sets the scene for a comparison, more specifically, of pluralist secularism in the Netherlands and India.

One place to begin tracing the paradoxes of European modernity is at the same place that Europe today takes as its mythic starting point: the violations of the Second World War. As with the Indian Partition, it is at once the enabling wound and the trauma that should not have happened. This is most obvious with regard to the problem of the Holocaust, a grotesque orgy of scientific racism and violence, political religion, technological spectacle and destruction. While Zygmunt Bauman has persuasively argued for understanding the Holocaust as the offspring of modernity, most of Europe's most influential thinkers would like to understand it as its interruption. [3]

From this perspective, the current project of Europe entails a re-commitment to the project and heritage of enlightened modernity, under the dedication "never again". This is a commitment passionately felt by many, but deeply blind to the violence of Europe's colonial history. Even as the repudiation of the aggressive nationalism, racism and mass passions that sustained Second World War has been made the collective moral reference point for the new (Western) Europe, engagement with the moral degradations of imperialism have been left to individual nations, to debate or ignore in the privacy of their own languages and lands.

This becomes a problem at the moment in which a second rupture in European modernity's smooth progression takes place: the colonial world's entry into Europe. The European narrative of modernity after all was based on the assumption of Europe going out into the world, but could never imagine the world coming to Europe and transforming it from within. At the same time, European modernity imagined the public domain as the domain of progressive, critical, elite reason, but failed to anticipate that today the most dynamic movements claiming the mantle of the enlightened European and modernity would be populist reactionary ones averse to the elite as much as to immigrants and Muslims. Nor could the European project of modernity that gave birth to and depended on the nation-state as its pre-eminent horizon of meaning and authority imagine today's grand European experiment in disciplining the interests of disparate nation-states within one grand union, balancing on the edge of the post-national.

Last but not the least, while European modernization theory predicted the decline in religious communities and in religious influence on the public domain, it utterly failed to anticipate either how exceptional this process of secularization would be in relation to the rest of the world or how attached Europeans *simultaneously* would remain to their Christian identities, in ways highly contradictory, contingent and subtle. [4]

In sum, Europe is more globalized, more populist, more post-national, more religious and more exceptional than its classic imagination of the modern future ever anticipated. While deeply shaped by its own narrative of modernization, Europe nonetheless diverges crucially from it in ways that are highly disruptive of its most fundamental assumptions and trajectories. At the same time, the ways in which these contradictions play themselves out vary tremendously from one country and region to the next. Though developments in France, Germany and UK are often taken as representative of the rest of Europe, they are of course anything but that. So while Europe may be richer and more developed than most of the world, European modernity as such is no more coherent, no more rational, and no more secure in its identity and achievements than the modernity to be found outside Europe.

Leaving the old account intact critically impairs our ability to understand the political play of religion and secularism in Europe, and the place of religious (notably Islamic) minorities in it. It is, to begin with, some version of this classic binary between an advanced West and a Rest hobbling to catch up that is today deployed by populists, pundits and politicians to symbolically and bodily eject the emergent minorities in Europe's midst. So, in public debates, much of this politics is often framed in terms of a tension between all that is European, enlightened, modern, democratic, law-abiding, just and secular versus all that is foreign, benighted, reactionary, autocratic, criminal, uneducated and religious.

In short, this is reduced to an opposition between the modern and the backward. Often presented as an empirical given, this comparison is in fact a deeply normative, moral and political argument that excels at leaving out uncomfortable facts. The most important of these are European modernity's own incoherence and its entanglement with the modernities of the Rest.

Crucially, even more subtle and careful accounts than we find in many public debates—including by those highly critical of aggressive practices of caricature, revulsion and marginalization of immigrants and Muslims—largely bypass these features of European modernity. Most striking and significant in this regard is perhaps the work of Charles Taylor, who in the political domain has done significant work to make possible structures and policies of inclusive religious pluralism in Canada, even as the great appeal of his writing wrests on the lucid and comprehensive coherence he creates through his narrative of the West's coming of secular age.

Crucially, this lucidity is enabled in part through Taylor's exclusion of both colonialism and race as critical aspects of modern Western thought, with the result that neither the significance of global missionary encounters to secularist thinking, nor of liberal colonial thinkers nor of Black Americans such as Martin Luther King and the civil rights movement more generally find their way into his account. In this sense, Taylor's narrative is deeply racialized in ways that it itself can neither acknowledge nor engage precisely because race is not within its horizon of meaning even as it tells us a story of Europe largely unaffected by its empires and the tremendous intellectual, cultural and military productions it aroused. Read in terms of its political significance—a not entirely unfair reading, given Taylor's career as a politician-philosopher—Taylor affirms the foundational historical framework of the very xenophobic and Islamophobic populist commitments to inclusivity challenge. While disagreeing fiercely on the value of pluralism, both agree that Europe has evolved apart from the Rest and that its tremendous project to re-imagine and remould the world through force of arms alongside the seductions of modern capital and liberalism are inessential to contemporary European self-understanding and the evolution of European secularism and modernity more generally. [5]

Just as crucially, considering European secularism and modernity at the empirical level, their incoherence has everything to do with the significant variations between countries in their religious-secular histories, concepts and institutions. This is reinforced by the striking gap between modernity as a discourse and modernity as a practice on the ground. So the simple exercise of choosing which country we might take as representative of European modernity and modern church-state relations quickly becomes mired in details and variety. How to decide between France, Germany, Italy, the Netherlands, the Atlantic Isles (UK), Poland,

Lithuania, Russia, or Turkey, or any other of the 54 from which we might choose? [6] On what basis might we make such a choice? And is such a privileging of one country fundamentally different from the process by which one region—Europe—is privileged relative to other regions in classic discussions of modernity? This question is particularly timely, given how often French laicity is taken as typical of Europe, while in fact it is deeply exceptional.

When it comes to questions of church- (nation-) state relations, national divergences are particularly crucial precisely because European countries have chosen such different routes for solving this thorny problem. These solutions have everything to do with the specificities of their patterns of state formation. As David Martin elaborated already some 30 years ago in his *A General Theory of Secularization* (1978), countries differ enormously in their particular histories and the role and place of religion in this' history has been at once contingent and essential.[7] Crucial factors include the pathways followed by the Reformation and counter-Reformation and whether a nation's revolution was "an act which divides internally" (as in France) "or unites against something external" as in America against England or in Holland against Spain. In each country, the socio-political—but also socio-affective—frameworks created by such histories would continue to structure the course of religion in relation to the state and society far into the future: setting off cycles of recurring hostility, distrust, fear and violence (as in France) or structures of compromise, adaptation and mutuality (as in Holland).

In terms of the religious regimes of European countries this has created situations that range from monopolies (Catholic, Orthodox, secular Left) to various forms of pluralism. Putting these developments together, David Martin establishes the following patterns in Europe:

1. The *English* pattern (medium religious pluralism, fairly low anticlericalism, fairly low cultic participation, high

stability of democracy, centre-left political orientation of Catholicism, religiously toned civil religion, retained church-state nexus, religious and then semi-secular school system, non-existent religious parties).

2. The *Scandinavian* Pattern (low religious pluralism, low/medium anticlericalism, very low cultic participation, high stability of democracy, secular civil religion, retained church-state nexus, secular school system with religious fringe, very minor religious parties). [8]
3. The *Mixed* pattern (high religious pluralism, fairly low anti-clericalism, high cultic participation, high stability of democracy, centre-left political orientation of Catholicism, mixed school system, influential religious parties).
4. The *Latin* pattern (very low religious pluralism, very high anticlericalism, high/low cultic participation, low stability of democracy, high communist influence and right from centre political orientation of Catholicism, strained or broken church-state nexus, increasingly secular school system and extensive religious parties).
5. The *Right Statist* pattern (e.g. Spanish and Portuguese fascism).
6. The *Left Statist* Pattern (in 'Marxist-Leninist' countries).
7. The *Nationalist* Pattern (churches of nations without secure state [Poland, Ireland, and Israel])

In the face of such variety in the modern European management of religion and religious minorities, it is impossible to say that there is a specific modern European formation for relating religion, nation and state. At the same time, the most striking feature, with regard to modernism, is the fact that the majority of European countries retain various forms of weak constitutional or legal church-state linkages to this day. In this sense—insofar as the separation of church and state is conceived as essential to modernization—the majority of Europe has yet to fully modernize. Alternatively, and more productively, we might say that Europe is as saturated in multiple modernities as the world far beyond its borders.

The Netherlands: Muslims and Negotiations of Secular Public Space

The Netherlands offers a particularly engaging example of this. Like India, the Netherlands was initially thought to be too diverse as a country to survive for long. Having gained its independence from Catholic Spain, it had no monarch, no national religion and no centralized "nation" but rather consisted of something like a strong confederation of diverse provinces. While positions of official authority were reserved for members of the Reformed Church and the public display of other religions was formally illegal, enforcement was selective and left religious minorities extensive freedom to follow their religious beliefs. 'Foreign' religions, including Sephardic and Ashkenazi Jews, German Lutherans, French Huguenots and English Puritans were able to build public places of worship, some quite impressive, while indigenous minorities—notably Catholics but at times also dissenting Protestants—needed to be much more circumspect. Following the French invasion in 1795, all existing religions were gradually given equal status, creating an increase in publicly visible religious pluralism. At the same time, the state continued to fund the Dutch Reformed Church, later also beginning to fund other churches, and exerted significant influence on its internal affairs.

The formal separation of church and state in 1848 enabled a return of the Catholic hierarchy. Gradually, there emerged an increasingly self-conscious resistance to what had become the dominant liberal-rationalist Protestant religious culture, on the one hand by Catholics and on the other hand by Protestants inspired by a neo-orthodox Calvinist revival. It was these developments that generated the Netherlands' first mass movements and increased democratization. The central issue revolved around the question of whether or not religious communities should be allowed to freely establish denominational schools, but also to have these funded by the state on an equal basis with "public" schools.

After several decades, the result was not only to establish

equal government funding for all schools irrespective of their religious identity but also the re-organization of society as a whole along denominational lines. Protestants, Catholics, Liberals and Socialists organized themselves into "pillars", each of which was understood to support the Dutch nation by being most true to its own identity, and constituting separate life-worlds with their own institutions for media, politics, education, leisure, welfare and so forth.

In practice, there existed enormous variety from one place to another in how exactly and how absolutely these structures were in place, even as large cities offered possibilities for mingling, dissent and freedom from the discipline of the pillars. This system played a critical role in achieving the equality and participation of Catholics and the working class. At the same time, its demands for conformity and the limits it placed on truly democratic (individual) politics, also could be stifling. By the 1960s, the system suddenly and dramatically collapsed, as people left their churches in droves, challenged established hierarchies in private and public life, experimented sexually, discovered new leisure activities and were seduced by the potency of sociology and Marxist thought to explain their world better than the religious ideologies locked into place by pillarization.

For much of contemporary Holland, this is the mythic origin of current Dutch society, the moment when individualism, equality and freedom from dogma and tradition were realized. On this account, religion figures as little more than authoritarian enforcement of conformity, irrationality, and submission to tradition. Nonetheless, to this day, pillarization continues to shape myriad organizations in the Netherlands, including political parties, even as the Dutch state continues to fund all schools regardless of denomination, recognizes all religions equally and works closely at moments with religious organizations in the interests of tackling social problems.

The paradoxes and contradictions of this history—in which modern democratic Holland first came into being through communal, religious mobilization and then through the repudiation of religion—have been little addressed in public life. Correspondingly, the unreflective conviction that Dutch public life is and ought to be secular, and owes its modern democratic character to secularism, has become widely shared. Crucially, just as the Dutch were secularizing and liberating themselves from the strictures of inherited hierarchies, a significant number of guest workers arrived from predominantly Muslim countries, notably Turkey and Morocco. Both the government and the workers assumed this would be a temporary arrangement.

By the 1980s, however, it started to become clear that something more permanent was involved. Beginning to settle in seriously, migrants reunited with their families, began to build mosques, to learn the pathways of the funding bureaucracies and to establish networks within the Dutch corporatist socio-political system. While sporadically politicians complained, these complaints were quickly dismissed as racist until 2000. From then on, in quick succession a manifesto against multiculturalism in a pre-eminent national newspaper, the subsequent rise and murder of the queer anti-Islam politician Pim Fortuyn, the attacks on the World Trade Centre of 9/11, the phenomenal political career of the anti-Islam Ayaan Hirsi Ali, the murder of the filmmaker Theo van Gogh and the establishment of a new cadre of anti-Islamic politicians and publicists utterly transformed established alignments and issues in Dutch politics and society, while dramatically altering not only the content but also the tone and style of public debate. After the rise and fall of several politicians and new parties, the ex-Liberal Geert Wilders—creative, daring, strategic, and unrelenting in his vituperative attacks on Islam—established the Party for Freedom and quickly succeeded in becoming both the third party of the land and joining the governing alliance as an official and essential ally.

In contrast to what is shown in the international media, this is a highly complex and quickly shifting field of interests, issues, positions, rhetoric, actors and alliances. A crucial aspect is the liberalization of the media, both the expansion of commercial media and the government's decreasing protection of public media from competition. Along with new social media, the effect was to enable both individuals and perspectives that previously would have been silenced to gain access to the public domain.

Simultaneously that public domain was itself fundamentally altered by the new social media: Geert Wilders' preference for communicating with journalists and his constituents through text messages and twitter allowed him to do what he does best: fire off verbally, creative attacks without exposing himself to the danger of either questions or public debate. The ideal of the public domain as the site of reasoned debate was in this way thoroughly disrupted: there was neither debate nor reasonableness. Wilders' access quickly became a means to challenge the established elite in all domains for having failed to protect that national interest of the Netherlands and her people. Established elite narratives and conventions themselves were exposed to increased competition, particularly from nationalist populists speaking in the name of the people. Much of the time elites were slow to adapt, increasing their loss of persuasive authority. (The overlap with developments in India—where there was a very similar transformation linking the opening-up and liberalization of the media, economics and the political domain to the rise of a populist nationalist movement in the late 1980s and early 1990s—is striking). [9]

Throughout this, Muslim minorities were overwhelming spoken about, while having little chance themselves to speak. Expressions of criticism towards the West or secular culture were strongly repressed, including through the threat of expulsion in the case of immigrant imams. At the same time, all cooperation between government and Islamic organizations had become both suspect and liable to intense scrutiny. In the process, the extent to which such cooperation between the state and religious organizations more generally still was the norm in the Netherlands became publicly visible to many who thought religious organizations had no role, or should have no role in public life and society. Time and again, there were calls for a "separation of church and state"—meaning a call to end all collaboration between government and religiously-inspired organizations and the complete privatization of religious thought and identity in public. The irony is that if this were to be carried out literally, it would entail an utter disruption of established Dutch modes of governance, not to mention the Christian Democratic Party and a number of more orthodox Protestant parties.

Analysis of the contradictions here: what was thought to be modern and secular turns out to be modern, secular *and* religious; it is at the point that Muslims begin to integrate and claim the rights given to other religious groups that those rights begin to be challenged, with regard to Muslims, but also more generally. This is paired with an impressive mobilization of citizen participation in the public domain—but at the expense of precisely of those qualities of the public domain—reasoned discussion—that are said to be under threat from religion/Islam. In essence, two forms of secularism are in contest here: (i) established Dutch modes and practices of inclusive, public religious pluralism and (ii) a fantasy of the complete privatization of religion and the state's radical segregation from all things religious.

This is a fantasy precisely because if you look at what happens in France, for example, it turns out that laicity entails tremendous state involvement in defining and directing religion in a continual negotiation with religious groups...So what the Muslim minority does in essence is confront what are imagined to be a secular Europe and secular state with their entanglement with and dependence on the religion. Precisely that which the Netherlands thought it had left behind, turns out to be all to present, not only in the Muslim alien, but in the very heart of the state.

This becomes particularly interesting once we start to compare regimes of secularism across the East-West divide. In doing so, there are three challenges to overcome: first, the tendency in analyses of the West to ignore the Rest; second, the tendency in analyses of secularism outside the West almost invariably to compare it with Western secularism, but then a highly essentialized and reductive version better suited to a ritually displayed icon than to a critical analysis; and third, the tendency to give in to the habit of methodological nationalism by gravitating towards frameworks and explanations that simultaneously foreground the exceptional nature of the national condition while at other moments elevating it to a universal one. In other words, there is the tendency for analyses to remain enclosed within the logic of the nation-state—rather than at an ontological distance from it. In part, this is because the logic of secularism is itself deeply dependent on that of the sovereign nation-state for its constitution and continuity, a point to which I will return below.

Keeping these challenges in mind, the position of Muslim minorities within such regimes of secularism offers one of the most fruitful possibilities both for comparative secularism and for an understanding of the transformations in Islamic identity and politics today. All too often, the tensions surrounding Muslim minorities are read through a national or regional lens —as European, South Asian, East Asian, Dutch, French, German, Indian, Chinese, Thai—but this obscures the extent to which these tensions overlap. Most especially, it obscures the fact that today Muslim minorities have become test cases for secular democracies in all regions of the world in which they are present.

This is not because Islam is an exceptionally aggressive religion (as asserted by a new group of intellectual entrepreneurs who have arisen since 9/11), but has much more to do with the historical coincidence of a tremendously energetic and, for some, highly appealing rise of Islamic revival movements whose influence has spread across the world simultaneous to the liberalization of national economies; the vast increase in possibilities for cultural consumption and expression that stimulate these Islamic movements both as something to be imitation and to be repudiated; new (social) media; and the emergence of post-national, transnational and diasporic forms of labour and citizenship that challenge established frameworks, authorities and certainties.

India: Muslims and Negotiations of Secular Public Space

Before discussing the position of Muslims in Indian secular democracy, it is essential to critically reflect on the frameworks we have for understanding Indian secularism. Comparison with the West has been central to almost all discussions of secularism in India. Rather invariably, reading Europe as the original source for modernity and secularism, the assumption is that there is a natural fit between "Europe", "modernity" and "secularism" that contrasts with the unnatural and problematic fit elsewhere. So, for example, (anti-communalist) anti-secularists, especially Ashis Nandy, along with T.N. Madan and Veena Das argue that "secularism" is an alien import to India at odds with indigenous history, culture and traditions of religiosity and religiously inclusive tolerance. [10]

While their arguments are thoughtful and careful, this obscures the extent to which within the West itself secularism has been a highly contested project—indeed, constituted through that very process of contestation—as it entails international borrowing, translation and transformation that is highly political. In practice, in fact, much of the secularized West has remained deeply entangled with various forms of public religion that to this day have been as impossible to privatize—notwithstanding their Christianity—as have Indian Hinduism, Buddhism, Islam and so forth. Alternatively put, completely privatized religion is, *in practice*, as alien to the West as it is to India. But this only becomes clear once we consider local Western practices and not just the ideology of secularism in its transnational, universalist guise.

An alternative approach to secularism in India is offered by Partha Chatterjee. Rather than arguing that secularism fits badly with Indian culture, he argues that Indian secularism necessarily diverges from that in the West. This difference is a problem to be foregrounded and analyzed before other discussion can proceed:

At the very outset, let us face up to a point that will be invariably made in any discussion on "secularism" in India, viz. that in the Indian context the word has very different meanings from its standard use in the English language...Thus, if one is to consider the "new" meaning acquired by the word secularism in India, it is not as though the plea of the advocates of secularism that the concept bears application to modern Indian state and society has won general acceptance and the concept has thereby taken on a new meaning. If that had been the case, the "original" meaning of the word as understood in its standard sense in the West would have remained unmutilated; it would only have widened its range of referents by including within it the specific circumstances of the Indian situation. The reason why arguments have to be made about secularism having a new *meaning* in India is because there are serious difficulties in applying the standard meaning of the word to the Indian circumstances. The original concept, in other words, will not easily admit the Indian case within its range of referents. [11]

One of the explicit intentions of Chatterjee's article is to show that "what has been taken to be marks of impurity in post-colonial institutions could be read as signs of a different modernity—the attempt to find, under new historical conditions, new forms of the modern state". What is striking here, however, is Chatterjee's willingness to make his argument through constituting an imaginary West untroubled by the inherent contradictions of nation-states and their secularisms. In this case, moreover, Chatterjee's position is not one of strategic essentialism but instead reveals itself as simply messy thinking. In the course of his essay, he evokes three distinct frameworks of secularism: the secularist practice of British colonial governance, the secularist ideals of anti-colonial Indian leaders, and the contemporary American elaboration of the separation of church and state.

Chatterjee's account of British colonial secularism, as it were, sets the scene for the state that is neutral towards all and avoids direct intervention as far as possible; the modern Indian nationalist project selectively builds on and transforms this, in part through justifying increased intervention in religious affairs via the moral authority of the national community; while the American framework forms the contrastive contemporary background for understanding the anomalies of the secular Indian state, particularly in regard to the issues of religious freedom, religious equality and state neutrality.

The unselfconscious insertion of the American framework is surprising, since it is exceptional in its own right, diverges significantly from contemporary British formations, and has no historical relation to the development of secularism in India. What it does offer Chatterjee, however, are a set of concepts from a country that shares with India a strong orientation towards the Constitution as a national socio-moral reference point, a long tradition of proud religious pluralism, and a central role for the judiciary in addressing the conflicts this pluralism regularly generates. All these, in a certain sense, make America more like India and less like Europe. In other words, even as America has a different post-colonial history (in relation both to its transformation of British colonial influence and its governance of pluralism and religion) from India, it shares India's divergence from the majority of European models. To then take the American concepts as somehow representative of the West, allows Chatterjee to foreground certain features of Indian secularism, but at the cost of drastically misreading the tensions between various Euro/American forms of governing religion and religious pluralism. [12]

The critical shortcoming of this approach is that while Chatterjee can foreground the insufficiency of liberal political philosophy in accommodating the Indian situation, he misses the extent to which it also at significant moments fails to come to grips with Western Europe's own "Europeanized" *and* globalized situation. Both of these transformations are raising many of the same dilemmas as Chatterjee foregrounds in India, regarding the rights of cultural and religious minorities in relation to issues of citizenship and the state. It is precisely for this reason that the Muslim is a "problem" as much here as there. That is to say, the issues that India raises for liberal political theory, are at times and moments the issues that Europe raises. At the same time, the problem, seen from this perspective seems not to be so much about the shortcomings of liberalism in the face of diversity, but the rupture of the pre-eminent framework for liberalism, namely the sovereign nation-state.

Most recently, Rajeev Bhargava has argued not only that Indian secularism is different from that in the West, but that it has something to teach the West. While this is certainly true, the approach Bhargava takes combines the worst of all approaches. He both misrepresents Western secularism—arguing that the American and French models are representative of the mainstream, while they are anything but that—and fails to address the deep challenges facing Indian secularism. While foregrounding the marginalization and discrimination against Muslims in Europe, Bhargava utterly fails to engage the tremendous violence against Indian Muslims. While Europe certainly struggles to imagine a place for Islam in Europe, it has not known anything like the riots and grotesque violence that have been perpetrated against Indian Muslims and the structural over-exposure of Indian Muslims to the precarization brought on by liberalization.

Discussion of Sachar Committee Report: 1st time official recognition of discrimination against Muslims...shift from issues of identity to issues of development...the political possibilities that this has opened up. And this is the critical issue in the comparison of the position of Muslims—could one say that the Sachar Report marked the recognition of Muslims as part of the national project of India? There are significant drawbacks that this is done within the framework of liberalization and development...but at the same time has generated significant political energy among Muslims, the choices and the discussions are shifting. However, Europe has yet to embrace Muslims as part of the national project and the project of Europe.

Endnotes

1. S.N. Eisenstadt (2000), "Multiple Modernities", *Daedalus* 129.1, (Winter): 1-29 and *Comparative Civilizations and Multiple Modernities* (Leiden: Brill, 2003), Dilip Parameshwar Gaonkar, *Alternative Modernities* (Durham, NC: Duke University Press, 2001), Lawrence Grossberg, "Imagining Modernities: Projecting a Multiple Understanding of Time and Space", *Springer in* 1(2007), available at: http://www.springerin.at/dyn/heft.php?id=50&pos=1&textid=1898&lang=en, accessed on December 17, 2015), Charles Taylor and Benjamin Lee (n.d.) "Multiple Modernities Project: Modernity and Difference", The Centre for Transcultural Studies, North-western University, available at: www.sas.upenn.edu/transcult/promad.html, accessed on December 17, 2015), Charles Taylor, *Modern Social Imaginaries* (Durham, NC: Duke University Press, 2003).
2. The utterly unexpected and engrossing transformations in North Africa and the Middle East are leading the way in this regard. Though hailed for their spontaneity, they build (especially in Egypt) on relatively recent networks linking multiple interests—secular and religious, labour and middle class, feminist and traditional—to each other not through shared ideologies, nor through shared leaders, but through a shared commitment to realizing civil relations and civil rights across these differences in ways that were impossible under autocratic governance. Charles Hirschkind, *The Ethical Soundscape: Cassette Sermons and Islamic Counterpublics* (New York: Columbia University

Press, 2006), also Charles Hirschkind, "New Media and Political Dissent in Egypt", *Revista de Dialectologíay Tradiciones Populares*, 65.1 (January-June 2010): 137-154. Asef Bayat, "Islamism and Social Movement Theory", *Third World Quarterly,* 26.6 (2005): 891-908, also Asef Bayat, "The 'Street' and the Politics of Dissent in the Arab World", *Middle East Report,* 226 (Spring 2003), available at: http://www.merip.org/mer/mer226/street-politics-dissent-arab-world, accessed December 17, 2015.

3. Among the most forceful arguments for this standpoint is that of the German philosopher Habermas, whose work is committed to the realization of modernity at its most productive, rigorous and just.
4. On the complex persistence of religious identity in Europe, see the work of Grace Davie, notably her highly influential *Believing without Belonging* and Daniél Hervieu-Leger's reformulation of this in the French context as "belonging without believing". Consider too, the intense debate on whether or not to include a reference to Christianity in the preamble to what was to be the European Constitution and the ongoing unease in much of Europe–though this is far from consistent–with regard to Turkey gaining membership as a secular (Islamic) democracy.
5. Crucially, Taylor presents this as a pragmatic choice for thoroughness in a way that largely bypasses the politics of such choices: "Crucial changes...need to be studied in their different civilizational sites before we rush to global generalization", *A Secular Age,* (Cambridge, MA: Belknap of Harvard UP, 2007) p. 1. This is at the same time to misconstrue the global as the sum of the world's parts, rather than a domain of its own, parallel to, interrupting and interrupted by the local, since the 19th century. By way of contrast, consider C.A. Bayly's discussion of the emergence of a global network of liberal thinkers, writers and activists in the early 19th century, generating citational practices that spanned the world: "Rammohan Roy and the Emergence of Constitutional Liberalism in India, 1800-1830", *Modern Intellectual History* 4.1 (2007): 25-41. More generally, on the tension between national and imperial frameworks in history—which in Taylor's case we could reframe as a tension between civilizational and

world history–from a diversity of perspectives, see Michael Geyer and Charles Bright, "World History in a Global Age", *The American Historical Review*, 100.4 (October 1995): 1034-1060; Jack P. Greene, "Colonial History and National History: Reflections on a Continuing Problem", *William and Mary Quarterly*, 64.2 (April 2007): 235-250; and Prasenjit Duara...Also useful is Arjun Appdurai, "The Past in Its Place", *Man*, 16.2 (1981): 201-219, on the role of history in the management of meaning and on the cultural organization of debates about the past.

6. In offering the possibility of 54 countries from which to choose, I here use the broadest conception of "Europe". Defining Europe is a conceptual, historical and political minefield, but the more general point here is that while this essay by and large refers to "Europe" while focusing on Western Europe, this is a matter of convenience and convention, rather than conviction.
7. David Martin (1978), *A General Theory of Secularization,* New York: Harper & Row.
8. An important note here, not discussed by Martin, is the highly divergent response to pluralism taken in Sweden relative in particular to Denmark following the arrival of significant waves of immigrants in the 1980s and 1990s. While both are Scandinavian, in Sweden ideals of human rights led to an active and fairly exceptional pattern of inclusive pluralism, while Denmark has responded much more nationalistically and exclusively, particularly in the political domain (as distinct from actual practices, which are tending to converge). Despite their high degree of secularization, the shared Lutheran identity of Danish people remains an important ethno-religious reference point relative, especially, for Muslim immigrants.
9. For an insightful analysis in the case of India, see Arvind Rajagopal, "Politics after Television: Hindu Nationalism and the Reshaping of the Public in India", Oxford: Oxford University Press, 2001.
10. See, in particular, Ashis Nandy, "The Politics of Secularism and the Recovery of Religious Tolerance," in Veena Das (ed.) Mirrors of Violence: Communities, Riots and Survivors in South Asia, Delhi: Oxford University Press, 1990, 69-93; Ashis Nandy, "The Twilight of Certitudes: Secularism, Hindu Nationalism and Other Masks of Deculturation".

11. Partha Chatterjee (1995), "Religious Minorities and the Secular State: Reflections on an Indian Impasse", *Public Culture,* 8: 13-14.
12. José Casanova has written on this in recent years, from a standpoint that has the tendency to celebrate American denominationalism for its associationalism, individualism, mobility, and democratic inclusivity relative to what he perceives to be the monopolistic, sedentary, turgid and exclusive European organization of religion into (national) churches that are unable to keep up with globalization. Despite the fact that Casanova's work is tremendously rich and wide-ranging, it is striking that he neither engages the deep structural racial divides in America as these continue to fundamentally shape everything from the forms of religiosity, its organization and meaning to the politics of religion (as we see in the recurring debates about Obama's Christianity as either a form of potential Black nationalism or Islamic subterfuge. Contests over the religiosity of minorities—African-American and Native American in particular—have been central to their governance within America's regime of race. Consider also the 19th century decision not to annex all of Mexico, under the assumption that brown Catholics could not be turned into good, democratic Americans. As a result, there is nothing in Casanova's work that would let us anticipate the intense wave of Islamophobia sweeping America today. At the same time, Casanova's perception of the sedentary, closed, monopolistic nature of European churches utterly fails to engage the history of European missionary activity as this not only travelled out into the world, but also returned to transform European religion and society. Where European religion truly as immobile as Casanova asserts, Christianity would not be the global religion it is today.

5

Exploring Muslim Modernities: Public Presence of Mosques in Delhi and London [1]

Hilal Ahmed

Introduction

This paper is primarily concerned with three sets of questions, which revolve around the intrinsic relationship between the public presence of Islamic built forms and the formation of Muslim identities. The first set of question is related to the idea of 'mosques', which is often discussed and analysed either as an Islamic religious place of worship or as an architectural object. The paper, however, focuses on the symbolic capacities of a mosque and asks a very fundamental question: how do mosques as symbolic sites shape the making and remaking of Muslim identities in different socio-political context?

The second kinds of questions are associated with the notion of *Muslim modernities*. The conventional dichotomy between Islam and modernity, which has also been established as an analytical framework, repeatedly tells us that Islam and modernity are two very different and almost contradictory projects. The goal of Islam, and for that matter Muslims, is to establish an Islamic state based on the supremacy of God, while modernity as a secular project strives for this-worldly reason, supremacy of individual and secular-democratic and egalitarian society. The paper tries to question this kind of essentialism and asks: Is it possible to recognize the religious-cultural engagements of South Asian Muslim communities simply as non-modern and/or anti-modern phenomenon? Or, do these cultural-political forms represent a very different version of modernities?

The third sets of questions are of comparative nature. I talk about a few mosques situated in Delhi and London as concrete examples to offer an ethnographic flavour to my larger argument. In a conventional paradigm of comparative studies, it is quite acceptable to compare these two cities—assuming that an analysis of a developed modern city could be useful in making sense of the issues and debates going on in a developing city. I do not subscribe to this rigid framework for two very obvious reasons. First, I do not think that the liner concept of modern time, which produces the notions of developed and developing would be helpful at all in our case. Delhi and London symbolise very different historical moments and encounters, which cannot be understood by engaging with the developed/developing kind of arguments. Secondly, my purpose is not *merely* to compare the cultural political experiences of Muslim communities in Delhi and London. Rather, I am interested in the specificities of various peculiar trajectories by which mosques are made, perceived and used. For that reason, it is important to find out a few broad points or rather markers by which the public presence of mosques in these two cities could be understood.

Let me make a clarification to further illustrate my fundamental objective. I focus on two kinds of south Asian Muslim communities: (a) Those Muslim communities, which stayed back in Delhi after the formation of Pakistan and prefer to call themselves *Indian Muslims* in India and conceptualised a new Muslim identity of 'religious minority'. (b) Those communities, which migrated to UK mainly in the 1960s from India and settled in London. These Muslims prefer to call themselves Indian Muslims in the UK and have been responding to the British multiculturalism through mosques. This focus on South Asian Muslims in two different contexts will help us in getting out the dominant picture of universal Islam.

I analyse the notion of public presence of mosque through

the changing inner and the outer architectural features and religious aesthetics of mosques. The inner of the mosque in this sense is a domain where religion and culture are interacted. While the outer is a domain where mosques as built forms respond to legal-constitutional discourse of secularism. Thus, two external features (legal-constitutional discourse of secularism and the city landscape) and two internal features (changing religiosity and changing language by which Islam is read and disseminated) are taken as reference points.

The paper is divided into three short sections. The first section looks at the existing literature on the idea of mosque and underlines the rigidity of methodological initiatives in this regard. The second and third sections discuss a few trends in Delhi and London. In the final section I try to spell out my argument.

What is a Mosque?

'What is a mosque?' [2] This very simple and straightforward question introduces us to two very different perspectives, which actually shape and constitute the dominant discourse on Islamic built environment. [3] Firstly, there is a *legal-technical* perspective on mosques, which revolves around the architectural attributes, archaeological significance, historical values and/or legal status of mosques. More precisely, this perspective conceptualizes mosques as architectural, historical, legal objects, and attempts to map out their placing in the wider secular discourses. In fact, a strict dividing line between the built space of a mosque and associated religious practices is drawn to comprehend the modern, objective, unbiased and rational meanings of such structures.

Mosques, consequently, are defined either as religious architecture/Islamic monuments or as legal/juristic person. Although this perspective originates in the writings of Orientalist scholars of Islamic art and history in the 19th century, it still influences the debates on Islamic architecture, conservation of Islamic monuments and the legal-constitutional discourse on Islamic religious places of worship. The literature on contemporary mosques suggests that this legal-technical perspective is moving in two new directions. One kind of writings is involved in redefining mosques as a site of cultural encounters and/or accommodations, especially in post-9/11 Europe and North America. A recent report entitled *Conflict over Mosques in Europe: Policy Issues and Trends* (2009) and Omar Khalidi's various writings on American mosques, especially his photo essay *Mosques in North America and Canada* (2001) are good example in this regard. The architecture of contemporary mosques, especially the mosques built in post-Second World War Arab world and East Asia is another new area for legal-technical perspective. Ismail Serageldin and James Steele's study *Architecture of the Contemporary Mosque: New Architectures* is an example of this genre.

There is also a *religious-ritualistic perspective*, which offers a *functional* meaning of a mosque. This perspective tries to establish a link between the Islamic religious principles and actual built space of a mosque. The waqf character of a mosque, demarcation of the sacred spaces (e.g. separating the innermost part of the mosque from the outer or less sacred parts such a *wadukhana* or toilet etc.), the general codes of conduct and ritualistic aspects such as performing *salat* (daily five time prayers) etc. are some of main concerns for this kind of writings. This perspective draws its legitimacy from the conventional pre-modern Islamic religious sources like *Hadith* (saying of the Prophet), various *Tafseer-ul-Quran* (explanations and commentaries on the Quran) and *fiqh* literature (literature on Islamic jurisprudence or *Sharia*) and produces specified commentaries on *waqf* (endowment), *nizam-e-masjid* (system of mosques) and/or *adab-e-masjid* (etiquettes of mosques). [4] Since Islamic principles are taken as a point of reference in this genre of writings, the mosque is seen as a site where Islamic faith is actually embodied. [5]

These two perspectives, despite being opposite to each

other in various ways, somehow stress upon a fixed and static image of mosque and try to interpret this *fixity* either in terms of built forms or religiosity. For example, the legal-technical perspective adopts a building centric position and gives more importance to the outer technical features of mosques. In this case, a mosque or rather the building of a mosque is *fixed* in such a way that any alteration in its recognizable architectural form(s) becomes a kind of destruction of its original/real artistic significance. In fact, this building centric approach has been the core established legal norm for modern conservation policies.

The religious-ritualistic perspective, which actually gives emphasis to customs and rituals, offers another kind of fixity to mosques. The emphasis on ritualistic purity, especially in relation to performing five times *salat* in mosques, confines mosques into those fixed spaces where Islam as a faith travels without any historical/cultural interruption. Although a hierarchy of mosques, mainly in terms of *holiness* is often set out to recognize the sacred status of *Masjid-ul-Haram* (Mecca), *Masjid-ul-Nabavi* (Prophet's mosque, Medina), *Masjid-ul-Aqsa* (Jerusalem), mosques are often seen as undifferentiated neutral entities. The cultural and sectarian influence on the internal making of mosques and the relationship between a mosque and those *believers* who do not practice rituals, are some of the areas, which are often not touched upon in these writings.

These fixed images of mosques either convert them into those 'historical monuments'/architectural objects, which do not have any relationship with Islamic rituals and practices and/or the *present* of Muslim communities, or transform them into static, timeless, sacred spaces, which do not have any semiotic or political function. I do not see that these fixed images could help us in mapping the changing nature of inner and outer universe of a mosque. Precisely for that reason, it is important to focus on the notion of public presence of mosques.

Public Presence of Mosques in Delhi

The mosques have a very interesting placing in the urban landscape of contemporary Delhi. On the one hand, we have Indo-Islamic historic mosques and tombs, which demonstrate the fact that Islam has an old relationship with this city. On the other hand, one encounters with big green minarets—a new architectural feature of the recently rebuilt mosques, which share the city sky with DTH dishes, towers belonging to mobile service providers and huge hoardings. Delhi's urban landscape, therefore, is not only dominated by the modern urban buildings—a symbol of progress in the conventional modernist paradigm—but also portrayed the *public presence* of the past and the present of city's Muslims in an unprecedented way. In this sense, the religious and cultural symbols or what is often called *heritage* of a minority community get represented extensively through historic and functional mosques.

Figure 1: An Official Image of Delhi

Source: Delhi Tourism.

In order to understand the making of this landscape, three particular historical moments can be identified. The Partition of the country in 1947, which converted the Delhi's significant Muslim population into a religious minority, was the first crucial moment. The communal riots that took place in the aftermath of partition redefined the socio-cultural map of the city. As a result, a few Muslim localities grew, which evolved a new definition of inner and the outer mosques in an interesting way. For example, the mosques, which were situated inside Muslim localities, became the prime focus of all the religious/social activities. Many new madrasas were established in these mosques and the Tablighi Jamaat (TJ)—a religious movement, which was started in Delhi in 1930s and subsequently spread to different parts of the country and abroad—started using the mosque space for their religious mobilisation.

Figure 2: The Public Presence of Mosque in Delhi

However, the protection of those mosques, which were situated outside the Muslim localities including the state protected historic mosques, was a crucial issue. In partition riots, many non-functional Muslim mosques had already been destroyed and there was a fear among the Muslims that their Islamic religious and cultural identity was not at all safe in Delhi. It was, however, found that Sufi shrines and tombs were not targeted in riots. The relative security of these shrines encouraged the Muslim leaders of that time to highlight *Sufi Islam* through those mosques, which were located near or around any known or unknown grave. This kind of grave-centric Islamic religiosity was compatible with emerging Nehruvian discourse of secularism, which was equally interested in protecting Muslim heritage and culture.

The post-Bangladesh war of 1971 actually marks the second moment when the public presence of mosque acquired a very different significance. In 1975, the Imam of Delhi's historic Jama Masjid, Syed Abdullah Bukhari openly refuted the legal powers of government-managed Wakf Board and established himself as a political authority of some kind. In the later years, he started a new election fatwa politics. Interestingly, he re-conceptualised the public address system (PAS) of the Jama Masjid as a mode to disseminate a new kind of essentialist political Islam.

Figure 3: Public Address System and Public Presence: Jama Masjid 1975

Source: TOI.

The PAS also played a very important role in re-shaping the Islamic religiosity. The TJ, which had become a powerful religious moment in mid-1980s, initiated a new waz/bayan culture. The TJ, which had been working quietly in these years, started exploiting its established mosque network to organize weekly/monthly lectures on basic Islamic issues such as*salat*and*roza*etc. This proliferation of TJ's propaganda not only strengthened its popularity but also established a new individuated Islamic religiosity, which gradually replaced the custom-centric Islam in Delhi. The PAS of mosques, thus, emerged as the most important feature of the public presence of mosques in this period, which further paved the way for a more elaborated media-centric religion in late 1990s, particularly after the emergence of local Islamic T.V. channels. The third moment began in the post-Babri Masjid Delhi in the mid-1990s. The religious demography and political profile of Delhi changed very rapidly in this period. The Hindus and Sikhs, who used to live in Muslim majority areas moved to relatively developed parts of the city. On the other hand, Muslims, particularly the middle class Muslims from neighbouring towns, started settling down in these Muslim localities. As a result, four completely Muslim majority areas have developed.

The new Muslim middle classes, unlike the elite Muslims of 1950s, were more practicing Muslims. For that reason, mosques have become the centre of their activities. In fact, these middle classes have redefined the meanings of TJ in a significant way. TJ is no longer a movement of poor villagers; it is an established elite religion, which has its own demonstrative capacities. That is the reason behind the emergence of a new Muslim identity—an identity of a globalized entrepreneurist Indian Islam.

This aspect is evidently reflected in the mosque architecture. In last two decades, almost all the functional mosques in Delhi have been rebuilt quite extensively—not only in terms of size but also in terms of design and architectural features. The global Islamic architectural characteristics, such as green minarets and domes etc. are replacing the traditional Indo-Islamic architectural forms. In fact, considerable amount of financial resources are spent in the outer decoration of these minarets and domes.

The most significant change is the increasing use of Hindi in the religious discourses. The Muslim middle classes are employing Hindi for mass religious mobilization. All the notice boards in mosques, signposts and even the epitaphs in

Muslim graveyards are now being written in Nagari script. The sell of Hindi version of Quran is increasing tremendously and the TJ's basic source book Fazaile Amal's Hindi translation is often read in mosque during the time of *Talim*.

Figure 4: A New Islamic Language

This cultural political engagement takes us beyond the standard minority right argument that the insecurities of minorities stem from lack of adequate representation of cultural and religious symbols in the public sphere, therefore, as it is quite stridently argued, that the cultural symbols of minorities should be given adequate legal protection. In this case, on the contrary, minority symbols, more specifically the most important Islamic religious icon—mosque—get represented even over-represented at least architecturally. At the same time, use of Hindi makes this configuration more complex.

Public Presence of Mosques in London

The story of mosques in London also revolves around three historical moments. The first moment begins in the late 19th century, when a small mosque *Shahjehan Masjid* was built in Woking, Surrey in 1889. [6] This was the very first public building constructed entirely for the purpose of Islamic religious practices in the city. Although the five times collective prayers continued to be a low profile affair, this mosque for the first time, brought Islam into the then British public sphere.

Figure 5: Shahjahani Mosque, London

Courtesy: Munaf Zeena.

It is important to mention that Muslims from Indian sub-continent played a very significant role in the public dissemination of Islam in Britain. The economically powerful and politically connected Muslims, mainly from various princely states of India initiated a series of public discussions in the 1920s for establishing a religious centre for Muslims in London. For example, the Begum of Bhopal was directly involved in the Shah Jahan Masjid project and Indian lawyer and author Ameer Ali was among those who initiated the campaign for the central mosque in London. These public discussions paved the way for the establishment of *Nizamia Trust*, which was set up with the help of Nizam of Hyderabad to collect money for the construction of a central mosque in the city.

The British government's approach towards the idea of a central mosque in London changed quite significantly in the 1940s. The government, which had been quite reluctant to give any kind of support to central mosque project, quite unexpectedly decided to offer public fund for this purpose in 1944. In fact, this initiative was highly publicized through print media and radio. Although, the central mosque project was completed much later because of a number of technical/political reasons, this project, which was directly linked to the British government's Arab policy, also affected the public face of Islam.

The central mosque project also redefined the public face of Islam. The Arab Islam emerged as the real Islam and the other forms of Islam(s) especially the Indian Islam(s) turned out to be the diluted forms of this real version. This virtual transformation of the image of Islam had some concrete political reasons. The partition of India had changed the geo-political map of the erstwhile British India. The princely states (mainly those which were ruled by the Muslim rulers), which had been a major source of funding for mosques and the dissemination of Islam in Britain, dissolved into the newly created nation-states—India and Pakistan. This virtual disappearance of independent Muslim rulers and landlords also affected the symbolic strength of the South Asian Muslim communities in London.

On the other hand, the new political equations in the Arab world helped Saudi Arabia to become the custodian of the holiest places of Islam. The increasing economic powers of the middle-eastern countries somehow cemented this version of Islam. This architecture of the Shah Jahan Masjid and the Central mosque underline this shift very clearly. The Shah Jahan Masjid was inspired by the architecture of Taj Mahal of Agra. Its minarets and domes clearly remind us of the historic mosques of the subcontinent. The architecture of the central mosque, however, reflects a very evident Arab influence. It is important here to note that Sir Frederick Gibbard, who was a British architect, designed the central mosque.

The Shah Jahan mosque and the central mosque project had a very obvious elite character. These mosques came into existence simply because there was a political consensus between the British state and the Muslim elites. For instance, the British policy on public mosque remained quitc evasive in the early 20th century. Muslim subjects were almost non-entity at that point and there wasn't any pressing need to legally define the space for alien faiths like Islam. The existence of Shah Jahan Masjid was very obviously responded to this ambiguous legal discourse.

The mosque was situated outside London and it was a place where Muslim dignitaries used to visit. In fact, the mosque became non-functional for sometime. However, in the 1950-60s this was not the case. The British policy towards its Muslims soldiers, who were killed during the War and its subsequent approach toward the Arab world created a new space for a new architectural form in the city landscape. The central mosque was the outcome in this regard.

Figure 6: London Central Mosque

Courtesy: Munaf Zeena.

The second moment started in post-1960s. Indian Muslims from Gujarat started coming to the UK in the aftermath of the Second World War. They were quickly absorbed in the British industries. The subsequent migration of Muslim Gujratis to UK in the 1970s, mainly via east Africa and Burma made them a noticeable minority community in London. These Gujratis were mainly involved in low-income jobs and businesses. It was not possible for them to collect money and build mosques at that point of time. That's why instead of constructing mosques, these people adopted a new form of collective religiosity. Private apartments and quiet places around the workplace became the sites to perform five time regular prayers. This makeshift and temporal arrangement for Islamic religious observance helped these immigrants constitute a community of a distinct type.

The sense of community was further increased through TJ. Since the movement was led by a few Gujratis (e.g. Maulana Palmpuri etc.), it also became popular among these immigrants. It had two practical reasons. First, the basic tenets of TJ were compatible with the kind of religiosity these immigrant communities were practicing. The TJ's emphasis on the 'construction of faith-not the construction of mosque' legitimised all makeshift private mosques in the 1960s. Secondly, it had an economic dimension too. It was not possible for immigrant workers to do any kind of philanthropic activity. TJ discourages all such activities and gives more importance to five times *Salat*. This salat-centric Islam thus became the core of Gujrati immigrants' religiosity in London.

The third moment began in the mid-1970s, when a number of mosques were established in London. This moment was actually marked by the experiences of the second generation of Gujrati immigrant community. This generation grew up along with a serious political discourse of 'racial equality', which paved the way for the policy on multiculturalism and cohesion of faith-based communities in later years. Mosques were more than a religious place of worship for them. It was a cultural space where they interacted with each other as members of a legally recognizable faith and ethnic group. These community orientations, which were also encouraged by the state's regeneration programs, transformed mosques into community centres. As a result, we find that almost all big mosques are built with a social service centre in London.

Figure 7: Masjid-e-Quba

Courtesy: Munaf Zeena.

The change in language of religion was an interesting aspect of the inner feature of newly built mosques. Since almost all the second generation Gujratis were English speaking, English became the main language for the internal dissemination of Islam among Muslims. It was very obvious because English was also the language for public discourse. But the most striking aspect was the re-emergence of Urdu as a language for Muslims. In almost all the madrasas, Urdu along with Arabic is taught. The mosque proceedings are held in English and Urdu and even the radio transmission of mosque activities are done in Urdu and English. Gujrati language does have space on mosques' notice boards—not for the second generation but for the older generations, which even now does not have command over either Urdu or English. The inclusion of Urdu and English into the community practices is also relevant. The state-funded regeneration funds, which aim to help local communities to participate in the developmental activities at local level, are often employed by the second Gujrati immigrants to teach ESOL courses (English for the Speakers of Other Languages) and Urdu to their communities.

Figure 8: Mosque Notice in English

Courtesy: Munaf Zeena.

This is a very peculiar cultural configuration, which affects the ways in which religion is embodied in the inner spaces of a mosque. On the one hand, Gujrati speakers still prefer to call themselves Gujratis of Indian origin. In fact, all the leading Indian Muslim organizations like the Indian Muslim Federation (IMF) and the Council of Indian Muslims (CIM) are lead by Gujrati Muslims. At the same time, this Indian origin is defined not in terms of Gujrati culture but in terms of Urdu—a language that was associated with Muslims in post-1947 India in a highly politicised manner. Similarly, TJ, which had a practical relationship with immigrant religiosity in the 1960s, is still the dominant form of Islam among them. Interestingly, the proceedings of TJ, including weekly *Gasht* (visiting Muslims of a particular locality and invite them for salat) and *Bayan* (a sermon delivered after the prayers) are performed in a new manner. Bayan is delivered in English and is often followed by refreshment!!!

Muslim Modernities and Mosques

What do these two cases reveal? We find that mosques' outer and inner domains do not remain motionless and fixed; rather the changing cultural-political requirements affect the ways in which mosques, as a symbolic entity is constituted. Is it possible to call these processes 'modern'? In my opinion, this question needs to be formulated differently because in its present form, it eventually leads us to another difficult and almost unsettled question, which is: *what is modernity*. Thus, I would like to pose the same question in a different manner. I ask: Is it possible to have a non-western story of modernity by which the discursive formation of mosques, and for that matter Muslim identity, can be understood? I think the possible answer is yes. The recent discussion on multiple modernities, particularity the work of Sudipta Kaviraj, tell us that the western experiences cannot be taken as a yard stick to map out the non-western cultural experiences. No doubt that modernity—in terms of political institutions as well as cultural practices—came to South Asia through colonialism. But it took very different directions. In fact, modernity as a cultural form, amalgamated in specific cultural religious practices in such a way that the distinction between modern and traditional eventually disappeared.

This argument, I feel, is useful for our case in two ways. First, it could suggest the changing dynamics of the public presence of mosques and shows that these worldly concerns, demographic changes and political considerations not only affect the outer architectural/symbolic features of mosques but also influence the internal constrictions of the Islamic religiosities. Thus, mosques represent the modernities of concerned Muslim communities.

Second, these Muslim modernities are not static and that's

why it would be completely incorrect to divide them into secular/religious, or developed/developing etc. We cannot say that the use of Hindi in Delhi mosques would encourage nationalism among Muslims or use of Urdu by the Gujrati Muslims in London would make them communal. What is possible for us is to capture the discursive moments in which a few cultural and political trajectories are amalgamated and produce a specific discourse. This is precisely what I have tried to achieve in this paper.

Endnotes

1. This is a revised version of the paper which was presented at the International Seminar on "Negotiating and Accommodating Religious Identity in Public Arena: Comparing Indian and European Experiences with Special Reference to Muslim Minorities" on February 10-12, 2010 Jamia Millia Islamia, New Delhi. I am thankful to D.L. Sheth, Rajeev Bhargava, Aditya Nigam, Simonetta Casci, Javeed Alam, Anwar Alam and Amir Ali for discussions on some of the ideas, which shaped this paper. Since the paper is a part of a much larger and almost evolving study of post-colonial Indo-Islamic modernities, the reflection of the argument presented here could also be found in my other recent writings.
2. English word 'mosque' comes from the Arabic word '*masjid*', which means a place for prostration (*sajada*). Since the early Islam, especially during the time of Prophet, discouraged symbols, figures, idol worship and even worship of the Prophet-built environment, specifically mosques or graveyards could not acquire any symbolic meanings. However, in the later period, mosques and graveyards gradually became the centres of all forms of Islamic commemorative practices. For an extensive discussion on this aspect, see Oleg Grabar, "The Earliest Islamic Commemorative Structures: Notes and Documents", *Orientalis,* Vol. 6, 1966.
3. The term 'Islamic built environment' is used here quite deliberately to not only cover the Islamic buildings such as mosques, tombs and shrines (*dargahs*) but also the less-studied areas such as Islamic graveyards in South Asia. In fact, Islamic built environment as a concept is employed here to identify these

two perspectives, precisely because of the *set manners* in which mosques as an object of inquiry is placed, analysed and understood in these two kinds of writings.

4. I am primarily concerned with the religious literature written in 19th and 20th century in South Asia, especially in Urdu, Bengali and Hindi. Maulana Zafeeruddin Mifthali's Urdu text *Nizam-e-Masjid* (1996) is a good example in this regard.
5. It is important to note that although this genre of writings place itself in the broader category of Islamic religious literature, their Islamicness does not entirely rests on the established pre-modern religious sources. This kind of writing emerges in a specific context and therefore oscillates between the Islamic sources and their own contextual requirements. Raziuddin Aquil's recent study on Indo-Islamic history underlines this point in the context of medieval *Adad* and *Akhlaq* literature. See, Raziuddin, Aquil, "In the Name of Allah: Understanding Islam and Indian History", Chapter 1, Penguin Books India, Delhi, 2009. I also find this trajectory in the later religious literature, especially the texts written in post-colonial north India.
6. A.L Tibawi (1981), "History of the London Central Mosque and the Islamic Cultural Centre 1910-1980", *Die Welt des Islams,* New Series, Bd. 21, Nr. 1/4.

References

Ahmed, Hilal (2009), "Muslims as a Political Community", Seminar No. 602.

——(2009), "Reception of Nehruvian Secularism and the Political Architecture of Jama Masjid", *Third Frame*, Vol. 2, No. 3, July-September (Special issue on Nehru and Minorities).

——(Forthcoming), "Conservation of Indo-Islamic Historic Buildings in India: An Evaluation of the Post-colonial Indian Conservation Policy and Legal Framework", an edited book on Culture and Development based on World Bank project on 'Policies and Financial Mechanisms for Culture in Sustainable Development Learning Initiative'.

——(2007), "Politics of Monuments and Memory in Post-colonial North India: A Study of Muslim Political Discourse on Jama Masjid and Babri Masjid", Ph.D. thesis, SOAS, University of London, London.

——(2008), Debating Muslim Representation, Seminar No. 532.

Allen, Charles (2006), "God's Terrorists: The Wahabi Cult and the Hidden Roots of Modern Jihad", Abacus, London.

Allievi, Stefano (2009), "Conflicts over Mosques in Europe: Policy Issues and Trends", Alliance Publishing Trust/Network of European Foundations, London.

Aquil, Raziuddin (2009), "In the name of Allah: Understanding Islam and Indian History", Penguin Books India, New Delhi.

Binder, Leonard (1988), "Islamic Liberalism: A Critique of Development Ideologies", (Chicago and London).

Burgess, Jas (1906), "The Orientation of Mosques", *Journal of the Royal Asiatic Society of Great Britain and Ireland*, April.

Creswell, K.A.C. (1953), "Problems in Islamic Architecture", *The Art Bulletin*, Vol. 35, No. 1.

Eaton, Richard M. (2000), "Essays on Islam and Indian History", Oxford University Press, New Delhi.

Eickelman, Dale. F. (2000), "Islam and the Languages of Modernity", *Daedalus*, Vol. 129, No. 1, Winter, pp. 119-135.

Eisenstadt, S.N. (2000), "Introduction: Multiple Modernities", *Daedalus*, Winter.

Esposito, L. John (2001), "Islam and Democracy", *Humanities*, Vol. 22, No. 6.

Euben, Roxanne (1997), "Pre-modern, Anti-modern or Post-modern? Islamic and Western Critiques of Modernity" *The Review of Politics*, Vol. 59, No. 3.

Farouqui, Ather (2006), "Redefining Urdu Politics in India", (ed.) Oxford University Press, New Delhi.

Gandhi, J.S. (2006), "Living with Urdu: Living without Urdu" in Ather Farouqui (ed.), 'Redefining Urdu Politics in India', Oxford University Press, New Delhi.

Göle, Nilüfer (2000), "Snapshots of Islamic Modernities", *Daedalus*, Vol. 129, No. 1, Winter.

Grabar, Oleg (1963), "The Islamic Dome: Some Considerations", *The Journal of the Society of Architectural Historians*, Vol. 22, No. 4.

Grabar, Oleg (1966), "The Earliest Islamic Commemorative Structures: Notes and Documents", *Orientalis*, Vol. 6.

Habermas, Jurgen (1981), "Modernity versus Post-modernity", *New German Critique*, No. 22.

Halevi, Leor (2007), "Muhammad's Grave: Death Rites and the Making of Islamic Society", Columbia University Press, New

York.

Hourani, Albert (1983), "Arabic Thought in the Liberal Age: 1798-1939", Cambridge: Cambridge University Press.

Jalal, Ayesha (2001), "Self and Sovereignty: Individual and Community in South Asian Islam since 1850", New Delhi: Oxford University Press.

Kaviraj, Sudipta (2005), "An Outline of a Revisionist Theory of Modernity", *European Journal of Sociology,* Vo. 46, No. 3, pp. 497-526.

Kepel, Giles (2002), "Jihad: The Trail of Political Islam", Cambridge: The Belknap Press of Harvard University.

Kerr, H. Malcolm (1966), "Islamic Reform: The Political and Legal Theories of Muhammad Abduh and Rashid Rida", Berkley and Los Angeles.

Khalidi, Omar (2008), "Mosques in North America", *American Studies Journal*, Vol. 52, Winter.

Kinberg, Leah (1986), "Interaction between this World and the After World in Early Islamic Tradition", *Oriens*, Vol. 29.

Maussen Marcel (2004), "Policy Discourses on Mosques in the Netherlands, 1980-2002: Contested Constructions", *Ethical Theory and Moral Practice,* Vol. 7, No. 2, April.

Mifthali, Mufti Zafeeruddin (1996), "Mosques in Islam", English translation of 'Nizam-e- Masjid', Qazi Publishers, Delhi.

Noorani, A.G. (2003), "The Muslims of India: A Documentary Record", New Delhi: Oxford University Press.

Nora, Pierre (1996), "From Lieux de Memoir to Realms of Memory", Pierre Nora (ed.), 'Rethinking the French Past: Realms of Memory, Conflict and Division', New York: Columbia University Press.

Riegl, Alois (1982), "The Modern Cult of Monument: Its Character and Its Origin", *Opposition*, No. 25, Fall.

Rippin, A. (1988), (ed.), "Approaches to the History of the Interpretation of the Quran", Oxford: Clarendon Press.

Robinson, Francis (2008), "Islamic Reform and Modernity in South Asia", *Modern Asian Studies,* Vol. 42.

Shahabuddin, Syed (2006), "A Trinity without a Church: Urdu Language, Urdu Education in India and Muslim Indians", in Ather Farouqui (ed.), 'Redefining Urdu Politics in India', Oxford University Press, New Delhi.

Sikand, Yoginder (2002), "Origins and Development of the Tablighi-

Jama'at (1920-2000): A Cross-Country Comparative Study", Hyderabad: Orient Longman.

Thanvi, Ashraf Ali (2006), "Quran Majid (Urdu)", Delhi: Islamic Book Service.

Tibawi, A.L. (1981), "History of the London Central Mosque and the Islamic Cultural Centre: 1910-1980", *Die Welt des Islams,* New Series, Bd. 21, Nr. 1/4.

Tillotson, G.H.R. (1998), "The Paradigm of Indian Architecture: Space and Time in Representation and Design", Surrey: Curzon Press.

Zubaida, Sami (1993), "Islam, the People and the State: Political Ideas and the Movements in the Middle East", London: I.B. Tauris.

Zubaida, Sami (2000), "Trajectories of Political Islam: Egypt, Iran and Turkey", *Political Quarterly.*

6

Religion and the Constitutional Order in the Orbit of the European Union: De-Constructing State Neutrality in Germany and Turkey

Kyriaki Topidi

Introduction [1]

"Peaceful coexistence in a diverse society requires that we learn to find a normal range of identity-related differences". [2]

A wave of secularization has hit Europe since the end of the Second World War. The trend has been connected to social modernization and in that sense it fails to predict or simply explain the current and widely discussed *religious revivalism.* [3] Contemporary arrangements of church-state relations are not particularly helpful in justifying the return of religion to the forefront. Religious fundamentalism enhances the impression of re-actualization of religion, especially in legal orders that have fervently preached that religion is strictly unnecessary in a secular and neutral state. [4] It is precisely the re-assessment of the wider place of religion that triggered the questioning of state neutrality. [5] The so-called 'de-privatization' of religion and religiosity, despite the detachment of believers from churches in Europe, suggests a new kind of public presence that defies the traditional state religion. [6]

Traditionally, the introduction of freedom of religion has been presented as the legal cornerstone of religious pluralism. Accordingly, the secularized state has taken upon itself the mission to guarantee equal religious freedom to all. Does that suffice? [7] Probably not because it fails to provide instructions on how to draw the line between a positive liberty to practice one's own religion and the negative liberty not to be subjected to the influence of the religious practices of others.

This paper assumes that there is an inherent interest in allowing religious expressions in a given society but not just for reasons of respect of individual rights. There is consensus in international law that individuals (should) enjoy a right to a free exercise of their religious beliefs. [8] Beyond that, however, there seems to be also an argument that the expression of religious beliefs contributes to the construction of identity.

The aim of the paper is to analyse through diverse national trajectories, such as the German and Turkish cases, the meaning of state neutrality, taking into account the challenges that national and supra-national actors pose to the legal rights and issues surrounding religious rights claims, particularly the increasing relevance of the European Union in this field.

Visions of Neutrality

The role of religion in a changing public sphere can be fashioned in a variety of ways: [9] from secular liberalism, where the state remains outside any religious consideration in its activities, to new forms of traditionalism, where the state embraces at varying degrees religion, it is possible to find different solutions to the question.

The rise of religion in multicultural contexts thus gives rise to disputes over symbols, access, recognition and even resources. These disputes are often translated into legal matters where courts and legal texts demonstrate *in concreto* the meaning and understanding of neutrality within each narrower context. The way states deal with neutrality and religious rights depends largely on the types of claims that religious groups are posing: on the one side there is the struggle for equality that is legally based on the contestation of discrimination on the basis of religious beliefs. On the other hand, there is also the option of claiming a right to difference that is comparatively a more 'aggressive' strategy. Finally, there is always the option of escaping the narrow confines of law and focusing on radicalized forms of religious action. [10]

In essence, these disputes come down to the question of settling the boundaries of the religious field and of who has the power to define these boundaries. [11] The complexity of the demarcation exercise is also due to the need to balance both the individual asserting his/her identity yet at the same time leave scope for the law to treat 'otherness' in the form of religious difference. [12] Occasionally, this signifies that in highly centralized states with an exhaustively defined public sphere, even the most insignificant religious claims will be conceived as threats to the secular nature of the state.

State neutrality is conventionally understood as a duty for the state to '*neither allow[ed] to favour nor to discriminate against certain professions of faith*'. [13] It should be noted, however, that 'secular' carries a different meaning depending on the constitutional arrangement between the state and church: in an *established church* model, it signifies the recognition of religious pluralism despite the state's affiliation with a particular religion; in a *cooperationist* model, secular means the equal treatment of all religions while in the *accommodationist* model, the state is expected to grant equal accommodations and exemptions. Finally, in the *separationist* model, the state banishes religions from the public domain and restricts their relevance to the private realm. [14] What is common in the vast majority of all Western states is their declared incompetence vis-à-vis religion irrespective of the prevailing arrangement between the state and the church. [15] One should be cautious however not to confuse the legal guarantees of individual or collective rights with their actual protection as the situation of Muslims and members of 'new religious movements' amply demonstrate today. [16] Two basic forms of state neutrality have dominated the scope of academic analysis: an active type and a negative one.

Active Neutrality: Usually used as a tool for integration of new minority groups, active neutrality does not imply state abstinence but instead active support of religious groups. The neutrality of the state consists in this case, the distribution of its support in proportion to the size or popular support for religious groups. [17] Conceptually, this type of neutrality is derived from the norm of respect for self-determination and autonomy of persons as well as from the respect for pluralism. [18]

Negative Neutrality: Neutrality in this context does not signify equidistance from the different faiths and systems of beliefs but instead a complete abstinence from consideration of the element of religion in the performance of the state's duties. State neutrality in this case functions de facto as an 'exit-option' [19] for the state and its institutions (particularly courts) who refuse to consider and address issues apparently too complex for the law to solve. Historically, the state accepts uniquely the secular burden of guaranteeing a certain type of protection for its citizens but declines to guide them with regards to religious convictions, which belong to the sphere of the so-called *forum internum.* [20]

Limits of Neutrality: State neutrality as applied in the Western world knows a number of limitations. These limits have been inevitably stressed by the constitution of multi-cultural societies. Insofar as the state shows preferential treatment to certain denominations for historical or cultural reasons, it automatically limits the exercise of the freedom of religion of others. The easy counter argument to this point is of course to argue that rights are not absolute. Neither is (declared) state neutrality: it has become increasingly difficult to argue that the neutrality principle represents an objective right. As the case studies on Germany and Turkey will further discuss, courts most often draw different boundaries depending on the view point. [21] In that sense, neutrality becomes more often than not a 'field of struggles' as it can be interpreted both as a device for inclusion of religious minorities and their exclusion. [22]

Principle of Neutrality at the Supra-national Level in Europe

Before immerging into the national constitutional

approaches to state neutrality, it is useful to shed some light on how the EU and the Council of Europe's European Court of Human Rights (ECHR) are shaping the environment of religious freedom in the European constitutional landscape, in the hope to explain divergences and mechanisms of interaction for both existing and aspiring Member States to the Union. [23]

It has been often remarked how legal frameworks beyond the nation-state have become increasingly relevant since the second half of the twentieth century. Certain authors go as far as to claim a 'universal personhood' that has emerged as a result of the diffusion of human rights norms from both (inter-) governmental and non-governmental organisations. [24] The case of the EU presents an essential element of complexity: for the purposes of drawing a European constitutional identity, national constitutional traditions have to be taken into account. Does that signify that the European identity should reflect exclusively or even predominantly Christian values, given its Christian historical and traditional past?

Such an approach would inevitably lead to a serious curtailing of non-Christian religious claims for recognition in the European public sphere. [25] In addition, such an assumption seems to ignore that the relationship between Christianity and secularism in the European political sphere over centuries, far from being non-conflictive, reached its current state of relative balance due to the mutual emancipatory inter-dependence developed between the two poles. [26] With religious rights within the context of neutrality, the norms in question are far from being uniform and continue to depend to a large extent on the domestic cultural, political and legal context.

European Court of Human Rights: The European Court of Human Rights, to whom the ECJ and the Union turn to often for inspiration and guidance in human rights issues, has been preoccupied in the last few years with a number of cases that involve Muslim women and their right to wear the headscarf and/or its more conservative variants (*jilbab* or *burqua*). The almost exclusive dealing with cases that involve the 'visual' manifestation of religious freedom is for the most the consequence of the practice of a number of state signatories to the Convention, such as Germany and Turkey that seek to implement a strict secularization of the public sphere. [27]

The case law of the Strasbourg court is overall unsatisfactory for those seeking answers on the religious needs and rights in multiethnic societies. The Court allows for a wide margin of appreciation for individual states to determine the extent of these rights, avoiding the real debate (or at the very least) the constructive questioning of the limits and content of such rights in multicultural societies. [28] It also assumes that the headscarf operates as a powerful symbol with the potential to exercise 'some kind of proselytizing effect', instead of a mere manifestation of religious beliefs, as well as an expression contrary to the principle of gender equality. [29] All in all, an adjudication and conflict resolution method that clearly sides with the protection of the rights and freedom of the majority.

From the standpoint of legal methodological interpretation, it can even be argued that the ECtHR has operationalized the principle of neutrality as a hermeneutical device to apply the principle of religious freedom although the Convention does not command a de jure duty of states to be neutral. [30] This has inevitably led to a problematic line of case law that tends to use neutrality either to preserve the autonomy of religious communities, or to legitimize the restriction on religious practices or even both. [31] Essentially, it is more and more clear that at the level of the European Court in Strasbourg, neutrality is not necessarily a shared pan-European value, citing the example of Orthodox legal culture which is prima facie not at ease with the concept. [32]

An alternative proposal by Zucca puts forward the notion of *inclusive secularism* as a remedy to the current incoherence, to avoid the boundaries between neutralist and any anti-religious approach. [33] Overall, there are open questions on the goals and effectiveness of supranational institutions in creating and enforcing a shared human rights policy in Europe, as the following section will further problematize. Neutrality *between* religions is a clear pre-requisite although neutrality *about* religion is not necessarily required for a healthy civic life, as will be discussed further. [34]

European Union's Approach to Religious Freedom

Conceptualizing State Neutrality with the EU: Against a background of cautious European attitudes toward religion and churches, the European project revitalized questions on the role of the state vis-à-vis religion in multiple and complex ways that no discipline can claim to explain comprehensively on its own. Guest workers from Turkey and North Africa and more recent immigrants from former colonies or Eastern Europe confronted European *exceptionalism* on religious matters with new religious and moral practices. [35] The established status quo of religion on a purely privatized scale became less relevant especially since the new migrants claimed legal protection to the practice of their religious beliefs.

Secularism was, thus, transformed into a more complex task for the state that had to take into account religious pluralism to a larger extent. The 'mobilization of religion' understood as the 'activation of legal norms and of the courts which have the task of preserving and enforcing these norms' [36] marked the gradual process of transformation of anti-discrimination and equality norms located initially within the legislation on the regulation of the internal market to more genuine provisions on religion such as the ones contained in Article 10 and Article 21 of the Charter of Fundamental Rights that reflects an anti-discrimination provision. [37] The Charter, now of legally binding force since the entry into force of the Lisbon Treaty, provides new impetus to religion by recognizing the right to exercise of religion in a comprehensive legal sense that reflects largely Article 9 of the ECHR.

At the same time, the development of the European polity added a transnational layer to the debate on the meaning of neutrality for a Member State (or a prospective Member State) to the Union. European treaties regarded religion as an important element of the European identity. Which religion the drafters of the treaties were referring to is of course still debatable.

During the drafting of the Charter of Fundamental Rights, controversy arose with regards to the preamble where the word 'religious' was included to describe the patrimony of the Union (and its identity by extension). The final compromise referred to 'the spiritual and moral heritage of the Union'. Later on, during the drafting of the (failed) Treaty establishing a Constitution for Europe, a similar situation was created between those that were for and against the inclusion of a reference to God in the preamble of the text. [38] The controversial character of a reference to God implied a dilution of the secular character of the Union as a political community and as such was highly objectionable. The final version of the Treaty signed in Rome on October 29, 2004 referred to '(…) the cultural, religious and humanistic inheritance of Europe (…)' without specifying anything further. [39] Weiler purports on this point that the failure to mention God or Christianity in the Preamble suggests an "EU-enforce laicité on European public life". [40]

More recently, Article 17 of the Lisbon Treaty stipulates that states retain competence on the management of relations between faith communities. [41] Paragraph 3 of the same article yet points to the need for the EU to 'maintain an open, transparent and regular dialogue with the churches and organisations'. [42] The intention in this context moves a step further than the ECtHR's approach and previous expressions within EU legal texts of constitutional character to religious rights—conflicts insofar as it recognizes the need to create a pan-European platform to address recurring themes concerning religious rights and freedoms. The mobilization of religion also operates on the level of the participation of religious organizations at the EU level. Article 11(2) of the Lisbon Treaty commits the Union to maintaining an "open, transparent and regular dialogue with representative associations and Civil Society". The need for this 'regular dialogue' is based *inter alia* on a perceived legitimacy of religious bodies and associations deriving from their "historic role as moral guardians and from their status as representative organisations". [43]

Religion within the EU and its institutions, however, is far from being an established and regular item of policy-making. [44] Internal and external pressures have indirectly created more favourable conditions to promote a religious rights *prise de conscience.* Such factors are the expansion of the EU political dimension and its elevation to a global player, the institutional transformations subsequent to the Maastricht Treaty, the development of a foreign affairs agenda that touched upon areas where Muslim culture is deeply enrooted or other incentives of the recent past such as the Turkish candidacy, the post-September 11 challenge and the immigration flows. [45]

Very often the question of (religious) identity of the EU has been treated in the past in 'procedural' terms by insisting on the common values of the Union rather than discussing the detailed content of rights that are derived from the values characterizing the Union. This treatment of religion and its ensuing rights nevertheless puts into a central position the political values of the EU as a polity and indirectly anchors the debate in secular terms. Ernesto Balluci argues that the new, post-modern Europe should be '*the age of the free meeting of minds, prepared to contribute to a common historical project, on the basis of a cosmopolitan ethos*'. [46]

So the immediate question that arises is of course the one concerning the content of the principle of neutrality under the new circumstances and its implications for the interpretation of religious rights. So far, the EU has remained attached to an ambiguous secular line of thinking which at the same time claims firm attachment to the human rights and fundamental freedoms as the lowest common denominator. With respect to Islam in Europe, however, policy evidence seems to suggest that the situation of Muslims living in Europe still does not constitute a priority and the engagement with intra-EU faith issues is an undesirable task. [47] The EU has, therefore, a clear preference for those forms of religion that are compatible with accommodation of the humanist and/or secular elements of European culture. [48] In simple terms, the Union has placed emphasis on the pacification of conflicts without attempting their resolution, hence the limits of its approach.

Place of Religion in EU's Hard and Soft Law Schemes: As is already well established, the EU and its European Court of Justice (ECJ) have adopted the ECHR as a baseline for EU policies in the area of freedom of religion. [49] This is attributed to the fact that the EU disposes of no express competence to introduce legislation in this area yet and is regularly confronted with questions surrounding the human rights dimension of its attributed competences.

Despite, however, a lack of firm legal basis on the subject of religious freedoms, and resonating developments in other human rights related areas, the assumption that the EU holds no role in this issue or the one that it can only obtain limited powers through the principle of subsidiarity has been heavily conditioned. Very tellingly, Article 17.3 of the Treaty on the Functioning of the EU (TFEU) formalized an ongoing dialogue between the religious groups of Europe (churches and organizations) with the EU.

The nexus between religion (and religious rights) with Europeanization as it occurs at the level of the EU is a complex one. There is academic research that claims that the link between the EU and religious diversity remains characterized by its constant evolution. [50] This evolutionary character is due to the fact that religious rights and religious identity are addressed at the Union level not directly, but in connection with other core areas of EU legislative activity, such as European citizenship, non-discrimination and fundamental rights, or immigration. Simultaneously, at the level of policy-making, religious identity surfaces in the debates on employment, social inclusion, education, culture, as well as integration of third-country nationals. [51]

Lack of a legally binding nature of measures taken that affect religious rights is therefore not uncommon, particularly for areas that the EU does not dispose of legal competence to enact measures. Predictably, the discussion on religion at EU level occurs at multiple, parallel and even competing levels. The already mentioned Article 17.3 of TFEU calls for the recognition of identity and contribution of religious groups, and calls for a dialogue, which does not have a fixed understanding of state neutrality and is respectful of each Member State's arrangements and practice of state neutrality in religious matters. In this same respect, and at the same time, the principle of subsidiarity serves as a 'natural' barrier to any attempted generalization on this point.

In stricter legal terms, it is beginning to become clearer that the general principles of EU law take precedence, however, over the claims for accommodation of Member States' religious or moral interests. [52] The EU Charter of Fundamental Rights [53] guarantees the freedom of religion in its Article 10 also mentioned above, which is at present legally binding. Yet it barely delineates the substance of the position and role of religion in the public space of Member States. At times, it is used as a marker to outlaw certain behaviour, especially incitement to hatred, [54] other times as a constraint to the discretion of Member States wishing to limit certain rights contrary to EU law, [55] and finally as a balancing tool vis-à-vis other rights (e.g. freedom of expression). [56]

These confrontations between rights are taking shape by virtue of a systemic transformation in the EU's legal and political edifice. The entry into force of the Charter of Fundamental Rights, along with the expansion of the competences of the Court of Justice of the EU or the results of soft-law tools are some of the essential elements of this evolutionary relationship between the EU and the notion and conception of religious pluralism.

Particularly with respect to soft-law measures, initiatives similar to the *EU Framework on Integration* that encourages the exchange of information and 'best practices' on integration of immigrants in the Member States, together with *European Integration Fund* encourage the practice of diverse cultures and religions, as guaranteed by the Charter of Fundamental Rights, subject, as previously, to "European values" and "other inviolable European rights or national law". [57] An obvious and predictable point made in this respect would question the content of "European values". To the extent that these values are centered on fundamental rights, religious diversity, democracy, equality and tolerance, there is little to object to. In cases, however, where these values encompass national or European liberal democratic histories and principles, there is immediately less clarity on what is expected from immigrants.

There could even be an inherent contradiction between these latter values and the principles of tolerance and religious diversity, in cases of ambiguity. [58] If we accept that integration is a 'two-way' process, the burden placed on the migrant 'other' becomes unclear and possibly too heavy to 'carry'. In this light and despite this ongoing process, there are arguments put forward that still suggest that religion remains considered (and treated) as a 'threat' or a source of insecurity in instances where it appears to clash with the so-called European values.

Another point of essential criticism focuses on the (measurable) lack of representation of non-Christian groups in policy formation, implementation and evaluation at EU level. This phenomenon is in straight contrast with the concomitant increase in the levels of agency of religious organizations involved in EU programmes and that benefit out of this involvement. [59]

In short, the role of religion at the EU constitutional level operates on three platforms: on that of recognition of religion as a constitutional value; institutionally, through the recognition of religious bodies; and in substantive law by means of the recognition of religion as part of a public morality which, under certain limitations, has a solid national base and discretion. Communal moral standards of law appear pluralist at EU level, with the limitations afforded under EU law principles (e.g. the freedom of movement) and that operate as a way to avoid national perceptions of religious freedom and morality. [60]

The following two case studies, of Germany and Turkey, one belonging to the EU and one in the immediate external border of the Union, attempt to approach and problematize the requirements of a cosmopolitan ethos in the EU through the national trajectories on neutrality without neglecting the concern that states often express for the maintenance of their religious identity.

Religious Neutrality in Germany

The principle of 'neutrality' occupies a central position in the German constitutional order. The juridical state-church relations are based on two fundamental principles: on the one hand there is recognition of a right to religious freedom that carries a positive and negative side to it (free exercise of religious beliefs from personal conscience to religious rituals as well as collective rights) and at the same time there is also an institutional separation between the state and the church.

Germany has adopted an interpretation of neutrality that provides an even-handed public status to the various religious groups yet at times seems to operate under the assumption that the German state has been and remains for cultural and historical reasons a 'Christian state' with the implications that this assumption carries at times to exclude other religions such as Islam for example. [61] The prohibition of a state church is contained in Article 140 of the Basic Law (in connection with

Article 137(1) of the Weimar Constitution) yet the separation is far from being as strict as in the US context. This 'cooperationist' perspective is reflected in the individual and collective religious and philosophical freedoms of Article 4(1) and (2) of the Basic Law. It is the constitutions of the Länder that are competent to decide on issues pertaining to the (neutral) position of the state in religious matters. Public instruction is considered a typical example in this respect. [62] The church in itself is supported by the state by withholding taxes from members' salaries (Article 137 [6]) as well as by allowing certain taxes to be collected for its benefit. [63] Finally, Article 3(3) of the Basic Law forbids the unequal treatment based on religious beliefs.

German Constitutional Court on State Neutrality: In 1995, a famous case was brought before the German Constitutional Court on the restriction of the exhibition of the Christian crucifix in public classrooms. [64] The questions posed in this case touched upon neutrality insofar as the interpretation of the norm in itself was concerned and also on whether the crucifix constituted a neutral symbol. [65] For the first point, the Court interpreted the state's role as an entity which should address religious matters to the extent that all parents agree and if not, allow dissenters to benefit from an alternative option. In essence, an active equality stance. As for the significance of the crucifix and cross as symbols, the Court rejected the cultural symbolism of it and instead held that it cannot be a neutral symbol due to its central position in Christianity. What this argument implies is that neutrality as a norm can operate as a standard of appreciation of religious symbols: even if a symbol carries a broader meaning, it fails the neutrality test if it represents primarily an expression of religious conviction. [66]

Any argument of separation of powers between the Länder and the Federal State that was used in previous case law [67] proved irrelevant in this case since the focal point of the court's analysis was the negative right to religious freedom. In the earlier

School Prayer decision, the proximity of the practice to Christianity was not considered as having crossed the constitutional limits of neutrality because the Christian faith was viewed as a historically influential factor that did not aggressively turn against other religious faiths. In sum, positive religious freedom prevailed over negative religious freedom.

In the circumstances of the 1995 case, it was translated as the right not to be confronted with religious symbols in the public sphere (here a public school). It has been argued by commentators that this aspect of freedom of religion has been explored to such an extent so as to become the *Groundwork* of the 'constitution of religion' (*Religionverfassungsrecht*), in itself one of the foundations of the principle of state neutrality. [68]

A second instance of confrontation between the 'Christian-Occidental' tradition and neutrality in Germany came on the occasion of the September 2003 decision of the Constitutional Court in the case of Fereshta Ludin, that had been denied the job of a public school teacher in the Land of Baden-Wuerttemberg because of her refusal to take off her veil in the classroom [KTI]. [69] Unlike France, in Germany the question was posed with regards to the right of teachers to wear religious dress, while it was considered a given that students had the right to do so. The Constitutional Court reversed the decision of all previous instances by arguing that the teacher's constitutional rights could not be restricted without a statutory basis, which was lacking in the present case.

The teacher's right to freedom of belief (Article 4 of the Basic Law) and her right to equal access to the public office (Article 33 of the Basic Law) prevailed *de facto* over the negative right to religious freedom of the students and the right of their parents to educate them according to their beliefs (Article 6 of the Basic Law), because the Court was of the opinion that it was up to the political branches of government to decide on the principles that should be applied when dealing with cultural difference. Joppke suggests a second reading of this often criticized case whereby the Court intended to hint at the unfairness of selectively targeting the Islamic veil while excluding otherwise the ban on all religious symbols from the school. [70] The latter solution of course would be highly congruent with the status quo in France, where a different type of neutrality, less open, is at place. In any case, subsequent Laender legislation disregarded the Court's reading of the law. [71]

Later case law, as recent as 2006, suggests taking the discussion a step further towards the complete disentanglement of religious rights from any historical and cultural arguments. [72] The legal question posed to the Federal Constitutional Court concerned this time the clash between the religious freedom of parents wishing to home-school their children and the general obligation to attend school. The Court performed the exercise of reaching a public decision without the constraint of its usual socio-legal justification by arguing that the state has a legitimate interest in the general capability of students as future citizens to enter into dialogue with others within the scope of democratic decision-making and involvement in the public sphere. The argumentation avoided clearly the notion of religion as a collectively exercised right and assumed that the basic conditions of instruction cannot be guaranteed by parents, as is the case for example in the United States.

The most recent decisions of the German Constitutional Court [73] dealt again with the question of the interdiction for teachers to wear a headscarf in public schools in two cases. On this occasion, however, the Court stressed unambiguously that the German constitutional understanding of open secularity does not presuppose or require that public schools are a religion-free zone. Secondly, while public servants, as state officers, are required to preserve neutrality, they still maintain their own individuals rights, measured against the general state interest to maintain neutrality towards citizens. This specific point demonstrates a clear evolution from arguments used in *Ludin*. Furthermore, the present cases clarified that any limitation to the freedom of religion (Article 4 of the Basic Law) has to be relied upon "sufficient concrete evidence" that the appearance of teachers wearing the headscarf would risk creating a disturbance to the peaceful atmosphere necessary in schools.

Any basis for the prohibition of such religious symbols could not rely convincingly, according to the Court, on the assumption that such a symbol is opposed to the constitutional values of gender equality, human dignity and the basic values of a liberal democratic society. [74] Thus, the headscarf as a religious symbol becomes a question of individual identity and of choice that does not involve the State that a Muslim teacher is serving in the context of the public school system. [75] Equally, as importantly, the Court found that the privileging of Christian symbols and traditions is unconstitutional, an argument often disguised in similar decisions of many national jurisdictions as a *cultural* one.

Essentially, the current understanding of neutrality in the German context entails a duty for the state to abide to religious neutrality but with a declared (and now constitutionally protected) openness to the diversity of religious faiths present on its territory. The basis used for that protection is an individual-rights one and is clearly connected to human dignity. The crucial novelty of the 2015 decisions is concentrating on the ways to draw "the line between state expressions on religious messages and individual expressions". [76] While this is a very standard analytical tools in the US constitutional context (free exercise and non-establishment clauses), it is much less common in the European content.

In sum, adding the various points made on state neutrality in the German educational context, it can be concluded relatively safely that the state is not allowed to define or judge the content of religious beliefs but in case of a conflict, could in principle allow for the introduction of religion in public education to the extent that it is culturally acceptable (e.g. school prayers are allowed for all groups before the beginning of school instruction). [77] Neutrality becomes a stricter concept where equal treatment is synonymous to taking into account 'the possible provocative effect of the crucifix for one particular student and identified this provocation as an illegitimate *coercion*'. [78]

Is then negative freedom of religion more than the sum of its parts? Ladeur argues that it has been transformed in a right not to be confronted with the *other.* [79] This is hinted at within the 2015 decision of the Federal Constitutional Court. In such a case, the balancing act that courts usually perform is insufficient to address the complexities of the relationship between a constitutional right to freedom of religion and the role of the state, especially in the context of a division-and-cooperation model. In *Wallace vs. Jaffree,* Justice O'Connor had foreseen this type of dilemma when he declared that: 'The solution to the conflict between the Religion Clauses lies not in 'neutrality', but rather in identifying workable limits to the government's license to promote the free exercise of religion'. [80]

Within the German context, there are voices that insist on making a strict differentiation between preferential treatment of one religion with '*the protection of values, traditions and customs that, although once originally rooted in a country's predominant religion, have lost their religious connotations and are no longer viewed as specific expressions of a religion but rather have become a part of the country's general culture that includes believers and non-believers*'. [81] In practice, this task is far from easy to achieve in the sense that it will systematically result in disregarding to various degrees, the religious rights of the minorities. In essence, this interpretation of state neutrality appears less neutral than it proposes to be because it privileges directly or indirectly a national culture permeated with Christian values. [82] On the other hand, religious freedom is far from being an unconditional right for at least two reasons: it is based on voluntary compliance and the neutral state being the exclusive holder of legitimate force, religious communities should abstain from compulsory means and second, there is a negative aspect to religious freedom that aims to protect the believer from his religious community with regards to what are labelled as the 'essentials' of the German Constitutional Order. [83]

Turkey and the Controversial Concept of Secularism

Turkey provides an interesting case study for two reasons: the first and obvious one is that it is the first predominantly Muslim country that aimed for EU membership. In this capacity, it has succeeded in stirring the debate about European identity as either secular or religious. The second one is that it disposes of a very distinct understanding of state neutrality and secularism while at the same time being governed by a pro-Islamist party (AKP) since 2002.

An Evolving Version of Secularism: Initially, supporters of Union membership claimed that the EU would constitute a firm guarantee of secularism and of a neutral state in Turkey, given that after 2002, Islamists and the AKP placed Europeanization on the top of their agenda while aiming for an enhanced protection of their religious activities. [84] The Turkish model, however, remains attractive particularly for the rest of the Muslim world, because, as the following sections will explain, it has been efficient in gradually (yet not unconditionally) allowing for the emergence of 'Islamist movements and parties that reflect tradition, a large segment of public opinion, and the country's developing democratic spirit', under the auspices of the desire to join the EU. [85]

Abdullah al-Ahsan argues that there is something inherently paradoxical with Turkey: it seems to have been drawn closer to Islamic values because of its commitment to join the EU, i.e. by cultivating Western values. [86] Arie Ooslander's 2003 report in the European Parliament on *Turkey's Application for Membership of the European Union* explained the same point in more neutral terms by arguing that *'the political values of the European Union are chiefly based on the Judaeo-Christian and humanist culture of Europe but (...) no one has a monopoly on the universal values of democracy, the rule of law, human and minority rights and freedoms of religions and conscience which can perfectly well be accepted and defended by a country where the majority of the population is Islamic*'. [87]

Although the republican history of Turkey has suffered a number of shocks, the surprise was considerable when in the 1995 general elections, the so-called Welfare Party, a pro-Islamic political formation, came first in votes. AKP leaders, as a result of their own legislative victory in 2002, in particular Gül (the former President of the Republic) and Erdoğan (the former Prime Minister and current President of the Republic), declared an understanding of *res publica* completely independent from religion, despite their ideological orientation, and demonstrated firm attachment to certain democratic rights and freedoms. [88] At the same time, following the same elections, Erdoğan regarded EU membership an absolute priority for Turkey as well as an important step for the modernization of the country. [89]

With a military that has taken upon itself the heavy task of serving as the guarantor of the secular republic order [90] and an Islamist political party in power, it is not unexpected that the internal legal and political landscape would be far from settled. To enhance the Turkish paradox, reforms in line with the Copenhagen criteria and the *acquis communautaire* were initially led by AKP despite its Islamist ideological tag, in defiance of past political attitudes of its predecessor parties. In a sense, this evolution subscribed to a parallel model of transformation that saw non-violent Islamist political parties in the South Mediterranean Arab countries reach power with political agendas shifted to 'ordinary' (i.e. non-religious) priorities and declining religiosity. [91]

Freedom of Belief and the Headscarf Issue: Identity or Political Symbolism? On March 7, 1989 the Turkish Constitutional Court annulled a law passed by the Parliament allowing female students to cover their heads for reason of religious belief. The Court's rationale was that the law at stake was contrary to the principle of secularism enshrined in Article 2 of the Constitution. [92] The historical experiences of the country afforded, according to the Court, constitutional status to the principle in dispute. The Court went on to define secularism as the '*principle which offers the individual the possibility to affirm his or her own personality through freedom of thought and which, by the distinction it makes between politics and religious beliefs, renders freedom of conscience and religion effective*'. [93]

Such an argument, however, ran counter to the absolute interdiction of the wearing of the headscarf for example in higher education establishments, [94] especially as the mere manifestation of one's convictions from the standpoint of a student and not so much that of a teacher or a public servant. [95] As the ECtHR stated in Şahin, '*a balance must be achieved which ensures the fair and proper treatment of people from minorities and avoids any abuse of a dominant position*', [96]—in sum a balance between universality and diversity.

Both legally and politically, the headscarf has become an issue of contention between secular and Islamist circles or between those in favour of an assertive form of secularism opposed to those more comfortable with passive secularism. For the former, the headscarf represents a political symbol that departs from the secular character of the state. As the Turkish Constitutional Court stated in 1997, secularism implies the '*separation of religion and worldly affairs*', the '*separation of social life, education, family and economy, law manners, dress codes etc. from religion*'. [97] For the latter, it is simply related to one's religious beliefs and by extension, identity. Furthermore, the banning of the covered students from higher education constitutes a human rights violation, according to Islamists, despite national and international *fora* ruling otherwise.

If law is supposed to reflect the society's opinion on certain matters then it is worth exploring the purpose of amendments passed by the Parliament in February 2008 changing Articles 10 and 42 of the Constitution. Article 10 guarantees equality before the law, including equal access to all public services, as the new provision stipulates. Article 42 concerns the right to education amended to include a sentence preventing the denial of access to education, unless for a reason openly stated by law. [98]

Both amendments were clearly at odds with the previous judicial decisions. The suggested amendments pointed at the intention of Islamist political leaders to 'rethink' the Western political values and insist on a rights-centered understanding of the individual in the society. The rights-based discourse was obviously related to their quest for legitimacy in Turkish politics. [99] The balance between tolerance and diversity remains problematic especially since on June 5, 2008, the Constitutional Court annulled amendments to both Articles 10 and 42 on the grounds that they were against the secular nature of the state. The neutrality and secularism battle appears to continue.

The Exercise of Religious Rights in Secular Turkey: Article 10 of the Constitution guarantees the principle of equality '*irrespective of (...) philosophical belief, religion and sect*'. Secularism is deeply rooted in the workings and processes of the Republic. *De facto,* this freedom has encountered restrictions in two directions: for non-Muslim minority groups, despite Article 40 of the Treaty of Lausanne, the state denies legal personality to non-Muslim religious institutions with repercussions to the status of their respective properties. [100] The 2008 Law on Foundations has mitigated the effects of restrictions, allowing religious foundations to apply for the restitution of their properties. [101] The law, nevertheless, has not addressed the issues of properties of foundations seized and sold to third parties or properties of foundations merged before the new legislation was adopted. Similarly, the ban on the training of clergy creates adverse effects to the exercise of the freedom of religion. For Muslims, the tight control of the state over religion also raises objections to the basic concept of secularism as guaranteed under the Constitution. A typical illustration of the controversy has been depicted in the headscarf issue.

An equally controversial issue, in conjunction with the right to education, is the fact that religious culture classes remain compulsory. In the light of the recent ECtHR decision on an application lodged by a family who were followers of Alevism, [102] religious diversity requires further measures for its protection. This observation is enhanced by the puzzling arguments of the Turkish government on the occasion of *Zengin* sustaining that '*the teaching of religion in schools is an appropriate method of combating fanaticism (...)*'. [103] More constructive in the overall assessment of the issue was the acknowledgement of the Turkish government that '*in the religious culture and morals lessons, the religious diversity which prevails in Turkish society is not taken into account*'. [104] Accordingly, but not surprisingly, the Court found a violation of Article 2 of Protocol 1 to the ECHR guaranteeing a right to education.

The sweeping August 2002 reforms touched upon perceptions of Turkish identity insofar as they embodied amendments in the direction of cultural diversity. [105] They even went further than EU membership requirements, questioning the ideological foundations of Turkish identity and its constant desire for westernized modernity. The confusion of unity with uniformity prevailing pre-2002 stands separately from any 'reconciling' role with the Muslim world that we may want to assign to Turkey. In other words, while it is definitely undisputed that Turkey is and remains a Muslim country, it is also a secular one—despite the rule of a pro-Islamist government for the last years—and as such, insisting on the paradigm of Turkey as a 'bridge between the Occident and the Orient' can only have limited effects. [106] Turkish identity, after all, is partly the consequence of Ottoman heritage, which historically has been treated as 'Europe's Other'. [107] Yet, national feelings and identity cannot be always rationally justifiable. The value of Turkey's example lies precisely at this point: allowing the circulation of values between parties involved by gradually abolishing the strict demarcations between 'us' and 'them'. [108] Transformation can only occur under such circumstances. The European Union is after all a social (and legal) construction that is based on *unity in diversity.*

In a way, the theological reform debate in Turkey was entangled to EU membership and was no longer taking place in a vacuum. [109] Its repercussions were visible in the balancing of secularism and Islamism, in the light of AKP governance. The modernization of pro-Islamic politics as evidenced by progressive and reformist law-making, fuelled the intellectual discussion about a secular Islamic alternative for Turkey within Europe. Can Islam as an essential defining value be compatible with the rule of law, democracy and human rights? The Turkish national goal of EU accession and the conditionality imposed by the Union in the form of the Copenhagen criteria constituted indeed one possible path in the direction of Islamic modernism. The position that 'an intellectual cannot be Islamist and an Islamist cannot be an intellectual', was beginning to lose ground. [110]

Particularly, for Islamists, the European project disposed of added value: it operated as a guarantee of their democratic rights, [111] although doubts about the sincerity of the EU's intentions towards Turkey's membership subsist. The real question, however, that was posed was the extent to which the promised stability would affect the Europeanization process and the ensuing attitude of Turkish people towards the West. And if so, would a trend develop in favour of a rights-based understanding of democracy? As importantly, would the current divide between secularism and Islamism gradually subside?

Moving away from the historically contradictory Turkish attempts to westernize, whereby sovereignty rimed with *limited* democracy, [112] it remains legally unorthodox that an incentive for change is provided by a (moderate) Islamist party. From the perspective of the EU, the value of Turkey's membership would constitute an important paradigm of a country in transition adhering to all the fundamental principles of liberty, democracy and the rule of law, striking a new balance between secularism, Europeanization and Muslim identity. [113]

The evolution of secularism, however, did not proceed squarely in this direction. Under the uninterrupted leadership of Recep Tayyip Erdogan, the AKP won three successive general elections between 2002 and 2011. During this period, the concept of *secularism* as constructed in the Turkish context has undergone a number of transformations. The constitutionally-protected concept, in the form of *laicism,* has acquired varying content and continues to pose intense debate and numerous questions, insofar as it questions the role of religion in the public sphere. The peak of the debate concerns issues of citizenship and ethics and the practice of secularism in Turkey is increasingly difficult to separate from the exercise of political power.

It is clear that a reconceptualization of secularism in Turkey is timely, especially since issues regarding both the freedom of religion from the government but also the freedom of government from religion are essential in democratic societies. Very predictably, a number of studies and authors suggest the return to a fresh discussion of what being secular means in Turkey today. Peter Berger's myth that modernism is the antithesis of religion is completely set aside, yet the new challenge ahead is how to deal with the growing capacity for political influence that religious actors are acquiring. [114]

Elizabeth Hurd's two paths of secularism are a useful tool to examine the role of religion in the public sphere. On the one hand, a first path of secularism relies on a "laicist trajectory, in which religion is seen as an adversary and an impediment to modern politics" and a second one, where religion operates as a source of unity and identity. [115] For the first, more assertive option, the ultimate goal is to create a neutral public sphere where the state is isolated (and to some extent also protected) from the influence and possible excesses of religion. The danger in cases where the public sphere is exposed to religious influences is that theological precepts may begin to form an authoritative public morality, dictating the "good" way of life for all. The second, passive form of secularism tries to "maintain state neutrality towards various religions", [116] imposing the duty on the state to foster in equal terms the expression of religious views and the exercise of religious rights for both religious and non-religious citizens, without becoming a religious state in itself.

The Turkish version of secularism is sourced from the concern that the state should be in a position to control religion. This is the clear heritage of Kemalism, which instrumentalised Islam in three ways, according to Yavuz: [117] first, the state was placed in a position to influence religion towards the goal of creating an enlightened Islam that would support the general modernization project for Turkey, second, Islam was used to contribute towards the creation of a national identity and third, it provided a legitimization niche for the state. With this triple objective, the General Directorate of Religious Affairs (Diyanet) was established in 1924 to oversee all matters related to Islam. [118] In short, it became what Barker labels the location of the "official Islam". [119] An interesting argument in this respect posits that in those early years of Turkish Republicanism in the 1920s, nationalism was intended and designed to replace religion. [120]

The Diyanet's role since the early 1980s has shifted and is currently to propagate the 'correct' Islam both within Turkey and among diasporic Turkish minorities abroad but also more recently in the Balkans and the Caucasus, in an attempt to assume a role as an actor of international affairs. [121] It maintains a holistic definition of Islam within Turkey, including in its conception the Alevi and Sunni minorities present on Turkish territory. The role of the institution has been further politicized in the context of the recent electoral campaign in Turkey. Perceived as the AKP's political tool, the Diyanet is often presented as a super-sized institution that is tasked with the mission to protect the moral values of the country. [122]

The recent governance of Turkey under an ostensibly pro-Islamist party, re-surfaces those aspects of Turkish secularism and begs a number of questions: could it be, that currently, religion is used in a way that it almost replaces the long-prevailing Turkish nationalism, quite in the opposite way of the Kemalist historical legacy? Are there any indications that religion, in a country that is comprised of a crushing and overwhelming majority of (practicing) Muslims, [123] is susceptible of becoming the vehicle for the expression of a comprehensive doctrine on what is "good"? [124] As importantly, where do the limits of the state's role lie in this difficult balance?

It is difficult to dispute that the role of the state in this context is not to crush the individual but to guarantee the individual's exercise of rights. [125] It is also established that in democratic states, religious institutions should not enjoy a privileged position that allows them to partake in the formulation of public policy although they should be free to express and promote those views, within the limits of law and the Constitution. More concretely, the role of the Turkish Constitutional Court should be re-assessed vis-à-vis its understanding of secularism. Should secularism remain a comprehensive worldview?

The 1937 Turkish Constitution officially proclaimed the Turkish Republic to be secular but one's understanding of secularism needs readjustment if the ultimate goal is the respect of religious rights on an equal basis for all, regardless of faith or worldview. The issue of Alevis has arisen a number of times and retains political (and legal) momentum. [126] In that respect, there has been reluctance both from the government as well as the Diyanet to recognize a separate religious identity to the group in question, expressed most commonly in the refusal to recognize *cemevis* (gathering houses) as the places of worship that Alevis have set for the practice of their faith. [127]

Recent reforms to the education system have also signalled the willingness of the ruling party to further bring to the fore, the religious element. After legislation in 2013 that banned any form of advertising of alcohol and following the entrance of the first female lawmaker in the country's Parliament wearing her headscarf, in September 2014, the government enacted provisions allowing female pupils as of the age of ten to cover their head using headscarves at school. [128] In December of the same year, the National Education Council of Turkey's Ministry of Education enforced basic religious knowledge course to first graders and implemented Ottoman languages as electives. [129] Other contested measures included the increase in the number of compulsory religious classes from one to two hours per week.

Overall, it is difficult to ignore that there is evidently greater scope for religion in the public sphere but this 'openness' is not without controversy. While the interpretation of secularism and state neutrality remains a genuinely constitutional matter, it is not an isolated practice within a 'power-free space'. [130] Gözaydin correctly points out that various secularisms and laïcisms emerge within ever-changing socio-political climates. [131]

Habermas' 'post-secular' label for the present era indirectly confirms the evolutionary societal adjustment of the concept of state-neutrality vis-à-vis religion. [132] Within Turkey, this conceptual fluidity, despite a promising initial phase already described under the first AKP term of government, renders the country "(...) as too secular for the Islamists, too Sunni for the Alevis and too Turkish for the Kurds (...)". [133]

Concluding Remarks

One of the recurring criticisms in the application of state

neutrality by individual Western-minded states is that it fails to address the collective dimension of religion. The headscarf decisions of the German and Turkish Constitutional Courts insist on the individualisation of faith and its decoupling from politics as the only means to secure equal rights for all citizens. But if we accept that state neutrality as currently applied is not entirely appropriate for multi-cultural societies, perhaps the starting point of our quest for a post-secular conception of neutrality should be placed precisely here.

Religious criteria of rightness have no place in the organisation and the legal system of the state as well as of the European Union but clarifying the modalities of cooperation and at times even subordination of religious norms to the principles of a free and egalitarian state would alleviate the burden of constant questioning as regards the role of religion in a neutral state. The difficulties that are inherent in the state's role as guarantor of religious freedom are different whether neutrality places religious beliefs entirely in the private sphere or whether it attempts to solve collisions of religious rights through indirect legal methods that do not always draw clear lines to the extent on which the religion of the majority carries more weight than that of the minority.

At times of contentious relations between communities in Europe, modern understanding of Islam in our continent have been a prominent topic of religious, political, social and even legal debates. Clearly the case of Turkey has accentuated the broader issue further, bringing fuzzy concepts such as Euro-Islam back to the fore. In this regard, mainstream literature distinguishes two 'variants' of Euro-Islam, relevant for this analysis: one that proposes the adoption of European liberal-democratic fundamental values as a remedy to emerge from a 'decaying' religion and its ensuing mental attitudes, [134] and another that seeks to embrace and re-surface the 'universally valid' fundamental values of Islam. [135]

If we accept that a constitutional identity both draws on and transforms a constitutional tradition, the European Union in the wider scheme of things could (and hopefully will) function as a factor of re-construction of state neutrality by opening up legal spaces, minds and arguments. For the moment, it remains a supra-national polity that operates as the sum of the plurality of national perceptions of state neutrality: it tries to accommodate but has not been yet able to reconcile the different constitutional traditions on the role of religion in the public sphere. It is not even clear whether it wishes to undertake this kind of 'reconciliation' project. What is clearer, is that religious rights will continue to claim their position in the public sphere, and depending on the national (or supra-national) constitutional context, will utilize highly contextualized socio-legal tools to maintain their place. The urgency to consider critically the constitutional role of religious belonging for individuals and groups stands firmer than ever.

Endnotes

1. Parts of the present introduction have been published in Kyriaki Topidi (2012), "Religious Diversity in Public Education: A Comparative European Perspective", in Cornelia Roux (ed.), 'Safe Spaces: Human Rights Education in Diverse Contexts', pp. 109-128, Sense Publishers.
2. Jocelyn Maclure and Charles Taylor (2011), "Secularism and Freedom of Conscience", Cambridge Mass: London, Harvard University Press, p. 47.
3. Grace Davie argues in favour a European exceptionalism explaining that: "*European patterns of religion are not a prototype of global religiosity; they are peculiar to the European continent. It follows that the relatively low levels of religious activity in modern Europe are not simply the result of early modernization; they are part of what it means to be European and need to be understood in these terms*", available at:
   http://huss.exeter.ac.uk/sociology/staff/davie/research.php,
   as quoted in Kippenberg, 2009, p. 212.
4. Ladeur (2008), at 249.
5. Leustean, (2008), at 248.
6. Kippenberg (2008), at 152.
7. Jürgen Habermas asked the same question in 'Religion in the

Public Sphere' (2005), Lecture at San Diego University, available at: http://www.sandiego.edu/pdf/pdf_library/habermaslecture031105_c939cceb2ab087bdfc6df291ec0fc3a.pdf, pp. 5-6.

8. Article 9 of the European Convention of Human Rights; Article 18 of the UN Pact on Civil and Political Rights; UN Declaration on the Rights of Persons Belonging to National or Ethnic Religious and Linguistic Minorities (1992); UNESCO's Declaration on Cultural Diversity (2001); the Convention on the Rights of Migrant Workers and Their Families (1990); Article 4 of the German Basic Law; First Amendment to the United States Constitution.
9. On this topic, see for example, Hackett (2005), pp. 659-682.
10. For more on these strategies, see Koenig (2009), pp. 300-301.
11. Reuter (2009), p. 6.
12. What Ladeur calls the 'symbolic order of the "Other", C.F. Ladeur (2008), p. 250.
13. Ladeur and Augsberg, (2007), p. 143.
14. Van der Ven, (2008), at 166.
15. Bader (2009) at 49.
16. Bader (2009), at 54.
17. For a discussion of this type of neutrality, see Van der Burg and F. Brom (2009).
18. Van der Burg and Brom (2009), at 9.
19. Ladeur and Augsberg (2007), at 144.
20. Ladeur and Augsberg interestingly argue that this move from the collective to the individual regarding religion has not occurred in the Islamic world and this de-politisation within Islam is still expected to come (Ibid., at 145).
21. A typical illustration of the elastic nature of state neutrality is to be found in the presumption that for the headscarf issue the state would be identifying itself with a particular dogmatic string of Islam while in the Crucifix case, a different boundary was suggested for negative religious freedom that involved the cultural argument of Occidental tradition in Germany and the cross as 'neutral' symbol that depended on the approval of parents. For more on this point, see Ladeur and Augsberg (2007), at 147-148.
22. Joppke (2007), at 314.
23. In Turkey's case, EU membership remains an item of the

country's external policy agenda, with fluctuating priority (Cf. EU External Action, EU Relations with Turkey, available at: http://eeas.europa.eu/turkey.

24. Koenig (2009), at 314.
25. For a similar point, see Augenstein (2009), at 5.
26. Augenstein (2009), at 13.
27. Hambler (2008), at 122.
28. See for example Leyla Sahin vs. Turkey, Appl. 44774/98, Judgement of June 29, 2004, where the Court distinctly stipulates in para 100 of the judgement: '*Where questions concerning the relationship between the State and religious are at stake, on which opinion in a democratic society may reasonably differ widely, the role of the national decision-making body must be given special importance*'.
29. See Dahlab vs. Switzerland, Appl. No. 42393/98, ECHR 2001-V, at 7-13.
30. Andrea Pin (2014), "Does Europe Need Neutrality? The Old Continent in Search of Identity", BYU L. Rev. 605 (2014), at 611.
31. Ibid., at 614.
32. Ibid., at 616-617. Pin takes the syllogism a step further by arguing that neutrality might not be after all the appropriate foundation for the protection of religious freedom, given the lack of agreement between States on its significance. She proposes instead the concept of *religious pluralism.*
33. L. Zucca (2012), "A Secular Europe", Oxford University Press, at.132.
34. Benjamin L. Berger (2014), "Religious Diversity, Education, and the Crisis in State Neutrality", 1, Paper 76, at 23.
35. Kippenberg (2009), at 212.
36. Groetsch (2009), at 234.
37. Article 10 of the Charter stipulates: '(i) Everyone has the right to freedom of thought, conscience and religion. This right includes freedom to change religion or belief and freedom, either alone or in community with others and in public or in private, to manifest religion or belief, in worship, teaching, practice and observance; (ii) The right to conscientious objection is recognized, in accordance with the national laws governing the exercise of this right'.
38. For a more detailed analysis of the drafting process, see Mandry

(2009), at 263-274. The final version of the Constitutional Treaty and the relevant section of the Preamble reads: "Drawing inspiration from the cultural, religious and humanist inheritance of Europe, from which have developed the universal values of the inviolable and inalienable rights of the human person, freedom, democracy, equality and the rule of law" [Council of the European Union, consolidated versions of the Treaty on European Union and the Treaty on the functioning of the European Union, Brussels, April 15, 2008, 6655/08].

39. CONV 850/03.
40. J.H.H. Weiler (2003), "Un'Europa Cristiana: Un saggio esplorative", Milan, BUR Saggi.
41. Article 17(1) stipulates, "The Union respects and does not prejudice the status under national law of churches and religious associations or communities in the Member States" [Cf. Article 17(1), Consolidated Version of the Treaty on the Functioning of the European Union, O.J. C115/47].
42. Article 17 TFEU reads: '(i) The Union respects and does not prejudice the status under national law of churches and religious associations or communities in the Member States; (ii) The Union equally respects the status under national law of philosophical and non-confessional organizations; (iii) Recognizing their identity and their specific contribution, the Union shall maintain an open, transparent and regular dialogue with these churches and organizations'.
43. Ronan McCrea (2009), "The Recognition of Religion within the Constitutional and Political Order of the European Union", LEQS Paper No.10/2009, September, at 19.
44. For more on this point, see Silvestri (2009), at 1212-1239.
45. Ibid., at 1216-1217.
46. As quoted in Roebben (2008), at 208.
47. Silvestri (2009), at 1225.
48. Ronan McCrea (2009), "The Recognition of Religion within the Constitutional and Political Order of the European Union", LEQS Paper No.10/2009, September, at p. 12.
49. Consolidated Version of the TEU, Article 6, September 5, 2008, OJ (C115) 19.
50. Sergio Carrera and Joanna Parkin, "The Place of Religion in European Union Law and Policy: Competing Approaches and Actors Inside the European Commission", RELIGARE Working

Document No. 1/September 2010, available at: http://www.religareproject.eu.

51. Ibid., at 2-3.
52. See indicatively, case C-268/99 of Jany and Others vs. Staatssecretaris van Justitie (2001), ECR I-8615 that stroke down as incompatible with EU law, the refusal of the Dutch government to issue residence permits to self-employed prostitutes from Poland on the basis of moral considerations.
53. O.J. (2010/C 83/02), March 30, 2010.
54. Cf. Council Framework Decision 2008/913/JHA.
55. See for example, the 2000/78 Employment Equality Directive, which provides a general framework for combating discrimination on the grounds of religion at work but which nevertheless allows certain exceptions in Article 2.8 of the Directive and elsewhere on the possibility to limit the exercise of religious freedoms in the workplace on the grounds of public interest, genuine occupation requirement or when the employer is a church or an organisation with an ‚ethos‘ based on religion. The ambiguities within these provisions do not preclude the possibility for legislative discrepancies in the Member States. Other relevant pieces of EU legislation operating in a similar pattern are Directive 2003/86 on the right to family reunification O.J. 2003 L 251/12 and Directive 2003/109 on the status of Third Country Nationals who are long-term residents. O.J. 2004/L16/44 and that sanction the exercise of religious rights in events of polygamy and subject to *integration measures* at the discretion of Member States. These measures condition access for TCNs to the right to family reunification and social solidarity, subject to the general principles of EU law on proportionality, non-discrimination and fundamental human rights (cf. Case C-540/03, Parliament vs. Council (2006), ECR I-5769).
56. Carrera et al. (2010), at p.8.
57. Ibid., at 17, for more on these initiatives.
58. For a similar point, see Carrera et al. (2010), at 19.
59. Ibid., at p. 26.
60. Further to the case of Jany, the case of C-159/90 SPUC vs. Grogan [1991], ECR I-4685 reminds us that: "It is not for the Court to substitute its assessment for that of the legislature in those Member States where the activities in question are

practised legally". (at paras 19 and 20 of the judgment).

61. Joppke (2007), at 314-315.
62. It should be borne nevertheless in mind that there are exceptions to this trend such as Article 7 para 4 of the Federal Constitution (*Grundgesetz)* that stipulates the right of religious communities to provide for religious instruction in public schools as part of the curriculum.
63. For more on the so-called Privilegienbuendel, cf. BVerfGE 102, 370 as quoted in Brugger (2007), at 39.
64. BVerfGE 93, 1 1 BvR 1087/91.
65. Van der Burg and Brom (2009), at 17.
66. Ibid., at 19.
67. See for example, the case on school prayer in public schools discussed in 1975 [BVerfGE December 17, 1975].
68. For example, cf. Ladeur (2008), at 2452.
69. BVerfG, September 24 2003, at 108.
70. Joppke (2007), at 330.
71. Ibid., at 331-332, in particular the law of Baden-Wuerttemberg.
72. BVerfGE June 6, 2006, 2 Entscheidungen des BVerfGE 1693 (F.R.G.).
73. Decisions of January 27, 2015, 1 BvR 471/10 and BvR 1181/109.
74. This was the case of para 57, Sections 4(1) and (2) of the School Law of North Rhine-Westphalia challenged in the set of the cases before the Court.
75. For more on this point, see the short commentary of the decision, available at: http://www.ezire.fau.de/2015_03_13_ezire_german-constitutional-court_headscarf_engl.pdf.
76. On this point, see Claudia Haupt, "The New German Teacher Headscarf Decision", *Int'l J. Const. L. Blog*, March 17, 2015, available at: http://www.iconnectblog.com/2015/03/the-new-german-teacher-headscarf-decision.
77. Ladeur (2008), at 2459.
78. Brugger (2007), at 77.
79. Ibid., at 2464.
80. 472 U.S. 38, 83 (1985).
81. Grimm (2008), at 2374. See also in the same direction, O. Gerstenberg, "Freedom of Conscience in Public Schools"

(2005), 3 *International Journal of Constitutional Law*, 94 et seq. in particular 96.
82. Augenstein (2009), at 21.
83. Grimm (2008), at 2380. These essentials are human dignity, the principle of equality, integrity of the person, the right to participate in public discourse and the formation of public will.
84. Kippenberg (2009), at 213.
85. Fuller (2002), at 59.
86. Al-Ahsan (2008), at 597.
87. As quoted in Silvestri (2009), at 1226.
88. Abdullah Gül, Interview, *Milliyet*, July 15, 2001.
89. Dagi (2002), at 27.
90. The army has staged in total four direct or indirect military interventions precisely to protect and preserve the secular features of the republic. The most recent, also qualified as a post-modern coup, took place on February 28, 1997, when the Turkish military succeeded in mobilizing public opinion to an extent to force the resignation of a coalition government led by the Islamist Welfare Party.
91. Emerson (2006).
92. Article 2 stipulates: '*The Republic of Turkey is a democratic, secular and social state governed by the rule of law, bearing in mind the concepts of public peace, national solidarity and justice; respecting human rights; loyal to the nationalism of Atatürk, and based on the fundamental tenets set forth in the Preamble*' [emphasis added].
93. Passage as quoted by the ECtHR in Leyla Şahin vs. Turkey, Application no. 44774/98, Grand Chamber Judgment, November 10, 2005, at paragraph 39.
94. In Şahin, the ECtHR found no violation of Article 9 ECHR arising out of the prohibition of the headscarf for students at university due to '*pressing social needs*'.
95. On this point, see Leyla Şahin vs. Turkey, Dissenting Opinion of Judge Tulkens, at paragraph 7.
96. Leyla Şahin vs. Turkey, at parapgraph 108 of the judgment.
97. Kuru (2007), at 142.
98. The added text reads, 'No one shall be deprived of the right to higher education because of their apparel'.
99. Dagi (2002), at 41.
100. European Commission (2009), "Progress Report on Turkey", at

21.
101.Ibid., at 27.
102.Hasan and Eylem Zengin vs. Turkey, application n. 1448/04.
103.Paragraph 59 of the judgment.
104.Paragraph 67 of the judgment.
105.The reforms included *inter alia* the abolition of death penalty in peacetime, allowed broadcasting in other languages and dialects than the Turkish language and authorized their learning as well. For an overview of the package, see ABGS, *Harmonization Laws, 57th Government,* Ankara, 2002.
106.Svensson (2008) at 18.
107.Reference is made here to the 16th-17th century history of the Ottoman Empire. For more on the point see Svensson (2008), at 19.
108.Stråth (2000), at 28-40.
109.See for e.g. Stahr (2006).
110.Ibid.
111.Nas (2001), at 186.
112.Dagi (2002) pertinently describes it as '*a popular but limited democracy in which the tutelage of the state elite and the army was justified (...) as republicanism*'.
113.European Commission, Communication to the Council and the European Parliament, Recommendation of the European Commission on Turkey's progress towards accession, COM 2004 (0656) final, at point 3.
114.J. Paul Barker (2012), "Re-thinking Secularism: Religion in Public Life in Turkey", *Turkish Journal of Politics,* Vol. 3, No. 1, Summer, 5-19, at 7.
115.Elizabeth Hurd (2008), "The Politics of Secularism in International Relations", Princeton: Princeton University Press, at 23.
116.Ahmet Kuru, "Passive and Assertive Secularism: Historical Conditions, Ideological Struggles and State Policies toward Religion", *World Politics,* Vol. 59: 568-594 at 571.
117.Hakan M. Yavuz (2009), "Secularism and Muslim Democracy in Turkey", New York: Cambridge University Press, at 146.
118.Act of March 3, 1924, no. 429 on the Abolition of the Ministries of Religious Affairs and Pious Foundations.
119.Barker (2012), at 11.
120.Erik Zurcher (2004), "Turkey: A Modern History", 3rd edition,

New York: I.B. Tauris, 2004, at 181-82.

121. Istar Gozaydin and Ahmet Erdi Ozturk (2014), "The Management of Religion in Turkey", The Turkey Institute, November, available at: https://serdargunes.files.wordpress.com/2013/08/gc3b6zaydin-the-management-of-religion-in-turkey.pdf.

122. The Turkish President Erdogan in a televised speech on April 25, 2015 on the occasion of the meeting of the Independent Industrialist and Businessmen Association declared: "(...) The main opposition party (CHP) has written in their election platform, 'The Diyanet will be at equal distance to all faiths'. The religion of this nation is clear. And the members of other religious communities have their own institutions, and those are clear. So why are they brining the controversy to the doors of the Diyanet?". Extract found in Pinar Tremblay, 'Is Erdogan Signalling the End of Secularism in Turkey?', April 29, 2015, available at: http://www.al-monitor.com/pulse/originals/2015/04/turkey-is-erdogan-signaling-end-of-secularism.html.

123. According to the ARDA World Values Survey, the percentage of individuals identifying themselves as religious rose from 74.6 percent in 1990 to 82.6 percent in 2005. Figures quoted in Barker (2012), at 13.

124. This question remains pertinent in the light of Erdogan's declarations on May 25, 2012 on the occasion of the International Parliamentarians' Conference on Population and Development (ICPD) in Istanbul on abortion and the practice of C-sections for women, as well as issues of population growth ('three children for every family').

125. Barker (2012), at 15.

126. In the case of Cumhuriyetçi Eğitim Ve Kültür Merkezi Vakfi vs. Turkey (application no. 32093/10), the European Court of Human Rights held unanimously that there had been: a violation of Article 14 (prohibition of discrimination) taken together with Article 9 (freedom of thought, conscience and religion) of the European Convention on Human Rights. The case concerned the possibility under Turkish law for places of worship to be granted an exemption from paying electricity bills and the refusal to grant this privilege to the applicant foundation. The Court found in particular that the applicant foundation had sustained a

difference in treatment without any objective or reasonable justification, and that the system for granting exemptions from payment of electricity bills for places of worship under Turkish law entailed discrimination on the ground of religion.

127. Gozaydin et al. (2014), at p. 17.

128. Dina al-Shibeeb (2014), "Did Erdogan Reverse Secularism in Schools in 2014?", Al-Arabiya News, December 22, 2014, available at: http://english.alarabiya.net/en/perspective/analysis/2014/12/22/Did-Erdogan-reverse-Ataturk-s-secularism-in-Turkish-schools-in-2014-.html.

129. The Ottoman language courses were made compulsory for imam-hatip religious schools. The Ministry of National Education also announced plans to open such schools for Turkish expatriates in other countries, following the spectacular increase of their number within Turkey.

130. Ishtar Gözaydin (2013), "Religion, Politics and the Politics of Religion in Turkey", Friedrich Naumann Stiftung Für Die Freiheit, Occasional Paper 121, available at: http://edoc.vitapol.de.

131. Ibid., at 9.

132. Ibid.

133. José Casanova (2001), "Civil Society and Religion: Retrospective Reflections on Catholicism and Prospective Reflections on Islam", 68:4, *Social Research*, at 1064.

134. Bassam Tibi is the main proponent of this interpretation of Euro-Islam. The main critique for this understanding of Islam within Europe regards it as a call for assimilation.

135. Tariq Ramadan is the most representative scholar in favour of this self-assertive conception of Euro-Islam that is nevertheless criticized for its lack of theological grounding.

References

Al-Ahsan, Abdullah (2009), "Law, Religion and Human Dignity in the Muslim World Today: An Examination of OIC's Cairo Declaration of Human Rights", *Journal of Law and Religion*, 24, pp. 569-597.

Augenstein, Daniel (2009), "The Contested Polity: Europe's Constitutional Identity between Religious and Secular Values", University of Edinburgh School of Law, Working Papers Series,

n. 13.

Bader, Veit (2009), "The Governance of Religious Diversity: Theory, Research and Practice", in Bramadat and Koenig (eds.), 'International Migration and the Governance of Religious Diversity', Montreal: McGill-Queen's University Press, pp. 43-72.

Barker, Paul J. (2012), "Re-Thinking Secularism: Religion in Public Life in Turkey, *Turkish Journal of Politics,* Vol. 3, No. 1.

Berger, Benjamin L. (2014), "Religious Diversity, Education, and the Crisis in State Neutrality", Osgoode Legal Studies Research Paper Series, Paper 76.

Brugger, Winfried (2007), "On the Relationship between Structural Norms and Constitutional Rights in Church-State-Relations", in Brugger and Karayanni (eds.), 'Religion in the Public Sphere: A Comparative Analysis of German, Israeli, American and International Law', Berlin: Springer, pp. 21-86.

Carrera, Sergio and Parkin, Joanna (2010), "The Place of Religion in European Union Law and Policy: Competing Approaches and Actors Inside the European Commission", RELIGARE Working Document No. 1, September.

Casanova, José (2001), "Civil Society and Religion: Retrospective Reflections on Catholicism and Prospective Reflections on Islam", 68:4, *Social Research.*

Dagi, Ihsan (2002), "Islamic Political Identity in Turkey: Rethinking the West and Westernization", Central European University, Open Society Institute, available at: http://pdc.ceu.hu/archive/00001804.

Emerson, Michael (2006), "Dear Turkey, Play it Long and Cool", CEPS Commentary, available at: http://enarpri.org/Article.php?article_id=551, December 15.

European Commission (2004), Communication to the Council and the European Parliament, Recommendation of the European Commission on Turkey's progress towards accession, COM 2004 (0656) final.

European Commission (2009), "Progress Report on Turkey", available at: http://ec.europa.eu/enlargement/pdf/key_documents/2009/tr_rapport_2009_en.pdf.

Fuller, Graham E. (2002), "The Future of Political Islam", *Foreign Affairs,* March/April, pp. 48-60.

Gozaydin, Istar and Ozturk, Ahmet Erdi (2014), "The Management of Religion in Turkey", The Turkey Institute, available at: https://serdargunes.files.wordpress.com/2013/08/gc3b6zaydin-the-management-of-religion-in-turkey.pdf.

Grimm, Dieter (2008), "Conflicts between General Laws and Religious Norms", *30 Cardozo Law Review,* Vol. 30:6.

Groetsch, Florian (2009), "The Mobilization of Religion in the EU (1976-2007): From Blindness to Religion to the Anchoring of Religious Norms in the EU", *Journal of Religion in Europe 2,* pp. 231-256.

Habermas, Jürgen (2005), "Religion in the Public Sphere", Lecture at San Diego University, available at: http://www.sandiego.edu/pdf/pdf_library/habermaslecture031105_c939cceb2ab087bdfc6df291ec0fc3a.pdf.

Hackett, Rosalind I.J. (2005), "Rethinking the Role of Religion in Changing Public Spheres: Some Comparative Perspectives", *Brigham Young University Law Review*, pp. 659-682.

Hambler, Andrew (2008), "A Private Matter? Evolving Approaches to the Freedom to Manifest Religious Convictions in the Workplace", 3, *Religion and Human Rights*, pp. 111-133.

Haupt, Claudia (2015), "The New German Teacher Headscarf Decision", *Int'l J. Const. L. Blog*, March 17, 2015, available at: http://www.iconnectblog.com/2015/03/the-new-german-teacher-headscarf-decision.

Hughes, Edel (2008), "The Secularism Debate and Turkey's Quest for European Union Membership", *Religion and Human Rights*, 3, pp. 15-32.

Hurd, Elizabeth (2008), "The Politics of Secularism in International Relations", Princeton: Princeton University Press.

Joppke, Christian (2007), "State Neutrality and Islamic Headscarf Laws in France and Germany", *Theor. Soc.*, 36: 313-342.

Kippenberg, Hans G. (2008), "Europe: Arena of Pluralization and Diversification of Religions", *Journal of Religion in Europe,* 1, pp. 133-155.

Kippenberg, Hans G. (2009), "Introduction: Religion and the Search for a Transnational Foundation of the European Community", *Journal of Religion in Europe,* 2, pp. 211-214.

Koenig, Matthias (2009), "How Nation-States Respond to Religious Diversity", in Bramadat and Koenig (eds.), 'International Migration and the Governance of Religious Diversity',

Montreal: McGill-Queen's University Press, pp. 293-317.

Kuru, Ahmet T. (2007), "Changing Perspectives on Islamism and Secularism in Turkey: The Gülen Movement and the AK Party", available at: http://www.gulenconference.org.uk/userfiles/file/Proceedings/Prcd%20-%20Kuru,%20AT.pdf.

Kuru, Ahmet T. (2008), "Passive and Assertive Secularism: Historical Conditions, Ideological Struggles and State Policies toward Religion", *World Politics*, Vol. 59, pp. 568-594.

Ladeur, Karl-Heinz (2008), "The Myth of the Neutral State and the Individualization of Religion: The Relationship between State and Religion in the Face of Fundamentalism", *Cardozo Law Review*, Vol. 30:6, pp. 2445-2471.

Ladeur Karl-Heinz and Augsberg Ino (2007), "The Myth of the Neutral State: The Relationship between State and Religions in the Face of New Challenges", *German Law Journal,* Vol. 8, No. 2, pp. 143-152.

Lason, Alexandra (2009), "Talking about the Christian Occident in the Context of European Unification", *Journal of Religion in Europe,* 2, pp. 285-308.

Leustean, Lucian N. (2008), "Challenges to Church-State Relations in Contemporary Europe: Introduction", *Journal of Religion in Europe,* 1, pp. 247-250.

Mandry, Christof (2009), "Instrument of Mobilization or a Bridge towards Understanding? Religion and Values in the Reform Process of the European Union", *Journal of Religion in Europe,* 2, pp. 257-284.

McCrea, Ronan (2009), "The Recognition of Religion within the Constitutional and Political Order of the European Union", LEQS Paper No. 10/2009.

Nas, Çigdem (2001), "Turkish Identity and the Perception of Europe", *Marmara Journal of European Studies,* Vol. 9, No. 1.

Pin, Andrea (2014), "Does Europe Need Neutrality? The Old Continent in Search of Identity", BYU L. Rev. 605.

Reuter, Astrid (2009), "Charting the Boundaries of the Religious Field: Legal Conflicts over Religion as Struggles over Blurring Borders", *Journal of Religion in Europe,* 2, at pp. 1-20.

Roebben, Bert (2008), "Fellowship of Fate and Fellowships of Faith: Religious Education and Citizenship Education in Europe", *Journal of Beliefs and Values,* Vol. 29, No. 2, pp. 207-211.

Silvestri, Sara (2009), "Islam and Religion in the EU Political System", *West European Politics,* 32:6, November, pp. 1212-1239.

Stahr, Volker S. (2006), "Synthesis of Islamic Thought, Secularism and Modernity: Turkey as a Laboratory of Islam?", available at: www.qantara.de.

Stråth, Bo (2000), "Introduction: Europe as Discourse", in Stråth (ed.), 'Europe and the other and Europe as the Other', Brussels: Presses Interuniversitaires Européennes, pp. 28-40.

Svensson Adam (2008), "Turkey as the European Other: A Constructivist Account of Turkey's Accession Process to the EU", Lund University, available at: http://theses.lub.lu.se/archive/2008/01/08/1199783717-29066-437/Turkey_as_the_European_other_080120.pdf.

Thio, Li-ann (2007), "Judges and Religious Questions: Adjudicating Claims to Wear Religious Dress in Public Schools", *Religion and Human Rights,* 2, pp. 119-148.

Topidi, Kyriaki (2012), "Religious Diversity in Public Education: A Comparative European Perspective", in Cornelia Roux (ed.), 'Safe Spaces: Human Rights Education in Diverse Contexts', Sense Publishers, pp. 109-128.

Van der Burg, Wibren Brom and W.A. Frans (2009), "In Defence of Neutrality", available at: http://papers.ssrn.com/sol3/papers.cfm?abstract_id=1463289.

Van der Ven and A. Johannes (2008), "Religious Rights for Minorities in a Policy of Recognition", *Religion and Human Rights*, 3, pp. 155-183.

Weiler, Joseph (2003), "Un'Europea Christiana: Un Saggio Esplorativo", Milan, BUR Saggi.

Yavuz, Hakan M. (2009), "Secularism and Muslim Democracy in Turkey", New York: Cambridge University Press.

Zucca, Lorenzo (2012), "A Secular Europe", Oxford University Press, Oxford.

Part III: Negotiating Citizenships

7

Citizenship and Affirmation of Group Difference: Constitutional Mode of Negotiating Religious Identities in India

Kumar Suresh

Situating the Argument

Citizenship constitutes site of both affirmation and contestation in heterogeneous societies. It is affirmed on account of its promises that it makes. It is contested the way it unfolds and operates in diverse societies. Citizenship in heterogeneous societies, adapted and negotiated through the creation of multicultural constitutional spaces, institutional mechanisms and policy framework, can lead to multicultural inclusion by combining the twin principles of identity and difference. Such negotiations are well articulated in the constitutional mode of accommodating and negotiating differences in India. It is submitted that this attempt of negotiations, in various forms and manifestations and at various levels including the multi-level structures of federal governance, has provided space to the minorities for expressing their particularities of identity and cultures. Whereas the linguistic and many ethnic groups are entitled for reasonable degree of political rights along with cultural rights as collective/group rights, the religious minorities are primarily entitled for cultural rights.

The historical context, especially the context of partition has shaped the public debate in such a way that guaranteeing political rights to the religious minorities as exclusive group rights has been taken as antithetical to the project of nascent national state. It is amply evident in the debates of the

Constituent Assembly of India. This has informed the public policy deliberations throughout the period after Independence. It has remained as one of the major bones of contention as well as one of the stumbling blocks in the direction of realising the idea of inclusive citizenship.

The under representation of Muslims in the structure of State and their relative deprivation on multiple parameters of economic and political empowerment interrogate the constitutional mode of citizenship. However, the constitutionally guaranteed space for cultural difference is not less important. It signifies departure from the classic mode of citizenship. It is no denying the fact, that there is a long way to go in the direction of translating the promises of formal citizenship to substantive citizenship, but the space for difference in the public sphere is a significant step in the Constitutional model in India.

The paper attempts to grapple with this constitutional mode of negotiation. It is suggested that there are at least three important ways through which religious identities are accommodated in the public spheres: (i) distinctive approach of secularism wherein secularism in its deeper meaning appears as a mode of multicultural living; (ii) cultural rights to communities, especially manifested in personal and customary laws of the communities; and (iii) Constitutionally guaranteed educational and cultural rights of minorities. In each of these cases, we find a complex negotiation of cultural difference along the principle of citizenship.

Citizenship as a Site of Affirmation in Heterogeneous Societies

The concept of citizenship has been symbiotically intertwined with idea of the hyphenated concept of nation-state. In the mould of nation-state, not only an all-encompassing political identity is created but also an attempt is made to homogenise the differences arising out of ethnic, religious, linguistic or similar social affiliations. The public sphere does not allow any expression of cultural difference; it is rather intolerant to politics of cultural difference. The revival and assertion of ethno-religious identity, movements for recognition and rights of self-determination, violent ethnic conflicts and breaking away of the large state systems are some of the cases in point which not only interrogate the all pervasiveness of the concept of nation-state but also the assimilative mode of citizenship.

Given the historical context and its articulation in different societal context, citizenship has emerged as a terrain of both affirmation and contestation. This paradox emerges out of the promises that citizenship makes. Citizenship theoretically unfolds a wide range of possibilities for the excluded and marginalized but the practices of unfolding and extending the arena of citizenship in different societal contexts have gone exactly against its emancipatory promises. The concept of citizenship is deeply rooted in the emancipatory project of modernity. The promises of modernity that the ethnic affiliations would dissolve into civic ties, religious identities into secular order, inequality arising out of communitarian context into equality of the citizenship rights, and a sharp separation between the public and private realms, are far away from the existing realities of the contemporary world. Therefore, if citizenship has appeared as an enabling identity in different historical context of discrimination and exclusion articulated through the language of rights and entitlements on the one hand, it has simultaneously created a condition of exclusion for the groups and communities, on the other. This is precisely the paradoxical context of citizenship that leads to its affirmation and interrogation in different societal and historical contexts.

It is premised here that citizenship could be both exclusionary and inclusionary at the same time. Much depends on the context in which the principle of citizenship takes roots and operates. It is inclusionary as it opens up possibilities of participation for every individual irrespective of social origin and cultural location. Theoretically, it delinks the State from ethnicity. But it may become exclusionary in heterogeneous and unequal societies if it is applied in its assimilative mould. The differential location of groups and communities in heterogeneous and unequal societies require negotiation of citizenship. The negotiation and adaptation of citizenship in a heterogeneous and unequal society is a requisite of inclusive citizenship.

It is further submitted that negotiation of citizenship with cultural difference and making it more sensitive to diversity is not necessarily limiting the scope of citizenship. Negotiation of citizenship in a heterogeneous and unequal society is an attempt of extending the realm of citizenship and making it more inclusive. India is one such case that has adapted the model of citizenship with affirming and recognising group difference in its post-colonial state and nation-building. Indian experiment with negotiation and adaptation signifies a context of situating citizenship outside its classic mould. This negotiation is reflected in the model of constitutional engineering, subsequent institutional innovations and public policy deliberations.

Therefore, the main focus is placed on this dimension. The central premise that is advanced here is that constitutional mode of negotiating differences and institutional mechanisms of effecting such negotiations are important in advancing the realm of citizenship. The Indian experience of this negotiation over the past sixty five years qualifies as a case of relative success. It is with this premise that the paper attempts to locate the sites of negotiation and adaptation of in the specific context of the post-colonial project of nation and state building in India. For this purpose, the paper critically examines the constitutional principles, institutional mechanisms and policy framework, which best reflect the negotiation of the principle of citizenship with cultural difference.

Context and Logic of Negotiation of Citizenship in India

Exploring and adapting a model, which could negotiate between equality and pluralism in the historical backdrop of partition, community conflict and mass violence was not an easy proposition for the leaders of the national movement and the framers of the Constitution of India. It was not that they were not aware of the limitations of accommodating the groups and communities having their mutual claims of identity and rights in the mould of a homogenized nation-state of the European construct. The idea of nation-state and its principles of equality and non-discrimination, secularism and uniformity of political and legal space was profoundly impressive and tempting for the framers of the Constitution and these ideas have transpired in the deliberations of the Constituent Assembly debates. [1]

It was nevertheless almost impossible to replicate the Western concept of homogenized nation-state and uniformity of legal and political space irrespective of diversity and unevenness of location of groups and communities. They had to face a formidable challenge of nation and state building and patterning of state-society relationships in the frame of its own historical context of diversity and difference. Striking a balance between the conflicting demands of autonomy and recognition of difference in the public sphere; and the imperatives of integration in the configuration of national cohesion was an uphill task.

Looking beyond the model of western nation-state and affirmation of group difference in the given context of diversity of religion, ethnicity, language, culture and caste was a complex problematic for a newly independent country and its project of nation and state building. The option in this context was not between the either-or dichotomy of citizenship and affirmation of group difference but the challenge was to negotiate, harmonise and connect citizenship to the affirmation of group difference. This was, in turn, a doubly compounded project of building and championing equality and citizenship and granting autonomy to groups and communities and allowing them sufficient space for public recognition of their difference and representation in the institutional structure of the State.

Creating space for difference within the expanding universe of equality of citizenship was a bold and unique experiment of the project of nation and state building in India. This attempt was a fundamental departure from the mode of assimilative citizenship. The underlying logic of this endeavour was creation of unity out of diversity of religion, caste, region, language and ethnic formation in India. As a corollary, anxieties of the minority communities and deprived and excluded groups had to be addressed in a mould, which could ensure equality in the public domain and constitutionally protect their specific aspects of identity and culture. This was not possible without negotiating the values of citizenship with the affirmation of positive difference. The logic of India's constitutional design bears the testimony of this negotiation.

Citizenship and Group Difference

The universe of equality of citizenship and space for difference is inextricably interwoven with the specific logic of India's constitutional design. It is not that the framers of the Constitution were not aware of the inherent and emergent tension between the constitutional claims of citizens' equality and recognition of difference, but the logic that informed the project of nation and state building had to be rooted in a way that could address the necessity of accommodating diversity. This becomes more evident if one goes through the deliberation of the Constituent Assembly debates. However, it needs to be highlighted that the affirmation of group difference and recognition of differential rights to minority communities and deprived groups were not intended towards narrowing down the scope and value of citizenship but towards the protection and inclusion of groups and communities. The concept of citizenship in this case was not restrictive but enlarging. It was seen as an enabling identity loaded with the inherent prescription of entitlement.

The idea of citizenship had specific value in the given context of unequal social order of India, for it envisaged the maximization of the realm of equal entitlement for individuals as a full and free member of the political community. However, equality of citizenship was not meant to undermine the positive value of diversity in a multicultural condition existing in India. A narrow understanding of the concept of citizenship and its mechanical application would have been limiting thereby undermining the very essence of citizenship. Therefore, the deliberations in the Constituent Assembly over the specific issues of minority rights and inclusion of deprived and excluded forms the complex logic of the constitutional design and incorporation of two principles of equality and difference. Both the principles appear to form an inseparable union and, therefore, they do not exclude but negotiate and complement each other.

A systematic reading of the constitutional philosophy and the debates of the Constituent Assembly in India unravel the logic of India's constitutional design. Citizenship and its equalitarian concerns are basic to the design. Equality is a prime and overriding concern of the Indian Constitution. [2] The incorporation of the "difference principle" [3] is an extension of the very idea of citizenship. [4] Autonomy and protection guaranteed to the minority communities and preferential treatment accorded to the deprived and excluded groups are intended towards accommodation and inclusion which, in turn, provides strong grounding to the principle of equality and enlarge the concept of citizenship.

Affirmation of group difference and preference is, therefore, not in contradiction to the principle of citizenship, though it appears as such in most of the cases of constitutional interpretation. Replication of the Western notion of citizenship in plural and unequal socio-cultural order in India would have been, in fact, nothing but reinforcing the structure of inequality and creating a series of exclusion and discrimination. The best possible way, therefore, that appeared before the framers of the Constitution were to strike a balance between equality and difference not in a confrontationist mode but in an accommodative design.

In this constitutional crafting, citizenship was seen as an encompassing identity privileging over any other identity. Priority given to the principle of equal citizenship in the public domain speaks out the mind of the framers of the Constitution. Prioritization of equality principle over the "principle of difference" was more appropriate and promising in the given condition of India's socio-cultural order, for it opened up the opportunity structure to all irrespective of one's social origin. Ensuring equality of status and opportunity and equal access to public domain was a major achievement towards the project of nation and state building in post-independent India. It marked a transformation from a community "mediated society" to a "direct access society". [5]

This transformation was emancipatory enterprise for the deprived and excluded groups of society. It was also directed towards addressing the question of minority protection because it accorded to them an equal status as individual citizens under the general dispensation of citizenship rights along with the guarantee of maintenance of identity and culture. However, it also envisaged a concern to protect the individuals against any inhuman practices and excesses of the community. Therefore, individuals were made to directly link to the State without mediation of her/his membership of caste and community. The instances of mediation and preference of community over the individual were meant for the purpose of their protection against any possibility of majoritarian cultural threat.

The enlarging concept of citizenship and the creating space for difference has appeared as an arena of contestation. The project of nation and state building and emancipatory appeal of the idea of citizenship has been under severe attack. The pluralist, multiculturalist, post-colonists and post-modernists critiques see the emancipatory project, negotiated through the principle of citizenship, as homogenizing and hegemonic. The critiques may have valid reasons for questioning the project of nation-state building in post-independent India because the processes of citizenship building over the last six decades have not been congruent with the vision and intentions of the framers of the Constitution.

However, problematizing the issue should not essentially be construed as the outcome of ill intentionality or as a homogenizing project. Much depends on how one situates the priority of citizens' equality over the group difference. Undermining the value of citizenship may have its own complexity. The Indian society has experienced the inequality of access and opportunity on account of ordained and legitimized principle of hierarchy and a series of discriminations and exclusions both within and outside the institutions. This appears to be prime concern because of which the founding fathers have accorded priority to citizenship and its equality. It has been negotiated with the principle of difference only as a means of striking equality in conditions of inequality, as means of accommodation and protection of minority communities and deprived and excluded groups. The constitutional crafting of "citizen plus" [6] not only marks the distinctive contribution of the vision of the framers but also moves beyond the western mode of citizenship building.

Sites of Negotiations

The Indian experience of reconciling with the twin concerns of citizenship and cultural difference over the last sixty five years has emerged as a case of considerable success. Naturally, the question arises as to what is distinctive about the Indian mode of accommodating diversity? Does the Indian case offer constitutional solution and institutional mechanisms to meet the challenges of diversity and difference and transforming conflict into a situation of peace and order in other cases of empirical approximations? Does it exemplify an alternative mode of conceptualising citizenship, which is inclusive and sensitive to cultural difference? Glancing over the constitutionally created space for minorities and deprived groups, the elaborate institutional arrangements and wide range of public policies affirm the answer in positive.

The constitutional mode of accommodating diversities in India best exemplifies an attempt of harmonising the twin concerns of equality and pluralism. The very preamble of the Constitution of India speaks out the preferences of accommodating diverse social groups. Equality, liberty, justice, fraternity, socialism and secularism are cardinal principles of patterning society and state in India. These principles are, at least in theory, extended in the multiple arena of state action, though there seems a wide gap between the professed policy and practice of the state.

Synoptically, the efforts of accommodating diversities in India can be seen in the following arenas: (i) cultural autonomy and promotion of pluralism as a dominant value (official recognition of diversity), reflected especially in the case of legal pluralism relating to customary and personal laws of different communities, language pluralism, and state policies towards education and culture; (ii) constitutional protection of minorities; (iii) federalism and multilevel institutional autonomy to territorially concentrated ethno-linguistic groups; (iv) constitutional safeguards and the policy of protective discrimination meant for accommodating the excluded and disadvantaged groups, officially designated as scheduled castes, scheduled tribes, other backward classes and persons belonging to scheduled areas, (v) some element of consociational mode of power sharing articulated through party system and coalition formation. These efforts have significantly sustained India as a democratic republic over the last six decades of democratic experiment.

Cultural Autonomy and the Protected Spheres of Communities

The idea of preserving cultural diversity and group specific practices is basic to the constitutional mode of accommodation in India. It is ingrained in the approach of cultural autonomy to community and legal pluralism to diverse religious groups. The advancement of the realms of cultural autonomy and the protection of minorities are ensured constitutionally. These rights favour the conditions of cultural autonomy and legal pluralism. The constitutionally created space for autonomy is advanced by limiting the role of the state in intervening in the affairs of the community. The sphere of cultural autonomy is not restricted only to any specified minority group but also appears as group rights guaranteed to the community for preserving and promoting the community specific components of identity and culture.

This context of autonomy ensures the flourishing of differences without the intervention of the state. This is strictly in accordance with the imperatives of integration in a multi-cultural, multi-ethnic, multi-religious and multi-lingual society. In the multicultural context of India, creating the sphere of autonomy for groups and communities and protecting them constitutionally and institutionally is envisaged as a prerequisite of multicultural accommodation and its political and institutional manifestations. This context of autonomy shapes the public space and informs the policies of the state in numerous ways. The fundamental rights of religious freedom and secular positioning of state on the one hand, and different affirmative measures of the state towards protection and promotion diversity and group difference on the other are important pointers in this regard.

The constitutionally guaranteed sphere of cultural autonomy in India can specifically be located into two inter-related contexts: (a) freedom of religion and conscience as ensured under Articles 25-28; and (b) cultural and educational rights guaranteed to minorities under Articles 29 and 30. The constitutionally guaranteed rights of religious freedom constitute a site of claims from both the perspective of citizenship rights of individual as well as the group rights of communities. However, it is this context that points out a complex relation between the State and the religious groups. In the given context of religious diversity and the presence of a large majority and small minority religious groups the State is supposed to act in a way in which equality between and among them is maintained without prejudice and discrimination.

This demands freedom of conscience and religion on the one hand and the equidistance approach of the state on the other. The State is, however, not to be seen as a passive spectator. The "non-interference" approach of the State in the religious affairs of the community is envisaged in a more constructive mould. The relationship between the State and the religion and the extent of the limits of religious freedom have been weaved in such a way so as to strike a balance between citizenship rights of individuals and group rights of the communities. This act of balancing can best be located in the content and intent of Articles 25-28.These Articles read as follows:

Article 25 (1): Subject to public order, morality and health and to the other provisions of this part, all persons are equally entitled to freedom of conscience and the right to profess, practise and propagate religion.

(2) Nothing in this article shall affect the operation of any existing law or prevent the State from making any law: (a) regulating or restricting any economic, financial, political or other secular activity which may be associated with religious practice; (b) providing for social welfare and reform or the throwing open of Hindu religious institutions of a public character to all classes and sections of Hindus.

Explanation I: The wearing and carrying of *kirpans* shall be deemed to be included in the profession of Sikh religion.

Explanation II: The sub-clause (b) of clause (2), the reference to Hindus shall be construed as including a reference to persons professing the Sikh, Jain or Buddhist religion, and the reference to Hindu religious institutions shall be construed accordingly.

Article 26: Subject to public order, morality and health, every religious denomination or any section thereof shall have the right: (a) to establish and maintain institutions for religious and charitable purposes; (b) to manage its own affairs in matters of religion; (c) to own and acquire movable and immovable property; and (d) to administer such property in accordance with the law.

Article 27: No person shall be compelled to pay any taxes, the proceeds of which are specifically appropriated in payment of expenses for the promotion or maintenance of any particular religion or religious denomination.

Article 28 (1): No religious instruction shall be provided in any educational institution wholly maintained out of State funds; (2) Nothing in clause (1) shall apply to an educational institution, which is administered by the State but has been established under any endowment or trust which requires that religious instruction shall be imparted in such institution; (3) No person attending any educational institution recognised by the State or receiving aid out of State funds shall be required to take part in any religious instruction that may be imparted in such institution or to attend any religious worship that may be conducted in such institution or in any premises attached thereto unless such person or, if such person is a minor, his guardian has given his consent thereto.

This set of rights envisages secularism as the fundamental principle and basic to the constitutional structure of India (specifically pronounced in the Bommai Case judgment of the Supreme Court). The principle of secularism is pronounced in the constitutional positioning of the state as 'religion neutral', meaning thereby that the state in India has no religion of its own. [7] This may have two different contextual implications: (i) no preference to be given to any religion and there is no privileging of one over the other. It additionally underlies that no religion would be unequally treated except in accordance with the demands of welfare and equalizing instance of the state, and (ii) non-intervention of the State in the religious affairs of the community, with exception of public order, morality and health.

However, the constitutionally guaranteed freedom of religion is not an absolute right. In order to maintain harmony and equality among the religious groups, it further maintains that the freedom of religion of one group should not violate the freedom of religion of the other group or groups. When read in conjunction with other provisions of the fundamental rights, it demands that freedom of religion guaranteed to the individuals and groups should not be limiting and curtailing to the citizenship claims of liberty and equality. The cluster of Articles (25 to 28) in conjunction with other provisions of the Constitution, attempts to maintain balance between the equal rights of citizenship and the essential aspects of religious activities of the communities.

Personal Laws and Legal Pluralism

The non-interference approach of the State in the religious affairs of the community is amply validated in the constitutional guarantee of the freedom of religion. As a derivative of the freedom of religion, different communities have been permitted to retain their specific cultural and community practices. Different sets of personal laws relating to marriage, divorce, adoption and succession of different religious groups and denominations and customary law of the tribal communities stipulate the case of legal pluralism. Though many provisions of different personal laws have been codified at different points of time either in the light of judicial intervention or as a part of social reform process, these are still important in governing the life of the communities.

Though the Constitution incorporates the principle of legal pluralism under the dispensation of religious freedom and cultural autonomy, the Directive Principles of State Policy makes provision for a Uniform Civil Code (Article 44) where the state is directed to strive for creating a uniform civil code (UCC).

However, the inherent institutional intention here is not of imposing majoritarian uniformity on different groups and communities, especially on the minorities but to create a positive atmosphere among the communities to pursue the goal of uniform civil code i.e. fostering national coherence. Though at times, this proposition may appear as over-stretched, it is a logical derivation of the deliberations of the debates in the Constituent Assembly on the one hand, and reading of the regime of personal and customary laws in conjunction with the group rights and minority protection available as fundamental rights under the constitution on the other.

But despite the tension between the individual rights of citizenship and the cultural rights of community, and between the 'national priorities' of the State and the community assertion of their identity rights and for the space of cultural autonomy, the very attempt of combining individual rights of citizenship and group rights of community is important. It especially indicates an attempt of grounding citizenship to the roots of cultural difference. Although the constitutionally created space for cultural autonomy and protection of minorities has been a contested terrain both for the homogenizing construct of the nation-state and the majoritarian politics of "cultural nationalism" and national homogeneity.

Citizenship and Minority Rights

The equal rights of citizenship provided in the Constitution enables the minority to claim equal treatment without the prejudice of their socio-cultural location and religious affiliation. The citizenship rights of equality guaranteed under Articles 14, 15(1) and 29(2) are particularly relevant in this regard. These rights entitle individual to advance his or her claims of equality in a condition of unequal and differential treatment, which are not otherwise spelt out or specified in the Constitution as clauses of exception. Article 14 guarantees equality before the law and equal protection of law. It says, "the State shall not deny to any person equality before the law or the equal protection of the laws within the territory of India". Similarly, Article 15(1) provides that, "the State shall not discriminate against any citizen on grounds only of religion, race, caste, sex, place of birth or any of them". And Article 29(2) further mentions, "No citizen shall be denied admission into any educational institution maintained by the State or receiving aid out of State funds on grounds only of religion, race, caste, language or any of them".

The clauses of equality under the generic context of citizenship rights are enabling rights, which are available to the minorities as a citizen. In the context of citizenship, an individual is considered as the claimant of the rights. The cultural and educational rights under Articles 29 and 30 of the Constitution, on the other hand, are particularly concerned with the protection of minorities as a group. The underlying assumption is of the recognition and protection of group difference. This is the richness of the Indian mode of combining the twin concerns of autonomy and integration. Though efforts of reconciling the equality principle of citizenship with the aspect of group difference is loaded with tension between the two different principles, it has largely been negotiated in the process of citizenship in the own historical context of "together in difference".

The minority rights as available in the Constitution are specifically located in Articles 29 and 30. These Articles read as follows:

Article 29 provides, (i) Any section of the citizens residing in the territory of India or any part thereof having a distinct language, script or culture of its own shall have the right to conserve the same; (ii) No citizen shall be denied admission into any educational institution maintained by the state or receiving aid out of state funds on grounds only of religion, race, caste, language or any of them.

Article 30 ensuring minorities to establish and administer educational institutions further provides, (i) All minorities, whether based on religion or language, shall have the right to establish and administer educational institutions of their choice.

(1A) In making any law providing for the compulsory acquisition of any property of an educational institution established and administered by a minority, referred to in clause (i), the State shall ensure that the amount fixed by or determined under such law for the acquisition of such property is such as would not restrict or abrogate the right guaranteed under the clause [added by the Constitution Forty-fourth Amendment Act, 1978]. The State shall not, in granting aid to educational institutions, discriminate against any educational institution on the ground that it is under the management of a minority, whether based on religion or language.

The complex interconnection between the rights of equal citizenship and differential rights of minorities amounts to a compounding problem in which the recurring judicial intervention has been a logical corollary. Whatsoever may be the interpretation and positioning of minority rights in contemporary Indian situation, it cannot be denied that the original intention of the framers of the Constitution was directed towards addressing the question of the distinct cultures, language and educational needs of the minorities.

Experiences of Negotiation

The experiences of negotiating the model of citizenship during the last six decades have been a mixed bag of success and failures. However, the extent of success overrides the areas of failures. One of the most important indicators of its success lies in its capacity of 'holding together' diverse groups and communities in a framework of a national state. The adaptation of citizenship in India has served as a principle of multicultural inclusion. Reconciliation of identity and autonomy in the framework of national state has fairly articulated the aspirations of distinctive identities of language, ethnic and religious groups. This becomes more apparent once we traverse though the trajectories of regional, linguistic and ethnic movements. If there are the problems, which have not been addressed throughout these years, these cannot be attributed essentially to the model of constitutional engineering.

The constitutionally guaranteed space for articulation of identities and rights has given channel for claim making. Citizenship has introduced an arena of claims, which is articulated through the language of rights and entitlements. In the given context of historical exclusion and discriminations, the enabling and elaborate citizenship rights and entitlements have proved to be a liberating experience for a vast mass of people. It was individuals' liberation from the suffocating inhuman and unjust clutches of 'community' as exemplified in India in the case of hierarchical caste system and its egalitarian ethos. The most important achievement that needs to be noted is the visibility of the excluded groups in the political structure. This has been made possible by the constitutionally guaranteed space provided to these groups in the form of reservation for political representation. It cannot be denied that inter-group inequalities and uneven development are still major issues that need redressal.

Endnotes

1. For a comprehensive view on the deliberations of the Constituent Assembly, see "Constituent Assembly Debates", Volumes I-XII, New Delhi: Lok Sabha Secretariat, Third Reprint, 1999.
2. See P.M. Bakshi (2002), "The Constitution of India" (with Selective Comments), Delhi: Universal Publishing Co., Fifth Edition, pp. 61-65.
3. The framework of "equality principle" and "principle of difference" and prioritization constitutes the central point of argument of John Rawls' Theory of Justice. The concept has been borrowed from him for analysing the logic of India's Constitutional design. For a comprehensive understanding of the concepts see John Rawls, "Theory of Justice", Oxford: Oxford University Press, 1973.
4. The most widely accepted definition and account of citizenship comes from T.H. Marshal's classic work, "Citizenship and Social Class and Other Essays", Cambridge: Cambridge

University Press, 1950. In the recent theoretical debates, citizenship and its emancipatory potentials, however, is subjected to interrogation on account of an inherent conception of homogenization and marginalisation of minority identity and cultures. Even then the very idea of citizenship is not outright rejected. The emphasis is shifting only in terms of making the concept of citizenship more inclusive and sensitive to difference. This can be, for instance, seen in the works of Will Kymlicka, Charles Taylor, Iris M. Young, Bhikhu Parekh and a host of other scholars.

5. See Charles Taylor (1998), "Modes of Secularism" in Rajeev Bhargava (ed.), 'Secularism and its Critics', New Delhi: Oxford University Press, 1998.
6. The phrase *citizen plus* was coined in the Howthrone Tremblay Report in the context of Canadian citizenship, which underlies the idea that apart from the entitlements of citizenship rights, the minority community should also be given additional rights to preserve their distinctive cultural identity. The concept has been discussed in Bhikhu Parekh, "Cultural Diversity and the Modern State" in Martin Doornbos and Sudipta Kaviraj (eds.), 'Dynamics of State Formation: India and Europe Compared', New Delhi: Sage, 1997.
7. Rajeev Bhargava (1998), (ed.), "Secularism and its Critics", New Delhi: Oxford University Press. Though the claims of secularism in clear words did not find specific place in the Constitution, prior to the Forty-Second Amendment of the Constitution, the basic philosophy and the reading of the provisions of the Constitution unambiguously reinforce the secular claims of the Indian State.

8

New Muslim Brokers in European Cities and Politics of Muslim Citizenship [1]

Konrad Pędziwiatr

The outgoing Secretary General of the Muslim Council of Britain, one of the country's organisations which strive to represent British Muslims vis-à-vis the government, [2] announced during his valedictory speech on June 4, 2006 that 'the age of the politics of Muslim identity is over', and called for Muslims to engage more actively in non-Muslim civil society. [3] The sociological research on Islam in Europe shows, however, that the age of Muslim identity politics is far from yet over and that some Islamic organizations continue to take the 'Muslim power' approach [4] mainly nourished by despair at the victimization of Muslims in different places of the globe, to attract new followers. [5]

At the same time, and here the former Secretary General of the MCB has a point, one may observe a growing trend amongst the Muslim organizations to move from a politics of identity, which is preoccupied with difference and otherness, towards a politics of identity that increasingly emphasizes also, elements of sameness. An analogous observation is also made by one of the editors of "European Islam: Challenges for Public Policy and Society", Amel Boubekeur, who points out that 'the cultural and religious otherness' is no longer the privileged means of expressing contestation by the political Islam in Europe. [6]

The key observation in the research into religion and active social citizenship amongst young organized Muslims in Brussels and London on which this paper is based was that, one may see in both analysed countries and cities not only a development of a civic consciousness among certain segments of their Muslim populations, [7] but also a construction of a new type of identity—Muslim civicness—and a move from the politics of Muslim identity, largely based on the emphasis of 'otherness', to the politics of Muslim citizenship that also increasingly stresses elements of 'sameness'. This has been done by young Muslims inter alia by 'reversing the stigma' associated with Islam and 'positivisation of religion of their parents'. [8]

I am going to argue that the aforementioned change in the public mobilization of Islam in Europe, is not so much related to the recent pressures on European Muslims to prove their loyalty and attachment to the their societies, but is above all a result of the re-definitions of the notion of citizenship, and of the fact that the largest Muslim communities in Europe are constituted today of a majority of people who are born and bred Europeans. The objective of this article will be to explore some processes behind a move from the politics of Muslim identity to the politics of Muslim citizenship.

Identity Politics and Citizenship

Before I do so, let me clarify some of the key notions used in the text and shed some light on the main features of the research, which constitutes the basis for this paper. One of such key notions is that of identity politics, which is a highly disputed concept, both in politics and in theoretical writing. In a large sense, identity politics refers to any political mobilization around a particular identity, be it ethnic, religious, civic, sexual (women's groups, gay movement) or functional (e.g. labour movement centered around the workers as a defined category). [9]

In this paper, the concept is used primarily to refer to the mobilization of young European Muslims in which the notion of citizenship plays an important role. This last concept assumes that the membership in a legally constituted political community should rest on the principle of formal equality. The principle of equality has been commonly defined in terms of a particular understanding of civil, political and social rights. The notion of positive freedom, understood as social rights, was introduced in the concept of citizenship by T.H. Marshall. [10]

One of the major drawbacks of the very influential Marshallian theory of citizenship is that it fails to address such salient issues of contemporary heterogeneous societies as politics of ethnicity and diversity. This issue was addressed, inter alia, by Pakulski [11] and Delanty, [12] who argued that a fourth dimension (apart from civil, political and social) of citizenship could be culture. They have pointed out that today there are other kinds of exclusion which cannot be accommodated by a model of social rights. The recognition of these forms of exclusion has committed many people to the view that policies of universal equality would not be adequate and that therefore some kind of radical difference is necessary in the recognition of the group rights. [13]

The emphasis on the last component of citizenship may also be found in the scholarship of Bryan Turner, who argues that citizenship confers not just a legal status but also "*a particular cultural identity on individuals and groups*". He aptly notices that the main focus of citizenship struggles has shifted in recent decades from class to claims to cultural identity and cultural history. Today's struggles have been not about the access to the means of production, but inter alia about sexual identities, gay rights, gender equality and aboriginality. [14]

I believe that with the advancement of the European born generation of Muslims into the public sphere and their refusal to privatise Islam, we could also add religion to this list. Furthermore, I agree with Nilüfer Göle and Tariq Modood who point out that Muslims emerging into identity politics generally follow the example of ethnic minorities, women, gays and lesbians in seeking space for their heritage and values in both public and private spheres. [15] The children of immigrants born in Belgium and Britain have been learning to take advantage of citizenship which is today one of the two, (besides the human rights) main discourses of entitlement. This exposes the growing tension between the discourse on equality (on civil, political and social levels), as a classical preoccupation of citizenship and recognition of difference, (equality on the cultural level) as a contemporary engine of citizenship.

The important question is: why has citizenship been such a valuable political tool for allowing various groups to make different demands? The answer can be found in the scholarship of T.H. Marshal who, in his classic exposition, spoke of "*an image of an ideal citizenship against which achievements can be measured and towards which aspirations can be directed*" (1950:29). It is thus nothing else but this 'ideal citizenship' that Muslims in various European countries have had in mind when demanding, for instance, that state authorities allow Muslim girls to wear hijabs at school or to provide financial support to Muslim schools. The politics of citizenship has increasingly been a politics of recognition, in which claims are made for cultural rights and Islam has begun to play an important role in that politics.

This politics of citizenship has been almost entirely urban politics. Numerous scholars have pointed out to close relationship between the city and contemporary citizenship. Michael Ignatiev, for instance, maintains that "*to speak of citizens is to speak of cities. It is in the city where we live as civic beings: it is the urban environment what releases in every minute the sensation of belonging or not belonging to something called political society*". [16] Also, James Holston emphasizes the importance of the urban experience for contemporary citizenship. He argues that as long as there are diverse populations' places and new politics of identity and difference "*the cities are challenging the nations, separating themselves and even replacing them, from an important space of citizenship to alive spaces, not only of their insecurities but also in their emergent ways*". [17]

The aforementioned authors share with many other scholars around the globe the same conviction that, although one of the essential purposes in the construction of a nation has been to disassemble the historical priority of the urban citizenship and to substitute it for the national citizenship—cities keep on being the strategic place for the development of the citizenship. That is also one of the reasons why the research, which constitutes the basis for this paper, has been carried out in two cities: Brussels and London.

In the course of the research, the author has interviewed more than 50 young Muslim Brusselers and Londoners active in and within the Muslim or wider civil society. The key informants were selected from within the emerging new Muslim brokers, that is the social actors of the second and third generations who participate directly or indirectly in the processes of decision-making that are important for the future of Muslim communities and wider societies. It concentrated in particular on these young Muslims who try, through various projects, to tackle some of the issues faced by their communities and societies and thus at least partially solve the problem of collective uncertainty. [18]

Through their social engagement, the young Muslim men and women begin to play in the analysed countries, a role of the new religious brokers. [19] The research looked particularly closely at the activists of *Ligue Islamique Interculturelle de Belgique (LIIB) and Présence Musulmane (PM)* in the case of Brussels and of *the Islamic Forum of Europe (IFE) and City Circle (CC)* in the case of London. Apart from the interviews with activists of the above mentioned organisations, the author also conducted interviews with members of other Muslim associations in order to more accurately locate the key material within a wider spectrum of Muslim identity politics in both cities.

Thus, a minimum number of interviews were carried out with members of *Federation of European Muslim Youth and Student*

Organisations, Al-Qawthar, L'Humanité Sans Frontiers, Astrolabe and *De Click* in Brussels and activists of *Muslimaat, Young Muslim Organisation, Muslim Association of Britain, Islamic Society of Britain* and *Hizb-ut Tahrir* in London. [20]

Key Dimensions of Muslim Civicness

One of the most significant shifts in the mobilisation of Islam in Europe is clearly visible in my research material, that is a move from the politics of Muslim identity to the politics of Muslim citizenship has been closely linked with the development of a civic consciousness among certain segments of the Muslim populations in Europe observed inter alia by Hassan Bousetta, Dirk Jacobs [21] and a construction of a new type of identity—Muslim civicness. This is a form of identity, which prevailed amongst the members of the new Muslim brokers in Brussels and in London. It has been emerging from the shadows of 'emancipatory politics', and mixing elements of Muslimness with those of active citizenship. It is an identity which has numerous features of a 'project identity' defined by Castells as "*a situation when social actors, on the basis of whatever cultural materials are available to them, build a new identity that redefines their position in their society and by so doing, seek the transformation of overall social structure*". [22]

The first and foremost feature of the Muslim civicness is that it fairly strongly supports national narratives. Its supportiveness for the national projects is not limited only to the emphasis of the importance of the identification with other compatriots, but also stresses the significance of the emotional attachment to the country in which one is living, its territory and various elements of the national culture, including national ceremonies and rituals. Thus, it quite firmly upholds the national identities and alike the traditional accounts on citizenship it links with a nation.

Probably most clearly, this feature of the Muslim civicness portrays the statement of one of my interviewees from Brussels who said, "*I am a practising Muslim and a practising*

Belgian" (Khalil). For this interviewee, as well as for many others, the religious and national identity did not contradict each other, but on the contrary, they were mutually reinforcing. That is also why many of them liked to say similar to what Kadir said that, "*I am very comfortable being British and Muslim*". In their views, the two identities—national and religious—were largely overlapping. Consequently, some of them strongly opposed more rigid definitions of secularism, which exclude religion from citizenship. One of them was Hadijah who stated, "*you cannot cut someone in the middle and say that this part belongs to the citizenship and that to religion. Muslimness and citizenship are inseparable entities*".

In general, they proposed to view the two 'entities' as functioning in harmony with each other and opted for the pluralistic definition of identity assuming the possibility of possessing multiple and hybrid identities. If they did distinguish between the two identities, like Rashid who pointed out, "*spiritual identity is vertical and the civic one is horizontal*", they did so only to stress that they closely and positively interact with each other.

Moreover, the support for the national narratives that characterised most of my interviewees in Brussels and London also signified their strong emotional attachment to their countries and localities. The significant support for the effective identification model of citizenship amongst my British and Belgian interviewees was one of the evidences of such attachment. Here, however, it is important to note that when my interviewees were stressing that they should be viewed as part and parcel of British and Belgian societies, they subscribed not to the unitary concept of a nation, [23] which does not leave a room for particular identities, but to the pluralistic definition of this term that takes into account the existence of such identities within a larger 'imagined community'. [24] The porousness of the boundaries of the Belgian and British national identities clearly helped my interviewees to claim 'being the same' and yet 'being different'.

By supporting the national narratives, the members of the emerging Muslim elites did not cease to identify with their co-religionists in other parts of the world. The sense of empathy and solidarity with Muslims living in other parts of the world was particularly strong amongst the British Muslims. A majority of my interviewees perceived the worldwide ummah as the community united by the common beliefs, ethics and morality, rather than as a form of political and religious authority. For them, identification with other believers of Islam in the world did not exclude the identification with other compatriots. In their opinion these two identifications were not mutually exclusive and it was perfectly possible to be at the same time attached to the religious and national community.

At the level of citizenship participation, persons who would not mind calling themselves practising Muslims and practising Belgians/Britons were characterized above all by the social activism, which was not limited to their own religious group, but which transgressed Muslim symbolic boundaries and aimed at all the members of the society. The gathered research material portrays some of the projects undertaken by the members of the emerging new Muslim elites in Brussels and London, which clearly went beyond the traditional *dawah* and creatively engaged with the wider society. Raising money for hostels for homeless in London, joining the campaign for the 'living wage' and feeding Brussels' homeless are only some of them. They portray how Muslim civicness manifests itself in practical terms. The young Muslims involved in these kind of projects were also happily volunteering for non-Muslims NGOs such as, for instance, the Amnesty International, Greenpeace or Citizens Organising Foundation. For many of them it was not that important whether it was 'an Islamic cause', but above all they wanted to be sure that it was 'a just cause'. They were willing to lobby not only for Muslim causes, but also for non-Muslim ones.

This impartiality was, for example, stressed by Murad who said, "*...if a Jew is attacked, Muslims have to fight with the* *injustice done to him as if he was a Muslim (...)*". The interviewees willing to engage in the fight for non-Muslim causes were also more likely than others to talk about the non-Muslim issues that should be fought for. If they spoke about injustice in the world they did not concentrate only on Muslims in such places as, for instance, Palestine, Chechnya or Uzbekistan, but saw the problem of injustice much more globally and not limited only to their co-religionists.

At the level of citizenship rights, the Muslim civicness manifests itself above all in the strong emphasis on the right to the sameness. The vast majority of the new Muslim brokers stressed that they would like to more fully participate in the sameness and to be included in the more flexible and open conception of 'us'. While maintaining their religious identity they wished to be recognised as citizens equal to others. They wanted their presence in the midst of the Belgian and British society to be banalised, or 'taken for granted'. They believed that banalisation of their religious otherness might provide them with enough room to more openly manifest their religiosity and at the same time to be active citizens. If they called for the right to the difference, they framed such requests very carefully so as not to set themselves aside from the wider society. They were also ready to resign from some of the privileges acquired by other religious groups (e.g. right to the state-funded religious schools). By and large, their requests had a character of the acculturative demands rather than dissociative ones.

One of the major features of the Muslim civicness at the level of citizenship obligations is that it puts emphasis on the importance of carrying for all the members of the society regardless of their religious allegiance, or on having obligations vis-à-vis all the citizens without distinction of creed. In other words, it stresses that in everyday activities one should not only care about his or her co-religionists, family or kin, but also about other members of the society. Numerous young Muslims interviewed in the course of the research were, for instance, pointing out that they had obligations not only towards members of their own religious community, but also towards other members of the society, and by asserting that the later obligations were equally important as the former one. Nabihah in Brussels, for example, argued that, "(...) *our work should profit not only Muslims but also others*", whereas Samar from London said, "*The obligation of a citizen is to contribute to the society; to do something meaningful. Not only make a difference to my life, but to make a difference to lives of others*".

The opinion of Thaqib from London that, "*Being a good Muslim and a good citizen is synonymous*", points out yet another significant feature of the Muslim civicness—that this identity perceives the demands of the faith and those of citizenship as highly compatible. Most of my interviewees in Brussels and London believed that if these demands were at times not compatible, then such sporadic incompatibilities were easily solvable. Moreover, many of them also argued that their religious convictions pushed them to fulfil citizenship obligations with greater attention and that religion made citizenship obligations more meaningful to them. The gist of this idea was captured by Khalil who spoke about Islam as "*an engine of citizenship*". In his view, which was widely shared by my interviewees in Brussels, as well as in London, it was religion, which gave a deep meaning to such rudimentary civil/civic duty as, for instance, casting a ballot. It also underpinned numerous more abstract civic obligation such as, for example, honesty, helpfulness, truthfulness, love of justice, industriousness, etc., which unlike the civil obligations cannot be enforced by the law.

Muslim Civicness as a Project Identity

Having pointed out the most significant features of Muslim civicness, it is time to shed more light on this identity that is being developed by numerous young Muslims in Europe and which was particularly popular amongst my interviewees. The popularisation of this identity has been one of the major factors contributing to the significant shift in the mobilisation of Islam in Europe from the politics of Muslim identity to the politics of Muslim citizenship. As I have argued earlier, the Muslim civicness bears many traits of the 'project identity'. [25] The Muslim civicness redefines the social position of Muslims engaged in its development and transforms social structures mainly by challenging the traditional public-private sphere divide (e.g. the popular understanding of the role of religion in the public life) and by calling for the transformation of the existing power structures between the 'established' and the 'outsiders'. [26]

According to the dominant narrative, the public sphere is not a privileged domain of religion, and especially so, if it is a religion of a relatively newly established minority group. [27] As Talal Asad reminds us, religious practice and belief are highly welcomed (since without the idea of religion the concept of the secular cannot do) but mainly in the private sphere or in the space where they cannot threaten political stability and the liberties of a 'free-thinking' citizen. [28] By asserting the importance of Islam not only in the private sphere but also in the public one, my interviewees clearly transgress the boundaries drawn by modern liberal states. By the very fact of mobilizing politics along religious lines they de-centre a fundamental public-private distinction of a modern liberal state, which sees religion as a matter of personal concern rather than public.

At the same time, they do not call for the total abolition of this distinction, like some more radical believers, but for its rebalancing. They seek a gradual transformation of the existing structures, rather than revolutionary change. By emphasizing the importance of religion not only in the private domain but also outside of it, they also suggest that political secularism is not religiously neutral and, as such, it should not be taken for granted. As numerous feminist scholars have shown, [29] the assumption that difference must be privatized works as a 'gag-rule' to exclude matters of concern to marginalized and subordinated groups (such as, for instance, women) who want erstwhile private gender relations to be the subject of collective deliberation and reform. Thus, what would earlier be called 'private' matters have become the basis of the struggle for equality.

By extension, *toute proportion gardée*, the same might be said of the religious practice of European Muslims. Their political integration in terms of equality inevitably involves challenging the existing boundaries of the public realm. As Tariq Modood aptly notices, such integration essentially flows from the process of discursive engagement, as marginal groups begin to confidently assert themselves in the public space, and others begin to argue with and reach some agreement with them.' [30] The focus of this process of discursive engagement is on participation in a discursive public space, while equality becomes defined as inclusion within a political community, not in terms of accepting the rules of the existing polity and its hallowed public-private boundaries, but rather in terms of some redefinition of the existing rules and boundaries. In this respect, the advances achieved, for instance, by feminism (with its slogan 'the personal is the political') have acted as benchmarks for subsequent groups who have introduced new categories of identity into politics such as Muslims.

The meaningful engagement of young European Muslims in a discursive public space has above all been possible due to their possession of substantial cultural capital. The embodied and institutional cultural capital has enabled members of the emerging new Muslim elites in Brussels and London to choose between different courses of action and to move beyond the formal to participatory forms of citizenship. In other words, substantial cultural resources have allowed them to enact their citizenship status or to take up a role of citizen and engage with it creatively from within their religious tradition. These resources have allowed them to become subjects without distancing themselves from one of the major sources of authenticity that they have at their disposal, namely their religion. Their sense of agency, or the belief that they can act, has been visibly strengthened by the possessed cultural capital. Acting as a citizen, especially collectively, as Ruth Lister rightly notices, in turn fosters such sense of agency. [31]

The form, which they could enact, that is legal citizenship, is also of crucial importance. The role of a citizen, enabled them to present themselves as equal and, to some extent, similar to others around them and thus, provided them with a significant tool to challenge the 'established', and try to at least minimally shake their domination in the discursive public sphere. As Elias and Scotson demonstrate in their study of 'Winston Parva' in East Midlands of England, this domination is not easily shakeable since the communal feelings of belonging and ownership, membership of important community roles, integration into informal (and formal) local networks and local knowledge, and many other resources give established groups an upper hand in the 'relations of definition' between themselves and newer groups.

All of these power resources also enable the established to make their evaluations stick and, as the practice shows, these evaluations are rarely favourable to those who are 'less established'. This is because established groups tend to generate 'group charisma', or a sense of their own superiority as a group, based on a 'minority of the best' as part of their social and self-identity. Their self-image tends to be based on evaluations rooted in the best aspects of the group whilst ignoring other elements that might contaminate such an image and, as such, it forms an important aspect of the group's internal solidarity and sense of community. This 'rosy' self-image of the established is sustained through the vital mechanisms of communal 'gossip' and everyday conversation. Established groups produce 'praise-gossip' [32] when discussing their own group, but use 'blame-gossip' [33] to describe other groups, which they do not consider as 'one of theirs' or 'established enough'.

The European Muslims viewed by many 'established' Europeans as outsiders, are often targets of stigmatizing labels. Their relative lack of substantial power resources (as a whole group) leaves them vulnerable to the gossip and stigmatization of more powerful groups. Over time, some of them have come to accept and take on the stigmatized form of identity created for them by the 'established'. They c see their own group as inferior and see themselves as inferior people, idealizing and imitating the established behavioural codes, manners and so on in order to raise their valuation. This, according to Elias and Scotson, reduces their power chances even further by reinforcing claims to the superiority of the established. Furthermore, the generational transmission of stereotypes ensures that 'outsiders' are continually reminded of their interior status.

The aforementioned scenario, however, does not take into account the fact that 'outsiders' with the passage of time also start (faster or slower) [34] to acquire some power resources and are not deemed to accept the forever stigmatising labels. This is clear, for instance, when comparing the situation of the black people in America after the Second World War and at present, when the African American candidate Barack Obama has become a new incumbent in the White House. The example of African Americans who, more than half a century ago, started to actively challenge their negative stereotypes and create their own positive evaluations (e.g. 'black is beautiful') [35] also demonstrates that the outsiders-established relations are not easily erasable and are often part of the long-term process of social change over many generations. Moreover, these long-term processes are subject to a reversal of the present trends, rather than being simply linear pathways which once embarked upon become somehow inevitable.

In the analysed cases of Muslims in Belgium and Britain, one may also observe a process of a narrowing of the gap between their own and the established power. At the same time, many of the established continue to view their Muslim compatriots born in Europe as outsiders. The new Muslim brokers possess some power resources that allow them to at least partially reduce the scale of the 'blame-gossip' generated by the established. Those who are developing Muslim civicness have learnt to reject the stigmatising labels of the established without rejecting the whole system created and largely run by them. [36]

This seems to be an efficient strategy for redefining their position in societies, which is a key goal of the project identities. Armed with legal citizenship, substantial civic skills and other resources, they are beginning to quite successfully 'break into the bounded Britain and Belgium'. [37] They are beginning to achieve some success not only in contesting the hegemonic constructions of the cultural and religious boundaries of the British and Belgian nations, but also in opposing elements of the 'blame gossip' generated by the established. The first task they accomplish, for instance, by demonstrating their in-depth knowledge of Belgian and British society and profound affection to their respective countries, whereas the second one, by writing to local and national newspapers or appearing in TV and Radio programmes and correcting some of the fairly widespread derogatory images of Muslims and Islam. [38]

Conclusion

In conclusion, however, it must be stressed that the relative success achieved by Muslim groups in shaking the domination of the 'established' in the discursive public sphere and rebalancing the relations between themselves and non-Muslim Belgians and Britons are not definite and irreversible. On the contrary, these achievements can be erased fairly easily and the significant gap between the power chances of the 'outsiders' and the 'established' can be re-created. This was particularly noticeable after the terrorist attacks committed in the name of Allah on September 11, 2001 (US), March 11, 2004 (Spain), July 7, 2005 (Britain), January 7, 2015 and

November 13, 2015 (France), and March 22, 2016 (Belgium). [39] The attacks marked the point when one could clearly observe an increase in the 'blame gossip' trying to force as many people of Muslim faith as possible to accept 'group disgrace'. At the same time, after the attacks it was possible to see numerous symptoms of a reversal of the process leading to the more equal balance of power between the established and outsiders. Interestingly, these temporary reversals in the processes of power rebalancing seemed not to discourage members of the Muslim communities already involved in the public sphere from even more active involvement.

As I have shown above, the members of the emerging new Muslim elites were particularly successful in turning the stigma associated with their religion into a source of empowerment or 'group charisma' rather than 'group disgrace'. It is important to stress that the channel of 'empowerment-through-stigmatisation' analysed in the earlier chapters is only open for those members of the Muslim communities who possess the necessary tools to deal with the stigma resulting, for instance, from the traumatic events. This also proves the phenomenon of the double capacity of cultural traumas observed by numerous scholars, [40] which in spite of their immediate negative, painful consequences, shows their positive, functional potential as forces of social becoming. [41]

On the whole, my interviewees possessed the necessary resources to turn the stigmas, such as those resulting from the aforementioned traumatic events, to their advantage. Those who were engaged in developing Muslim civicness even in the most unfavourable circumstances took pains to stress a strongly held religious belief and used Islamic practice in order to interact more effectively with the rest of the society. The late Ottavia Schmidt di Friedberg described such attitudes, which characterised also some of her interviewees, as 'riding the tiger'. [42] In my opinion, this metaphor aptly captures not only the risks involved in maintaining such an attitude, but also the difficulty in using one of the major emerging global symbols of contestation of the West (i.e. Islam) to interact with the members of European (Western) societies.

In February 2008, the cover of *The Time* magazine (Vol. 171, No. 6) featured faces of members of the European Muslim elites and some of my interviewees with the title 'Europe's Muslim Success Story'. Today, this 'success story' is shared only by a small proportion of the European Muslims and members of their communities, while a majority experience serious levels of exclusion and disadvantage. The improvement of the situation of the Muslim communities in Europe will depend not only on the effective struggle against at least some of the forms of exclusion and disadvantage faced by the members of these communities, but also on the results of the Muslims' efforts to re-invent and position themselves as citizens and full members of the European polities. The latter objective is particularly difficult to attain. Before European Muslims achieve this goal, they will need to yet work tirelessly to reconstruct popular images, assumptions and representations of their religion and their communities within wider societies. The members of the new Muslim elites have been already doing so and they will surely not rest until they achieve some tangible results.

Endnotes

1. An altered version of this chapter was published in *COLLeGIUM: Studies Across Disciplines in the Humanities and Social Sciences*, 11, (2012) 83-99.
2. For more information about this and other Muslim organisations in Britain claiming to represent 'the country's Muslims' vis-à-vis the government, see Pędziwiatr (2007a).
3. Sacranie, I. (2006), Valedictory Speech of the Secretary General of the Muslim Council of Britain, available at: http://www.mcb.org.uk/uploads/SECGEN.pdf.
4. Modood, T. (2003), "Muslim and the Politics of Difference", in S. Spencer (ed.), 'The Politics of Migration: Managing Opportunity, Conflict and Change', London: Blackwell Publishing.
5. One such organisation is, for instance, Hizb ut-Tahrir. For more information about the organisation, see Taj-Farouki (2003),

Wiktorowicz (2005) and Karagiannis and McCauley (2006.

6. A. Boubekeur (2007), "Political Islam in Europe", in S. Amghar (ed.), 'European Islam: Challenges for Public Policy and Society', CEPS, Brussels, p. 40.
7. H. Bousetta and D. Jacobs (2006), "Multiculturalism, Citizenship and Islam in Problematic Encounters in Belgium", in 'Multiculturalism, Muslims and Citizenship: A European Approach', Routledge, London pp. 23-32.
8. These strategies are explored in depth in Pędziwiatr (2008).
9. Calhoun (1994), "Social Theory and the Politics of Identity", New York University, New York.
10. T.H. Marshal (1950), "Citizenship and Social Class and other Essays", CUP, Cambridge.
11. J. Pakulski (1997), "Cultural Citizenship", *Citizenship Studies*, t. 1, pp. 73-86.
12. G. Delanty (2002), "Two Conceptions of Cultural Citizenship: A Review of Recent Literature on Culture and Citizenship", *The Global Review of Ethnopolitics*, t. 1, no. 1, pp. 60-66.
13. It refers to rights specific to particular groups of people (e.g. women, ethnic and religious minorities) which protect and enable realisation of the particular needs interests and priorities of these groups. These are the rights, which Isaac Berlin saw as embodiment of the third form of freedom [e.g. Young (1990), Kymlicka (1995) and Isin and Wood (1999)].
14. B.S. Turner (1997), "Citizenship Studies: A General Theory", *Citizenship Studies*, t. 1, no. 1, p. 8.
15. N. Göle (2003), "The Voluntary Adoption of Islamic Stigma Symbol", *Social Research*, t. 70, no. 3; T. Modood (2003), "Muslim and the Politics of Difference", in 'The Politics of Migration: Managing Opportunity, Conflict and Change', S. Spencer (ed.), Blackwell Publishing, London.
16. F. Bianchini (2001), "Cultural Citizenship and Urban Governance in Western Europe", in N. Stevenson (ed.) 'Culture and Citizenship, Sage, London.
17. J. Holston (1999), "Cities and Citizenship", NC: Duke University Press, Durham, p. 189.
18. For an overview of scholarship on local elites see, for example, Tilleux (2003).
19. By religious brokers I mean individuals who play a key role in the articulation of the identity narrative discourse.

20. For detailed conceptual and methodological information about the research, see Pędziwiatr (2008).
21. Bousetta and Jacobs observe that, paradoxically, the radicalism of the jihadist discourse of bin Laden and his followers has stimulated a form of civic consciousnesses among Muslims (2006: 32-33).
22. Ibid.
23. For more information about the concept of a nation conceived in this way, see Brubaker (1988).
24. B. Anderson (1983), "Imagined Communities: Reflections on the Origin and Spread of Nationalism", Verso, London.
25. M. Castells (1997), "The Power of Identity", Blackwell, Oxford, p. 9.
26. N. Elias and J.L. Scotson (1994), "The Established and the Outsiders: A Sociological Enquiry into Community Problems", Sage Publications.
27. It is not without importance which religious group strives for more room in the public sphere. Some newly set up Christian evangelical communities find it much easier to claim such a space than, for example, Muslim groups. The former ones are, in fact, re-claiming it, while the latter ones claiming it for the first time in the history of the analysed countries.
28. T. Asad (2003), "Formations of the Secular: Christianity, Islam, Modernity: Cultural Memory in the Present", Stanford University Press, California.
29. E.g., Benhabib (1992), Fraser (1992), Lister (1997) and Voet (1998).
30. T. Modood (2004), "Multiculturalism, Muslims and the British State", in S.J. Sutcliffe (ed.) 'Religion: Empirical Studies', Ashgate, p. 247.
31. R. Lister (1997), "Citizenship: Feminist Perspectives", Macmillan, London, p. 38.
32. 'Praise-gossip' means that the best elements perceived by the established group form the basis for discussion and evaluation whilst negative elements are not openly discussed.
33. 'Blame-gossip' is exactly the reverse, as outsider groups are discussed and assessed in terms of what are considered to be their worst elements.
34. This largely depends on the structure of a given society. One may expect that in a society with high social mobility such a

process should be relatively fast. The state and to a lesser extent supranational bodies (e.g. European Commission, United Nations) act as important mediators in the relations between the 'established' and the 'outsiders'.

35. The shifting balance of power between white and black groups in America is clearly explored, with the usage of the established-outsiders framework, by Dunning (2004). For an analysis of the civil rights movements from the social movements' perspective, see McAdam et al. (1996) or McAdam (1999).
36. Those who develop uncompromising Muslimness, on the other hand, tend to reject not only the stigmatizing evaluations, but also the whole system within which they are generated.
37. This expression I have borrowed from Sean McLoughlin (1997) analyzing how representations of belonging of the Muslim in Bradford challenge the hegemonic constructions of the racial, cultural and religious boundaries of Britain.
38. How widespread such images are in Belgium and Britain may be gleaned from, for example, Allen and Nielsen (2002) or EUMC (2006).
39. One could add to the list of 'turning points' in relations between Muslims and non-Muslims in the West, the religiously motivated murder of Theo van Gogh on the streets of Amsterdam on November 2, 2004. Although of much smaller scale, this event had a tremendous impact on the collective memory of not only the Dutch, but all Europeans.
40. P. Sztompka (2002), "Socjologia-analiza spoleczenstwa", Znak, Kraków; J.C. Alexander (2004), "Towards a Theory of Cultural Trauma", in J.C. Alexander et al. (ed.) 'Cultural Trauma and Collective Identity'.
41. According to Sztompka, the 'constructiveness' or 'destructiveness' of such an ambivalent social phenomenon as trauma depends on four major factors: the strength of initiating traumatogenic change, the gap between old and new cultural syndrome, the size of the traumatized groups, the scope of individual resources (education, connections, rootedness, financial capital), and the openness of the channels of mobility, which allow individuals to escape the traumatized groups or social positions and liberate themselves from trauma (2004: 194).
42. O. Schmidt di Frieberg (2002), "Being Muslim in the Italian Public Sphere: Islamic Organisations in Turin and Trieste", in W.A.R.

Peters Shadid and Leuven (eds.) 'Intercultural Relations and Religious Authorities: Muslims in the European Union'.

References

Allen, C. and J. Nielsen (2002), "Summary Report on Islamophobia in the EU after 11 September 2001", Vienna: EMUC.

Anderson, B. (1991), "Imagined Communities: Reflections on the Origins and Spread of Nationalism", London: Verso.

Asad, T. (2003), "Formations of the Secular: Christianity, Islam, Modernity", Stanford: Stanford University Press.

Benhabib, S. (1992), "Situating the Self", Cambridge: Polity.

Bianchini, F. and J. Bloomfield (2001), "Cultural Citizenship and Urban Governance in Western Europe", in N. Stevenson (ed.), 'Culture and Citizenship', London: Sage.

Boubekeur, A. (2007), "Political Islam in Europe", in S. Amghar, A. Boubekeur and M. Emerson (eds.) 'European Islam: Challenges for Public Policy and Society', Brussels: CEPS.

Bousetta, H. and D. Jacobs (2006), "Multiculturalism, Citizenship and Islam in Problematic Encounters in Belgium", in 'Multiculturalism, Muslims and Citizenship: A European Approach', London: Routledge.

Brubaker, R. (1988), "Citoyennetè, identitè française et principe d'exclusion", In C. Withol de Wenden (Ed.), 'La citoyennetè', Paris: Edilig/Fondation Diderot.

Calhoun, C. (1994), "Social Theory and the Politics of Identity", New York: New York University.

Castells, M. (1997, 2004), "The Power of Identity", Oxford: Blackwell.

Delanty, G. (2002), "Two Conceptions of Cultural Citizenship: A Review of Recent Literature on Culture and Citizenship", *The Global Review of Ethnopolitics,* 1(1), 60-66.

Dunning, E. (2004), "Aspects of the Figurational Dynamics of Racial Stratification: A Conceptual Discussion and Developmental Analysis of Black-White Relations in the United States", In S. Loyal and S. Quilley (ed.), 'The Sociology of Norbert Elias', Cambridge: Cambridge University Press.

Elias, N. and J.L. Scotson, J.L. (1965), "The Established and the Outsiders", London: Frank Cass & Co.Ltd.

EUMC (2006), "Muslims in the European Union: Discrimination and Islamophobia", available at:

http://eumc.europa.eu/eumc/material/pub/muslim/Manifestations_EN.pdf.

Fraser, N. (1992), "Rethinking the Public Sphere", in C. Calhoun (ed.), 'Habermas and the Public Sphere', Cambridge: MIT Press.

Göle, N. (2003), "The Voluntary Adoption of Islamic Stigma Symbol", *Social Research,* 70(3).

Holston, J. (ed.) (1999), "Cities and Citizenship", Durham: NC: Duke University Press.

Isin, E.F. and P.K. Wood (1999), "Citizenship and Identity", London: Sage.

Karagiannis, E. and C. McCauley (2006), "Hizb ut-Tahrir al-Islami: Evaluating the Threat Posed by a Radical Islamic Group that Remains Non-violent", *Terrorism and Political Violence,* 18(2), 315-334.

Kymlicka, W. (1995), "Multicultural Citizenship", Oxford: Oxford University Press.

Lister, R. (1997), "Citizenship: Feminist Perspectives", London: Macmillan.

Marshal, T.H. (1950, 1992), "Citizenship and Social Class", Cambridge: Cambridge University Press.

McAdam, D. (1999), "Political Process and the Development of Black Insurgency: 1930-1970", Chicago: University of Chicago Press.

McAdam, D., J.D. McCarthy and M.N. Zald (1996), "Comparative Perspectives on Social Movements: Political Opportunities, Mobilizing Structures, and Cultural Framings", Cambridge: CUP.

McLoughlin, S. (1997), "Breaking into Bounded Britain: Discrepant Representations of Belonging and Muslims in Bradford", Unpublished Ph.D. thesis, University of Manchester, Manchester.

Modood, T. (2003), "Muslim and the Politics of Difference", in S. Spencer (ed.), 'The Politics of Migration: Managing Opportunity, Conflict and Change', London: Blackwell Publishing.

Modood, T. (2004), "Multiculturalism, Muslims and the British State", in S.J. Sutcliffe (ed.) 'Religion: Empirical Studies', Ashgate.

Motzkin, Fischer Y. (ed.), "Religion and Democracy in Contemporary Europe", London: Alliance Publishing Trust.

Pakulski, J. (1997), "Cultural Citizenship", *Citizenship Studies,* 1, 73-86.

Pędziwiatr, K. (2007), "Creating New Discursive Arenas and Influencing the Policies of the State: Case of the Muslim Council of Britain", *Social Compass,* 54(1).

—(2008), "The New Muslim Elites in European Cities: Religion and Active Social Citizenship Among Young Organised Muslims in Brussels and London", VDM Verlag Dr Muller GmbH & Co KG.

—(2008), "Publicizing, Secularizing and Integrating Islam in Europe".

—(2008), "European Diversity, Religion and Citizenship", *European Judaism,* Vol. 41, No. 2, 79-84.

—(2008), "From Politics of Muslim Identity to Politics of Muslim Citizenship", in J. Nowicki, Porębski. C. (ed.) 'L'invention de l'autre', Paris: Editions du Sandre.

—(2008), "Nation-Building Processes in Palestine", in A. Kostka (ed.) 'Visions of Palestine', Krakow: Tischner European University.

—(2008), "L'activisme social des nouvelles élites musulmanes de Grande-Bretagne", *Hermes,* 51, 123-131.

—(2008), "Politicizing Islam in Europe: Case of the Muslim Council of Britain", *Zeszyty Naukowe WSE,* 2(3), 154-169.

Sacranie, I. (2006), Valedictory Speech of the Secretary General of the Muslim Council of Britain, available at: http://www.mcb.org.uk/uploads/SECGEN.pdf.

Schmidt di Frieberg, O. (2002), "Being Muslim in the Italian Public Sphere: Islamic Organisations in Turin and Trieste", in Shadid, W.A.R., S. van Koningsveld (eds.), 'Intercultural Relations and Religious Authorities: Muslims in the European Union', Leuven, Peeters.

Sztompka, P. (2002), "Socjologia-analiza społeczeństwa", Kraków: Znak.

Sztompka, P. (2004), "The Trauma of Social Change", in J.C. Alexander, R. Eyerman, B. Giesen, N.J. Smelser and P. Sztompka (eds.), 'Cultural Trauma and Collective Identity', Berkeley: University of California Press.

Taj-Farouki, S. (2003), "Islamists and the Threat of Jihad: Hizb ut-Tahrir and al Muhajiroun on Israel and the Jews", in B.S. Turner (ed.) 'Islam: Critical Concepts in Sociology', London:

Routledge.

Tilleux, O. (2003), "Contribution à l'étude des modes de fonctionnement des élites locales", *Recherches Sociologique,* 1, 3-28.

Turner, B.S. (1997), "Citizenship Studies: A General Theory", *Citizenship Studies,* 1(1), 5-18.

Voet, R. (1998), "Feminism and Citizenship", London: Sage.

Wiktorowicz, Q. (2005), "Radical Islam Rising: Muslim Extremism in the West", Oxford: Rowman & Littlefield Publishers.

Young, I. (1990), "Justice and the Politics of Difference", Oxford: Princeton University Press.

9

Muslims and Naturalization Process in France

Anne Fornerod

At first sight, it may appear peculiar enough to openly put side by side French naturalization and religious affiliation, if we consider that French law is characterized by the constitutional principle of *laïcité* which implies a neutral relation with the religious phenomenon. Indeed, French administration officially does not take into account any religion, as a result of the neutrality that guides its action. Among the various patterns of the legal frameworks ruling the State-Churches relationships, French *laïcité* is very often depicted as an embodiment of a strict separation between public authorities and religious bodies. This conception may be the result of a political approach blurring the proper legal dimension of the principle of *laïcité*. This one appears in the Constitution of 1946 and lies today in the still in force Constitution of 1958. Although the constitutional text provides no definition, it is commonly agreed that *laïcité* is composed of three elements: neutrality, freedom of religion and pluralism (Council of State 2004: 272 and seq.; Council of State 2010: 18). The Constitutional Council gave somehow another definition in a decision of November 19, 2004, reading that the constitutional provisions 'forbid to anyone to invoke one's religious beliefs in order to be free from respecting the common rules, which regulate the relationships between public authorities and individuals'.

However, the real legal significance of *laïcité* cannot be yet fully assessed. If one can read here the rejection of the community closing in on itself phenomenon, [1] it could also reflect in law the fact that for several years now, the legal dimension of *laïcité* has been questioned in the context of crisis of the nation-state political model, since it is often made of a component of the republican identity. It could also be analysed as an illustration of the general statement that 'around the world, we are witnessing a revitalization of religious issues, which includes, in particular with respect to contemporary Islam, a re-politicization of religion' (Ladeur 2009: 2445). Accordingly, the political dimension of French *laïcité* is seemingly overlapping its legal definition or at least increasingly developing itself alongside. [2]

The link between acquiring French nationality and being a Muslim, handled with here, enlightens this tendency. The examination of a French nationality application leads the administrative authorities to deeply control the way of life of the person involved in this process. The religious dimension of the applicants' way of life is not exempted as it was proved several times. An overview of the main features of nationality law will precede an analysis of the pertaining case law in order to find out why and how belonging to Islam is taken into account within a matter intrinsically related to national identity. Beyond, it sheds light on the fact that the nationality law is a legal field closely linked to political considerations, which may include the principle of *laïcité*.

Acquiring Nationality: Assimilation and Religion

The basic features of nationality law (A) allow understanding how its enforcement may give rise to an examination of the religious affiliation of the applicants (B).

(A) Basic Features of Nationality Law: The Concept of Assimilation: There are three ways of acquiring French nationality, regulated by the civil code (Article 21 and seq.): the automatic one (by reason of birth or residence in France for example), the acquisition by reason of a declaration, and, at last, the French nationality granted by public authorities which is properly called naturalization. The first one does not call for further comments. On the other hand, the following ones should be focused on and analysed in light of the condition of assimilation. Indeed, an insufficient assimilation may justify a refusal of naturalization but also found the opposition procedure of the government in case of acquisition of French nationality by reason of marriage. [3]

Despite its fundamental importance in nationality law, the condition of assimilation required by the civil code has no legal definition. This criterion draws on the administrative regulation applicable during the inter-War years and the political regime of Vichy [4] (Bruschi 1996: 163; Fulchiron 2000: p. 85; Weil 2002: 81). Today, the knowledge of the domestic language is the main element clearly mentioned by law. More precisely, in fact, the July 24, 2006 Act added some provisions according to which 'the effective situation of polygamy of the foreign spouse or the conviction pursuant to the crime defined in Article 222-9 of the Penal Code are constitutive of a lack of assimilation' (now Article 21-4 of the Civil Code). [5] Without any legal definition, it is necessary to refer to case law and administrative regulation, which display noticeable complementarities. For example, according to an administrative circular of 1952 and reiterated twenty years later, a foreigner is assimilated when 'by its way of speaking, his way of life, his state of mind or his behaviour towards the French institutions he distinguishes as less as possible from the other citizens' (Olekhnovitch 1995 : 882).

More recently, but not very differently, a circular of February 24, 2005 related to the investigations carried out by the administrative services, indicates that assimilation 'may be defined by a full adhesion to the rules and the values of tolerance, *laïcité*, freedom and equality of the welcoming society; by a participation in the activities of this society and not only to its economic life'. The way of life is assessed through the 'applicant's behaviour in general and during the hearing before the administration, his social relations, his behaviour in family and his hobbies'. The text goes on with particularly relevant elements here. Namely, the civil servant in charge of the inquiry is enabled to put forward 'the affiliation to movements, which advocate a radical practice of religion or violent acting, and, for the woman, the fact to confine oneself to home, to be forced or to voluntarily wear conspicuous religious symbols, or to be prevented from communicating with male persons'. Thus, it clearly appears that religion may be an element, among others, to assess the degree of assimilation of the applicants. The link between religion and French nationality is old and was established often painfully. [6]

Today, the religious affiliation is still present in the nationality issue. Contrary to the preconceived idea that French State behaves without any reference to religious matters, the nationality issue shows how the national community and its values may be shaped by the place ascribed to religion in society and the way the State deals with it.

(B) Acquiring Nationality and Religion: General Overview of the Relevant Case Law

Firstly, it has to be emphasized that practising a religion has never been considered as a lack of assimilation in itself. For example, the Council of State thus held in a case of November 24, 1997, that 'the fact that the applicant belonged to the association of 'Islamic students of France', took part in radio and television broadcasts and conferences in order to make know better the Muslim religion, that moreover, had supervised the review 'the Muslim', if true, cannot be analysed as a lack of assimilation'. [7] By browsing the relevant contemporary case law, it emerges that Islam is the sole religion brought up in the array of relevant cases, which brings together religious practice and acquisition of nationality. Among the various appeals lodged before the courts, it is possible to distinguish between those involved in the wearing of religious dress and the others and, at the same time, between the cases pertaining to naturalizations and those facing the nationality acquisition by marriage. For all these cases, it appears that the administrative judge clearly puts side by side the religious affiliation of the applicant and the fundamental values of the Republic, including the *laïcité*.

It is noticeable that the case law contains a range of decisions in which citizenship was denied to applicants assumed to be belonging to fundamentalists groups. In this case law, the administrative court of Nantes of October 14, 2008 handled a denial of naturalization. According to Article 21-15 of the Civil Code, 'the acquisition of French nationality by a decision of the Government results from a naturalization granted by decree at the request of the alien'. In this case, the judge rejected the appeal lodged by the applicant against the minister's decision denying him the French nationality on the ground that 'he still actively advocates in favour of a radical Islam and propagated thesis incompatible with the values of tolerance and *laïcité* in the French society and refuses to recognize the principle of *laïcité*—the fundamental principle of the French Republic'. [8] According to a Home office's report, this man was one of the leaders of a place of place of worship in Amiens, managed by the association of the Muslims of Picardie, affiliated to the UOIF [Union of the Islamic Organizations of France]...and his behaviour reveals a lack of integration by his refusal to recognize the principle of *laïcité'*. It must be noticed that this ground was not questioned by the applicant. [9] Most of the other comparable cases are of the same vein.

The cases pertaining to the religious dress code could, in appearance, let believe to a more open attitude of the administrative judge. For example, the Council of State annulled the refusal to grant the French nationality to a Tunisian man who asserted himself as a strict believer and whose wife wore the Islamic veil. [10] Moreover, wearing the veil won't prevent a woman from obtaining the French nationality. [11] To our knowledge, no court decision does of it as an insufficient assimilation. [12] In fact, a sharper examination of the applicant's behaviour often implies to go beyond the statement that she wears the Islamic veil. In 2003, the administrative Court of Appeal of Nantes confirmed the rejection of the application of an Algerian woman since she was an active member of an organization advocating a radical practice of religion and more precisely the wearing of the veil in every space, including at school. [13]

In this perspective, an administrative regulatory of May 12, 2000 regarding naturalizations was astonishingly precise about the assessment carried out by the civil servants. Indeed, it stated that they must not only mention that the applicant wears the veil but also indicated whether it is 'the traditional headscarf in use in the Maghreb/North African countries or in Turkey', whether it is 'the *hidjab* which covers entirely the head and the neck and is, like the chador, a sign of belonging to fundamentalist Islam'. [14] In such situations, the applicant is required to explain the meaning of wearing this kind of dress. A case during the year 2008, illustrated how the administrative judge sometimes takes the religious convictions of the applicant into account. This important court decision raised a lot of debates and may be considered as an interesting first step in the current thinking about wearing the full veil... and the governmental and parliamentary will to enact an overall ban. [15]

According to the Civil Code, the foreign spouse (Article 21-2) may acquire French nationality provided that he or she fulfils several conditions, including a good knowledge of the French language. Nevertheless, since 2003, the Government may 'on grounds of indignity or lack of assimilation other than linguistic', oppose the acquisition of French nationality by the foreign spouse within a period of one year. Indeed, after the foreign spouse has made the declaration in order to acquire the nationality, the administrative services of the prefecture carry out an investigation in order to appreciate the level of assimilation and also the behaviour and the loyalty of the applicant. Madam M., who is Moroccan, had married a French man and, as it is legally required, applied for French nationality. In a very short ruling, the Council of State upheld the government's administrative decision and judged that 'even if Madam M. has a good knowledge of the French language, she has however adopted a radical practice of her religion, incompatible with essential values of the French community, particularly the principle of equality of the sexes. Therefore, she does not meet the condition of assimilation entrenched in Article 21-1 of the Civil Code'.

In addition, the Council of State deemed that the governmental decree was not in breach of the religious liberty. This judicial case contained no detail about her clothes but simply spoke of the radical religious practice. It transpired from the public reporter's findings only that Madam M. 'leads an almost cloistered life: she hardly ever receives visitors and her life mainly consists of looking after her children and cleaning the house'.

From this point of view, by focusing on the behaviour, this case belongs to a set of former decisions turning down the French nationality because of the applicant living without any relation with the national circles and remaining confined to his/her family (Fulchiron, 2000: 25). This kind of requirement reflects the voluntary approach of nationality, seen/considered as an expressed desire to belong to the community of the citizens, inherited of the Revolutionary period. The final solution of 2008 is all the more striking and questionable since the judge clearly justified the opposition of the government on the religious dimension of her way of life. [16]

More recently, the Government adopted a decree, which could lead to a similar solution. Relying on the legal provisions of Article 21-2 of the Civil Code, it decided to deny French nationality to a man who forced his French wife to wear the full veil, deeming that he 'deprived her of the right to go and come with uncovered face and rejected the principles of *laïcité* and equality between men and women'. [17] The communication made about this decision may be explained by the overall context of public debate about wearing of the full veil, held in France at the same time. In case the decree was brought before an administrative court, it should nevertheless be analysed not with regard to the recent advice about the project of general banning on full veil delivered by the Council of State—deciding here as a consultative authority—but through considering its position—as a judge—in a case law imbued with many particularities.

The possible solution could be deduced in the light of either the above mentioned case Madame M. or the former case law applicable to men as well. Indeed, the singularity of the case Madame M. comes from the fact that she has been strangely reproached not to respect the principle of equality between men and women when it is commonly agreed that this principle is usually applicable to situations in which women are victims of such a non-respect. It would, therefore, be logical that the principle could be opposed to the man targeted by the decree. It is nevertheless important to underline that the link established by the government between the behaviour of the wife of the applicant and his request may be irrelevant with regard to the former case law, which leans on the principle of the personal dimension of acquiring nationality.

This principle implies an individual examination of the application and prevents *a priori* from taking into account the behaviour of the family's other members. [18] On the other side, this case law guiding principle knows exception, [19] and the level of investigation provided by the administrative services may justify taking into account such an element. It may indeed come under the 'familial behaviour' (Olekhnovitch 1995: 383). [20] Concerning precisely the Islamic religion, a decision of 2009 delivered by the administrative Court of Appeal of Nantes clearly relied on the husband's attitude and way of life to dismiss the appeal of a woman who applied for naturalization. Indeed it was established that her husband, who had been previously denied French nationality, was said 'to head an association linked to an Islamist Moroccan movement, advocating a rigorous practice of Islam'. The judge deemed that the woman 'necessarily agreed with those thesis and practices incompatible with the French community's values of tolerance and *laïcité'*, despite the claim of the woman that her situation could not be assessed in the light of her husband's opinion and activities. [21]

Eventually, the problem is not whether but how the religion is considered. The religious beliefs, and especially practices, have unavoidable consequences on the behaviour—this one being then put in perspective with what the respect of the national values requires. If this corresponds to a basic feature of nationality law, one can nevertheless wonder whether it is still relevant to speak of the neutrality of the State.

Which Neutrality of the State?

This 'fading' neutrality might be the result of the nationality law logic. It might also belong to a global tendency to interpret the religious symbols.

(A) Nationality Law is, in its Essence, a Reflection of a Political Context: Nationality law being also 'the criterion to determine the population of the State', is often marked by political preoccupations (Dionisi-Peyrusse, 2008: 4) and hence the reflection of a political context. The nationality law's evolution has always been determined by circumstances: answer to the need of soldiers, to fill the demographic deficit and so on (Weil, 2002: 272). The balance between taking aliens and the criterion to grant nationality has for long influenced the latter, however with much more intensity during the last decades. The case law above mentioned as well as the administrative regulation, reflect actually how the state copes with access to nationality, which has been marked for twenty years now by the issue of extra-European aliens' integration and the concern to see the principle of *laïcité* to be respected.

Because of the failure of the integration politics, unemployment and troubles in the suburbs, the differences in cultural customs and behaviours have been considered more and more as a threat to the national community's values. The repercussions on nationality law are so to say unavoidable and this one is accused of allowing access to the French community too easily without the guarantee that the new comers really endorse the national identity. A particular conception of the national identity is at stake here. Indeed, two conceptions of the national identity stand side by side, one or the other prevailing, according to the considered times. The first one rests on the participation of the new comers to a community of citizens, entitled with political and civic rights while the second one includes an ethnical dimension, taking into account the cultural, linguistic or religious belonging (Zeghbib, 2005: 96).

Hence, it is not surprising that the principle of *laïcité* comes to the fore when such consideration of the origin is applied to aliens coming from countries said to be 'Muslim'. A major part of the last immigrants have indeed very often in common come from labelled 'Muslim' countries. They are not only aliens but also Muslims (Bertossi, 2007: 5). Moreover, religion and original culture are mixed. According to an important report carried out in 1988 by the Commission of the Nationality, Islam 'is more than a mere religion: it is a rule of social life, a legal, philosophical and economic rule as well. This rule may be in contradiction with morals, domestic legal framework, and even with the values of a non-Muslim society' (Dionisi-Peyrusse, 2008: 83-84; Long, 1988: 37). A space is therefore created where being an alien, cultural differences and religion—and in fact, especially Islam—are mixed: the link between national identity and *laïcité* is established and the latter could appear as a mean to manage religious diversity in which stands a religion 'from abroad'. One could observe the same type of combination when the debate around *laïcité* rose from 2003 and peaked in 2004.

If it focused on *laïcité*, the debates led nevertheless to the integration of aliens' issue. In a letter dated from 2003, the former President of the Republic Jacques Chirac, made *laïcité* the focal point for various demands like 'the neutrality of public services, the respect of pluralism, religious freedom, freedom of expression, strengthening cohesion and fraternity among citizens, equal opportunities, fight against discriminations, sex equality and woman's dignity'. Facing serious difficulties to ensure the integration of immigrants—but also of French citizens—the State relies on *laïcité* to renew the traditional places of integration such as school, public services and even the institutional forms of religion. Failing in reaching a kind of unity around the elements of the motto of the Republic—especially equality and fraternity—the State may only observe how the feeling of belonging to the nation has vanished in favour of the belonging to other communities, whose real existence still needs to be proved. The difficulties of the State in fighting effectively against discriminations and meeting the conditions of the 'republican theories of equal citizenship' (Bowen, 2006: 29) leads to discourses based on the defence of values and emphasizing the need for safety. It follows uncertainty about the meaning and the contents of *laïcité*, even from a legal point of view. The recent tendency to interpret religious symbol strengthens this uncertainty that affects the contents of *laïcité* as a legal principle.

(B) The Uncertainty about the Legal Meaning of the Principle of *laïcité*: This overview of the case law combining nationality and Islamic religion could be in fact indicative of a current double tendency regarding the *laïcité*'s contents: the first one consists of questioning the neutrality of the State towards religion whereas the second one corresponds to a new definition of *laïcité* provided by the Constitutional Council in 2004.

One can wonder whether the *laïcité*, regularly emphasized in public discourse, is really synonymous with neutrality as it is alleged to be. Beyond the French situation, it is largely agreed that this neutrality means above all that, on the one hand, the State must withdraw from religious issues and the internal regulation of faith-based institutions. On the other hand, it is also of common knowledge that those religious actors should not interfere with the definition of the public sphere, in the sense that common values are not directly determined by the religious representatives (Sen, 2005: 295). Accordingly, the public authorities should not be entitled to mark the boundaries of what is religious, instead of the religious communities themselves. Nor are they legitimate to decide the relevance of the values conveyed by religious bodies and individuals. The courts' assessment should only deal with the behaviours and acts, which may be contrary to the public order (Messner, Prélot and Woehrling, 2003: 434).

Concerning nationality law, the courts' reasoning judge goes into religious considerations in view of the respect of the national values. Coming from the competent public authorities, there is nothing really surprising here since they are entitled to use their discretionary power on this matter. In reality, it reveals a recent tendency to venture on the ground of the interpretation of religious signs that goes beyond nationality law. It was openly asserted that while the veil at schools issue was discussed, the impossibility for the administrative judge to decide of the meaning of a veil was an obstacle in fight against discrimination between men and women, given that the veil could be indicative of such discriminations. By passing the 2004 Act, 'for the first time, the legislator—influenced by the schools' directors—has given to the administration, the power to venture in the religion and freedom of conscience field, through the interpretation of religious signs'. [22] The rare case law has already provided some examples of contradictions in such interpretation. [23]

The stake is hence to know where possibly settle the boundaries between what is related to real religious beliefs and what deals with foreign cultural or social habits. By having entered the ground of religious signs interpretation, has the judge not opened a Pandora box? This assumes importance at a time in which it has become difficult to determine the right place of the legal principle of *laïcité* between secularism—mainly used in the sociological studies to describe a society where values are no longer defined by spiritual and religious bodies—and politics.

Within the above mentioned triptych defining *laïcité*, neutrality emerges as the predominant element in the sense that it could be qualified of its 'active' element. [24] Implementing the two other elements could closely depend on the right use of neutrality. Pluralism, which allows ensuring an equal treatment to all religious groups, is one of the guiding dimensions of a balanced legal framework implementation. How will the State legitimately cope with the demands of the increasing religious diversity, if it gives up, even partly, its neutral position? Moreover, what to think of a State committed to ensure the effective freedom of religion if religious practices may be held not compatible with the principle of *laïcité,* which precisely includes this freedom? And yet it is the risk run by associating this principle to public policy—meant here as the reflection of social values—which is the sole possible limit to the exercise of liberties (Prélot, 2010).

Another aspect of the way *laïcité* is currently dealt with lies in the definition provided by the Constitutional Council. According to its decision of November 19, 2004, the constitutional provisions 'forbid to anyone to invoke one's religious beliefs in order to be free from respecting the common rules, which regulate the relationships between public authorities and individuals'. It goes back to the Rousseau's conception of the political organization of society, in which no intermediate group or affiliation should stand between the citizen and the state, representing the general interest.

Even if it was not of course expressly said, nobody failed to notice that this '*anti-communautarisme*' addressed the Muslim community. The matter of concern here is the divergence with a previous legal and well accepted definition provided in particular by the Council of State (the highest Court for administrative matters), and shared by an overwhelming part of the literature in law, which makes *laïcité* a triptych: neutrality, equality/pluralism and freedom of religion. The demands of the social and political assimilation applied to persons belonging to Islam sheds light on the growing gap between both the legal and the political dimensions of *laïcité*. Not randomly stands this principle, in the heart of a discourse about what should be the national motto. It is, therefore, astonishing to see how *laïcité* has been several times defined as affiliated to the 'vivre-ensemble' ('the living together'), which belongs to the definition of what is a nation provided by Ernest Renan in his famous speech of 1882. [25]

The introduction of the values and principles, which would drag national identity into the debates about *laïcité* enlightens the case law related to nationality and could explain why it entails many examples in which 'the essential values of the national community' are opposed to 'the radical practice of religion'. On the other hand, the regular presence of such cases underlies the double process of re-politicization of *laïcité* and the intrinsic features of nationality law. Nevertheless, the principle of *laïcité* remains an easy but wrong answer.

Endnotes

1. It is expressed in French by the word *communautarisme*. Appeared less than ten years ago in the dictionaries, this word consists of a neologism derived from the English and American 'community'. It belongs to the political discourse and takes on a negative connotation. According to the general agreed meaning, *communautarisme* depicts the tendency of the new comers (or former immigrants) to join and stay in the group sharing the same origin, at the expense of the national community belonging.
2. See the parliamentary information report on behalf of the Commission about the practice of the full veil wearing on the national territory, January 26, 2010, National Assembly, n°2262, p. 93.
3. While naturalization corresponds to a discretionary decision by the State to grant–or not–nationality, the nationality by reason of marriage is a right of the applicant that the Government is entitled to oppose to, within a delay of two years (Article 21-2 of

the Civil Code).

4. Thus, named after the city where the French government settled while the French territory was a German occupation from July 1940 to August 1944.
5. Article 222-9 of the Penal Code reads that "Acts of violence causing mutilation or permanent disability are punished by ten years' imprisonment and a fine of €150,000. In fact, these provisions take aim at the practice of excision.
6. It is enough here to remind how thousands of Jews lost their French nationality just before the World War II. Concerning more precisely the Muslims, it is instructive to look back to the legal framework in force during the 'French Algeria' regime which distinguished between colonizers and Algerians. See Bozzo, Anna (2006). "Islam et citoyenneté en Algérie sous la IIIe République: logiques d'émancipation et contradictions coloniales (l'exemple des lois de 1901 et 1905)", in Luizard, Jean-Pierre (ed.) 'Le choc colonial et l'islam. Les politiques religieuses des puissances coloniales en terres d'islam', Paris: La découverte and Weil, Patrick (2002), "Qu'est-ce qu'un Français? Histoire de la nationalité française depuis la Révolution", Paris : Grasset.
7. Council of State, November 24, 1997, Monsieur Mamadou, n. 158917.
8. Administrative Court of Nantes, October 14, 2008, n. 0702875.
9. For an older case, thus illustrating a kind of continuity, see Council of State, October 14, 1998, M. Nourredine X., n. 175186: the naturalization was denied to an Algerian national and married to a French woman, since he was an active proponent of an extremist movement and advocated in the neighbourhood, particularly in the mosque of Angers, some thesis revealing a rejection of the essential values of the French society.
10. Council of State, November 19, 1997, M. Raouf X., n. 169368. See also Council of State, March 23, 1994, n. 116144.
11. Council of State, February 3, 1999, Madame X., n. 161251.
12. Administrative Court of appeal of Nantes, April 19, 2001, Monsieur X., n. 00NT00457:

    The fact that the spouse wears the veil cannot be opposed to her husband. The alleged fact that he would have imposed the wearing of the veil to his daughters at school is denied by him and is not confirmed by the elements of the file'. Taking into account the behaviour of other members of the family is *a priori* contrary to the principle of individuality of nationality, which implies an individual assessment of the file. See Council of State, September 26, 1986, Ngoc Que, n. 54518. Nevertheless, beyond the fact that this rule knows exceptions (Council of State, October 4, 2000, Madame Pham, n. 204298), it looks like the level of administrative investigation might justify taking into consideration such elements, which belong to the 'familial behaviour'. See also Olekhnovitch (1995): 383.

13. Administrative Court of Appeal of Nantes, April 11, 2003, n. 02NT01010.
14. Circular n. 2000-254 of May 12, 2000 related to naturalizations and reinstatements in French nationality and loss of French nationality.
15. The garment at issue in this judicial proceeding was not the *burqa* but the *niqab*, even if it was very often if not systematically mentioned this way.
16. From this point of view, it seems that the government's will to separate as much as possible the current bill to ban the full veil wearing and *laïcité* failed. Despite the various declarations in this sense coming, among others, from the Muslim official body (French Council of the Muslim Faith), according to which the full veil is not prescribed by the Koran, it has become difficult to maintain a distinction between Muslim religious practices and wearing the *niqab* or *burqa.*
17. See the official press release of the Ministry of Immigration, Integration, National Identity and Co-Development, 'Confirmation d'un projet de décret transmis au Premier ministre', of February 2, 2010, http://www.immigration.gouv.fr/, accessed on March 6, 2010. See also *Le Monde*, 'Besson refuse par décret de naturaliser un homme imposant le voile à sa femme', February 2, 2010. It should be noticed that the word 'naturalization' is improperly used here since this decree was passed for the acquisition of nationality by reason of declaration applicable to a man married to a French person.
18. Council of State, September 26, 1986, Ngoc Que, n. 54518.
19. Council of State, October 4, 2000, Madame Pham, n. 204298.
20. See Administrative Court of Appeal of Nantes, 19 April 2001, Monsieur X., n. 00NT00457. This case is nevertheless not

totally relevant here since the judge apparently refused to take into account the veiled daughter, because of the lack of reliability of the information.

21. Administrative Court of Appeal of Nantes, December 29, 2009, Madame Khadidja X., n. 09NT00018.
22. R. Keller (2008), "Le port d'un bandana ou d'un turban sikh dans un établissement scolaire", Conclusions sur Conseil d'Etat, 5 décembre 2007, M. et Mme Ghazal, *Revue Française Droit Administratif*, p. 529. The administrative judge took the opportunity implicitly provided by the 2004 Act to decide on the meaning of a religious sign in a case of 2007 of Ms. Ghazal. It involved a pupil who had refused to remove not her veil but a kind of headscarf called 'bandana'. It was judged that the director of the school was entitled to exclude her from the school since the bandana could be considered as a religious symbol replacing an Islamic veil. We face here a striking example of interpretation of such a sign of religious affiliation by public authority acting in the name of a secular State. It is noticeable that this tendency was also observable at the European Court of Human Rights level, especially in the criticized Dalhab case (*Dahlab v. Switzerland*, n. 42393/98, ECHR, February 15, 2001), which involved a Swiss teacher wearing the veil in the classroom.
23. While the wearing of a headscarf by a female pupil was given a religious meaning, the wig worn by a teacher for religious purpose was judged compatible with the *laïcité* of the public education. Administrative Court of Versailles, March 10, 2006, n. 0503198.
24. See, for example, how Pierre-Henri Prélot emphasizes on the neutrality, which he places at the core of the legal meaning of *laïcité*. Prélot (2006): 114 and seq.
25. Ernest Renan (2007), "Qu'est-ce qu'une nation?", Marseille : Le mot et le reste. The original texte was written in 1882.

References

Bertossi, Christophe (2007), "Les musulmans, la France, l'Europe: contre quelques faux-semblants en matière d'intégration", in 'Migrations et Citoyenneté en Europe', Paris: Institut Français des Relations Internationales (IFRI), Friedrich Ebert Stiftung, pp. 1-15.

Bowen, John R. (2006), "France's Revolt: Can the Republic Live Up to its Ideals?", *Boston Review*, January/February, pp. 29-32.

Bruschi, Christian (1996), "L'acquisition de la nationalité française à raison du marriage", in Fulchiron, Hugues (ed.) 'Etre français aujourd'hui. Premier bilan de la mise en œuvre du nouveau droit de la nationalité', Lyon : Presses universitaires de Lyon.

Council of State (2004), "Annual Report: A Century of laïcité", Paris: La documentation française.

Council of State (2010), "Review of Legal Possibilities to Ban Full Veil", Paris: La documentation française.

Dionisi-Peyrusse, Amélie (2008), "Essai sur une nouvelle conception de la nationalité", Paris: Defrénois.

Decouflé, Jean-Clément (1992), "Historic Elements of the Politics of Nationality in France", Noiriel, Gérard and Horowitz, Donald L. (ed.), 'Immigrants in Two Democracies: French and American Experiences', New York: New York University Press.

Fulchiron, Hugues (2000), "La nationalité française", Paris: Presses Universitaires de France.

Keller, Rémy (2008), "Le port d'un bandana ou d'un turban sikh dans un établissement scolaire. Conclusions sur Conseil d'Etat", 5 décembre 2007, M. et Mme Ghazal', *Revue française de droit administratif*, pp. 529-534.

Messner, Francis and Prélot, Pierre-Henri and Woehrling, Jean-Marie (eds.) (2003), "Traité de droit français des religions", Paris: Litec.

Ladeur, Karl-Heinz (2009), "The Myth of the Neutral State and the Individualization of Religion: The Relationship between State and Religion in the Face of Fundamentalism", *Cardozo Law Review*, Vol. 30, No. 6, pp. 2445-2471.

Long, Marceau (ed.) (1988), "Etre français aujourd'hui et demain. Rapport remis au Premier minister", Paris: La documentation française.

Luizard, Jean-Pierre (ed.) (2006), "Le choc colonial et l'islam: Les politiques religieuses des puissances coloniales en terres d'islam", Paris: La découverte.

Marceau Long (ed.) (1988), "Être français aujourd'hui et demain. Rapport remis au Premier minister", Paris: La documentation française.

Olekhnovitch, Georges (1995), "La notion d'assimilation au sens des dispositions du Code civil relatives à la nationalité française",

Revue critique de droit international privé, No. 4, pp. 880-896.

Prélot, Pierre-Henri (2006), "Définir juridiquement la laïcité", in Gonzalez, Gérard (ed.), 'Laïcité, liberté de religion et Convention européenne des droits de l'homme', Bruxelles: Bruylant.

Renan, Ernest (2007), "Qu'est-ce qu'une nation?", Marseille: Le mot et le reste.

Sen, Amartya (2005), "Argumentative India: Writings on Indian Culture, History and Identity", London: Allen Lane/Penguin.

Weil, Patrick (2002), "Qu'est-ce qu'un Français? Histoire de la nationalité française depuis la Révolution", Paris: Grasset.

Zeghbib, Hocine (2005), "Identité et nationalité: les ambivalences du droit", in Zeghbib, Hocine (ed.), 'Être étranger en Europe du Sud', Aix-en-Provence: Édisud.

10

Protecting Muslim Minorities in the Work Place: Europe and India [1]

Katayoun Alidadi

Introduction

Employment is far more than a means of subsistence; it is recognized as a vital driver of social integration. [2] What's more, what one does for a living is a central feature of personal identity.

In today's work place, religion manifests itself in a myriad of ways, as workers are increasingly asserting recognition of their religious identities as employees. For policy makers, this presents a challenge. Should they hold on to the existing normative framework and for the most part refuse to accommodate religious claims? Or should they accept that societal changes call for a 'deconstruction' of the framework to a certain extent? [3] In fact, this dilemma is said to be 'so challenging to many polities precisely because it reflects a style of religious commitment that contradicts the norms of secularization'. [4]

For many believers, the issue seems to be how to reconcile demands of the work place with their religious duties, thus the premise being that work and religion are in competition if not in contradiction. In the current market paradigm, the worker is equated with 'human capital', a resource in the production process subject to matching managerial techniques. [5] In this conception, religion is a fish out of water in the work place. However, this has not always been the case and for a long time work itself was attributed a religious quality. [6] Relations between work and religion in the Western conception of work have transformed, and in fact switched into opposites at the beginning of the modern era.

Relatively recent Muslim minorities in Europe have gained large visibility and have presented the above dilemma for policy makers. India, with its longstanding religious and cultural diversity, is similarly confronted with claims from its Muslim religious minority.

Muslims have played a role throughout India's history and to that extent differ greatly from Muslims in the West, most of whom are relatively recent immigrants. Nonetheless, Muslim participation in the workforce has been shown to be problematic in both Europe and India. For instance, it is well-known that Muslims in Belgium, most of them immigrants, are disadvantaged in particular when it comes to employment. The Sachar Report has re-revealed that Muslim Indians have in various respects been deprived compared to other socio-religious communities in India, [7] and remain excluded from the reservations for scheduled castes based on the theory that Islam as a religion does not know castes. [8]

This explains the need for effective remedial measures in the work place to protect Muslims against the discriminations they face today as well as to uplift them as compensation for past systematic disadvantages. An adequate system of minority protection is said to be based on two pillars: [9] the first being non-discrimination in combination with the relevant human right(s), here religion, but also ethnicity, race and even language (as these intersect and overlap with religion to a large extent), and the second being specific rights to protect and promote minority identity. [10] Adopted measures can differ substantially from nation to nation depending on the concrete background and social dilemmas, but a comparative examination is helpful to open up horizons.

Muslims in Europe and India

Muslims in Europe: Immigrants Facing Employment Challenges: There are some 31 million Muslims in Europe (50 countries and territories), making up 5.2 percent of Europe's total population. [11] While Muslims in Western Europe are mostly relatively recent immigrants (or their offsprings), Muslims in Russia, Albania (80 percent), Kosovo (90 percent), Bosnia-Herzegovina (40 percent) and Bulgaria are indigenous. This means that 6 in 10 European Muslims are indigenous. Russia has the largest Muslim population of 16 million, and in fact most European Muslims live in Eastern and Central Europe. In Western Europe, Germany is home to an impressive 4 million Muslims. France has a higher percentage of Muslims but an overall lower number. [12]

By and large, the diverse minority Muslim presence in Europe today is a result of subsequent immigration waves after the Second World War. For the first time in history, Muslims as a substantial minority migrated to non-Muslim countries and set up house in search of better prospects for themselves and their children. [13]

It is estimated that between 350,000 and 400,000 Muslims live in Belgium. [14] Most Muslims in Belgium are of Moroccan, Turkish and Algerian origin. [15] There is no clarity as far as the actual self-identified number of Muslims because the Belgian Census does not measure religious adherence. The Belgian Census does distinguish between Belgians and individuals holding a different nationality, but this is not an apt way to determine the number of Muslims as many of them have obtained the Belgian nationality, enabled through increasingly flexible nationality legislation since 1984. [16] It is sure that Islam is the second largest religion in a historically and still predominantly Catholic country. [17]

The socio-economic situation of Muslims in Belgium is problematic, with Islam [18] being present especially amongst disadvantaged communities in urban areas. [19] 'The automatic association of ethnicity, Islam and poverty was widespread in Europe long before September 11, just as was the resurgence of xenophobia and race-oriented nationalism'. [20]

Compared to the local population, the immigrant population has a lower participation and employment level.

[21] A disproportionately high percentage of immigrants are unemployed in Belgium and it takes longer for them to find work. Significantly, 38 percent of Turks and Moroccans and 29 percent of 'other non-Europeans' living in Belgium were unemployed. This is in contrast to 7 percent of the local population and 12 percent of the Europeans. [22] According to a more recent data, the labour market participation rate of Moroccan and Turks at 29 percent shows a worrisome gap compared to 65 percent of autochthonous Belgians. [23]

The employment level of women with foreign nationalities on the Belgian labour market is extremely low: less than 40 percent compared to almost 60 percent for Belgian women. [24] Turks and Moroccans are over-represented in the lowest echelons of the labour market. Most are employed in trade, restaurant business and construction, conducting manual labour under temporary contracts. [25] But even higher skilled immigrants have a higher chance of being unemployed. [26] They are less employed in the service sector. [27]

Belgium is hardly exceptional in this regard. In the UK, the ethnic minority population has a higher unemployment rate than the white population, with recession periods disproportionately affecting them. [28] In France, the unemployment rate for young second-generation Moroccan and Algerian immigrants is twice the national average (40 percent as opposed to 20 percent). [29] As a general trend, Muslim immigrants are forced into less-skilled, unstable and low-paying jobs.

Muslim in India: Sparkling Bleak Prospects: India, with just under 161 million Muslims, is home to the third-largest population of Muslims worldwide. [30] Based on the 2001 Indian Census with self-identification, this makes for 13.4 percent of India's population. [31] Uttar Pradesh alone has more than 30 million Muslims, and in Kashmir, the Muslims are in a majority. International migration plays only a minor role in the growth of the Muslim Indian population. [32]

Under the influence of the Hindu caste system, the Muslim community in India developed social stratification and was internally sub-divided into four groups, often placed in two large categories of 'ashraf', meaning noble, and 'ajlaf' or 'degraded and unholy'. A third category, the 'arzal' or the very lowest classes of Muslims, was counted in the 1901 Census. [33] 'The ashraf are those without any social disabilities, the ajlaf are akin to OBCs among Hindus while the arzals are the 'very lowest castes', equivalent of SCs among Hindus'. [34]

While the dismal status of European Muslims has been well-documented, [35] the public perception on the socio-economic position of Muslim Indians was more confounded because of the iconic successful Muslims in Indian society. [36]

The Sachar Report established a literacy level far below the national average, the highest school drop-out rates, and great under-representation in the premier colleges of India. [37] It comes to no surprise then that employment participation is low to extremely low, both in regular jobs as well as in the management and professional cadre. [38] Their share in Indian government [39] is 'abysmally low' at all levels compared to their population share while 'in a pluralistic society a reasonable representation of various communities in government sector employment is necessary to enhance participatory governance'. [40] The fact that unemployment rate amongst the Muslim graduates is the highest of all socio-religious communities is disconcerting. [41]

In the Sachar Report, the socio-economic position on millions of Muslims in India appears to be to be 'abhorrent', indicating at least that India's minority protection has failed to ensure the advancement of its largest minority group. [42]

In the employment field, it found Muslim regular workers to be the most vulnerable with no written contract and social security benefits. As we saw above, Muslim immigrants in Belgium, with only temporary contracts and low-paid jobs, often also see themselves forced in arrangements with little job security. Muslim Indians receive lower daily earnings in both public and private jobs compared to other socio-religious communities, and a large number of Muslim workers are engaged in self-employment and street vending and, in the case of Muslim women, in home based work—all situations with little economic security. [43] The living standards of Muslims are low with substantial portion of families in urban settings living in one-room accommodations.

The Committee dubbed its findings 'a shocking testimony to six decades of institutional neglect and bias', [44] exemplified by a clear and significant inverse correlation between the proportion of the Muslim population and the availability of educational infrastructure (pp. 141-143) and banking facilities in small villages. [45]

There were several earlier qualitative reports that highlighted the dismal socio-economic state of much of India's Muslim population and called for urgent remedial measures. [46] The importance of the Sachar Report thus lies in the fact that it rang the alarm bell once again and reintroduced the plight of Muslims in the public eye and in all levels of politics. [47]

Muslim Minority Protection: From Formal to Substantive Equality

In the absence of a generally agreed upon legal definition of 'minority', it is accepted that it requires 'stable ethnic, religious or linguistic characteristics which are different from the rest of the population, a numerical minority position, non-dominance and the wish to preserve the own, separate cultural identity'. [48]

Muslims in Europe as well as in India are clearly a numerical minority and certainly not socio-economically dominant as illustrated above by the various reports raising concerns about their advancement in the work place. Notwithstanding internal differences within the communities among others with regard to origin and degrees of religious adherence, stable religious characteristics set them apart from the majority. The wish to preserve separate cultural identity is expressed on several occasions, and has been the source of tension. Thus, Muslims in Europe and in India constitute a 'minority' in the legal sense of the term, meriting protection both in the form of anti-discrimination provisions as well as specific measures in favour of preservation of their identity as a group.

Both Belgium and India have ratified the International Labour Organisation's 1958 Discrimination (Employment and Occupation) Convention nr. 111, [49] and thus agreed to 'pursue a national policy designed to promote, by methods appropriate to national conditions and practice, equality of opportunity and treatment in respect of employment and occupation, with a view to eliminating any discrimination'. [50]

Europe has focused on the first pillar of anti-discrimination to realize equality of opportunities for all, including Muslim workers, and to a certain extent opened up to substantive equality through a widening construal of the concept of discrimination. The focus on anti-discrimination fits within the tradition of protecting individual rights and liberties. However, when it comes to positive action schemes, Europe has exhibited hesitations and second thoughts.

In contrast, India has set up an extensive reservation program in educational facilities and government employment, which aims to facilitate—to a certain extent—social mobility of historically disadvantaged groups. Unfortunately, the reservation program that was created as a temporary measure 65 years ago to address the dismal position and protection of India's most vulnerable classes today has become a politicized battlefield. Today, supporters of reservations want to implement similar schemes in private employment. However, the minority protection possibilities provided by effective anti-discrimination legislation are often untapped.

Protection and Advancement in the Work Place in Europe

Anti-discrimination under the EU Race and Employment Equality Directives: Several international instruments to which European member states have acceded include the principle of non-discrimination and equality before the law. [51]

Initially, the EC treaty contained no general prohibition of discrimination as the European Union project was primarily concerned with setting up of a common market. [52] However, the EU institutions have increasingly moved towards a human rights perspective, with EC (now EU) equality and non-discrimination law developing throughout the years. In 1997, Article 13 was inserted in the EC Treaty (now Article 19 of the consolidated version of the EU Treaty), [53] empowering the Council to 'take appropriate action to combat discrimination based on sex, racial or ethnic origin, religion or belief, disability, age or sexual orientation'. The Council has adopted three directives thus far on basis of Article 13 (the so-called 'Article 13 Directives'). These are the Race Directive, [54] the Employment Equality Directive (also called the General Framework Directive), [55] and the Equal Treatment Directive. [56]

For our purposes, the Race Directive and the Employment Equality Directive carry particular importance. Both Directives set minimum standards [57] and allow member states to go beyond and provide greater protection. The concrete provisions will thus depend on the implementation by individual member state. Similarly, in Europe there is a wide divergence with regard to positive measures as the Directives do not mandate but only allow for such measures to be taken. With regard to proactive measures to increase the participation of its minority religious community in the work sphere, Northern Ireland has played a vanguard role.

The Race Directive prohibits four types of discrimination, namely direct discrimination, indirect discrimination, harassment and instructions to discriminate on grounds of racial [58] or ethnic origin.

The distinction between direct and indirect discrimination, which does not appear in the EU Treaty itself, has been developed by the European Court of Justice through its case-law since the 1960s. [59] That distinction, created to enhance the effectiveness of the legal framework, has become a cornerstone of EU anti-discrimination law. [60]

Under both the Directives, the principle of equal treatment equals the lack of direct and indirect discrimination. [61] There is direct discrimination when 'one person is treated less favourably than another...in a comparable situation' and the grounds for the distinct treatment is race or ethnicity. [62] Direct discrimination cannot be justified, but when the conditions for 'genuine and determining occupational requirements' are met, the difference in treatment does not constitute direct discrimination. [63] Occupational requirements must relate to the nature of the work or the context in which the work is carried out, but the objective must be legitimate and there is also a proportionality test.

An example of difference of treatment on basis of race/ethnicity not constituting discrimination could be an employer looking for actors with dark skin tone for a commercial on promoting diversity. [64]

Indirect discrimination is a more complex term. Certain rules, requirements or practices may appear neutral, i.e. they do not treat individuals different on basis of race or ethnicity, but in effect individuals of a certain ethnicity are disadvantaged by the operation of that rule, requirement or practice. [65] For instance, a job posting in Belgium could require applicants to have Dutch as their 'mother tongue' or be 'native speakers'. [66] While a Moroccan man is not formally treated different than a Belgian job seeker, in the sense that the same requirement applies irrespective of race or ethnic origin, it is clear that it is much more likely that this requirement disqualifies Moroccans. Even if the job seeker was born, raised and schooled in Belgium, he might have another native tongue.

The concept of indirect discrimination has been a vital tool in combating structural discrimination and promoting equality of opportunity. However, much depends on the application of the proportionality assessment in the justification test.

Indirect discrimination can be justified by fulfilling a three-prong test that the Court of Justice had developed in its 1986 landmark judgment, BILKA, in the context of gender discrimination. [67] Once infringement is established (i.e. it is proven that a rule affects a certain group in a far greater way), the respondent needs to prove that the rule is based on 'objectively justified factors unrelated to any discrimination on the [particular protected discrimination] ground'. [68] In the BILKA judgment, the challenged company decision was made because of economic reasons. Determining whether 'the measures chosen...correspond to a real need on the part of the undertaking, are appropriate with a view to achieving the objectives pursued and are necessary to that end', and thus that there was any infringement, was to be left up to the national court. [69]

In our example above, the quest for a 'native speaker' is not justified. Even if language would be an important qualification for the job, non-native speakers can be fluent in Dutch. Thus, the requirement is not necessary to achieve the goal of smooth communication with clients. [70]

Further, harassment and instructions to discriminate also are covered under the prohibition of non-discrimination. [71]

The scope of the Race Directive is broad and recognizes that discrimination at work comes in various forms. Besides lack of opportunity in getting jobs at the recruitment and selection stage, [72] there are barriers to education and training opportunities that set ethnic minorities back. [73] Racial and ethnic origin discrimination is prohibited in relation to: (a) conditions for access to [public and private] employment, to self-employment and to occupation, including selection criteria and recruitment conditions, whatever the branch of activity and at all levels of the professional hierarchy, including promotion; (b) access to all types and to all levels of vocational guidance, vocational training, advanced vocational training and retraining, including practical work experience; (c) employment and working conditions, including dismissals and pay; (d) membership of and involvement in an organisation of workers or employers, or any organisation whose members carry on a particular profession, including the benefits provided for by such organisations; [74]

Besides the employment field, the Race Directive also covers education, social protection including social security and healthcare, social advantages and access to and supply of goods and services, including housing. [75]

The Employment Equality Directive differs from the Race Directive in two main respects: the protected grounds are different and the scope of application is more limited. The Employment Equality Directive sets a framework for combating direct and indirect discrimination on the grounds of religion or belief, disability, age or sexual orientation in the employment setting alone. [76] This means that while ethnic and racial discrimination are prohibited in a wide array of settings, like housing, healthcare and services, only religious discrimination in the work place and related settings is envisaged.

This must be qualified. First, member states can go beyond the common denominator, which is the Directive. For instance, Belgium has expanded the scope of application for religious discrimination to the same scope as racial and ethnic discrimination, making religious discrimination to the same extent actionable. [77]

Second, there is a close interconnection between ethnicity and religion. With most Muslims in Europe being of North-African or Turkish descent, religion is closely intertwined with and hard to separate from race and ethnic origin so that even in member states where religious discrimination has a limited scope of protection, there is the option to proceed on another basis.

The fact that protection from discrimination on basis of religion or belief is confined to the employment field in the Directive, in contrast to what is the case with racism, has been criticized as being 'illogical' considering the move in EC law from a market integration model of social policy to one based on social citizenship. [78] The European Commission on its end has proposed a new directive that would enlarge the scope of the Employment Equality Directive. [79]

In EU anti-discrimination law, an opening towards

substantive equality can be found in the concept of indirect discrimination. One concept closely related to indirect discrimination, and highly relevant to religious minorities, is that of reasonable accommodations. Reasonable accommodations can be considered a modality of the right to equality and non-discrimination. [80] Developed as a corollary of the prohibition of indirect discrimination, the reasonable accommodation concept finds its original and most prolific base in the work place. [81]

The Employment Equality Directive foresees reasonable accommodations for disabled individuals, but not religious accommodations in the work place. In the US, where reasonable accommodations originated, reasonable accommodations were initially adopted in the work place for religious minorities under Title VII of the Civil Rights Act of 1964, and later extended to disability accommodations under the Americans Against Disabilities Act. [82] For the time being, Europe has decided to introduce one protective innovation at a time, starting with the less controversial one since accepting religion-driven reasonable accommodations (and thus actively facilitating and promoting integration in the work force) requires a significant switch of mentality compared to widely accepted non-discrimination principles.

Nonetheless, it is clear that reasonable accommodations in the work place in Europe can be a vehicle for progress in the European work place where many work place laws, regulations, company policies and customs are based on the dominant Christian calendar, dress codes and traditions. A number of countries in Europe have decided to extend reasonable accommodations for religious reasons, going beyond the Directives. [83]

At this time, the Commission is financing a research project entitled 'RELIGARE-Religious Diversity and Secular Models in Europe: Innovative Approaches to Law and Policy', led by the Catholic University Leuven, to examine how the EU, in the midst of expansion and migration fluxes, should deal with claims for recognition of religious identity in family life, work place, public space and financing of churches. [84]

With anti-discrimination legislation, there is a legitimate concern that provisions will remain dead language. As, in practice, discrimination is often difficult to prove and to penalise, specific rules seek to facilitate and promote its enforceability. Member States need to 'provide for effective, proportionate and dissuasive sanctions' and 'adequate judicial protection against victimization'.

Still, if enforcement remains solely in the hands of the victims, who rarely have the time, money and motivation to pursue legal action, clearing legal hurdles might still not do the trick. That is why under Article 13 of the Race Directive, member states must designate an agency ('a body for the promotion of equal treatment of all persons'), possibly in addition to associations, trade unions and other bodies, to provide independent assistance to discrimination victims, to legally pursue a claim on behalf of the victims, to conduct country surveys on discrimination, and to publish reports and make recommendations.

In Belgium, the Centre for Equal Opportunities and Opposition to Racism was given this role and has frequently taken legal action on behalf of victims against perpetrators of discrimination, providing a real impulse to the build-up of relevant case law. [85]

Positive Action in Europe: Controversial and Restricted

The aim of the EU Directives is to provide a fair playing field and thereby increase efficiency in the work place. The Employment Equality Directive clarifies that in any case it 'does not require the recruitment, promotion, maintenance in employment or training of an individual who is not competent, capable and available to perform the essential functions of the post concerned or to undergo the relevant training...' [86]

The question is whether legal tools as anti-discrimination legislation in practice create more opportunities for minorities and thus will result in a diversified work place. Or, on the contrary, whether we should accept that normal market principles do not operate effectively in this context, so that 'special measures' are indispensable to lend a helping hand to disadvantaged groups.

Despite the fragility and dangers of positive action, it can be argued that anti-discrimination is simply not enough, and various data suggests the limits of an 'equal playing field'. Studies have shown discriminatory practices in both private and public sector, but often discrimination is unapparent or even unconscious. [87] Negative stereotypes held by managers in charge of the selection process will disadvantage minorities. [88] Research on discrimination in the labour market traditionally looks at explicitly subjective attitudes and stereotypes of employers, but more recent research wants to gain insight in implicit prejudices which can lead to discriminatory attitudes among employers. Covert experiments on racial discrimination where identical resumes from two fictive candidates (one white, another a minority candidate) are sent to hiring companies shows the discrimination at the recruitment level. [89]

A recent Swedish study [90] found that employers clearly have more negative attitudes towards Arab-Muslim men as they have towards obese individuals, and that they associate both Muslims and obese people with a lower work performance. The parallel between Islam and obesity is an interesting metaphor as it indicates that Muslims carry a certain weight with them that somehow makes them less efficient and less valuable as employees. This type of research shows that Muslim job applicants are facing particular disadvantages in the recruitment processes as they have to fight the potential prejudices an interviewer might have. Stereotypes and implicit assumptions about Muslims thus operate on a subconscious level that anti-discrimination as a legal tool is unable to stand against.

Within the EU legal framework, member states are not obliged to proactively take positive measures but positive action is allowed within certain limits. The Directives state that 'with a view to ensuring full equality in practice, the principle of equal treatment shall not prevent any Member State from maintaining or adopting specific measures to prevent or compensate for disadvantages'. [91]

There has only been case law from the European Court of Justice on positive action with regard to gender discrimination. From that case law, it appears that positive actions, 'as a derogation from an individual right', are interpreted strictly. [92] The European Court of Justice has rejected positive action schemes (based on gender), which through automatisms at the selection stage lead to 'equal results'. [93] What is allowed, however, are quota prior to the point of employment selection. [94] Positive actions at the time of selections have to be 'flexible in nature and guarantee an objective and individual assessment of all candidates'. [95]

As said, when it comes to positive action, Northern Ireland has played a vanguard role. Northern Ireland's Fair Employment (Northern Ireland) Act (FEA), 1989 is considered an example of a good positive action practice in Europe. A report for the British Department of Work and Pensions authored by, among others, Tariq Modood, reviewing some positive action examples in the EU and North America, reads: 'The developments in Northern Ireland suggest that the introduction of proactive equality instruments accompanied by the political will to bring about social change can have an observable impact on employment equity...may be particularly pertinent for Britain...when many Muslims...complain of religious discrimination, when the most disadvantaged groups in the labour market are Muslims...'. [96]

It should be noted that the Employment Equality Directive contains specific provisions covering North Ireland's particular situation, specifying that differences in treatment in the police services 'shall not constitute discrimination insofar as those differences in treatment are expressly authorised by national legislation', and that 'the provisions on religion or belief in this Directive shall not apply to the recruitment teachers in schools in Northern Ireland insofar as this is expressly authorised by national legislation regards the recruitment of school teachers'. [97]

Based on the wording, these provisions suggest that the differences in recruitment treatment in Northern Ireland based on religion of applicants in the absence of an exemption would run counter to EU anti-discrimination principles. Thus, other member states would not be able to, let alone be encouraged to, take on similar measures in the absence of historical division between religious communities.

The EU anti-discrimination framework is more than a proclamation of equal opportunities, especially considering the potentials of the notion of indirect discrimination, which is a cornerstone of the system. However, in order to achieve social equity, EU has not gone so far as to oblige member states to institute better treatment for certain groups. Lastly, the EU is arguably moving towards a more proactive equality policy, e.g. the broad mainstreaming provision in the EU Treaty indicates that policy makers need to make equality a priority throughout EU initiatives. [98]

Compensatory Discrimination in the Indian Work Place

Derived from a Constitutional Mandate: Under the traditional Indian caste system, an individual was equated with the type of work assigned to him. [99] The caste structure of Hindu society divided people in distinct birth groups of individuals in particular occupation(s) with particular rules of behaviour. While there are thousands of castes and sub-castes, the population is traditionally divided into 4 hierarchical groups: [100] the Brahmins (originally the priests), the Kshatriyas (the warriors), Vaishyas (tradesmen) and the Shudras (servants and artisans). The casteless, the Dalits, find themselves in an extremely vulnerable position with no possibility for upward mobility, which explains that issues of integration and accommodation in professional positions were unknown.

In an attempt to deal with the legacy of the Indian caste

system, India's central and state governments on basis of a Constitutional mandate have adopted 'one of the most comprehensive affirmative action programmes'. [101] A percentage of posts, not exceeding 50 percent as per the Supreme Court of India, [102] in civil service, the public sector, and state and private educational institutions (except the minority institutions), is reserved for so-called backward communities and the scheduled castes and tribes ('OBCs,' 'SCs/STs'). Entrance (and sometimes promotion) requirements are relaxed in different ways for individuals who prove [103] they belong to one of these administrative categories, [104] with still large numbers of backlog vacancies. [105]

It should be noted that even though the Constitution aimed to dismantle the caste system, [106] it instead created new categories through the reservation system for scheduled castes (SCs), scheduled tribes (STs) and other backwards classes (OBCs). The categories have been defined and understood more or less along the same lines of the old castes. This has brought 'casteism' to the forefront. Consequently, caste-related issues have continued to dominate the limelight even after 65 years of India's independence. [107]

The Sachar Report raised once again the sensitive issue of reservations for Muslims. [108] Muslims are disqualified from the reservation schemes set up for SCs, but not for STs and OBCs. In what follows, we will focus on reservations for scheduled castes. [109]

Fight for Inclusion in Reservations for Scheduled Castes

The Sachar Report falls short of explicitly recommending the extension of the SC reservations to Muslims, but it did recommend that 'anomalies' in the reservation constituencies be addressed to equalize minority communities with similar social and occupational status. [110]

Reservations, also referred to as 'compensatory discrimination' or quota, are a form of affirmative action under Indian law for the benefit of historically oppressed groups with the aim to give a fair representation to the weaker sections of the society in legislative assemblies, educational institutions and public employment. As explained, reservations are constitutionally enshrined and seek to address India's historic societal and occupational segregation.

A percentage of open positions in assemblies, educational institutes and civil service are reserved for the particular beneficiary group, although it is not guaranteed that seats will be filled. [111] Reservations also apply to job promotions. [112] Educational reservations under Indian law clearly go much further than controversial affirmative action programs in the admission policies of American colleges and universities. [113]

Reservations in India, similar to positive action in Europe, frequently evoke adverse sentiment. The issue, especially with regard to university spots, has repeatedly mobilized protesters. [114].

The Constitution foresees the reservation of seats in the central and state legislative bodies, [115] urges reservations in educational institutions, [116] and mandates reservations in state and central civil service for scheduled castes. [117] The term 'scheduled caste' is an administrative euphemism for sub-castes collectively referred to as Dalits, [118] who are the most marginalized segment of India's population.

Article 341 of the Constitution states that the President may, by public notification, specify the 'castes, races or tribes or part of or groups within castes, races or tribes', which shall be deemed SC in relation to a particular State. The Government has done this through the Constitution (Scheduled Castes) Order, 1950 (C.O. 19), which lists hundreds of castes per state and territory.

The Constitution Order, in its 3rd paragraph, states: 'Notwithstanding anything contained in paragraph 2, no person who professes a religion different from the Hindu, the Sikh or the Buddhist religion shall be deemed to be a member of a scheduled caste'.

The initial text did not include the Sikh and the Buddhist

religions; those were added in 1956 and 1990 respectively. This practically means that Muslim or Christian [119] Dalits are excluded from the SC reservations, and conversion to Christianity or Islam legally disqualifies Dalits from the benefits of reservation for scheduled castes. Understandably, this has caused a lot of uproar, especially after the Sachar Report corroborated on the abominable socio-economic position of Muslim Indians. [120]

Currently, there are 15 percent reservations for SCs in public sector employment and higher education. The issue is not just whether Muslim and Christian Dalits must receive a piece of the pie, but also whether that pie itself should be enlarged.

The Sachar Committee suggested that it will be 'most appropriate' to absorb the lowest category 'arzal' Muslims [121] suffering maximum social deprivations, among the scheduled castes by amending the Constitutional Order and bringing Dalits of all the religions under one umbrella. Since previous attempts to include other Dalits in the list of scheduled castes had failed, [122] the Government appointed a Commission with Indian Justice Ranganath Mishra as the chair to specifically look into this issue.

Recently, the Mishra Commission similarly recommended to 'de-link the scheduled caste status from religion and make the scheduled caste net fully religion-neutral like that of the scheduled tribes', arguing that 'caste is in fact a social phenomenon shared by almost all Indian communities irrespective of their religious persuasion. Many of the particular castes are found simultaneously in various religious communities—equally facing problems of social degradation and mistreatment both by their co-religionists and the others'. [123]

The position of the National Minority Council (NMC) is also that Muslim Dalits should for 'moral, logical, empirical and practical' reasons be included in the reservation scheme for SCs/STs. [124] A sociological study commissioned by the NMC had found that 'Muslim and Christian Dalits are continuously discriminated against and excluded, and the intense social humiliation they face differs from those faced by their counterparts in other religions. The same is the position of the National Commission for Scheduled Castes (NCSC).

Nonetheless, paragraph 3 of the Constitutional Order, 1950 remains in effect at the Central level, [125] with the issue currently under review before the Supreme Court of India. [126]

Zoya Hasan, a Professor at the Jawaharlal Nehru University, points to three main reasons why Muslims were initially excluded from the reservations for SCs. First, it was said it would jeopardize secularism. Second, it was said that since there was no parallel caste system amongst Muslims there was no similar basis of oppression and discrimination to justify special measures. Third, the argument was advanced that national unity would be put at risk, reminiscent of the partition with Pakistan. [127]

She also notes that 'reservations ultimately were a casualty of Partition'. While the British had separate representation provisions for Muslims in various legislative bodies, the Constituent Assembly rejected the idea of continuing reservations for Muslims. The terms scheduled castes and scheduled tribes were 'renegotiated and redefined', and religious minorities were excluded because unlike lower castes they were not seen as part of the Hindu community. [128]

Hasan argues that it is thus social discrimination of a group within the Hindu caste system rather than the concept of 'minority' that is the legitimate drive for affirmative action programs in India. Conservation and promotion of cultural diversity of minorities is seen as a separate sphere from the justice and equity sphere of affirmative action.

Nonetheless, adherents of the two other religions born in India, Sikhs and Buddhists were successful in advocating the inclusion in the reservations scheme in 1956 and 1990. These inclusions have also rendered the argument for exclusion of Muslim and Christian Dalits, which is contradicted by reality,

[129] internally inconsistent as the Sikh and Buddhist religions, in theory at least, do not know castes either.

It has been said that opening reservations for Dalit Muslims [130] would encourage conversions. Even if this were true, that would raise highly problematic issue as it would involve a government policy entangling in religion by restricting the freedom of religion, which should be understood to include the freedom to change religions.

Paragraph 3 thus not only seems to violate the freedom of religion and non-discrimination on basis of religion clauses of the Indian Constitution, [131] but also several international instruments [132] that India has committed itself to.

What has perhaps confused the debate is that some Muslim groups have advocated for the whole Muslim population to be included in the SC category. While the 'Muslim community' as a whole could be a relevant group meriting certain forms of minority protection (e.g. cultural, non-discrimination) in the face of inter-group inequalities, for measures such as reservations, it will be justified to only extend those benefits to a sub-group determined by a mix of social and economic factors.

Hasan argues that Muslims should not seek quota for the whole Muslim community, [133] even if there is a fear that 'unless Muslims get on the backwardness platform, they would have to compete for a diminishing proportion of unreserved seats with the larger pool of Hindu upper castes', because governments are willing to extend reservations to Muslims on the basis of caste, but not religion. Understandably, Muslim Dalits are opposed to including the entire Muslim community as they fear the elites of that community would monopolize the benefits of government jobs. If the goal is to create real opportunities for upward social mobility, it is imperative to come up with adequate cross-sections that fit within the logic of the existing reservations structure as well.

The public opinion in India is divided on reservation. Interestingly, opponents have argued that reservations or a separate quota for Muslims in employment were just a means to achieve formal or identical equality, while the aim should be 'substantive equal outcome', while others argued that good educational facilities combined with non-discriminatory practices are adequate for Muslims to compete in regular admission competitions. Proponents differ in opinion as to which group of Muslims—only Dalit Muslims or every Muslim—should benefit from the SC reservations. [134]

The Indian example shows challenges and sensitivity in delineating affirmative action to the appropriate beneficiary groups. The issue regarding the constituencies benefiting from the reservations has been tumultuous with many groups organizing to get a piece of the pie. Ironically, it has been stated that India is the 'only nation in the world where people fight to be called backward rather than forward'. [135] This is the contradictory effect of the overreaching of positive action on Indian society; instead of being a temporary measure that ends when the emancipation of the historically disadvantaged portion is at a reasonable level, reservations have found secondary purpose on election platforms and have been repeatedly abused by politically influential castes to the detriment of those genuinely indigent. [136]

Conclusion

Recognizing the need to integrate workers from diverse religious backgrounds in the work place, for fairness, political, economic and national reasons, [137] various initiatives such as anti-discrimination legislation, affirmative action and reasonable accommodations related to the work place seek to empower disadvantaged sections of the workforce, increase proportional participation and even appease minorities.

Adequate minority protection presents the uncomfortable dilemma of equal rights versus special rights. Europe, with its aim to realize equal opportunities for all in the work place, has mainly adhered to non-discrimination. India's reservation scheme is a prime example of awarding special rights to minorities. Reservation schemes in India were not designed for religious minorities but rather to eradicate the backwardness of historically social and economically disadvantaged groups such as the Dalits under the administrative front of scheduled castes. What's more, the most vulnerable Indian Muslims have been excluded from reservations from the scheduled caste category and are now struggling to clasp their fair share, similar to what Sikhs and Buddhists have obtained.

In Indian politics, with a discourse gravitating between delineation on basis of caste and on basis of religion, affiliation to Islam seems to be a disadvantage. The issues of Dalits and Muslims in India each bring about a particular time sensitive and dynamic discourse to the political arena by appealing to the caste theme.

With historic, cultural and political backgrounds so divergent, it is not surprising that different routes have been taken to protect minorities, in general, and religious minorities, in particular, in the work place. Policies cannot be severed from their backgrounds and in order to be effective they require some level of approval by the constituency. The media plays an important role in the process, and societal reactions will sooner or later have to be dealt with. Still, there is room for the law to be innovative, advancing and emancipating. Law is not only the reflection of what the society accepts at a given time but also what that society should aspire to be. In the end, how a society treats its vulnerable groups reveals a great deal about a state project.

Endnotes

1. An altered version of this article was published previously as: 'Opening Doors to Muslim Minorities in the Workplace? From India's Employment Quota to EU and Belgian Anti-Discrimination Legislation', *Pace International Law Review*, 146, (2011).
2. See Council Directive 2000/78/EC, (preamble consideration) (9) (Employment and occupation are key elements in guaranteeing equal opportunities for all and contribute strongly to the full

participation of citizens in economic, cultural and social life and to realizing their potential).

3. Alain Supiot, *Orare/Laborare*, 30 Comp. Lab. L. and POL.'Y J. 641, at 652, referring to the US Supreme Court in Reynolds vs. US, 98 U.S. 145, 166-67 (1878); (Can a man excuse his practices to the contrary because of his religious belief? To permit this would be to make the professed doctrines of religious belief superior to the law of the land, and in effect, to permit every citizen to become a law unto himself. Government could exist only in name in such circumstances).
4. Kenneth D. Wald, "Religion and the Workplace: A Social Science Perspective", 30 COMP. LAB. L. and POL.'Y J. 471, at 474.
5. Supiot, supra, at 649.
6. Supiot, supra, at 641.
7. Prime Minister's High Level Committee, Cabinet Secretariat, Government of India, Social, Economic and Educational Status of the Muslim Community of India: A Report, 237 (November 2006), (hereafter 'Sachar Report').
8. Besides the fact that this is not the reality in India, there are several other problems with this reasoning and its consistency within the reservations framework, see Infra.
9. Kristin Henrard (2009), "Minorities and Socio-economic Participation: The Two Pillars of Minority Protection Revisited", *International Journal on Minority and Group Rights,* 16, 549-576.
10. See Kristin Henrard, "Equal Rights versus Special Rights? Minority Protection and the Prohibition of Discrimination 14", EU Publications, European Network of Legal Experts in the Non-Discrimination Field, 2007, (referring to inter alia F. Benoit-Rohmer, 'The Minority Question in Europe: Towards a Coherent System of Protection of National Minorities', 16; Henrard, 'Devising an Adequate System of Minority Protection' (...), 8-11; Pentassuglia, Minorities in International Law, Council of Europe, 2002, 91-93.
11. The Pew Research Centre Forum on Religion and Public Life, Mapping the Global Muslim Population: A Report on the Size and Distribution of the World's Muslim Population, October 2009, (hereafter Pew Research Study), available at: http://pewforum.org/docs/?DocID=450.

12. Pew Research Study, p. 21, estimate between 3 and 4 million Muslims in France based on recent immigration data and a 2005 Generations and Gender Survey projected forward to 2009.
13. See, Olivier Roy (2003), "De Globalisering Van De Islam", 53.
14. The Belgian government relied on a 350,000 figure for the purpose of the first election of a representative organ for the Muslim community in Belgium, available at: http://www.kuleuven.ac.be/icrs/religies/wr_eng_islam.htm. The 400,000 figure was issued by the King Baudouin Foundation. The Pew Research Study estimated it to be home to about 281,000 Muslims, constituting 3 percent of its population. The estimate was based on European Social Survey, 2006 and not on census information; the small sample size of this source make estimates less reliable, so number could be over or underestimated.
15. See more elaborately, Katayoun Alidadi, "The Western Judicial Answer to Islamic Talaq: Peeking through the Gate of Conflict of Laws in the U.S. and Belgium", 5 Ucla Jinel 1, at 15-16; Jocelyn Cesari, "The Securitization of Islam in Europe", Research paper no. 15 Ceps Challenge Program, p. 2, 'Most Muslims are immigrants or have an immigrant background' available at: http://www.eumap.org/library/static/libr3/u/0/5/1826_1_g.pdf.
16. See, Centrum Voor Gelijkheid Van Kansen en Voor Racismebestrijding, Statistisch en Demografisch Verslag (2008); Migraties en Migrantenpopulaties in België 126, 129, June 2009.
17. According to a 1999 European survey, only 63 percent of the Belgian population regards itself as member of a religious community and 57 percent as members of the Catholic Church. Only 1.7 percent and 0.3 percent of Belgians consider themselves as protestants or orthodox. In the 1990 value survey, 68 percent considered themselves as part of the Catholic Church. In 1981, the number was 72 percent. This shows a steady decline in religious affiliation within Christianity. See, http://theo.kuleuven.be/page/icrid_religies/#andere.
18. Islam is among the six religions officially recognized by the Belgian state (since 1974). Official recognition carries administrative and financial advantages.
19. Koning Boudewijn and Stichting Synthesenota (2004), "Islam en Moslims in Belgie", Lokale Uitdagingen and Algemeen

Denkkader, 5.
20. Cesari, supra, p. 22.
21. Liesbet Okkerse and Anja Termote (2004), "Hoe vreemd is vreemd op de arbeidsmarkt: Over de allochtone arbeidskrachten in België", Statistische Studiën nr. 111.
22. Id. (numbers are for 2002 and 2003).
23. Open Society Institute (2009), "Muslims in Europe: A Report on 11 EU Cities", 113, December, hereafter 'OSI', p. 110.
24. Centrum voor gelijkheid van kansen en voor racismebestrijding, Nieuwkomers...Welk perspectief op werk, verslag seminarie December 13, 2007.
25. Id.
26. Id.
27. Id.
28. T. Modood et al. (1997), "Ethnic Minorities in Britain: Diversity and Disadvantage", Policies Studies Institute.
29. OSI, p. 111.
30. The 1901 Indian Census listed 133 social groups entirely or partially made up by Muslims, see Sachar Report, p. 192.
31. Pew Research Study; Sachar Report Chapter III; While only 10-13 percent of the total Muslim population are Shia Muslims, most Shias (between 68 percent and 80 percent) live in just four countries: Iran, Pakistan, India (estimated 16-24 million Shias, 10-15 percent of India's total Muslim population) and Iraq.
32. Sachar Report, 41.
33. Sachar Report, p. 192.
34. Sachar Report, p. 193; Yoginder Singh Sikand, "Caste in Muslim Indian Society", in T.Wignesan (ed.), 'The Asianists Asia'.
35. Yoginder Sikand (2006), "Advocating Rights of Muslims in India: Problems and Challenges", July 12, available at: http://www.indianmuslims.info/articles/yoginder_sikand.html.
36. "Muslim Indians Inc.: Their Market and Global Business Impact", June 18, 2007, available at: http://www.dinarstandard.com/current/IndianMuslims061507.ht.
37. Sachar Report, pp. 52, 58 and 69.
38. Sachar Report, pp. 94 and 104.
39. Sachar Report p. 163; In India, government/public sector employment is still the preferred employment for most people due to a variety of reasons. Apart from having a long term

regular income and retirement benefits providing economic security, the higher positions in government jobs offer the employee, privileged positions in society...The perquisite of an official residence or housing is another reason.

40. Sachar Report, pp. 163 and 171.
41. Sachar Report, p. 74.
42. Id.
43. P. 91 and 96; related to this point, the report also identifies difficulties of Muslims getting credit for their enterprises.
44. See Executive Summary of Sachar Report, p. 2.
45. Sachar Report, pp. 141-143.
46. Unlike what is stated in the Sachar Report, it does not seem to be the first of its kind. In 1978 and 1980, high level Committees with similar mandates as the Sachar Committee were set up. The report of the Gopal Singh Committee (appointed by Indira Gandhi) was issued in 1983 but for a long time not released to the general public and its recommendations were not executed when the report finally became public. Several reports by the National Minorities Commission (1995, 1996 and 1999) showed that the proportion of Muslims in different sectors was disproportionately low and recommended corrective measures. http://ncm.nic.in/un_declaration.html; See Syed Tahir Mahmood (2006), "From William Hunter to Rajinder Sachar: Reports and Reports but No Results", *The Milli Gazette*, November 19, Asghar Ali Engineer, supra.
47. See Ranjit Hoskote (2006), "The Price of Exclusion", *The Hindu*, December 31.
48. Henrard, p. 5 (EU publication); Henrard, "Minorities and Socio-economic Participation", supra at 550; Kristin Henrard, "Devising an Adequate System of Minority Protection: Individual Human Rights, Minority Rights and the Right to Self-Determination", KLI, 2000, 30-31.
49. Belgium has ratified the convention in 1977 and India in 1960.
50. Article 2, ILO, Discrimination (Employment and Occupation) Convention No. 111; Article 5 states that special measures shall not be deemed discrimination.
51. See Council Directive 2000/43/EC preamble consideration (3) referring to the Universal Declaration of Human Rights, the United Nations Convention on the Elimination of All Forms of Discrimination against Women, United Nations Covenants on

Civil and Political Rights and on Economic, Social and Cultural Rights and by the European Convention for the Protection of Human Rights and Fundamental Freedoms. In addition, Council Directive 2000/78/EC, preamble consideration (4) also refers to Convention No. 111 of the International Labour Organisation.

52. Two specific forms of discrimination, closely tied to the economic project, were prohibited: first, discrimination based on nationality and, second, gender wage discrimination which could be explained by the fact that nationality discrimination contradicts free movement of persons in the common market, and practices of wage discrimination could distort competition (goods could be more expensive in a country with equal pay legislation).
53. Official Journal C 115 , 09/05/2008 P. 0001-0388; Article 19 EUT (ex Article 13 TEC):
(1) Without prejudice to the other provisions of the Treaties and within the limits of the powers conferred by them upon the Union, the Council, acting unanimously in accordance with a special legislative procedure and after obtaining the consent of the European Parliament, may take appropriate action to combat discrimination based on sex, racial or ethnic origin, religion or belief, disability, age or sexual orientation.
(2) By way of derogation from paragraph 1, the European Parliament and the Council, acting in accordance with the ordinary legislative procedure, may adopt the basic principles of Union incentive measures, excluding any harmonisation of the laws and regulations of the Member States, to support action taken by the Member States in order to contribute to the achievement of the objectives referred to in paragraph 1.
54. Directive 2000/43/EC of the Council of June 29, 2000 implementing the principle of equal treatment between persons of racial or ethnic origin, OJ L 180, July 19, 2000, 22.
55. Directive 2000/78/EC of the Council of November 27, 2000 establishing a general framework for equal treatment in employment and occupation, OJ L 303, December 2, 2000, 16.
56. Directive 2004/113/EC of the Council of December 13, 2004 implementing the principle of equal treatment between men and women in the access to and supply of goods and services, OJ L 373, December 12, 2004, 37; for gender equality a positive and proactive approach is foreseen under the Amsterdam Treaty

(thus Article 13 directives have been said to stand on 'weaker grounds').

57. Article 6, Directive 2000/43; Article 8, Directive 2000/78.
58. Preamble consideration (6) reads that 'the European Union rejects theories which attempt to determine the existence of separate human races. The use of the term 'racial origin' in this Directive does not imply an acceptance of such theories'.
59. EU publication, "Limits and Potential of the Concept of Indirect Discrimination", p. 5; however, the concept of indirect discrimination was not invented by the ECJ but has its roots in other international human rights treaties (see p. 12, referring to Tobler, 2005 a: 89).
60. EU publication, "Limits and Potential of the Concept of Indirect Discrimination", p. 5.
61. Article 2, 1 EU 2000/43; Article 2, 1 EU 2000/78.
62. Article 2, 2 (a) EU 2000/43; Article 2, 2 (a) EU 2000/78.
63. Article 4 EU 2000/43; member states may foresee in the 'occupational requirement' exception.
64. See p. 17, Annual Report, 2008, Belgian Centre.
65. Article 2, 2 (b) EU 2000/43.
66. Belgian Centre for Equal Opportunities and Opposition to Racism, Discriminatie op de arbeidsmarkt omwille van herkomst, huidskleur, nationaliteit, 15, Brussels, April 2009.
67. Case 170/84 Bilka-Kaufhaus GmbH vs. Hartz (1986) ECR 1607 (involving a German department store company—Bilka-kaufhaus GmbH—excluding part-time employees from its occupational pension scheme, effect of policy being much greater on women than men, as women are more likely than men to work part-time to meet family duties.
68. Id., 1627, r.o. 31.
69. Id., 1628-1629, r.o. 36-37.
70. Centre, supra, Discriminatie op de arbeidsmarkt omwille van herkomst, huidskleur, nationaliteit 15.
71. Articles 2, 3 and 2, 4 EU Directive 2000/43; harassment being 'unwanted conduct related to racial or ethnic origin...with the purpose or effect of violating the dignity of a person and of creating an intimidating, hostile, degrading, humiliating or offensive environment'. Examples of instructions to discriminate could be when employers ask temp agencies not to send them candidates from a certain ethnicity (case in Belgium with several

temp agencies).

72. Grosso Modo, employment discrimination occurs at 3 points in time; at the recruitment and selection; with regard to the conditions of employment; and around the time of termination of employment contract; see Annual Report, Centre, pp. 10-13 for the Belgian examples.
73. Mike Noon, supra, pp. 267-269.
74. Article 3, 1, (a)-(d).
75. Article 3, 1, (b)-(h).
76. Article 3, 2 (This Directive does not cover differences of treatment based on nationality and is without prejudice to provisions and conditions relating to the entry into and residence of third-country nationals and stateless persons in the territory of Member States, and to any treatment which arises from the legal status of the third-country nationals and stateless persons concerned).
77. Law of July 30, 1981 on the punishment of certain acts inspired by racism or xenophobia, *State Gazette* August 8, 1981 (amended in 2007, 2003, 1994 and 1993); Law of May 10, 2007 aimed at fighting certain forms of discrimination, *State Gazette* May 30, 2007, (replaced the Law of February 25, 2003, State Gazette, March 17, 2003) (amended in 2009).
78. Gwyneth Pitt, "Religion or Belief: Aiming at the Right Target?", in Helen Meenan (ed.) (2007), 'Equality Law in an Enlarged European Union: Understanding the Article 13 Directives', 229.
79. COM (2008) 426 final, Proposal for a Council Directive on implementing the principle of equal treatment between persons irrespective of religion or belief, disability, age or sexual orientation.
80. Emmanuelle Bribosia, Julie Ringelheim and Isabelle Rorive, "Aménager la Diversité: Le Droit de L'Egalité face à la Pluralité Religieuse", 78 Rev. Trim. Dr. H. 319, 322.
81. Woehrling, supra, pp. 330-336.
82. For the evolvement of reasonable accommodation for religion in the work place in the US, see Gretchen S. Futrell, "Bring Your Dogma to Work Day: The Work place Religious Freedom Act of 2007 and the Public Work Place", 7 First Amend. L. Rev. 373, at 382-384.
83. Bribosia, supra, 366 cites Sweden as the prime example for an EU state with legal provisions for reasonable accommodations

for religious minorities in the work place.
84. See project website www.religareproject.eu.
85. E.g. Centrum voor Gelijkheid van Kansen en voor Racismebestrijding vs. Firma Feryn NV, OJ C 223 of August 30, 2008, p. 11.
86. Preambule consideration (17) of EU Directive 2000/78 (without prejudice to the obligation to provide reasonable accommodation for people with disabilities) [no similar provision in Directive 2000/43].
87. Richard Jenkins (1986), "Racism and Recruitment", Cambridge University Press.
88. Id. Jenkins; Centrum, Annual Report Discrimination, 2008, p. 11 (for instance, 'Blacks are lazy', 'Foreigners are untrustworthy').
89. The Belgian Centre for Equal Opportunity and Opposition to Racism launched an awareness campaign to bring covert discrimination of immigrant young jobseekers at the recruitment level to public attention; Centre for Equal Opportunity and Opposition to Racism, 'Cast Me' Campaign, available at: http://diversiteit.be/index.php?action=artikel_detail&artikel=29; http://www.discriminatieophetwerk.be/index.php?pageId=1.
90. Institute for Labor Market Policy Evaluation (IFAU), "Ethnicity and Obesity: Evidence of Implicit Work Performance Stereotypes in Sweden", Uppsala, 2007, available at: http://www.ifau.se/upload/pdf/se/2007/wp07-20.pdf.
91. Article 5 EU Directive 2000/43; Article 7.1 EU Directive 2000/78.
92. European Court of Justice, Kalanke vs. Freie Hansestadt Bremen, 1995, p. 3078.
93. EU publication, "International Perspectives on Positive Action Measures: A Comparative Analysis in the European Union, Canada, The United States and South Africa", p. 23.
94. Id. p. 23, referring to Badeck vs. Hessischer Ministerprasident (2000) pars. 55 and 63 (50 percent of training spots meant for women and requiring at least 50 percent of interviews to be with women was accepted).
95. Id. p. 23, referring to Marshall vs. Land Nordrhein-Westfalen, par 35.
96. Ravinder Singh Dhami, Judith Squires and Tariq Modood (2006), "Developing Positive Action Policies: Learning from the Experiences of Europe and North America", Department for

Work and Pensions Research Report No. 406.

97. Article 15, Directive 2000/78.
98. Article 10 EU Treaty states, 'In defining and implementing its policies and activities, the Union shall aim to combat discrimination based on sex, racial or ethnic origin, religion or belief, disability, age or sexual orientation'. However, see Mark Bell, "EU Anti-racism Policy: The Leader of the Pack?", in 'Equality Law in an Enlarged European Union: Understanding the Article 13 Directives', Helen Meenan (ed.) (2007). Generally, there has been rapid progress on the level of anti-discrimination legislation, but that has not been matched in other areas as mainstreaming (as going beyond the anti-discrimination framework to achieve equality in practice).
99. Supiot, supra, p. 643.
100. See K. Zweigert and H. Kötz (1998), "An Introduction to Comparative Law", pp. 314-315; Laura Dudley Jenkins, Supiot, supra, p. 643, referring to Christophe Jaffrelot (2003), "India's Silent Revolution: The Rise of the Lower Castes in North India".
101. Arun Shourie (2006), "Falling Over Backwards: An Essay against Reservations and Against Judicial Populism".
102. Balaji vs. State of Mysore (1963).
103. For an example declaration see, http://www.rrbbpl.nic.in/Download/dec_form_obc.pdf.
104. Government of India, Department of Personnel and Training brochure, pp. 4-5, available at: http://www.persmin.nic.in/writedata/CircularNotification/ScanDocument/43011_103_2008-Estt.(Res.).pdf.
    For example, relation of 5 years in upper age limit, exemption from payment of examination/application fees, relaxation in qualification of experience at the discretion of the UPSC/competent authority, relaxations in standard of suitability etc.
105. Id. pp. 5-6 describing the special recruitment drives to fill the backlog vacancies for SCs/STs/OBCs, and especially the 2004 recruitment drive (74,008 backlog vacancies).
106. Article 17 abolishing the practice of untouchability and making it a criminal offence.
107. See Human Rights Watch (2007), "Hidden Apartheid: Caste Discrimination against India's Untouchables", February, (listing various atrocities against Dalits in modern India), available at:

http://www.hrw.org/en/news/2007/02/12/india-hidden-apartheid-discrimination-against-dalits.

108. BJP leader criticizes Sachar Report, *The Hindu*, December 2, 2006. BJP State president P.K. Krishnadas described the Sachar panel report as 'distorted, politically motivated and dangerous', and said that reservation on the basis of religion would harm the country and be obsolete. 'Muslim community has never been discriminated against in India. History tells us that India was once ruled by the Muslims'.

109. Reservation for scheduled castes is currently 15 percent, for STs it is 7.5 percent, which leaves a maximum of 27.5 percent for the OBCs as the Supreme Court has held that the sum of reservations should not exceed 50 percent. The OBCs currently have a 27 percent reservation. Reservations for STs and OBCs are largely caste-neutral as Muslims are included in the lists and not disqualified as is the case for the SC reservations.

110. Sachar Report, p. 241, "No Constitutional amendment would be necessary to include Muslims, it would suffice to amend the 1950 Presidential Order".

111. Kevin Brown, supra, p. 44 in the context of higher education: 'It is one thing to reserve seats...for Dalits, but it is another to assure that they occupy those reserved seats'; see also, Government of India, Department of Personnel and Training, Reservation for Scheduled Castes/Scheduled Tribes and Other Backward Classes Brochure, pp. 5-7, available at: http://www.persmin.nic.in/writedata/CircularNotification/ScanDocument/43011_103_2008-Estt.(Res.).pdf.

112. State of Kerala vs. Thomas (1976), upholding a Kerala government order exempting SC/ST government clerks from passing compulsory tests required for job promotions for a period of two years and giving them two more opportunities to pass the examination...Justice K.K. Mathew considering that the Constitution also guaranteed 'equality of result'. It was later ruled that compensatory discrimination should not be extended to promotions, prompting a Constitutional amendment in 1995 to grant SCs/STs this benefit.

113. Kevin Brown, supra.

114. In 2006, large-scale anti-caste based reservation protests took place all over India in opposition to the decision of the Central Government to reserve 27 percent of seats in central and private

institutes of higher education for other backward classes.

115. Article 330 et seq., Part XVI (special provisions relating to certain classes); provisions were meant to be temporary but are regularly extended for 10 year terms.

116. Article 15 (4), Article 46 (Directive Principle) of the Indian Constitution.

117. Article 16(4A), "Article 335 states that claims of the SC/ST shall be taken into consideration consistently with the maintenance of efficiency of administration in making of appointments in civil service. Added in 2000 was the clarification that this would not prevent 'relaxation in qualifying marks in any examination or lowering the standards of evaluation for reservation in matters of promotion of SC/ST.

118. 'Dalit' is a self-designated term that in Sanskrit means 'oppressed' or 'broken'. The Dalits, also called the 'untouchables', 'outcastes' and more recently 'slumdogs', comprise of an estimated 165 million (based on 2001 Census), available at:
http://www.censusindia.gov.in/Census_Data_2001/India_at_Glance/scst.aspx.

119. Dalit Christians account for nearly two-thirds of the 27 million Christians in India.

120. See Subodh Ghildiyal (2006), "Quota for Dalit Christians/Muslims?", *The Times of India*, May 27, 2006, available at:
http://timesofindia.indiatimes.com/india/Quota-for-Dalit-Christians/Muslims/articleshow/1577114.cms.

121. Muslim Indians are internally subdivided into three groups viz., ashraf, ajlaf and arzal.

122. In 1996, the Government prepared a draft amendment bill, Bill No. 17 of 1996, intending to include Dalit Christians by amending the Constitution (Scheduled Castes) Order, 1950. However, the amendment bill could not be passed in the Parliament.

123. National Commission for Religious and Linguistic Minorities Headed by Justice Ranganath Mishra, Report, May 21, 2007.

124. National Commission for Minorities (2008), "Reservations Must for Dalit Muslims and Dalit Christians", NMC Study, Press Release, April 8, available at:
http://ncm.nic.in/pdf/press%20release%203.4.08%20reservation.

pdf.

125. In the year 2000, the Bihar State Assembly passed resolution for granting SC status to Dalit Christians and Dalit Muslims; in the year 2006, Uttar Pradesh State Assembly passed resolution for the same; in the year 2009, Andhra Pradesh state government had passed resolution in its assembly for granting the SC status to Dalit Christians and Dalit Muslims.
126. Writ Petition (Civil) No. 180/2004, Centre for Public Interest Litigation vs. Union of India and Others, case has been delayed several times.
127. Zoya Hasan (2005), "Reservations for Muslims, Redressing Disadvantages", Symposium on Reservations and the Private Sector, 549, available at: http://www.india-seminar.com/2005/549/549%20zoya%20hassan.htm.
128. Hasan, supra.
129. The Mishra commission report stated, 'Even though Christianity and Islam do not recognise the caste system or untouchability, the ground reality in India is different'.
130. The same goes for Dalit Christians who are likewise excluded.
131. Articles 14, 15, 25 of the Indian Constitution; see Mishra Commission.
132. Universal Declaration of Human Rights, Articles 2 and 18; International Covenant on Economic, Social and Cultural Rights (ICESCR), which states in its Article 3 that the government will 'ensure the equal right of men and women to the enjoyment of all economic, social and cultural rights set forth in the present Covenant'.
133. Moreover, the 50 percent maximum reservation established by the Supreme Court (1992) will necessarily limit what can be foreseen without an unlikely Constitutional amendment.
134. Some Muslim leaders oppose reservation for Dalit Muslims denying there is a caste system among Muslims, so that any reservations should be given for entire Muslim community, see Asghar Ali Engineer, supra, available at: http://www.csss-isla.com/archive/archive.php?article=2006/dec1_15.htm.
135. N.R. Narayan Murthy, Infosys Chairman, available at: http://obcreservation.net/ver2/anti-reservation-mainmenu-97/personalities-mainmenu-78.html.

136. See Nagarajan, supra, at 486 and 509; (this abuse being most noticeable at the state level and now threatens to extend to the central level with groups lobbying to be included in the list even though they are not disadvantaged).

137. See Sachar Report, calling the problem of educational and economical backwardness of Muslim Indians a national problem, with immediate remedial action being in the national interest.

Part IV: Muslims, Multiculturalism and Politics of Islam

11

Islamic Responses to Multiculturalism: An Analysis of Qur'anic Citations

Husain Qutbuddin

The various flavours of multiculturalism offered by South-Asia and Europe have evoked a range of responses from Islamic denominations, such as the Deobandi, Barelwi, Salafi, and Shia schools of thought, and their affiliates and sub-denominations, as well as South Asian and European Islamic institutions such as the All India Muslim Personal Law Board, and the Muslim Council of Britain. These responses are typically substantiated with verses from the Qur'an and examples from the Sunna (exemplary life story of the Prophet), sources that are believed to be the roots of guidance by virtually all Islamic communities. [1] This paper will present some of the verses that are popularly cited for justification and conduct a meta-analysis of their interpretations, to demonstrate the flexibility that is present on the Qur'anic level for offering support to a myriad of positions, and frequently even contradictory ones. It will suggest that socio-cultural, political and economic backgrounds and circumstances have a substantial role with regard to which of the possible interpretations are considered 'true' and 'applicable' by respective denominations. [2]

The notion that the interpreter's background unavoidably takes part in his/her interpretation, especially when the subject of study is scripture, may be obvious to many readers, particularly those familiar with the fields of pragmatics and literary theory. However, it has not been explored *hands-on* with specific regard to Qur'anic interpretation by contemporary Islamic communities in South Asia and Europe, who seek to find in the Qur'an 'what God enjoins for today'. A lack of awareness of such a notion in the public sphere, particularly in large portions of the media as well as in political circles, has meant that Islam is seen as more or less an objective reality, whose 'true nature' can be determined simply by examining its source texts, or the actions of some of its adherents, and whose followers in general can be judged based on such a determination. By showing that the interpretations put forward by Islamic communities cannot be extricated from their respective circumstances, I will assert that the focus urgently needs to shift from discussions on the 'truth' about Islam, to those of the factors that lead respective communities to choose particular interpretations over others.

My primary sources of information are interviews with prominent members of the respective groups, sermons and lectures heard live and on the Internet, websites, which officially pronounce *fatwa*s (legal rulings) according to a particular school, and the texts that are frequently cited for precedents. *Fatwa*s are an especially excellent avenue of research since they offer answers to questions that are posed by ordinary adherents of a school regarding mundane issues such as whether it is permissible to marry a person from another Islamic sect, whether it is acceptable to share one's food and drink with a Jewish or Christian person, whether it is forbidden to wear certain types of clothes such as jeans, etc. The replies to such questions can be used to identify a school's attitude and behaviour in fine-grained terms—at least on the theoretical level—towards other communities and cultures.

Before listing some of the verses that are popularly quoted for justification of particular responses, a word on the nature of the Qur'an and its revelation as related by traditional Islamic narratives may be appropriate. The Qur'an was revealed piecemeal to Prophet Muhammad (d. 632 AD) over a period of more than a decade in Mecca, where he and his followers were a persecuted minority, and a subsequent span of 10 years in Medina, where he attained political power, and Islam's dominion gradually expanded to include almost the whole of Arabia.

Many of the verses responded to particular situations; for example, some verses addressed the Muslims' victory or loss in a particular battle, others responded to specific questions that were asked by Muslims or non-Muslims, and yet others enjoined the Muslims to behave and act in a certain way towards members of particular communities. As the situation and socio-political environment of the community changed, the Qur'an responded with newer directives that replaced previous ones, and were sometimes contradictory to them. The dating as well as the reasons for the revelation of particular verses are documented in texts belonging to the genre of *asbab al-nuzul* ('occasions of revelation'), and the accounts therein frequently present more than one distinct alternative as to when and why a verse may have been revealed. Theories of *naskh* ('abrogation') were developed by Muslim jurists to ascertain which of the opposing directives remained applicable in post-Muhammad. Broadly speaking, the later directives were considered—at least on the theoretical level—to remain valid and functional, whereas the ones that were replaced were considered abrogated and therefore inoperative.

The following are some of the verses that one finds frequently cited for advocating particular positions vis-à-vis how one should conduct oneself in multicultural societies. Carefully argued for positions would be those that take into account theories of *naskh*, and that address and provide an interpretation for most of these verses, especially for ones which seem to put forward injunctions that oppose those that are being advocated.

To arrive at an interpretation and a judgement regarding that which a verse entails for today, the interpreter may generally perform several steps. Chief among these may be: assigning a meaning to each of the words in a verse; working out the implications that can be derived from such an assignment; applying juridical methods such as *naskh*, *qiyas* ('analogical reasoning'), and *maslaha* ('the common good'); [3] arriving at an injunction that is put forward as valid for today.

#	Qur'anic Verse	Translation [4]	Common Usage
1.	يا أيها الناس اتقوا ربكم الذي خلقكم من نفس واحدة	O People, Fear your Lord who has created you from one being (4:1)	To argue for peaceful co-existence, sometimes democracy
2.	إن الله يأمر بالعدل والإحسان...	God enjoins justice and kindness... (16:90)	
3.	لا ينهاكم الله عن الذين لم يقاتلوكم في الدين ولم يخرجوكم من دياركم أن تبروهم وتقسطوا إليهم	God does not forbid you, regarding those who have not fought you in religion's cause and have not ousted you from your houses, that you be kind and be just to them (60:8)	
4.	إنا خلقناكم من ذكر وأنثى وجعلناكم شعوبا وقبائل لتعارفوا	We have created you from a male and a female and have made you into nations and tribes so that you know each other (49:13)	
5.	وعد الله الذين آمنوا منكم وعملوا الصالحات ليستخلفنهم في الأرض	God has promised those who believe amongst you and perform good deeds that He will make them successors of the land (24:55)	To ask Muslims to endure a 'bad' government; contrastingly, to encourage participation in politics

6.	وطعام الذين أوتوا الكتاب حل لكم...والمحصنات من الذين أوتوا الكتاب من قبلكم	The food of the People of the Book is lawful for you…and in wedlock women from the People of the Book [are lawful] (5:5)	To advocate eating and sharing food that is prepared by Jews and Christians; and to allow marrying Jewish and Christian women
7.	من أهل الكتاب أمة قائمة يتلون آيات الله ... أولـئك من الصالحين	Among the People of the Book is an upright community, who recite the signs of God…They are among the righteous (3:113-14)	To endorse befriending Jews and Christians
8.	يا أيها الذين أمنوا لا تتخذوا اليهود والنصارى أولياء...	O you who believe! Do not take the Jews and Christians as your friends (or allies)… (5:51)	To argue against taking non-Muslims as friends or allies
9.	لا تتخذوا عدوي وعدوكم أولياء...	Do not take my enemy and your enemy as friends (or allies)… (60:1)	
10.	إنما المؤمنون إخوة فأصلحوا بين أخويكم	Verily, the believers are brothers, so make peace between your brothers (49:10)	To urge different Islamic sects to unite, and to stop violence against each other

11.	من قتل نفسا بغير نفس أو فساد في الأرض فكأنما قتل الناس جميعا	One who kills a soul without [it being in retaliation for] another soul or corruption done in the land, it is though as if he has killed the whole of mankind (5:32)	To argue against suicide bombings, and killing civilians
12.	فاقتلوا المشركين حيث وجدتموهم	Kill the polytheists wherever you find them (9:5)	To justify the killing of civilians

At each step, authoritative sources may be brought in for justification: for example, to support a particular assignment of meaning, another verse from the Qur'an or a tradition of the Prophet (known as '*hadith*') may be cited. These steps are not necessarily performed in a sequence or independently of each other: for example, an interpreter may decide on the implications he/she needs to derive and then assign a meaning that is conducive to this derivation. [5]

Each of the steps is far from being a predictable process, where a certain input is guaranteed to yield a predetermined output. On the contrary, the factors that shape a particular judgement can be shown to be, for the large part, highly subjective. Here, I will focus primarily on the first step, concerned with meaning assignment, to demonstrate that the interpreter's background and circumstances play an unavoidable role in shaping his/her interpretation. I will avail of concepts elaborated in the field of pragmatic communication, which—unlike literary theories such as post-structuralism, which consider the notion of a text conveying any solid meaning that is intended by its author as unviable—delves deep into examining how meaning *is* communicated from a speaker/author to a hearer/reader, identifies the steps that the latter performs in the process of context selection and comprehension, and outlines where and how misunderstandings and ambiguities may arise. [6]

Relevance Theory, put forward by Sperber and Wilson in 1986, has been widely-acclaimed by pragmaticians as being the one out of the available pragmatic theories that most accurately accounts for verbal as well as written communication, especially in its detailed account of the role of context. [7] For the purpose of this synoptic essay, it will suffice to outline a few of its basic principles, although the argument that is presented here could be strengthened even more by presenting it in detail.

Relevance Theory advances three fundamental steps that one performs in the process of assigning meaning to each word in a sentence. [8] First, one *disambiguates* the word by working out its semantic import. This typically entails choosing one of its 'dictionary' meanings. For example, *jihad* can disambiguate to, amongst other things, 'internal struggle to better oneself' or 'physical battle with an enemy'. [9] Second, if the word is a noun, one works out that to which it *refers*. For example, in the sentence 'I participated in the *jihad*', uttered by a person after the battle of *Badr*, [10] the word 'the *jihad*' refers to the battle of *Badr*; in the sentence 'the lawfulness of *jihad* is a complex issue', stated in the context of discussing warfare under Islamic law, the word '*jihad*' refers generally to the legal concept of physical battle. [11] Third, one particularises the *sense* of a word. For example, if the sentence 'I participated in the *jihad* is uttered at the time of *Badr*, 'the *jihad*' has the sense of fighting with swords etc. whereas if it is spoken today, it would be in the sense of some type of modern warfare. [12]

At each stage, as may be apparent from the examples, the textual and extra-textual context of the sentence that is being interpreted helps one choose an appropriate assignment, in conjunction with linguistic, syntactic and morphological analysis. The extent of the participation of context in interpretation can be verified by placing the same sentence in different situations: for example, a sentence such as 'you are not ready for *jihad*' uttered before the battle of *Badr* has very different assignments at each stage compared to those it would have if it were uttered by a Sufi ascetic to his/her disciple in mediaeval times. The context generally may include—with varying degrees of importance depending on the text—knowledge of the author's biography and history, of his/her intended audience, and of contemporary events and socio-linguistic environments. Acquisition of the appropriate context is crucial for interpretive exercises where the goal is to identify—to as close a degree as possible—the meaning that has been intended by the author.

In texts for which the context is more or less determinable, the assignments can be made more or less straightforwardly and unambiguously. In those for which it is unclear or hard to acquire, such as is often the case with literary and historical texts, the assignments are more contentious and open to interpretation. Even with such difficult cases, however, the potential context is generally limited to that which can be reasonably estimated to be in the cognition of the author—knowledge of events that occurred after the author's time, for example, in most cases cannot be said to be a part of this. [13]

The Qur'an's author is believed to be the All-Knowing God, and it is taken as addressing the whole of mankind including humans today, and to be applicable until the day of judgement. Neither the cognitive capacity of its 'Author' nor of its intended audience can therefore be reasonably objectively delimited for the purpose of estimating a valid context for interpretation. This is in addition to the fact that its original contexts of revelation are themselves generally a matter of high dispute. The context that one does choose to apply for interpretation and deriving guidance for today is therefore a highly subjective choice, and typically, the Qur'an is intimately drawn upon for support by myriad ideologies, from the most conservative to the most liberal. [14]

To highlight this point, I will list some of the

interpretations put forward for Qur'an 5:51. The demonstration will show the flexibility in the Qur'anic language especially when one tries to infer what it says for today. It will indicate that at best, the verses suggest possibilities of action, which, without a reasonably objective way of estimating a valid context, cannot be particularised to any one injunction that can be confidently attributed to the intentions of the 'Author'. The interpretation that one affirms as being 'the true one' inevitably depends on preferring a particular context over all others, which is an unavoidably biased exercise.

	يا أيها الذين آمنوا لا تتخذوا اليهود والنصارى أولياء	O you who believe! Do not take the Jews and Christians as your *awliya'* (5:51)
#	**Interpretation of keywords**	**Injunctions/implications derived for today**
1.	**Jews and Christians**: refers to particular Jewish and Christian tribes at the time of the Prophet who were hostile towards the Islamic community, but not universally to all Jews and Christians. ***Awliya'***: friends and allies	The verse prohibited one to take Jews and Christians as friends and allies but only at the time of the Prophet, and in reference to particular tribes, because of certain socio-political circumstances. The verse is specific to its original context of revelation, and does not forbid one to interact positively with Jews and Christians today.
2.	**Jews and Christians**: refers generally to all Jews and Christians, including those of today. ***Awliya'***: allies	The verse prohibits one to form alliances with Jewish and Christian governments but does not forbid one to befriend ordinary civilian populations of Jews and Christians today.
3.	**Jews and Christians**: refers generally to all Jews and Christians, including those of today. ***Awliya'***: friends	The verse discourages one from befriending Jews and Christians today, but does not proscribe forging alliances with Jewish and Christian governments if it is politically advantageous.

<table>
<tr><td>4.</td><td>Jews and Christians: refers generally to all Jews and Christians, including those of today.
Awliya': friends</td><td>The verse discourages one from befriending Jews and Christians today, but does not forbid voting for political candidates who belong to these faiths.</td></tr>
<tr><td>5.</td><td>Jews and Christians: refers generally to all Jews and Christians, including those of today.
Awliya': friends in the religious sense</td><td>The verse prohibits one to befriend Jews and Christians on 'religious grounds', but one is allowed to befriend them on 'human grounds' today.</td></tr>
<tr><td>6.</td><td>Jews and Christians: refers generally to those Jews and Christians who are at war with Muslims, such as those in the West and in Israel today.
Awliya': friends and allies</td><td>The verse prohibits any positive interaction with Jews and Christians in the West and in Israel, who are 'at war' with Muslims around the world today.</td></tr>
<tr><td colspan="3">Remarks:
The interpreter has to decide to whom 'Jews and Christians' refers. Here, there are three interpretations illustrated: one that limits the reference to parties at the time of the Prophet; one that extends the reference to any and all Jews and Christians, including those of today, many of whom hold beliefs that are vastly different from the ones held by the Jewish and Christian tribes of Arabia; and one that encompasses parties who are at war with Muslims, including those perceived to be at war with Muslims today in a socio-political environment vastly unlike the one in tribal Arabia.

The interpreter also has to decide on the disambiguation of awliya' and particularise its sense. Here, in one instance, awliya' is disambiguated to 'friends', and its sense is interpreted—either explicitly or implicitly—to include the particular sense of friendship in today's societies, giving forth the relevant implications regarding what it may mean to be a friend today. In another instance, awliya' is disambiguated to 'allies', and its sense is interpreted—again either explicitly or implicitly—to include the particular sense of political alliances that are forged by governments of different countries today, and in the sense of voting for a candidate in a modern democracy.</td></tr>
</table>

By virtue of it being considered the message of God for all time, the Qur'an is, as demonstrated, susceptible to being interpreted in multiple contexts, including those which have arisen only in modern times. Yet because of this, it is virtually impossible to reasonably objectively delimit the intended context as one does with 'human' texts. Even if one is able to settle on a meaning that a verse put forward in its original context—a fairly difficult task if not an impossible one in many cases, given the lack of contemporary sources including ones that record *asbab al-nuzul*, and the disagreements between later sources—one then has to ascertain whether that verse is intended for application to newer contexts in later times, especially those of today. Observe, for example, that even though interpretations 1 and 6 are very similar, the former chooses to restrict the context of application to the Prophet's time, whereas the latter does not, without there being any reasonably objective way of justifying either.

Furthermore, even if one decides to apply the verse today, the particular injunctions that are derived will inherently depend upon one's own perceptions that are drawn from one's socio-cultural, political, and economic background. For example, the actual ruling that one derives from interpretation 6 is essentially dependent upon one's views as to who precisely is at war with Muslims; also, the specific commands that one obtains via the interpretation of *awliya'* as 'friends' or 'allies' depends on one's understanding of what it means to be friends in the modern world, and whether or not, for example, modern concepts such as democratic voting constitute an alliance. Evidently, to objectively pin down an intended context of interpretation is practically impossible. The context of interpretation that is selected and preferred is therefore a subjective choice. [15]

Qur'anic verses and sayings of the Prophet that are frequently brought in by interpreters to support their respective selections are inescapably dependent upon similarly complicated interpretive exercises themselves, and do not offer an escape from subjectiveness. Furthermore, principles of Islamic law, argued extensively over more than a thousand years in texts belonging to its vast and rich genre, are highly disputed, and therefore do not generally offer an objective parameter either. *Maslaha*, for example, is more or less agreed upon as a vehicle for deriving legal rulings by most Islamic schools, and moreover, is used with verses such as Qur'an 5:51 to justify preferring one interpretation over another. However, that which is in the common good is a patently subjective point: what is in the 'common good' according to one may not be so according to another, and depends on who one sees as falling under the reference of 'common', and whether one is considering the short-term or the long-term, as well as on one's expectations of the future. [16]

Owing to these factors, when one discusses Muslim responses vis-à-vis multiculturalism, one cannot, in an unqualified manner, state that 'the Qur'an prescribes a particular position', and, by extension, that 'Islam enjoins a specific action'. Arguments regarding the 'true Islamic position' may be appropriate between various Islamic sects, [17] but when such discussion transpires in the public sphere, in political, social, and economic arenas of debate, and particularly in the media, it incorrectly presupposes that there is an objective Islamic position regarding issues pertinent to the modern world, and that one can justifiably argue about the nature of this position. Such a presupposition renders one susceptible to perceiving the actions of a few Muslims, or examining the source texts directly, and then passing a judgement regarding Islam for which one then holds all Muslims responsible. In other words, it makes one prone to stereotyping. The need here is not only to recognise the diversity in the Muslim world especially with respect to its responses to the issues of the modern world, but go further and realise that there is no objective 'Islamic position' that one can discuss. If examining the nature of Islam at the time of the Prophet is a complex issue that is stricken with difficulties, examining 'Islam's position' vis-à-vis modern issues is nothing but an absurdity.

As an illustration, consider, on the one extreme, those such as the Danish Geert Wilders, and the Indian R.V. Bhasin, who categorically state that Islam preaches hatred and separatism, and that Muslims are prone to violence because of the 'realities' of their faith. On the other extreme, there are apologetic statements by those who feel they need to defend 'Islam' from the actions of some of its followers: "It is obligatory upon the Muslims...to explain that [the practice of suicide bombing] is free from Islaam [*sic*], and that Islaam [*sic*] is free from these actions" (Shaykh Salih al-Suhaymi); "In the face of the despair that engulfs us with the media's relentless cynicism, we must redouble our efforts to reach out in local communities and demonstrate the realities of our [peaceful] faith" (Muhammad Abdul-Bari). Even though such defensive statements are sometimes crucial to curtail negative reactions by the public towards all Muslims, they, perhaps unwittingly, convey that there is an objective 'Islamic position' that one can debate.

I have shown in light of pragmatic principles that due in particular to the belief that the Qur'an is authored by God and contains guidance for all time, and the subsequent proliferation of potential contexts, an interpreter's circumstances vitally contribute to the interpretations that he/she chooses as the ones that are 'true' and intended by God from the myriad possibilities afforded by the text's language. [18]

The focus of debate in the public sphere—having the potential of influencing public opinion and directing governmental policy—needs to be not on 'Islam's position' vis-à-vis issues of modernity, and how that supposedly dictates Muslims 'to act in a certain way', but on the factors that lead respective communities to prefer certain interpretations over others. With respect to whether a Muslim should be peaceful or violent towards certain parties today, there is no objective Islamic standard that promotes either position; there are

Muslims who choose interpretations that enjoin peaceful relations and others who choose the opposite, and both of these choices are necessarily shaped by their respective socio-cultural, economic, and political circumstances. Studies by groups such as the Working Group on Tackling Extremism and Radicalisation conducted by the UK Home Office, for example, have suggested—albeit not in correlation with issues of Qur'anic interpretation—that it is primarily US and European foreign policy in the Middle East that has caused 'radicalisation' amongst a number of Muslim youth. Such studies need to increase and gain more attention if such 'radicalisation' is to be curbed. [19]

Endnotes

1. For the Shia, a third root source is the sayings of their Imams.
2. These backgrounds and circumstances may be shaped by several factors, including, of course, the previously existing interpretations considered canonical by the denomination.
3. Islamic jurisprudential schools substantially differ on the methods that they consider valid for the derivation of law.
4. The translations of Qur'anic verses are my own, and generally reflect the meaning that is assigned to them in the primary sources.
5. Even though my primary concern here is the Qur'an as it is used for the derivation and justification of law, not all injunctions are necessarily shown by Islamic schools to have been derived from it. The methods that are put forward for deriving law generally outline ways by which one should proceed in the event that no textual basis for a rule is found in the root sources.
6. Using concepts that are defined in the field of pragmatic communication is a better option than relying upon one's own intuitive understanding of how textual communication operates. This is because such concepts are examined and commented upon by a large number of scholars in the field, and have a lesser chance of sustaining internal contradictions and inconsistencies in their description of the process of communication. The science of *Hermeneutics*, amongst whose proponents are Bultmann, Gadamer and Heidegger, also has useful ideas for interpreting historical texts. However, pragmatic theories

attempt to account for the process of communication at a more fundamental level than hermeneutical ones.

7. Relevance Theory claims to be able to account for all human communication, regardless of language. It has been shown to be able to explain communication in multiple languages, including Arabic.
8. These steps are not performed in a sequence; rather, they are executed simultaneously and in parallel.
9. Consider another example: in the utterance 'I will give you a bat', the word 'bat' can disambiguate to 'a club for hitting a ball in a game' or 'a nocturnal mouse-like mammal with wings'.
10. *Badr* was the first battle fought by Prophet Muhammad and his followers against the Meccan tribes.
11. Another example: in the utterance 'I bought McDonalds', the word 'McDonalds' can refer to the burger company as a whole (for example, perhaps if the CEO of Burger King is talking), or to a sandwich from one of its outlets.
12. Another example: in the utterance 'I caught a fish', the word 'fish'—in most cultures—would be interpreted in the sense of a living fish, whereas in the utterance 'I ate a fish', it would be taken in the sense of a cooked fish. Determining whether or not a word is used metaphorically also falls under the exercise of ascertaining its sense.
    Note that the examples here provide relatively simple interpretive alternatives. The context, however, may usually be more complex. For example, if 'I ate fish' is said by someone who has just come out of a Sushi restaurant in a country where fish is usually eaten cooked, the sense of 'fish' in the utterance may nevertheless be taken as 'raw fish' because of the fact that Sushi is made of uncooked fish.
13. In cases where the interpreter knowingly supplies a context which the author could probably not have envisioned, as is often the case in literary interpretation, the resulting meaning cannot with any reasonable degree of confidence be attributed to the intentions of the author.
14. This phenomenon is not limited to the Qur'an; it is present vis-à-vis virtually all scriptures.
15. The problem of the elusiveness of an objectively determinable and valid context is highlighted by the fact that to discredit opposing interpretations, one finds that each side most often

accuses the other of taking the verse 'out of context' or of selectively choosing certain verses at the expense of others.

16. *Maslaha* is frequently seen as guided by *maqasid al-Shari'a* (the aims of Islamic law), which are generally seen as constituting the preservation of life, property, progeny, mind and religion.
17. Even though Islamic sects widely acknowledge the existence of divergent opinions with regard to the interpretation of the Qur'an and the Sunna particularly vis-à-vis the derivation of law, the objective accessibility of these sources is generally not seen as compromised. Verses that are interpreted to put forth operative legal rulings are generally classified under the *muhkamat* (clear/unambiguous) verses of the Qur'an.
18. Note that the argument in this paper has relied primarily upon an analysis at a fundamental level of the process of communication and interpretation, in conjunction with examples of Qur'anic citations that occur in responses to issues of multiculturalism. A study that focuses more on empirical analysis—examining specific interpretations by individual denominations in light of their specific backgrounds and circumstances—can be undertaken in the future to further corroborate the conclusions presented here.
19. A focus on the factors that affect which interpretations are chosen is also indispensable when studying the various 'reform movements'—from the conservative to the liberal—that have arisen in the Islamic world. This is to ascertain the issues that motivate particular 'reformists' to choose one interpretation over another, and to understand the reasons for why they have or have not gained popularity with respective Islamic communities. For example, advocates of reinterpreting Islam according to 'Western values' of modernity, such as Asaf Ali Fyzee, Fazlur Rahman Malik and Nurcholish Madjid, are often labelled by more conservative Islamic groups as apologetic, with vested interests in the 'West', and therefore 'unimportant'.

12

Muslim Responses to Multiculturalism in India and Europe

Anwar Alam

Introduction

Multiculturalism has been a dominant discourse in recent years—both at the level of theory and praxis—to address the question of integration of ethnic, linguistic and religious minority communities within the structure of nation-state. Irrespective of context of origin of discourse of multiculturalism—whether it is related to the failure of liberal assimilationist model of integration to assimilate all ethnic and religious minorities, the process of globalization that intensifies the discourse of 'identity', the political assertion of feminism and LGBT community or the development of theory of multiculturalism that exposes the myth of liberal notion of 'culturally-neutral' nation-state, it is the physical presence of Muslim immigrant communities, the number of which estimated to be around 15-20 million in Western Europe, [1] and its growing demand for cultural and religious expression in public sphere that has shaped the intellectual and political debates on multiculturalism in the European hemisphere. Thus, much of multicultural flavour that was reflected in the public policies of European states, albeit within their respective national tradition of state secularism and Church-State relationship, during 1980s and 1990s, was primarily addressed to meet some of the religious and cultural demands of Muslim immigrant community. [2]

However, the series of terrorist attacks in Europe since late 1990s including 7/7 (London bombings) and 11/13 (Paris massacre), mostly committed by members of second or third generation European Muslims in conjunction with transnational Islamic terrorist network witnessed the progressive decline in the public commitment of European states to the issue of multiculturalism, leading to public acknowledgment of failure of multiculturalism on the part of German Chancellor Merkel, [3] French President Sarkozy [4] and the British Premier Cameron [5] to integrate Muslim immigrant communities—a political trend that continues till date. The success and failure of political multiculturalism has been hotly debated in the academia and in mainstream media ranging from 'death of multiculturalism' [6] and 'retreat of multiculturalism' [7] to the contestation to such conclusions. [8]

Though the political rhetoric over integration of Muslim immigrant communities is being increasingly shifted towards re-assertion of traditional colour blind liberal assimilationist model of integration, this has not offset the gains that has accrued to the Muslim community due to multicultural policies pursued by the European states during 1980s and 1990s except tightening the criterion of citizenship, [9] imposing greater restrictions on the public visibility of those Islamic practices that outrage the gender and humanistic sensitivity of host societies such as niqab [10] and increasing the greater surveillance and policing over Muslim immigrant neighbourhoods, particularly its underclass. Neither the reversal to liberal assimilationist model has led the European governments to employ 'ethnic and race relations framework'—the dominant liberal integrationist model, particularly in the UK, that has been historically applied to integrate the immigrant communities—to the Muslim immigrant community. Rather, the government continues to engage with Muslim community as 'religious group' within the frame of 'limited multiculturalism' as evident from the government's frantic search for 'effective moderate national Muslim interlocutor' to negotiate the cultural, religious and other demands of Muslim community with the government.

Unlike the European landscape, where multiculturalism

was primarily conceived as 'policy response' to emerging diversity, in the Indian context the multicultural values and norms has historically been a mode of governance, which runs deep from ancient Hindu Kingdoms to medieval Muslim Mughal era to modern British colonial rule to post-colonial secular India, to essentially a segmented and plural society. This historical multicultural norm of governance has also been applied to the Muslim community in post-independent India as evident from Constitutional provisions pertaining to group and minority rights as elaborated in Kumar Suresh's article and noted in the introduction of this volume, particularly in terms of political practice of Indian secularism that includes public recognition of religious and cultural values/symbols and affirmative public policies.

More specifically, the discourse of multiculturalism and secularism in India becomes a discourse of minority rights with focus on the Muslim community. Nonetheless, as India has embarked on the project of nation-state with its inherent majoritarian values and norms in the governing institutions, this has adversely affected the plural and multicultural fabric of Indian society and often marked by growing majority (Hindus)-minority (particularly Muslims) tensions and violence.

Many in India have questioned the efficacy of Indian multiculturalism and to integrate the Muslim communities, particularly in view of growing home grown Islamic militancy including the militancy in Muslim dominated province of Jammu and Kashmir and the Shahabano case [11] that witness probably the largest Muslim mobilization in post-independence history of India.

Problematizing the Singular Islamic versus Plural Muslim Respcnses

Thus, what is evident from the above is that Muslims as a 'religious group' is the crucial component in shaping the discourse of multiculturalism in Europe as well as in India. In this context, narratives about multiculturalism in both parts of continents have two dominant but identical features. From the liberal-democratic perspective the discourse of multiculturalism offers a 'multicultural citizenship along with regime of minority rights' that help in integrating the member of minority communities within the structure of a nation-state. On the other hand, in terms of majoritarian-nationalist perspective, the discourse of multiculturalism in effect promotes and perpetuates 'exclusivism', 'ghettoization', 'separatism' and 'parallelism' among the members of minority communities that hinders the prospect of meaningful integration within the structure of a nation-state. However, there is hardly any attempt to locate the Muslim responses from below to multiculturalism in both parts of the world.

While there is a growing number of textual Islamic responses (mostly based on exposition of Quran and Hadith) that either accepts/accommodates or rejects the discourse of multiculturalism, democracy, pluralism and secularism based on their Islamic exposition of *notion of self and other* and doctrine of *Tawhid/Sovereignty*; however this Islamic textual analysis does not capture everyday Muslim experiences and responses while living under the political regime of democracy, secularism and multiculturalism. Moreover, the textual Islamic analysis singularizes the Muslim responses and experiences as it presumes Muslims as a 'homogeneous faith community'. In reality, Muslim experiences and responses, like any other socio-religious groups, are plural and conditioned by class, sect, regional, national, gender and other variables. Furthermore, while Muslim minority community, like any minority religious group, desires a multicultural and secular political governance that allows them a modicum of space to preserve and promote their religious, cultural and linguistic identity, it is worth probing whether the community imbibes a multicultural outlook and principle of relative truth vis–a-vis other social and religious groups or not?

Before one proceeds further to explore the multiple layers

of Muslim responses as well as generalized everyday Muslim responses to the issue of secularism and multiculturalism in India and in Europe, a brief elaboration to the notion of political multiculturalism, as well as, the relationship between self and other is required in order to structure the Muslim responses to these concepts.

Notion of Multiculturalism and Relationship between Self and Other

Defining multiculturalism is problematic as it means different things depending upon different contexts. In sharp contradiction to the notion of pluralism, multiculturalism unmasks the 'value neutrality' of liberal state and demands the equal recognition and representation of group/community rights/pluralities and its culture in public sphere and political arena. It is the thrust on 'equality' that differentiates the modern form of multiculturalism with the traditional version of multiculturalism as practiced during the period of Empires. It advocates the notion of multicultural citizenship and multicultural nationhood. At a broader level, it aims at reconciliation of cultural diversity and political unity. [12]

The thrust and scope of the multiculturalism in each country varies depending upon their specific national traditions, character of nationalism and relationship between minority and majority. Thus, in France it is heavily coloured by tradition of *laicism* and assimilationism, in Germany by specific nature of nationhood in terms of nation versus *Auslander* (foreigner) and in Britain by the tradition of accommodation and group representation. [13] In India, multiculturalism goes beyond the British political tradition of accommodating group concerns and operates principally in terms of recognizing the religious and cultural identity and symbols in public sphere as well as establishing federal-multicultural model of governance that includes regional, linguistic, caste, religious and tribal considerations while framing public policies concerning governance. [14] However a critical inquiry into these existing political multiculturalism towards the social and political integration of minority communities reveals its emphasis on 'integrationist framework' which though allows the ethnic minority groups to maintain their linguistic, cultural and religious identity but does not empower them to be an equal partner in shaping the national culture and tradition.

A multicultural perspective requires a comprehensive understanding of the relationship between 'self' and 'other'. A religious response to multiculturalism or any other discourse is too internally conditioned by its conception of *self* and *other*. To this extent, the relationship between *self* and *other* has been recognized as '*Cartesian problematic*' in the domain of philosophy and '*the problem of representation*' in the social science literature. Anthropological study on this subject matter has demonstrated how the understanding of *self* represents in parts, the appropriation and internalization of the *other*. [15] It is this dialectical relationship between *self* and *other* that influences the particular construction of identity. As Berger and Luckmann [16] pointed out: The self is a reflective entity, reflecting the attitudes first taken by significant others towards it; the individual becomes what he is, addressed as by his significant others. It entails a dialectic between identification by others and self-identification, and between objectively assigned and subjectively appropriated identity.

However, it was Edward Said [17] who provided the inter-cultural representation of the relationship between *self* and *other* within the context of power and knowledge and envisaged three possible forms of relationship between the two. First, the *other* is better; and as such, should be seen as superior to the *self*. A second possibility is that *self* is better than the *other*, which is potentially capable of improvement; s/he should be encouraged to learn from self. Third, but beyond this relationship of knowledge and power is the possibility of the recognition of the moral equality of cultures so that the *self* and *other* could learn from one another as equals.

How and where does Islam figure in the above cited three possible forms of relationship between *self* and the *other*? An answer to this question may be found in the Islamic representation of other religions and cultures based on the textual sources—*Koran* and *Hadith* (sayings of Prophet) that is otherwise a dominant norm in the academia. But as El-Zain noted: "Islam", "Economy", "history", "religion" and so on do not exist as things or entities with meaning inherent in them, but rather as articulations of structural relations, and are the outcome of these relations and not simply a set of positive terms from which we start our studies". [18]

Therefore, a single, monolithic, orientalist solution to the complex issue of (Islamic) representation of *self* and *other* will at best be a mere simplification of the otherwise complex social reality.

Rather, the Islamic representation of *self* and *other* and the relationship between the two would be 'socially constructed', bounded by the notion of 'time and space' and plural in forms depending upon such factors as doctrinal and sectarian differences, class, caste (in Indian context), status (whether minority or majority, citizen or immigrant) rural, urban, gender and regional locations of individual, groups or organizations—all those who are involved in the articulation of relationship between *self* and *other* in Islamic terms or what I have called 'Scholarly Islam' as against 'Everyday Islam'. [19] Within this gamut of Islamic representation of *self* and *other*, a Muslim response to the issue of multiculturalism and secularism is obtained through the interaction of textual Islamic narrative from above and specific living realities of himself/herself from below.

Muslim Responses to Multiculturalism: Liberal Dimension

While the Islamic texts such as Quran, Hadith literatures and other classical works by Islamic jurists have dwelt upon the rights and obligations of non-Muslim subjects under

Muslim rule within the framework of *dhimmi* (initially confined to Jews, Christians and Sabians or what is called 'People of the Book' but later added to many other communities such as Hindus [20] (depending upon the political context), there is much less engagement in Islamic theology dealing with rights and obligations of Muslims living under non-Muslims rule. As a result, the issue of 'securing a Muslim way of life' under non-Muslim rule has become the most important agenda for discussions among the Islamic scholars across the world where Muslims are living today as religious minority under the non-Muslim majority rule.

It is a concern with 'living a Muslim life' or 'preservation of imagined Islamic identity' under the non-Muslim rule that primarily shapes, conditions or determines the responses of various individual Muslims or Muslim groups to the principles and norms of political governance depending upon their respective understanding of 'what constitutes a Islamic/Muslim life', often conditioned by class, sect, national, regional, gender, rural and urban location of the concerned individual Muslim or Muslim groups. Within this larger context, Muslims response to multiculturalism in European nations, particularly in Britain, Germany and France, and in India has mostly been a response to pattern of secular rule and secularism in these countries that provides a differentiated space for religious life for different religious communities depending upon the historical relationship between religious communities, nation and state.

Muslim response to multiculturalism can be broadly classified into two categories: an ideological and everyday religious response. The former, a minority intellectual trend, broadly consists of two facets of process of Islamic constructions: liberal and radical. The liberal facet of Islamic constructions within the minority context—both in India and in Europe—has decisively rejected the relevance of old classic Islamic model of *Darul-Islam* (Abode of Islam) versus *Darul-Harb* (Abode of War) in the present world. Instead, many

Islamic representatives and voices of this trend including that of Fethullah Gulen, (b. 1941), Tariq Ramadan (b. 1962), Farid Esack (b. 1958), Muhammad Talibi (b. 1921), Maulana Wahiduddin Khan (b. 1925) and Asghar Ali Engineer (1939-2013) have increasingly advocated 'diversity' and 'pluralism' as primarily 'divinely intended', based on several Quranic verses, the important among them being: 'Had God Willed, He would have created one community', 'God has made you into nations and tribes, compete among themselves for the sake of Allah' and 'We believe in what has been revealed to us and what has been revealed to you; Our god and your God is One'.

Further, they have proposed alternative Islamic conceptions such '*Darul Aman*' (a state at peace with Islam), '*Darul Shadha*' (to bear witness the truth of Islam), '*Darul Ahad*' (land of the pact) and '*Darul Hizmet*' (to serve the humanity) in order to provide the Islamic legitimation of living of Muslim minority under non-Muslim majority context. The thrust of their Islamic discourses is that the principle of democratic pluralism, diversity, tolerance, peaceful coexistence, brotherhood, universal human rights, love, compassion, service, and loyalty to the nation-state are the *core values* of Islam as grounded in normative values of Quran, Hadith, Islamic Schools of Law, goals of Sharia, life of Prophet Muhammad and Companions in Mecca and in the initial years of Madina including what is called 'Madina Constitution or Pact', Rule of Four Rightly Guided Caliphs and dominant facet of political rule of Muslim Empires in the past.

The liberal facet of Islamic ideological constructions represents the aspirations of dominant section of formerly educated, rich and middle class Muslims who are well integrated in the opportunity structure of the host societies. In the European context, it is the model of *Darul Shadha*—associated with writings of Tariq Ramadan [21]—and *Darul Hizmet*—associated with Fateullah Gulen [22]—that have gained currency among the well-to-do segment of second and third generation of Muslim immigrant communities. Though Ramadan is primarily a product of western, secular knowledge system and Gulen, a trained *alim, imam*, preacher and product of Islamic knowledge system, however both have developed a Islam inspired civil society discourse, unlike the discourse of Islamism, and enables or empowers Muslim to move in any trans-cultural, trans-religious or trans-secular space across the globe without being fearful of losing their faith or Islamic identity.

With relation to the West, both have vociferously advocated that the West/Europe with its democratic regimes, civil liberty and human rights provides far better conditions and rights to observe Muslim faith, participate in public affairs and negotiate their demands in democratic way than which is obtained in the Muslim countries. In a recent newspaper article, Gulen has called for a critical, contextualised reading of Islam and stated that 'the Muslim citizens of Europe want to live in peace and tranquillity. Despite the negative climate, they should strive to engage more with their local and national governments to help work towards more inclusive policies that better integrate their community with the larger society'. [23]

More than 'Islamicizing the modernity' or 'Islamicizing the French or British or European identity', these Islamic discourses create the possibility of being Muslim and British/French/European together by avoiding excessive-ritualistic-cum-identity dimension of Islam. In these discourses, the Islamic resources of *Ijtihad and dawa* has emerged as the principal instrument in the hands of liberal Muslims to engage and interact with 'religious other' or 'secular other' in the form of inter-cultural and inter-faith dialogue both from the point of view of presenting Islam before the host societies as essentially an ethical, moral, humanistic discourse and serving the 'common universal goods and values' as well as gaining acceptance and integration of Muslim community in the host societies.

These Islamic liberal, moderate Islamic discourses intends

to contribute to the process of integration of Muslim minority community by advocating the accommodation of Islam within the exiting legal structure of Church-State relationship, helping to remove the misperception or fear among Muslims about secularism as 'threat' to conservation and preservation of Islamic way of life, addressing the question of social and economic discrimination and deprivation among segments of Muslims within the legal structure of citizenship, condemning the incidents of terrorism conducted by radical Muslims as 'un-Islamic', placing high premium on education as 'the' source for becoming 'good Muslim/sgood citizens' and ensuring upward mobility in the opportunity structure. In the process, these discourses have paved way for three political trends, which are visible mostly among the segments of middle and upper middle strata of Muslim communities in Europe.

The first is related to the creation of representative platform of Muslim communities to meet the European government's demand for 'single Muslim/representative institutions' to negotiate the matter related to faith and also other social issues related with the Muslim community. Thus, the large number of national Muslim bodies in European countries such as Muslim Council of Britain (MCB), German Council of Islam, French Conseil Français du Culte Musulman (CFCM), Exécutif des Musulmans de Belgique etc., which is visible today has come into existence through the combination of hard work of moderate Muslim leadership from below and the support of the government from above. Though these institutions continue to suffer from legitimacy deficit and credibility in the eyes of some segment of Muslim communities and have proved deficient in preventing the growth of Islamic radicalism/militancy/terrorism among sections of Muslim youths within Europe, they do play an important role in moderating the public opinion among the Muslim population within the European hemisphere.

Speaking from within the system, these Muslim organisations and individual Muslim voices are lobbying hard with the European governments for extending legal protection of religion (such as Blasphemy law in UK) and religious rights and facilities—which is constitutionally available to other religious groups—to Islam and Muslim groups on the ground of existing regime of civic, religious and human rights as well as existing pattern of Church-State relations within the host European countries. In addition to this, Ramadan has repeatedly called upon the European governments to acknowledge 'Muslim/Islamic' contribution to the making of European modernity, which in turn would help the integration of immigrant Muslim community.

Second, a great number of Muslim and Islamic scholars, assisted by the respective European governments as well as the European Union, are involved in the creation of a homogenized, codified, singular conception of *Sharia* that conforms to the European value system or what is called the construction of Euro-Islam. [24] The idea of Euro-Islam signifies a European version of Islam that would conform to the fundamental democratic and secular values of Europe. Third, there is growing participation of Muslim communities in the political process of the host countries and Muslim communities have started sharing the power structure at least at the local level of governance structure.

In India, the dominant Muslim response to the given multicultural political reality has been traditionally articulated in the Islamic theory of '*darul ahad*, (land of the pact), derived from Prophet Muhammad's pact *(ahad)* with the Jews of Medina after his *hijra* (migration). The theory was first articulated by Maulana Hussein Ahmed Madni (1879-1957), principle of Dar al-Ulum, Deoband; [25] and leader of Jamaiat Ulema-Hind [26] and Maulana Abdul Kalam Azad (1888-1958), President of Indian National Congress from 1940-1946 and subsequently served as education minister in independent India, that subsequently became the basis for Muslims to live under non-Muslim secular rule in independent India. Highlighting the cultural understanding of '*Umma*' they articulated and advocated the notion of 'composite territorial nationalism' in the light of Islamic doctrine of governance based on Medina constitution [27] within which Muslims can live with non-Muslims without any fear or danger to Islamic life and opposed the division of the country on religious lines. [28]

According to this thesis, Muslims and non-Muslims have entered upon a mutual contract in India since Independence to establish a secular state under which Muslims would be free to exercise their religious obligations, at least in personal sphere. [29] In other words, allegiance of a Muslim citizen to the non-Muslim state is conditional upon the recognition and protection of Muslim identity, at least in personal sphere. Any cursory observation to the 'Muslim politics' in post-Independence period of India would reveal how the traditional *Ulema* not only jealously guarded the domain of Muslim personal laws from the intrusive interference from the government in the name of reform but over the years has also expanded the realm of personal laws and symbolic expression of Islam in public sphere as evident from inclusion of birthday of Prophet Muhammad as national holy day in 1990.

Since the Indian Constitution itself postulates the notion of 'multicultural citizen', Muslims in India, unlike Muslim immigrants in Europe, do not suffer from any contradiction in living simultaneously with both Muslim and Indian identity. Neither, unlike in Europe, they felt the pressure of representing themselves in a single body as the Government of India at various levels, by virtue of its political practice, conducts negotiation with religious groups or sects within the religious groups depending upon the political contexts. Moreover, the community articulates any attack on their 'life, liberty, property and freedom' including religious freedom as violation of practice of Indian secularism. In this regard, the Government of India has constituted National and State level Minority Commissions to register and investigate the cases related to violation of rights of minority communities.

In fact the discourse of secularism in India, to a large extent, is a discourse on minority rights. Nonetheless, like Muslim immigrants in Europe, the political loyalty of Muslim community is suspected among some liberal, secular and communal segments of majoritarian Hindu segment. One continues to find the political rhetoric of '*Nationalist Muslims*' versus '*Separatist Muslims*', which was constructed in the pre-Partition days of Colonial India, vis-a-vis Muslim community in the public domain. [30]

However, it would be fair to observe that the practice of secularism along with the regime of minority rights, the scope of which has been gradually expanded by successive judicial pronouncement and the political practice of Indian secularism, has helped the integration of Muslim community in the Indian state despite the growing economic, political and social deprivation among the Muslim community as highlighted in various governmental commissions. [31] Moreover, by participating in the political process, Muslim communities keep negotiating their religious, political, economic and social concerns with ruling political actors and oppositions alike some of which are sometimes accepted or rejected depending upon the political context and the political weight of the demands. [32]

Moreover, since the community does not suffer from cultural and religious deprivation barring a few incidents of destruction of mosques during Hindu-Muslim riots including the infamous demolition of Babri masjid in 1992 and the government's surveillance over madrasas, it does not see Indian state and society as 'enemy of Islam', which partly explains the absence of large-scale trend of Islamic radicalism among Indian Muslim youth despite the favourable internal and external conditions that exist in India for the same. [33]

Limitation of Liberal Facet of Islam in Integration of Muslim Minority

However, notwithstanding the increasing acceptance of

value of pluralism and multiculturalism within liberal face of Islam that helps in advancing the agenda of integration of Muslim community in the host societies, the discourse continue to suffer from 'superiority of Islamic self' both within Europe and in India. Thus, it is ironical that one finds the celebration of Ottoman *millet* system and its bizarre, even nonsensical, comparison with the present-day multiculturalism that calls for the equal treatment and recognition of all cultures in the public sphere, among some of the liberal Muslim academia and intelligentsia living in Europe, essentially to demonstrate the superiority of the Islamic system of governance that was supposedly *magnanimous*, [34] *fair* and *just* vis-a-vis the present day Western/Christian system of rule that is considered *discriminatory*, *unfair* and *unjust*, particularly to the Muslim communities.

In a similar manner, the Muslim Kingdom in India has been represented in many of liberal Muslim's writings as 'generous' and 'maginamous'—treating the culture and religion of non-Muslims groups with respect within the notion of *'dhimmi'*(non-Muslim subjects under the Muslim rule). This 'Muslim sense of superiority' in the Indian context was best expressed by Maulana Abul Hasan Ali Nadwi (1913-1999), one of the most influential contemporary Islamic thinkers of the Muslim world. In a response to an interview conducted by Christian W. Troll on the issue of accommodation and status of Muslims in a non-Muslim nation-state such as India, Maulana Nadwi remarked, "Considering the role they (Muslims) have played in the history of India, ruling the country successfully and blamelessly for 800 years, and taking into account the superior religious and moral equipment God has bestowed upon them as the final and best umma, possessing Qur'an, hadith, and sira as well as the fully developed sharia, they are bound to be asked by their co-citizens to give decisive leadership. Living in a republican (*jumhuri*) set up, they hold the balance in lawmaking and other areas of national life".

Moreover, its thrust on 'communitarianism' in the name of multiculturalism hinders the prospect of internal democratization of community, particularly its gender-relations, which is a vital aspect of integration. This is true for both Muslim communities living in India and Europe. The politics of communitarianism has two aspects. First, it has inherent tendency to promote the process of homogenization within the Muslim community by totalizing the category of 'Muslim' and 'Islam'. Both in India and Europe, the self-styled leadership of the Muslim community has mostly raised the issues related to Islamic faith and identity. [35] It may be noted here that the emergence of Political Islam is, in part, connected with this process of 'homogenization' and 'ideologization' of Islam in the contemporary period. [36] Second, it has an inherent tendency to suppress the internal dissent, alternative Islamic view points, dissenting minority Islamic sects and orientations or demand for gender justice in the name of unity of community.

In fact, its attitude towards the principles of pluralism varies from 'reluctant acceptance' to 'outright rejection' of the *idea* of equal recognition of relative definition of Truth, [37] if not in terms of internal legal and doctrinal pluralism that exists within Islam. [38] Almost all liberal scholars of Islam uphold the 'idea of Absolute Truth (of Islam)' at the cost of Principle of Relative Truth, which underlines the possibility that Truth also exists among other religious traditions. In this context, it may be noted that Pakistan in many ways symbolizes the rejection of India's plural and multicultural ethos. The spirited opposition of late Mahmood Madani, the architect of Islamic doctrine of *darul-ahad*, to the idea of Pakistan was based on consideration that such division would harm the purpose of Islamic dawah: Islamicization of the Indian society.

Muslim Response to Multiculturalism: Radical Dimension

The traditional Islamic formulation of *darul Islam* versus *darul Harb* continues to influence radical facet of Islamic constructions in both European and Indian context in varying degree. Under the radical frame of Islamic discourse, Islamic history, doctrines, values and norms are primarily looked upon and interpreted from ideological and political frame leading to the development of political Islam or Islamism with an eventual goal of creation of Islamic state and Islamization of society by utilizing all possible means: legal, illegal, constitutional, peaceful and violent. While the radical facet of Islam is still a minority trend in the Western society, however the net effect of their actions, particularly the violent ones, outlived their marginal and minority presence in the society and as such hampers the process of integration as it negatively affects the mutual perception of interactions. The appeal of such discourse is found among segments of lower Muslim middle class immigrant community, which suffers from a greater degree of alienation on account of various reasons including severe economic marginalization.

Unlike the liberal facet of Islam, the representation of the West suffers from negative image in the writings of radical representatives of Islam. Under the doctrine of *Jahaliyya*, first propounded by Maulana Maududi, the architect of Jammat-e-Islami in South Asia, and later expanded by Sayyid Qutub—the ideologue of Muslim Brotherhood in Egypt—the West is projected as suffering from 'cumulative internal disorder' represented by 'laxed morality', 'sexual obscenity', 'vulgar consumerism', 'rampant racism' etc. and contrasted with 'pure', 'simple', 'honoured' and 'respectful' Islamic life. There are plenty of negative statements one can find in the speeches and writings of radical representatives of Islam living in the West. [39] For instance, an important functionary of Milli Gorous, Turkish Islamic movement in Europe, in Berlin argued in 2005 that: "Every 40 minutes a suicide takes place somewhere in Germany. This is the result of the fact that we live in a materialist system, therefore there is need for an Islamic organization which can guide the way towards Islam". [40] Konrad, the co-editor of this volume, has conducted extensive interview with such Muslims and organisations in the European cities and called them as 'uncompromising Muslimness' and those with liberal attitude as 'Muslim Civicness'. [41]

Since Christians and Jews constitute 'a people of the book', the representation of the West in terms of *darul* Islam vs *darul harb* has not been debated heavily even among the radical facets of Islam, unlike India where the debates concerning whether India falls within the domain of *darul* Islam or *darul Harb* continues to take place, partly on the ground that India is predominantly the land of polytheists and idol-worshippers across the liberal and radical spectrum of Islam. [42] As a result, representation of 'majority Hindus' among Islamic scholars in India ranges from '*Kafir*' (non-believer) [43] or *mushrikin* (the idol worshippers) to '*Ahle-a-kitab*' (People of the Book). [44]

In the radical writings of Islam, the notion of *da'wah* emerged as the most important Islamic duty for the Muslims living in a minority context with an eventual vision of transforming the non-Muslim majority into Muslim through the work of *da'wah,* leading to the establishment of Islamic state and society. It treats minority status of Muslim as 'de facto situational reality', 'a temporary phenomenon', and then proceeds to engage with the concepts of 'pluralism', 'multiculturalism' and 'diversity' with an eventual conclusion: either to accept these concepts as 'pragmatic necessity' or to reject them on the basis that they contradict the "Islamic" *prescription* of good life. [45] In India, Jammat Islami and a host of other Islamic organisations conduct regulars *dawa* activities in the form of seminars and conferences with a sole purpose to present themselves as a democratic force and morally superior.

The radicalization of a segment of Muslim youth further consists of two trends: the apolitical Salafist conservatism and Salafist Islamic militancy/terrorism. The former refers to growing identification with religiosity in terms of behavioural expression (having long beard, mosque attendance, wearing hijab or veil or niqab etc.) and keeping minimum contact with the outside world. In a way, they prefer to withdraw from society and lead an isolated religious life. The latter is a violent Islamic reaction to what they consider a *jahilliıya* society, the members of which includes both Muslims and non-Muslims. There are multiple reasons behind the emergence of these trends among segment of Muslim youth, the elaboration of which is outside of the scope of this paper.

However suffice would be here to mention the both apolitical Salafist conservatism and Salafist Islamic terrorism in both Europe and India is in part a result of perceived religious victimization/discrimination/marginalization, which is often sharpened by the global jihadi Islamic discourses and networks. This trend is confined to segment of upwardly mobile, urban, formerly educated lower and middle class youth who suffer from hopelessness to improve their life situations in this world.

Muslim Response to Multiculturalism: An Everyday Life Experiences

Beyond this ideological construction of Islam by both liberal and radical facet of Islam, there exists an 'Everyday Islam' or 'Islam in every day life', which refers to the reality of 'lived Islam' [46] that resides in the great mass of Muslims cutting across class, caste, sect, gender, and region, rural, urban and other social categories. It is handed down by generation to generation in the form of practice, and is connected with the life process of common Muslims and have developed the 'internal social code', that is considered Islamic, to interact and negotiate within themselves and with other social groups of the society. By and large, they live peacefully, pay taxes, law abiding, follow the governmental rules and exhibit a high degree of political loyalty to their nations and believe in the political system of democracy and secularism. [47]

Common Muslims acknowledge the general concepts developed by the Islamic scholars, but they choose to live according to more particularistic notions of Islam, which conforms to the patterns of their daily experience. As Olivier Roy remarked, "Although there is a long tradition of exegesis and fatwa on what a Muslim should or should not do when confronted with a non-Muslim environment and practices, most Muslims find a way to deal with that without contacting fatwaonline.com". [48] Similarly, in the Indian context, late Muhammad Mujeeb long ago noted: "A bird's eye view of the variety of beliefs and practices and customs among Indian Muslims will convince us that it was not the Shariat of Islam that they adopted but the manners and customs and to some extent even their belief that became the Shariat of Islam, of their Islam". [49]

It is thus hardly surprising that the first generation of "single male Muslim" migrants in Western Europe did not make any demand of "Islamic presence" in the public sphere, not because they were "illiterate", "poor", or had less knowledge of Islam; or primarily saw themselves as "economic migrants" for a temporary period to eventually return to their native place; or lacking the historical sense of Islam but because they never saw, even in the sojourn, their historically established Islamic/Muslim identity as being threatened by outside forces as they were "accustomed" to performing what they considered as an "Islamic duty" in any given space.

It is only with the intervention of ideological Islamic scholars, whether liberal/moderate or radical/conservative, that facilitated in channelizing the "frustrated social existence" of second and third generation European born Muslim youths into the "Islamic cause", some of whom went into the direction of Islamic militancy. Similarly, the new research on 'Partition of India' has indicated that a large number of Muslims who migrated from India to now Pakistan did not have a sense that they were creating a new nation with regime of passport and visa but primarily motivated with consideration of better condition and facility to lead an 'Islamic way of life'. [50] The growing Islamization of section of present day Muslim generation of India is at best the result of homogenization of otherwise fuzzy plural identity of individual Muslim—partly induced through the external agency of self-proclaimed Islamic leaders—whether liberal or radical—of the community and global Islamic networkings.

In fact, the general perception among the Muslim masses has been that issues such as the veiling of women, interest-free banking, banning of alcohol, regular attendance at mosques in the Indian setting and the issue of Islamic instruction in the public school, the construction of the mosque, the recognition of Islam in public sphere, the issue of headscarf in the European setting respectively or the Islamic ideological debate concerning the 'status' of Muslims living in non-Muslim country in both the continents—whether *Darul al-Islam, Darul al-Harb, Darul al Aman, Darul al Ahad, Darul al-Shahada, Darul Hizmet* etc.—that preoccupy the forces of liberal and radical facets of Islam, are virtually irrelevant to them. In fact, the Saidian's third possibility of the relationship between *self* and *other* in the form of recognition of moral equality of all cultures lies in the very domain of this notion of Everyday Islam.

Similarly, the vast magnitude of Muslim immigrants including the European born Muslims, like the Indian Muslim mass, though concerned with things called "Islamic", are much bothered about their daily life existential situations—the issue of unemployment, rampant racism, citizenship, housing etc. It is through these daily courses of existential struggle that they learn the art of mutual accommodation, adjustment and living together without undergoing the ideological learning process of liberal or radical facet of Islam. Within Europe, Muslims, particularly youth, are developing 'hybrid identity' as reflected in the development of Turkish 'hip-hop and rap' and Arabic 'Rai' music, as well as, in the publication of bi-lingual literature. In India, Muslims are accustomed to live with hybrid identity, as testified by variation in the Muslim lifestyles across India, without any understanding that such hybrid life compromises their Islamic identity.

Islam in everyday life may appear to be conservative in its social ethos from the modernist perspective but accepts the logic of pluralism. There is considerable historical and ethnographical evidence that the common people everywhere, irrespective of individual religious identity, have long been comfortable with religious plurality. They acknowledge religious difference as the experienced reality: they do not consider it good or bad. As Malik has rightly stated, "There is a difference between multiculturalism as a lived experience and multiculturalism as an enforced ideology". [51] In other words, social harmony, or agreement, is built on the basis of difference. The average Muslim mass, irrespective of the context, learned the value of accommodation and adjustment through the struggle of daily life process without resorting to ideological legitimization of their conduct. Thus, multiculturalism is experienced in everyday life of Muslims as what Gilroy [52] calls 'convivial forms of multiculturalism' in which differences are actively negotiated and relationship with other is based on the principle of recognition and respect for difference.

It is not just a political framework that formally regulates inter-cultural or inter-religious relations but 'a collectively shared system of values, ideas and practices'. [53] Considerable amount of research with reference to India and Europe have demonstrated that accommodations and adjustments bearing cultural exchanges, shared value-orientations and lifestyles at micro level have been worked out by the people in the course of their everyday life in both the intra-religious (within Islam) and inter-religious (between Muslims and non-Muslims) contexts. [54] Given this trend, it would not be an exaggeration to claim that unlike liberal facet of Islam that has the *unintended* effect of eroding the diverse, hybrid identity of Muslims, the fuzzy, non-ideological Islam of everyday has potential to produce a 'Muslim French', a 'Muslim German', a 'Muslim British', a 'Muslim European' and a 'Muslim Indian'.

Conclusion

Thus, what comes out from the above analysis is that there is no single Muslim response to the idea of multiculturalism. Rather responses to such issues depend upon the social, class, regional or sectarian location of Muslims—both individual and group. Moreover, even though Muslims as a minority group prefer to be governed under the multicultural framework as it provides a modicum of space to the community to preserve and promote their Muslim/Islamic identity, some continues to display a sense of 'superior Islam self' vis-a-vis others, which hampers them from developing a multicultural outlook and thus hinders them from integrating fully in the host societies. However, notwithstanding these limitations, the possibility of integration of Muslim minority communities in the host societies lies greater within the domain of 'everyday Islam' than in 'liberal facet of Islam' as outlined above.

Endnotes

1. Almost a similar number of Muslims live in Central and Eastern part of the Continent. However, the character of these communities is different hence the volume focuses mainly on the Western communities. For detailed statistics, see PEW, "The Future of the Global Muslim Population", PEW, New York 2011.
2. This included provision of *halal* food in public schools, facility for prayer hall, construction of mosques in the form of prayer halls, burial places, religious holidays for Muslims, religious service in army, hospital and jail, right to wear hijab in educational institutions and public work places, recognition of Islam as official religion in Belgium and Austria, public funding of privately run Muslim schools and support to Islamic instructions in public schools in some cases etc.
3. 'Merkel says German multicultural society has failed', October

17, 2010, available at:
http://www.bbc.com/news/world-europe-11559451, accessed on December 29, 2015.

4. 'Nicolas Sarkozy declares multiculturalism had failed', *The Telegraph*, February 11, 2011, available at: http://www.telegraph.co.uk/news/worldnews/europe/france/8317497/Nicolas-Sarkozy-declares-multiculturalism-had-failed.html , accessed on December 29, 2015.
5. 'State multiculturalism has failed, says David Cameron', February 5, 2011, available at: http://www.bbc.com/news/uk-politics-12371994, accessed on December 29, 2015.
6. Arun Kundani (2002_, "The Death of Multiculturalism", *Race & Class*, 43, pp. 67-72.
7. Christian Joppke (2004), "The Retreat of Multiculturalism in the Liberal State: Theory and Policy", *British Journal of Sociology* 2, 55, pp. 237-257.
8. Nasar Meer and Tariq Modood (2009), "The Multicultural State We're In: Muslims, 'Multiculture' and the 'Civic Re-Balancing' of British Multiculturalism", *Political Studies*, 57, pp. 473-497. Also, Modood, Tariq (2011), "Post-Immigration 'Difference' and Integration: The Case of Muslims in Western Europe", London: The British Academy.
9. This includes language test, knowledge of national history and tradition, social and behavioural tests vis-a-vis common/national values etc., See the Cantle Report (2011) in the case of UK and Law on Civic Integration on New Comers (1998) in the case of Netherlands. Similar programmes were sought to be instituted by various European governments whether—left or right—including all Scandinavian countries, Belgium, Austria and Germany.
10. Europe, France, Belgium, Austria, Switzerland and Netherlands have placed full nation-wide ban on wearing niqab or burqa, while in Italy and Spain the ban is confined to a region/state.
11. This case relates to lady called Shahbano who was divorced by her husband in her old age. The matter reached the Supreme Court. The Court interpreted the sacred text of *Koran* and *Hadith* and passed the judgment for her future maintenance to be charged upon her ex-husband'. The All India Muslim Personal Law Board raised the issue that a secular institution does not

have a *right to interpret* the *Koran* and the *Hadith* and hence the court judgment amounts to interference in the matters of personal law that has been sanctioned by the Constitution to the Muslim communities. The movement became so powerful that it forced the then Rajiv Gandhi government to annul the Supreme Court judgment by passing a very retrogressive law called Muslim Women Protection Law (1989). On the implication of Shahbano case for national politics in Indian, see, Veena Das (1997), (ed.), "Critical Events: An Anthropological Perspective on Contemporary India", Oxford University Press. Delhi.

12. See, Charles Taylor/Amy Gutmann (1992), "Multiculturalism and the Politics of Recognition", Princeton University Press; Will Kymlicka (1995), "Multicultural Citizenship: A Liberal Theory of Minorities", Oxford University Press, also (1994) (ed.), "Minority Rights", Oxford University Press; Bihku Parekh (2000), "Rethinking Multiculturalism, Cultural Diversity and Political Theory", Palgrave.
13. Ibid.
14. Lloyld I. Rudolph and Sussanne Hoeber Rudolph, "Living with Multiculturalism: Universalism and Particularlism in an Indian Historical Context", in Richard A. Sheweder, Martha Minow, and Hazel Rose Markus (ed.) 'Engaging Cultural Differences: The Multicultural Challenges in Liberal Democarcies', Rusesell Sage Foundation/New York, 2002, pp. 43-62; also, Harihar Bhattacharya, "Multiculturalism in Contemporary India", *International Journal on Multicultural Societies* (IJMS), Vol. 5, No. 2, 2003, pp. 151-164.
15. R.S. Khare (1999), "The Other's Double: The Anthropologist's Bracketed Self Notes on Cultural Representation and Privileged Discourse", *New Literary History: A Journal of Theory and Interpretation,* Vol. 23, No. 1, pp. 96-110.
16. Peter Berger and Thomas Luckmann (1967), "The Social Construction of Reality: Everything that Passes for Knowledge in Society", London: Allen Lane, p. 32.
17. See Edward Said (1978), "Orientalism", New York: Pantheon Books and Edward Said (1994), "Culture and Imperialism", Amsterdam: Atlas.
18. Abdul Hamid El-Zein (1977), "Beyond Ideology and Theology: The Search for the Anthropology of Islam", *Annual Review of Anthropology*, 6, p. 251.

19. Anwar Alam (2007), "Scholarly Islam and Everyday Islam: Reflection on the Debate of Integration of Muslim Minority in Western Europe and India", *Journal of Muslim Minority Affairs,* Vol. 27, No. 2, August, pp. 241-260,
20. Scholars like al-Biruni (d. 1048), Mirza Mazhar Jane-e-Janan (d. 1780) and Dara Shikoh (d. 1659) believed Vedas, the Hindu scriptures, to be divinely inspired and considered Hindus as people of the Book who had prophets like other revealed religions. See Aziz Ahmad (1969), "Studies in Islamic Culture in the Indian Environment", Oxford: Oxford University Press, pp. 78-80.
21. Tariq Ramadan is a Swiss citizen and a grandson of Hasan al-Banna, the founder of the Muslim Brotherhood in Egypt. Trained in a Western and Islamic philosophy, Ramadan has written many critically acclaimed Islamic literatures dealing with theme of integration of Muslim immigrants living in Europe and has influenced young Muslim generations in Europe. Some of his important writings are: (a) "To Be European Muslims", Leicester: Islamic Foundation: Markfield Conference Centre, UK, 1999 and (b) "Western Muslim and the Future of Islam", Oxford. Oxford University Press, 2004.
22. Fethullah Gulen is an influencial Turkish Islamic scholar, currently living in the United States, who has inspired a powerful Islamic çivil social movement called Hizmet movement with its educational chain of schools, coaching institutes and university and inter-faith dialogue centres in more than 160 countries. For the exposition of view of Gulen, see, Paul Weller and Ihsan Yilmaz (2012) (ed.), "European Muslims, Civility and Public Life: Perspectives On and From the Gülen Movement", Continuum International Publishing Group, London.
23. "Muslims, We Have to Critically Review Our Understanding of Islam", December 17, 2015, available at: http://www.todayszaman.com/op-ed_muslims-we-have-to-critically-review-our-understanding-of-islam_407253.html, accessed on December 31, 2015.
24. Mathias Rohe (2004), "The Formation of European Sharia" in Jamal Malik (2004) (ed.), 'Muslims in Europe: From the Margin to the Centre', London: Transaction Publishers.
25. One of the famous traditional Islamic seminary in the Muslim

World.

26. A body of Ulema linked with Dar al-Ulum, Deoband, created during the Khilafat Movement in India (1919-1922), had opposed the idea of partition of the country. After Independence, it was closely allied with the Indian National Congress.
27. See Ali Bulac, "The Medina Document", in Charles Kurzman (1998) (ed.), 'Liberal Islam: A Source Book', Oxford University Press. Various Islamic and Muslim scholars have drawn heavily upon the Meccan verses of Quran that speaks of love, tolerance and dialogue. Many of them have hailed the Madina Constitution as the first multicultural constitution in the world.
28. See Maulana Hussein Ahmad Madani (2005), "Composite Nationalism and Islam", translated by Mohammad Anwar Hussein and Hasan Imam, Delhi: Manohar Publications. Also, Ian Henderson Douglas (1988), "Abul Kalam Azad: An Intellectual and Religious Biography", New Delhi: Oxford University Press.
29. On this aspect, see Syed Shabuddin and Theodre P. Wright Jr., "India: Muslim Minority Politics and Society", in John L. Esposito (ed.), 'Islam in Asia: Religion, Politics and Society', New York: Oxford University Press, 1987, p. 157; W.C. Smith (1957), "Islam in Modern History", Princeton, NJ: Princeton University Press, p. 285; Christian W. Troll, "Sharing Islamically in the Pluralistic Nation-State of India: The Views of Some Contemporary Indian Muslim Leaders and Thinkers", in Yvonne Yazbeck Haddad and Wadi Z. Haddad (eds.), 'Christian-Muslim Encounters', Gainesville: University of Florida Press, 1995, pp. 245-261.
30. See, "Culture Minister Mahesh Sharma Speaks: Despite Being a Muslim, A.P.J. Abdul Kalam was a Nationalist", *Indian Express*, September 18, 2015, available at: http://indianexpress.com/article/india/india-others/culture-minister-speaks-despite-being-a-muslim-kalam-was-a-nationalist/#sthash.q994PJ6c.dpuf, retrieved on December 31, 2015.
31. See, "Congress Committee Report, 1957", "The Gujral Committee Report, 1976", "The Gopal Singh Panel Report, 1983", "The Sachar Commission Report: Social, Economic and Educational Status of the Muslim Community of India, 2005", and Ranganath Misra National Commission for Linguistic and

Religious Minorities, 2007

32. This has been reflected in many major government initiatives: from grants to minority educational institutions to giving 'minority status' to various Muslim educational institutions; extending the benefit of affirmative policy to OBC Muslims in the opportunity structure of the state, the inclusion of Urdu in the Constitution's Eighth Schedule, the declaration of Urdu as the second official language in many states, the setting up the National Council for Promotion of Urdu Language Board (1996), the setting up the Maulana Azad National Urdu Central University (1998), the Protection of Religious Place of Worship Act, 1992, the upgradation of Jamia Millia Islamia as a Central University (1988), the Muslim Women Protection of Right on Divorce Act, 1989; the Prevention of Terrorism (Repeal) Ordinance, 2004; setting up various commissions to look into the grievances of Muslims, the National Minority Development and Financial Corporation, 1992, the setting up the National Commission for Minority Rights (1978), reconstituted as the National Commission for Minorities (1992), the National Commission for Minority Educational Institutions, 2004 etc.
33. Anwar Alam (2007), "Political Management of Islamic Fundamentalism: A View From India", *Ethnicities*, Vol. 7(1), pp. 30-60,
34. More on merits and demerits of millet system in W. Kymlicka and E. Pfostl, "Multiculturalism and Minority Rights in the Arab World", Oxford University Press, New York.
35. In India, 'Muslim politics' veers around preservation of Urdu, minority character of Muslim universities, Muslim Personal law, re-construction of Babri Masjid, representation of Islam in history textbook etc. See Anwar Alam (2003), "Democratization of Indian Muslim: Some Reflections", *Economic and Political Weekly*, Vol. xxxviii, No. 46, November 15, pp. 4881-4885. The major demands raised by Muslim organisations in Europe is mentioned in the beginning of this paper as well as in the introduction of this volume.
36. Anwar Alam (2009), "Modernity, West and Political Islam: A Critique", *Third Frame: Literature, Culture and Society*, Vol. 2, No. 1, January-March, pp. 36-56.
37. In the western context, this observation is drawn from my fieldwork conducted in Berlin, Germany (July-August 2005),

Paris, France (March-April 2005), Bristol and London (May 2005), and Amsterdam and Lieden, the Netherlands (September 2005), which was funded by AVH Foundation, Germany. It would suffice to point out that the reluctance and even rejection of the framework of pluralism and multiculturalism was not only obvious in terms of according equal recognition and respect to other faiths and social groups like women and those who have different sexual orientation like lesbians and gays, but even in terms of according equality to intra-Islamic/Muslim groups. Modood found similar ambivalent attitude among the Muslim groups towards the issue of pluralism and multiculturalism. See, Tariq Modood (2007), "British Muslim Perspectives on Multiculturalism", *Theory, Culture and Society,* March, 24:187-213.

38. This internal legal pluralism within Islam has been reflected in the development of four legitimate schools of law: Shafi, Maliki, Hanafi and Hanbali.
39. On the world view of radical Islamic organisations and their representation of the West, see, E. Karagiannis and C. McCauley (2006), "Hizb ut-Tahrir al-Islami: Evaluating the Threat Posed by a Radical Islamic Group that Remains Non-violent", *Terrorism and Political Violence,* 2006, Vol. 8, No. 2, pp. 315-334; S. Taj-Farouki, "Islamists and the Threat of Jihad: Hizb ut-Tahrir and al-Muhajiroun on Israel and the Jews", in B.S. Turner (ed.), 'Islam: Critical Concepts in Sociology', Routledge, London, 2003; Q. Wiktorowicz (2005), "Radical Islam Rising: Muslim Extremism in the West", Rowman and Littlefield Publishers, Oxford.
40. Field work, Berlin, 2005.
41. See, Konrad Pedziwiater (2010), "The New Muslim Elites in European Cities: Religion and Active Social Citizenship Among Young Organised Muslims in Brussels and London", VDM Verlag Dr Muller GmbH & Co. KG, pp. 405-410.
42. For details, see, "Scholarly Islam and Everyday Islam: Reflection on the Debate of integration of Muslim minority in Western Europe and India", *Journal of Muslim Minority Affairs,* Vol. 27, No. 2. August 2007, pp. 247-248.
43. In extreme cases, even non-conformist Muslims could be considered unbelievers. The interesting thing in Muslim categorization is not only that believers are categorized

according to their particular "religion", but also that the various religions themselves are described or constructed according to typically Islamic criteria. Muslims have had an Islamo-centric view of religions other than Islam.

44. Thus, scholars like al-Biruni (d. 1048), Mirza Mazhar Jane-e-Janan (d. 1780) and Dara Shikoh (d. 1659) believed Vedas, the Hindu scriptures, to be divinely inspired and considered Hindus as people of the Book who had Prophets like other revealed religions. See Aziz Ahmad (1969), "Studies in Islamic Culture in the Indian Environment", Oxford: Oxford University Press, pp. 78-80.
45. See the most recent works in this regard by two important Indian Islamic scholars who are also office bearers of Jamait-Uleme Hind, the Indian branch of Jamait-e-Islami, the most dominant representative of political Islam in South Asia. Fazlur Rehman Faridi (2003), "A Reject All Recipe: Living as a Muslim in a Plural Society", Chennai: Islamic Foundation Trust; Maulana Sayyed Jalaluddin Umri (2005), "Ghayr Islami Riyasat Aur Musalman", reviewed in *Islam and Muslim Societies: A Social Science Journal*, Vol. 1, No. 1, pp. 212-215.
46. Imtiaz Ahmad and Helmut Reifeld (2004) (eds.), "Lived Islam in South Asia: Adaptation, Accommodation and Conflict", Social Science Press, New Delhi.
47. See, Bhikhu Parekh (2009), "Feeling at Home: Some Reflections on Muslims in Europe", *Harvard Middle Eastern and Islamic Review,* Vol. 8, pp. 51-85, also Tariq Modood, "Multiculturalism, Britishness and Muslims", January 27, 2011, available at: https://www.opendemocracy.net/tariq-modood/multiculturalism-britishness-and-muslims, accessed on December 31, 2015. In the Indian context, see, S.K. Mitra (2001), "Constitutional Design, Democratic Vote Counting and India's Fortuitious Multiculturalism", Heidelberg Papers in South Asian and Comparative Politics, Working Paper, 4, pp. 1-33.
48. Olivier Roy (2005), "Globalised Islam: The Search for a New Ummah", New Delhi: Rupa & Co., p. 20.
49. Mohammad Mujeeb (1985), "Indian Muslims", New Delhi: Munshiram Manoharlal Publishers Pvt. Ltd.
50. See, Ashis Nandy (1985), "The Death of an Empire", *Persimmon: Asian Literature, Arts, and Culture,* Vol. III, No. 1,

Spring; also, Anam Zakaria (2015), "The Footprints of Partition: Narratives of Four Generations of Pakistanis and Indians", Harper Collins, New Delhi.

51. Kahlid Malik, Lecture given at Institut Français, London, November 16, 2002, quoted in Siobhán McPhee, "Muslim Identity: The European Context", Sussex Migration Working Paper No. 34, September 2005, available at: https://www.sussex.ac.uk/webteam/gateway/file.php?name=mwp34.pdf&site=252.
52. Paul Gilroy (2004), "After Empire: Melancholia or Convivial Culture?", London: Routledge.
53. See Sandra Jovchelovitch (2007), "Knowledge in Context: Representations, Community and Culture", New York: Routledge; also, Wolfgang Wagner and Nicky Hayes (2005), "Everyday Discourse and Common Sense: The Theory of Social Representations", New York: Palgrave MacMillan.
54. Jamal Malik and Helmut Reifeld (2004) (ed.), "Religious Pluralism in South Asia and Europe", New Delhi: Oxford University Press; also, Imtiaz Ahmad and Helmut Reifeld (2004) (eds.), " Lived Islam", New Delhi: Social Science Press.

13

Role of Muslim Class Relations in the Politics of Islam in France and India

Z. Fareen Parvez

This paper is a comparative study of the politics of Islam and the nature of "Islamic revival" in India and France, focusing specifically on the role of Muslim class relations. It draws upon ethnographic research and interviews conducted in mosque communities and Islamic associations in Hyderabad, India, and Lyon, France. Both cases are marked by increased Islamic piety, the growth of Salafist Islam among the poor, and tension with the secular state. I argue that the relationship of Muslims to the state and to Islamic practice differs across class, with the poor in both cases increasingly alienated from the state. However, the close Muslim class relations in Hyderabad, marked by elite paternalism and political competition, ensured a degree of integration of the poor into the political field. In Lyon, however, the class divide, marked by an "abandonment" of the Muslim poor, maintains the political withdrawal and isolation of Muslim communities. In elaborating the role of class on the politics of Muslim minorities, this paper moves away from the existing focus on globalization and identity.

Much of the literature that focuses on the politics and piety of minority Muslims, especially in Europe, favours accounts of immigrant Muslim communities, such as the struggle to assimilate and reconcile conflicting identities (Gerholm and Lithman, 1988; Nielsen 1999), and analysis of controversial incidents, such as the Salman Rushdie affair (Kepel, 1997)—instead of a more state-centred political analysis of Islamic movements. Some of the literature treats the issue as a problem of clash of identities (Davis and Krauthammer, 2005). Thus, it is oriented towards exploring the kinds of organizational structures and state policies that would develop a "European" Islam, free from the influence of Islamic countries and with tempered forms of religiosity that would better fit into the dominant conception of the public sphere. Olivier Roy's work on minority Muslims has also indirectly invoked notions of identity with its focus on "globalized Islam" and the needs of migrant and "floating" Muslim populations to carve out a religious space in society within the confines of a secular state (2004, 2006).

Others, also focusing on globalization, have depicted Islamic movements as the use of religious tradition to provide meaning and identity amidst a context of cultural confusion—where such confusion, in the cultural and personal realms, is caused by globalization (Coleman in Tibi, 1992; Mohammed, 2002). For example, family structure, gender codes, and sexual mores have all been challenged by globalizing economies (Benhabib, 2002). This paper departs from these approaches by examining instead the role of the state, local histories, and class relations specifically in the Muslim-minority cases of France and India.

Based on ethnographic research in Lyon, France, and Hyderabad, India, I argue that the nature of Islamic Revival and Muslim responses demands in these cases is significantly shaped by Muslim class relations. The argument is three-fold: (i) In both cities, there is a vibrant middle-class Muslim community that makes demands of the state. The nature of these demands is shaped by national models of minority integration and economic histories. In Hyderabad, the politics of Islam is a middle-class politics of redistribution, whereas in Lyon it is a middle-class politics of recognition. (ii) Poor Muslims in both the cases are alienated from the state and reject state engagement. They have also experienced a growth of particular Salafist forms of Islamic practice that stem in part from their marginality. [1] However, in Hyderabad, there is a growth of Islamic civil societies among the poor, while in Lyon there has been a retreat of civil societies. (iii) The close Muslim class relations in Hyderabad, marked by middle-class paternalism and political competition among elites, ensures a degree of integration of the poor into a politics of redistribution and a dynamic struggle over Islamic practice and discourse. In Lyon, however, the class divide, marked by an "abandonment" of the Muslim poor, maintains the political withdrawal and isolation of Muslim communities.

France and India are ideally suited to explore the dynamics of minority Islam and its politics despite their great differences. They are both secular democracies that have been challenged by religious policy demands by Muslims, who comprise their largest minority populations. The percent of Muslims in Hyderabad and Lyon varies from 10-30 percent of the population and greater in certain neighbourhoods. Both countries have experienced widespread Islamic revivals, marked by a growth of Islamic associations, mosques, conferences, literature, and women's veiling. They have also instituted post-9/11 surveillance of Muslim neighbourhoods and experienced episodes of violent civil conflict involving poor Muslim areas. Moreover, in both the cases, Muslims have suffered dramatic downward mobility since the 1970s and discrimination, coinciding with state retrenchment of welfare. But the cases ultimately diverge due to different models of minority integration and local histories, which I argue have led to divergent Muslim class relations.

France's model of secularism, laïcité, calls for a rigid separation of church and state such that the recognition of Islam has been a slow and painful process. Laicité is also part of the ongoing effort to uphold national values of *liberté, fraternité* and *et egalité*. In this context, religious identification and organizing are often obstructed and viewed as sectarian (Bowen, 2006; Salvatore, 2007; Amiraux, 2008; Joppke, 2009). The 2004 banning of the headscarf in public schools and 2009 Commission on the burqa are but two examples. [2] Alongside extreme spatial segregation of the poor, who remain in urban peripheries and housing projects, Muslims remain divided across class. In India, there is a peculiar model of secularism ("composite nationalism") that in fact recognizes religious laws and grants full freedom to religious communities (Hasan, 1997; Hasan, 1998; Sunder Rajan, 2000).

Thus, organizing on the basis of Muslim identity is easily accomplished. In Hyderabad, the existence of Muslim political parties who compete for electoral power, alongside the city's unique history as a princely state in the colonial period, has led to class relations based on paternalism and sense of shared identity. The rest of this paper presents these divergent outcomes through three discussions: the politics of the middle-class, the creation and retreat of civil societies among the Muslim poor; and the different forms of class relations that influence the Islamic political field and religious practice.

Methodology

Data for this paper is based on 20 months of participant observation (total) at three sites in primarily two neighbourhoods in each city: Islamic schools, neighbourhood mosques, and Islamic welfare associations. These three institutions are often tied together. I studied poor neighbourhoods as well as middle-class mosques, located closer to the city centres. The poor areas of Hyderabad include a slum neighbourhood called First Lancer and the Babanagar area in the old city section of Hyderabad. In Lyon, I studied Les Minguettes, a neighbourhood in Lyon's de-industrialized *banlieue* of Vénissieux as well as a mosque community in Villeurbanne, close to the city centre. [3]

By becoming familiar with mosque communities, I was able to not only hear the *qhutbas* but also learnt about the different social and economic issues community members face, their activities and experiences with Islam, and their perspectives on the relationship between minority Muslims and the state. Both Lyon and Hyderabad have dozens to hundreds of Islamic associations, ranging from those struggling for acceptance of Islamic law to welfare and immigrant support groups, in the case of France. Part of the ethnography was attending Islamic classes and welfare training (in the Indian case), association meetings and conferences, speaking with members of ten to fifteen associations in each city, and learning the details of these organizations' missions and their placement in the broader field of Islamic activism and civil society. The ethnographic component was supplemented by 30 semi-structured interviews with mosque and association leaders, Islamic political party and philanthropical leaders (in the case of India), Islamic school-teachers and students, and regular mosque attendees.

Middle-Class Politics: Redistribution versus Recognition

In both Hyderabad and Lyon, there is a vibrant Muslim middle-class activist community that makes claims of the state. But there are two major differences between the cases. First, in the Indian case, elite and middle-class activists have remained largely independent from the state, while in the French case, Islamic associations are either state-creations or in some way penetrated by the state. Second, they are distinct, in that the former concentrates on claims to economic and social redistribution, while the latter focuses on religious recognition. These differences stem clearly from the divergent policies toward religious minorities discussed earlier. In India, Muslims enjoy full rights to religious practice, notwithstanding occasional right-wing threats to obstruct practice based on Sharia.

However, the Muslim population tends to grossly suffer as regards the disproportionate rates of illiteracy and poverty, despite the presence of a Muslim elite land-owning class (which lacks such a counterpart in France). Hyderabad's peculiar recent history is, from one perspective, a story of Muslim dislocation. The area was ruled as a Muslim princely city-state, free from British domination, during the colonial period. Following the forced administrative turnover by the post-Independence government, the 1950s and 1960s saw a dramatic exodus of wealthy Muslims to Pakistan and the United States. This ensured the replacement of Muslims by Hindus in government and military positions. The remaining options for most Muslims were to join the informal economy and/or find menial jobs such as rickshaw pulling and auto driving. Today, the majority of the city's Muslims live in the Old City under conditions of abject poverty.

Because of this history of Muslim socio-economic power, particular to Hyderabad (as opposed to other Indian cities), as well as the national model of secularism that allowed for political organizing on the basis of religious identity, there developed a solid elite and middle-class Muslim community and political parties. The MIM (Majlis-e Ittihad al-Muslimin), the major political party organized around Muslim identity, claims to represent poor Muslims in the city and has a major public presence. Philanthropic activity, which both the MIM and Islamic welfare associations embrace, has become a significant part of Muslim activist culture. It operates through a strong sense of paternalism towards the poor. This paternalistic sentiment has been partly facilitated by the unique history of Hyderabad, whereby there is nostalgia for the pre-Independence era of Muslim power and an attachment to the Old City artisan culture that flourished under princely rule.

In turn, this paternalistic culture of charity has led to the construction of schools, clinics, banks, and women's training centres in textile work and other skills. Primary schools and colleges, with significant reservations for Muslims, are among the most important activities—in a context in which the state is widely accused of withdrawing from poor Muslim neighbourhoods, shutting down schools, neglecting extreme infrastructural problems, and deliberately assigning unqualified teachers to these areas.

Again, in response to state retrenchment, many Muslim

men have taken work contracts in Saudi Arabia and other Gulf countries. Poor Muslim women, often left behind, increasingly participate in local welfare and textile training centres operated by the city's Muslim elite. Muslim activists undertake these projects independently toward the goal of autonomous civil societies, but they also make claims of the state, for example, campaigning for Muslim reservations in educational institutions and policies like food subsidies.

In sum, redistributive projects and claims of the state are what dominate the middle-class agenda and definition of the politics of Islam. At the same time, this is an ideal-type depiction of the city's Islamic political field. Both the MIM and occasionally, the philanthropic elite, also make symbolic gestures toward the defence of Islam and religious recognition apart from distributive concerns. The MIM, in particular, stages demonstrations and calls for strikes. For example, December 6 is an annual day of strike in remembrance of the Ayodhya Babri Masjid, which was destroyed that day in 1992.

In contrast to the Hyderabad case, the French Muslim activist network is deeply penetrated by the state and given little discursive or legal room to organize on the basis of Muslim identity. Smaller mosque associations in Lyon are typically connected with, or dependent on, the Grand Mosque of Lyon or CRCM (Conseil Régional du Culte Musulman Rhone-Alpes), the regional branch of the federal, state-created CFCM (Conseil Fédéral du Culte Musulman). The Grand Mosque, though independent, is nonetheless monitored by and in close communication with the state. [4]

These organizations are counter balanced by l'UOIF (Union des Organizations Islamiques de France), an umbrella Islamic organization that typically struggles against the state and claims greater representation and loyalty of French Muslims. All of these major parties, however, focus on issues of religious recognition as opposed to economic questions. This is despite the fact that most French Muslims are of poorer and working class backgrounds. Immigrant Muslims arrived after World War II to work in heavy industry, filling labour shortages in auto factories, railways, and construction. Today, following decades of deindustrialization, most immigrant and second-generation Muslims in the banlieues suffer entrenched marginality and discrimination and are disproportionately unemployed, with the unemployment rate in some neighbourhoods (such as Les Minguettes) surpassing 50 percent. Thus, it is not necessarily the case that Islamic activism would have taken the form of recognition claims instead of distributive.

Nonetheless, the recent history of obstructing Islamic practice in the name of either *laicité* or women's rights has led to a defensive, often necessary, focus on recognition. The middle-class associations I knew in Lyon were occupied in securing municipal permission to initiate mosques and Islamic schools, such as Al-Kindi, an Islamic high school, which the municipality obstructed for over a year over dubious concerns related to building codes. Private Islamic education is rare but favoured among some Muslims in light of the banning of the headscarf in public schools. Mosques, though increasingly accepted, are also stalled for long periods of time. When I was in Lyon, the leader of CRCM had recently succeeded in negotiating with the Vénissieux municipality for the construction of a mosque for the local Turkish community.

Moreover, several mosques around Lyon were monitored and shut down in the aftermath of September 11. For example, one of my informants, Mounir, was a 25-year old janitor and son of Algerian parents who lived in a housing project. [5] For years, Mounir and his father attended a small mosque in his housing project. The mosque was forcibly closed at the mayor's direction in 2004 with vague promises for the construction of a new mosque. His was one of several mosques in the banlieues that suffered a similar fate. Mounir would complain that the state is anxious for there to be only one or two major mosques that can be more easily surveilled. He complained, "The government just wants one grand mosque for the entire community of Lyon. They think it can be like a church". He pointed out that a local mosque is essential to Islamic practice, as it requires prayer fives times a day and not simply once a week.

Mounir complained further about a Tablighi prayer space in his banlieue that was obstructed. [6] It had been rented from a Catholic Church association, and when the Church's lease expired, the association wished to move forward and sell it to the Tablighi group. The mayor of Bron tried desperately to obstruct the purchase but eventually, legal assistance from the international Tablighi movement enabled the purchase to proceed. The obstruction of mosques occurs alongside general monitoring of Islamic organizations. Another informant, a volunteer at a well-known middle-class Islamic association and library in Lyon, recounted that the centre occasionally receives telephone calls from local law enforcement agencies for security enquiries. This context of 'securitization' has further pushed religious rights and recognition to the top of Muslim middle-class agendas.

Finally, there are other political and social activities, oriented around religious recognition. For example, groups such as EMF, a student group affiliated with l'UOIF, defend Muslim women university students, who wear the hijab, in cases of harassment or unequal treatment by professors. (The headscarf is permitted at the university level). Further, Muslim youth groups and mosque associations hold cultural activities such as picnics, musical events, and leadership training—all designed to sustain Islamic identity where it is otherwise a continual target of disdain.

Civil Societies among the Muslim Poor

While the Muslim middle-class in Hyderabad and Lyon engaged the state on the terrain of either redistribution or recognition, I found that the poor in both cases rejected all possibilities for politics, finding them both profane and dangerous. This rejection is supported by their Islamic discourse, which emphasized salvation over worldly progress or material life, as well as their tense relationship with the state. In Hyderabad, state retrenchment especially in the realm of education, in addition to police harassment and arrests of Muslim youth in Old City neighbourhoods, has created intense mistrust of state engagement. Police patrol around central mosques in the Old City during politically charged moments (such as the controversy over the Danish publication of cartoons depicting the Prophet Muhammed) or during Friday prayers has become common.

During my research, I was continually struck by the number of poor Muslims who would immediately, defensively, tell me: "I have nothing to do with politics". Aside from the effects of surveillance, there was also the common mantra I heard from numerous poor informants that further led them to an anti-politics stance: "government doesn't do anything". At the same time, poor Muslims vote in high percentages, although I was told that many are coerced into voting for the MIM party. Although my informants viewed all politics as corrupt, many supported the MIM because, they claimed, it was better to have some representation as opposed to none.

Similarly, in Les Minguettes, outside of Lyon, three major security incidents had left residents jaded and mistrustful of any interaction with state agents. The French arrests of two young men who were sent to the Guantanamo prison camp occurred in Les Minguettes. (They were returned to France in 2004 and 2005, convicted in 2007 of criminal association, and released on appeal in 2009). There were the arrests of several family members who ran a housing project mosque. Their apartment was raided as they were accused of having ties to Chechen militants. Their mosque, which I attended during the fieldwork, was left unorganized and stained by its ill-repute.

Finally, Abdelkader Bouziane, the former imam of Mosquée Hasan, was deported in 2004 for posing a threat to public order. This occurred after the publication of an interview with him by a city-based magazine in Lyon in which he discussed the right of men to hit their wives ("only below the face") in cases of adultery. Notwithstanding Bouziane's problematic views, the magazine article was without context, and his remarks were made mostly at the journalist's prodding. But it caused an outcry throughout the country, and Bouziane was expelled from France after having lived there for 25 years. According to Ahmed, a former long-time Muslim activist in the neighbourhood, "the whole community felt scared and demoralized".

While the Muslim poor in Hyderabad and Lyon thus share a rejection of politics and state engagement, at the level of civil society they have undergone inverse phenomenon: Hyderabad has seen the creation of Islamic civil societies, while Lyon's banlieues have experienced a severe retreat and collapse of Islamic as well as secular associations. The collapse of civil society in the French case, according to my informants, was due precisely to the state's surveillance and devouring of associations in the banlieues, post-9/11.

In the 1980s and 1990s, under Mitterand's socialist administration, Les Minguettes in fact enjoyed a period of intense social activism and flourishing civic associations. This included Islamic associations as well as projects initiated by secular associations such as SOS-Racisme and DiverCité, active on behalf of immigrant rights. France's first and largest national demonstration for immigrant and racial justice was in fact initiated in Les Minguettes in 1983. The "marche des beurs", as it was called by reporters, followed a series of riots in the neighbourhood after a local teenager was injured by a policeman. Although few recall this event today, the name Les Minguettes continues to be attached to the memory of 1983. "There was so much hope back then", recalled Ahmed. "Today, it's all gone. There's nothing".

Ahmed's popular Islamic youth association in Vénissieux had once hosted weekly activities including family events, scholarly tutoring, youth clubs/sports and after-school activities, and training in debate and public speaking.

According to Ahmed, as local youth began feeling politically empowered, their presence appeared more threatening to André Gerin, the then mayor of Vénissieux. In the aftermath of 9/11, this network of Muslim activists was attacked by the state and placed under surveillance, eventually leading to their decline. Ahmed, like a number of former activists, was blacklisted throughout Lyon as a fundamentalist and potential terrorist. His defence of the two brothers who were sent to Guantanamo led to greater notoriety for him and a public confrontation with Mayor Gerin in which other Muslims were pitted against him. His association collapsed and today, said Ahmed, "I have a family now, kids to support. I can't put my family at risk. For all of us, it became too hard to find work or even have respect. And I'm tired. I can't do it anymore". He mused:

"What did we want when we were younger? To get out of the banlieue...to be *le bon francais, avec la bonne baguette* [a respectable Frenchman with a baguette under his arm]. Now, there are exactly two structures left in Minguettes: the drug dealers and the mosques. And the mosque leaders are totally incompetent and uneducated. They don't have the means to be politically active or organized".

Ahmed's particular trajectory reflects the decline of Les Minguettes, its structures of civil society and the hopes that bonded together Islamic (as well as secular) associations. It also shows the precise mechanisms by which the state itself demoralized and broke apart networks of youth and Muslim leaders, leaving only a drug market and unorganized mosques in their wake. Today, wandering around Les Minguettes, one immediately senses this collapse of civil society, the lack of social space and relative sterility of the neighbourhood of housing projects.

The state's regulation of mosques and Muslim activists also coincided with the banning of the headscarf in schools and a growing discourse about the oppression of Muslim women. Conversations in mosques or covering one's hair were no longer considered private matters. The most recent step in eroding Islamic civil society has been attacking the burqa and more generally, Salafist Islam, with which it is associated. This did not come as a surprise to any of my informants. Soon after the commission on the *burqa* was announced, a local bank in Les Minguettes put up a sign with an image of a woman in *niqab* with an 'X' crossed through it. In light of the 2004 banning of the headscarf, Sara, a close informant who wore the niqab, stated: "It's starting again".

Sara and many other Salafist women, whose movement has grown significantly in Les Minguettes, have created a moral community anchored in neighbourhood mosques. Although from one perspective this may be considered the creation of a civil society, I argue that these mosque communities are not promoting a collective identity but rather, a very private and individualized relationship with God. Moreover, a fundamental mistrust tends to permeate their sessions.

For example, when I was doing my research at Mosquée Hasan in Les Minguettes, several people outside the mosque community told me with no doubt that there were state agents who attended the women's classes on a regular basis. I was initially incredulous that there was a spy among the group of Salafist women that I was coming to know. Eventually, when I saw the degree of privacy that each woman sought to maintain, it no longer seemed so outrageous. No matter how much we came to know and like each other, nobody ever really knew the private details of each other's lives. There was always an element of uncertainty and mistrust. For these reasons, I argue that it is problematic to view these mosque gatherings as the creation of civil societies. Nonetheless, Salafist discourse and gendered practices have grown in Lyon's poor peripheries.

In Hyderabad, the opposite scenario is taking place in poor Muslim neighbourhoods. The presence of philanthropic projects and further, the effects of labour remittances from Saudi Arabia and Gulf countries, have facilitated the building up of Islamic civil society institutions. Labor migration from

Hyderabad to the Gulf has a long history but has increased significantly in the last fifteen years. Hyderabad is second only to the state of Kerala with regard to sending migrant workers to Gulf countries. Poor men, and sometimes women, secure temporary contracts to work in numerous service and manual labour industries.

Although both Hindus and Muslims work in the Gulf, there seems to be a disproportionate number of Muslim migrants. I was told stories of Hindus in fact pretending to be Muslims and changing their names so as to secure a contract. Workers send remittances or bring back savings, and often they donate to local mosques and madrasas—a crucial intervention given the state retrenchment from public education. Many of the mosques in the First Lancer slum neighbourhood that I frequented were constructed in the last two decades and have benefited immensely from Gulf remittances and donations from Arab relatives or visitors. In the Old City, the neighbourhood of Babanagar now sports the nickname, "Little Dubai".

In the context of surveillance and retrenchment I discussed, the ethos that defines the city's Muslim population revolves around the notion of a Muslim community and responsibility. The idea that the larger Muslim community has a responsibility to preserve Islamic institutions and support Muslim welfare arises in numerous diverse and random settings. Walking into a small photography studio in First Lancer, I spot a bumper sticker on the wall: "To help Jamia Nizamia is the foremost duty of Muslims". Jamia Nizamia is India's second largest Islamic university, training hundreds of men to be Islamic teachers and leaders each year.

Neighbourhood mosques are critical in asserting this notion of responsibility. All throughout the city, small mosques in Muslim enclaves amplify their announcements. The liberty with which they do so is somewhat unique to Hyderabad. Although amplification is outlawed in the city, there is a mutual understanding between the police and

Muslim neighbourhoods that the law will not be enforced. I was told by a member of the MIM political party that this was in exchange for allowing the makeshift Hindu temple that was illegally constructed at the floor of the Charminar, the city's central monument built under Muslim rule. Given this arrangement, mosques are able to make their presence even more public than might otherwise be the case. Announcements from the mosques in First Lancer would blare through the loudspeakers everyday. Many of these were requests, or imperatives, to give money or provide physical assistance for a Muslim family.

Typically, these were burial or wedding expenses. Obligations toward wedding expenses are also customary and reinforced by mosques, again by announcements and collection efforts. Donating to the neighbourhood mosque is a part of this obligation, especially when funds go toward local charity projects and poor families. Thus, leaders make weekly or bi-weekly announcements requesting funds for infrastructural projects and other necessities. When an announcement and speech was made at one of First Lancer's mosques requesting infrastructural repair for a madrasa and future welfare centre, a number of people volunteered to do the work and construction, and this is how it was later completed.

There has also been a growing trend in which poor mosques are instituting women's training centres, specifically in textile skills. Poor neighbourhood mosques are accomplishing this on their own, while in other cases philanthropical organizations are starting these programs in Muslim neighbourhoods. Whether in these textile training centres or junior high schools started by philanthropists, women and girls are increasingly participating, learning, and excelling, alongside engaging Islamic discourse. They are given the chance to earn income upon "graduating", and perhaps more significantly, socialize and meet other women. These are generally modelled after government self-help schemes. Masjid Al-Iman, another mosque in First Lancer, has operated a women's "stitching centre" for several years. Approximately, fifty poor women attend everyday to learn tailoring and embroidery skills from two teachers. None of the women attended the equivalent of high school, and many cannot read or write. In their own unfortunate words, they are "useless".

But as a part of the training curricula, they are taught basic Urdu/Arabic literacy, and some Quranic reading and explication. One of the ideas behind this phenomenon is to create opportunities for poor Muslim women to work without having to go outside and "clean other people's homes". Many are able to perform paid textile work from home. According to my informants, this fits with the desire for gender segregation as well as avoiding the indignities of domestic labour, especially where this would entail Muslim women working for Hindu families. Additionally, women in these centres receive some Islamic education. Anwar, a local leader in First Lancer, was wishing to institute a women's tailoring centre through his mosque. He viewed it as a chance to impart Islamic learning and discipline.

He was unwittingly, almost amusingly, frank in his motivation: "Once the women are gathered for some purpose, since we are associated with the madrasa, we can impose one hour to learn, to learn what is Islam, the rules of prayer, rules of fasting, how to cover their face. That can be imposed when you're dominating. When we're teaching them free of cost, then they're in my domination. Because I'm principal of the madrasa, I can implement my rules. Muslims are soft-hearted. If I tell someone 'you have to spend one hour learning the Quran', they'll never say no. But it's too difficult for them to come out just for the sake of the Quran. To pull them out [of their homes] in the name of this world is easy. People always look for materialistic benefits".

As this quote shows, intertwined with the goal of redistribution and charity is also a community disciplining toward greater Islamic practice and rigor.

Poor women's groups are often at the forefront of this movement and creation of collective identity centred in Islamic discourse. For example, the women's wing of Jama'at-I-Islami Hind (JIH) is the most well-known and active of these. [7] It has numerous Islamic campaigns, Quranic classes, women's textile training centres, primary school projects for girls, and scheduled "inspections" of girls' madrasas. I attended a state-wide conference, assisted by Students' Islamic Organization (SIO) and JIH and attended by 40,000 poor women. The speeches were impassioned and strove to create a sense of collective responsibility. The regional director gave a fiery opening address: "My sisters! We have to struggle to keep Sharia and Sunnath [the way of the Prophet] near to us. It is *your* responsibility to push evil away from you.

Today, Islam has many enemies and those who want to oppress it and give it a bad reputation...my sisters, together we can stop this storm"! The conference included numerous stalls and banners promoting sex segregation and women's veiling. One large banner stated: *We use purdah to cover our bodies, not our minds.* It had a picture of a woman in *niqab*, next to an office chair, a computer, and a group of surgeons around an operating table. It conveyed the common message that Muslim women can be equally educated and participate in professional fields, so long as they wear the *niqab.* In sum, women's groups, Islamic associations, as well as hundreds of poor mosques and *madrasas* have built up a network of civil societies that combines redistributive projects with the enforcement of collective responsibility and identity and an Islamic discourse that emphasizes gendered practices.

Divergent Class Relations: Paternalism versus Disconnect

What is the relationship of the Muslim middle-class in each case to these trends and religious practices among their poor brethren? In both cases, a form of Salafist Islam has spread among the poor, most visibly in the form of women's wearing of the burqa, men's vesture and beards, as well as strict sex segregation. And in both cases there was strong middle-class disdain for these practices. While in Lyon this was explicitly discussed in terms of a mainstream versus Salafist divide, in Hyderabad, it was viewed as an unfortunate and influence of Saudi Islam.

Hyderabad's middle-class and elite Muslim philanthropists I came to know were avowedly secular and despised what they viewed as lack of integration and extreme forms of practice. "Backwards", "ignorant", and "allergy-inducing" are a few of the words I heard to refer to the Islam of poor Muslims, especially in the Old City. These practices, much like those in Les Minguettes, include strict women's veiling, beards and caps for men, and a salvation discourse that discounted the importance of material, worldly progress.

This disdain, however, was channelled into an overall paternalism, marked by efforts to change the beliefs and behaviour of poor Muslims. This was evident in many different settings. Mr. Husseini, a prominent philanthropist in the field of education, was very vocal in critiquing practices like the hijab and certain beliefs that he believed were barriers to community progress. He says to his students who wear an Islamic cap, "you shouldn't wear this. You don't look like a student". "I don't want to make religion an institution. Religion should stay in the heart". During a visit to one of Mr. Husseini's middle schools in a poor Muslim neighbourhood in the Old City, I noted posters all over the walls outlining different scientific processes from the pulmonary system to nuclear fission—the secular orientation of the school was clear. Prayer and Arabic education are optional. Mr. Husseini stopped to make conversation with a big group of adolescent students. "What do you want to do when you graduate"? he asked. "Doctor"! one student shouted out. "Teacher"! said another. "What about an advocate [lawyer]"? asked Mr. Husseini. "This is against Islam", one girl interjected. He quickly tried to convince her otherwise. "Anyway, who can Muslims turn to when they are in trouble? We have to have advocates to defend us".

In Babanagar, one of the poorest sections of the Old City, there is a women's centre and primary school started by Mr. Haq, a prominent local philanthropist. The principal, Madame Rabia, was a young educated woman, raised in the New City and hired by Mr. Haq's foundation board. At the staff meeting one morning, the teachers (from the Old City) for the Islamic and Arabic classes had raised the issue of Madame Rabia's not wearing the hijab. Ideally, she would wear the *niqab*, according to them. She was a petite woman who instead wore a sari everyday and kept her long dark hair uncovered and in braids. In this, she was the one exception to all of the women who had any role at the centre. The particular teachers, all men, had apparently campaigned around the Babanagar neighbourhood defaming Madame Rabia and telling parents that she was "un-Islamic". They also criticized her programs, such as celebrating students' birthdays and always speaking in English with them.

As a result some parents started to complain and rejected her authority. Kulsoom, a member of the philanthropical foundation, assured her, "Don't worry. They won't get their way. Mr. Haq is on your side and will fire them [the teachers] if we need to. They're ignorant. They don't understand Islam. They don't realize that wearing the hijab is an extremely personal decision, and no one's supposed to tell us how or when to do it". Madame Rabia insisted, "I always wear the whole burqa when I go to Charminar [Old City centre]. But my parents and in-laws were modern—they always encouraged me to work, learn English, have a life". Kulsoom eventually left the office, and Madame Rabia said to me: "You see, after all, these teachers are so backwards, so ignorant [jahil]. They have no idea that these kids need to know English, learn science, or they'll never get jobs. This is why Hindus will always be better off than us. The Old City will always remain poor, as long as they keep this mentality about religion. They will only eat rice and sleep and read the Quran—and this is why Muslims will always be backwards"!

As this incident demonstrates, there is a clear struggle occurring between poor—and gendered—Islamic practice and middle-class "mainstream and secular" beliefs and practice. But ultimately, the powerful role that philanthropists play renders their practice and ideology hegemonic. The relationship between the classes is simultaneously hegemonic, in an ideological sense, and paternalistic. Distributing charity remains the crux of the relationship. Mr. Haq, for example, was himself orphaned at a young age and raised in the Old City. While he immigrated to the US and became wealthy, he said he was "haunted" by memories of children in the Old City. The first time I visited the Babanagar centre, there was a welcome reception that the students and women planned for Mr. Haq and the Board members. The Board members sat and listened as several girls took to a microphone and recited poems, songs, and prayers. "Mr. Haq, may God keep blessing you and your family with life and health. You care about us poor people, you are giving us the chance to earn respect, to be useful". The members then handed out Ramadan presents to the students and gifts for the teachers.

Although there is a real sense of paternalistic affection in Hyderabad, there is at the same time an intensely competitive political field in which Muslim leaders compete on the terrain of distribution. Elite philanthropists find themselves in competition with the local MIM party for legitimacy among the masses of poor Muslims. This sometimes turns violent, as the MIM is accused of violent harassment of local philanthropists. The latter, in turn, encourage their "constituents" to hold the MIM accountable for local conditions, such as education and sanitation. I attended an inaugural ceremony for a women's textile training centre in First Lancer for which about one hundred residents of the slum community patiently awaited the arrival of Mr. Haq.

Following the opening prayers, they listened to the politically charged and impassioned speeches by members of Mr. Haq's philanthropical board. "We Muslims must never be dependent on anyone and *must* learn to stand on our own! We mustn't be drawn into petty squabbles, as I have always tried to avoid. I am only doing what God wants me to do". Another member announced the possibility of establishing a local college in this neighbourhood and reminded the listeners, "You have political [MIM] representatives based right here. You must hold them accountable"! Indeed, aside from public rhetoric, middle-class activists and teachers assist poor students and women to apply for welfare benefits such as food subsidies and grants for the purchase of sewing machines and other items. In doing so, I argue they encourage a form of political participation among the poor.

In the case of Lyon, this form of class relations was essentially absent. Lyon's middle-class mosque community that I knew also held disdain for Salafist Islamic practice among the poor, accusing them of superficiality. But there was little interaction between "Islam of the banlieues" and the mainstream Islam practiced by the middle-class. Islam in this case is deeply bifurcated. Jameel, a young and prominent activist in Lyon's middle-class Muslim community, argues that Salafist practice is spreading in the banlieues because it is "easy and superficial" and does not require much thought or wisdom. Jameel went as far as to say that he hardly considers Salafists real Muslims, as they busy themselves only with bodily positions and vesture. He also argued that the practice of the niqab was a grave misinterpretation of Islam. However, during my research at the mosque in Les Minguettes, I found that the teachings of Salafist women were far from superficial and were largely oriented toward patience (*sabr*) in the face of suffering and how to find happiness in a life defined intrinsically by suffering (*la vie musibah*). This focus on life's temporality and the fact of suffering was unique to the Salafist community in the poorer mosques and was common also to the poor in Hyderabad.

Another common contention with Salafist Muslims was their relative isolation and refusal to politically engage the state or wider French society. Nadia, a 30-year old woman of Algerian origin, active in Lyon's mosque communities, found Muslim isolation in the banlieues very troubling: "They don't care about the future of Islam in France. They just turn their backs and then make their wives stay inside". According to Maryam, also a dedicated activist in one of the city's mosque communities, "[Salafists] don't see themselves as French. They don't call themselves French. Before turning to Islam, they faced a lot of discrimination, at work, in school, and so they don't feel French. But it takes strength of character, a certain maturity, to be able to say 'you can close your door on me, but I will struggle so that you understand me and understand that I *am* French". Indeed, the Salafist Muslims I knew in Les Minguettes hardly identified as French. When I first met Amira, who wears the niqab and is a young woman of Algerian parents, I mentioned I was staying in Lyon proper. "Lyon?" she questioned. "You can't find a good mosque there. They're all French, *real French*"!

But unlike the situation in Hyderabad, there exists neither the type of wealth, political competition, nor culture of paternalism among Lyon's Muslims. While there is certainly competition for prestige and power between the major middle-class and state-appointed associations, it is not clear what is at stake; moreover, it does not entail a redistributive component. [8] As discussed earlier, this was not necessarily the case in the 1980s and 1990s. Indeed, there was a sense of regret among middle-class activists over the isolation and virtual abandonment of the banlieues. L'UOIF, the country's largest Islamic organization and highly active in most cities, no longer has active programs in Lyon's housing projects and poor neighbourhoods. Although it prides itself on its many achievements on behalf of Islamic institutions, youth programs, and political engagements, it is surprisingly absent from the neighbourhoods of housing projects.

Ali, a prominent and long-time activist on behalf of Muslims in the banlieues, criticized his fellow middle-class

Muslims as pliable and ready to betray themselves to the state. "We call this new class of 'beurgeoisie' Muslims 'bobarts'. They don't care about the poor but just want to make money for themselves, even though making sure everyone has food in their stomachs is the foremost duty of all Muslims". Jameel, and others in this activist circle, also regretted the "growing individualism" within the Muslim community. According to Ali, organizations like l'UOIF simply have not prioritized the status of poor Muslims and the rampant unemployment that plagues them. He was angry with l'UOIF for its denunciation of the 2005 urban riots, calling this a striking example of the organizations' disconnect from the banlieues. CFCM also remains focused on Islamic institutions and ease of worship rather than socio-economic issues.

Even secular associations, like the well-known DiverCité, have very little presence in the banlieues. DiverCité is a national association created to draw attention to poor neighbourhoods (*quartiers*), to support legal and illegal immigrants, and combat racism. It is most active in Paris but also has regional groups. Ali, Jameel, and Khalil all worked with DiverCité, and they reluctantly admitted that the group no longer has projects in Lyon's banlieues. Its work revolves primarily around conferences and spreading awareness through the media. Debates over Islam appeared central to the internal confusion that has weakened DiverCité's trajectory. After a period of strong membership and activism in the banlieues in the 1990s, ideological differences within the association have unravelled its cohesion. DiverCité's weakening in the quartiers has coincided with the growth of Salafist practice.

At a two-day meeting of DiverCité in Lyon, the long debates between members made clear to me that the group is struggling with issues of reaching out to banlieue residents. During one meeting, Ali was very vocal and passionate as he spoke several times about his concerns. DiverCité has tried to form coalitions with other groups, such as feminist associations—Ali argued that these associations have made many offensive comments regarding the veil and were suffering from "Islamophobia". He also stated his concern that DiverCité was becoming too elitist.

One woman spoke at length about the need for DiverCité to create its own agenda apart from other associations and to be open about the veil—but she suddenly followed this sentiment by stating that she did not want "Maghrebin" (from the Maghreb), "intégriste" (fundamentalist), "Musulman" (Muslim) men to threaten the agenda of the group or make women feel uncomfortable. Ali in turn passionately reacted to this depiction and stereotype to point to it as an example of exactly what he found problematic with the group. The meeting was imbued with such vexed conversations in effect about DiverCité's abilities to represent the working-class in light of the salience of religious (and ethnic) identity. It ended with a somewhat hollow round of expressing hope for the future and excitement towards future organizational events.

Khalil, who was once active alongside Ali and had worked with DiverCité, decided to forego his activism due to his disillusion and failed efforts to ameliorate conditions in the banlieues. "Three generations of Muslims tried and failed to better their conditions, and now things are worse than ever. And there's a logical turn to Salafism". Khalil's father was a construction worker and immigrant from Tunisia. He faced multiple forms of discrimination and racial violence, which led to the murder of his elder brother and a gunshot wound to Khalil's chest in a separate incident. He gradually "gave up on France" and his hope for bettering Muslim conditions. He still feels angry, he said, when he goes to the store and people rudely stare at him and his wife, who wears the hijab.

Recently, he moved to Egypt out of desire to live in a Muslim country. "There's a saying in French", Khalil said. "We say, '*we accepted the contract*'. I did everything you asked me to do, I ate pork, I almost married a white woman, I left my religion, I did *everything* you wanted—and got nothing in return". If France refuses to recognize and respect the prevalence of Islam, according to Khalil, conditions for Muslims, specifically in the banlieues, will never change. "If you want to understand me, why I do the things I do, why I think the way I think, then you have to understand my faith." Now, he says, "The only thing we can do to possibly change our course is prayer".

In sum, Lyon's poor neighbourhoods have been disconnected from the middle-class politics of Islam and from the secular, radical social activism that helped define Les Minguettes in the 1980s and 1990s. Social programs that existed during those decades, managed either by Islamic associations or groups like DiverCité, are now largely absent. Efforts to engage unemployed youth have proven too difficult from both the middle-class religious and secular angles. It is in this context that Salafist 'preachers' and those espousing disengagement from the state have captured greater attention in Les Minguettes.

Conclusion

This paper was an exploration of the role of social class in the politics of Islam and the forms of Islamic discourse and practice that have grown in these two case studies of minority Islam. Existing literature has largely focused on the role of globalization and the need for minority Muslims in secular states to redefine their identities. From this dynamic, comes the tension over how to best "accommodate" Islam, especially as there is a growth in Salafist or Wahhabi practices among the poor. Instead of turning to theories of identity and globalization, I argued that the relationship between middle-class and poor Muslims is a key to understanding trends in Islamic practice and the degree to which minority demands are either channelled or suppressed. The nature of these class relations in turn depends on local political-economic histories, state policies, as well as national models of secularism.

While the Muslim middle-classes in Hyderabad and Lyon engage the state, respectively, in a politics of redistribution or recognition, the poor in both cases are especially alienated from the state and marginalized. However, the Muslim poor in Hyderabad are building a network of Islamic civil society institutions, typically intertwined with elite philanthropy. Muslim philanthropists facilitate the creation of independent civil societies, while at the same time exerting ideological disciplining among the poor and questioning practices such as the burqa. In Lyon's urban peripheries, in contrast, poor Muslims practice Islam and attend their mosques in the aftermath of the collapse of civil societies and the advent of great state surveillance of their institutions. They remain estranged and isolated from the network of middle-class mosque communities and activists. In sum, although questions of identity in rapidly changing secular societies are indeed salient for Muslim communities in both cases, the practice and politics of Islam, I argue, are more deeply rooted in state policies and class relations.

Endnotes

1. The Salafist movement, increasingly prominent in poor minority Muslim neighbourhoods, is based on the desire to emulate the Prophet Muhammed and follow the teachings of the earliest generations of Muslims. Historically, the Salafist movement refers to a reform movement within Sunni Islam to return to the original teachings and practices of the Prophet Muhammed and the Quran. Its origins as a movement are debated, with some citing 18th century Arabians and others citing 19th century intellectuals in Egypt. It is also internally debated as to which Islamic groups, schools of thought, and practices, may be considered Salafist. Salafism has historically been a pietist and apolitical movement, after some involvement in state politics in the late 19th and early 20th centuries (Stemmann, 2006). See, Hourani (1983) and Euben and Zaman (2009). The types of practices that have become more prevalent among the poor are similar in Lyon and Hyderabad, although in Hyderabad, they are more commonly referred to as part of the Ehle Hadith movement instead of Salafist.
2. The term "burqa" is commonly employed by Indian Muslims but is not employed by those in the French Muslim community who

are familiar with women's veiling practices. The word is currently used in France to refer to either the full body covering including the face, except the eyes, or a mesh-fabric covering over the eyes. These are the specific practices that were debated in the French Assembly. Among adherents, they are referred to as a "niqab" or "sitar" (which covers the eyes). Most of the women in France among whom I conducted fieldwork wore the "djelbab", which refers to a long hair and body covering that leaves the face exposed. Some of them also wore the niqab. In India, most of the Muslim women whom I researched wore a niqab. In this paper, I switch back and forth between the terms. There is little distinction made in political and popular debates between these practices.

3. The term "banlieue" refers to the suburban peripheries of France's urban centres. For an analysis of the socio-political construction of the 'problem of the banlieues' in France, see Tissot (2006). See Wacquant (2008) for an analysis of the differences between French banlieues and the American ghetto.
4. However, it maintains a greater degree of independence than the Grand Mosque of Paris, which is widely accused of being an arm of the state. For example, the rector of the Paris Mosque supported the national commission to discuss the possibility of banning the burqa.
5. All proper names have been changed to ensure anonymity.
6. Tablighi Jama'at, founded in India, is the largest transnational Islamic movement. It deliberately shuns engagement with the state in favour of missionary-style preaching (Metcalf, 2001).
7. JIH is a sub-Continental Islamic religious and political organization, formed in 1941. Despite episodes of hostile relations with the Indian state, its history has remained relatively stable. JIH had a women's wing from its inception, but it wasn't firmly established until the 1970s. See Grare (2001).
8. This is not to deny the charitable activities that major mosques in Lyon undertake, such as hospice visits and provision of free meals during Ramadan. However, these do not constitute the majority of their activities nor define their relationship to Muslims in the banlieues.

References

Amiraux, Valérie (2008), "De l'Empire à la République: à propos de 'l'Islam de France", *Cahiers de recherche sociologique*, 46: 45-60.

Assemblée Nationale (2009), "Mission d'information sur la pratique du port du voile intégral sur le territoire national", available at: http://www.assemblee-nationale.fr/13/cr-miburqa/08-09/index.asp.

Benhabib, Seyla (2002), "Unholy Wars", *Constellations*, Vol. 9, No. 1: 34-45.

Bowen, John (2006), "Why the French Don't Like Headscarves", Princeton: Princeton University Press.

Davis, Paul and Krauthammer, Daniel (2005), "Continental Clash: As Cultural Tensions Mount, Europe's Aging Population Must Deal with an Influx of Muslims", *Harvard Political Review*, 31(4): 14-15.

Euben, Roxanne L. and Zaman, Muhammad (2009), "Introduction in Princeton Readings in Islamist Thought: Texts and Contexts from al-Banna to Bin Laden", Princeton: Princeton University Press.

Gerholm, Tomas and Lithman, Yngve Georg (eds.) (1988), "The New Islamic Presence in Western Europe", London: Mansell Publishing Limited.

Grare, Frédéric (2001), "Political Islam in The Indian Subcontinent: The Jamaat-i-Islami", New Delhi: Manohar Publishers.

Hasan, Mushirul (1997), "Legacy of a Divided Nation: India's Muslims since Independence", Boulder, CO: Westview Press.

Hasan, Zoya (1998), "Quest for Power: Oppositional Movements and Post-Congress Politics in Uttar Pradesh", Delhi: Oxford University Press.

Hourani, Albert (1983), "Arabic Thought in the Liberal Age", Cambridge: Cambridge University Press.

Joppke, Christian (2009), "Veil: Mirror of Identity", Cambridge: Polity Press.

Kepel, Gilles (1997), "Allah in the West: Islamic Movements in America and Europe", Stanford: Stanford University Press.

Metcalf, Barbara (2001), "Traditionalist Islamic Activism: Deoband, Tablighis, and Talibs After September 11", Social Science Research Council, available at: http://www.ssrc.org/sept11/essays.

Mohammed, Ali (ed.) (2002), "Islam Encountering Globalization", London: Routledge.

Neilsen, Jørgen S. (1999), "Towards a European Islam", New York:

St. Martin's Press, Inc.

Roy, Olivier (2004), Globalized Islam: The Search for a New Ummah", New York: Columbia University Press.

—(2006), "Islam in Europe: Clash of Religions or Convergence of Religiosities"? in Krzysztof Michalski (ed.), 'Conditions of European Solidarity: Religion in the New Europe', Central European Press.

Salvatore, Armando (2007), "Authority in Question: Secularity, Republicanism, and 'Communautarisme' in the Emerging Euro-Islamic Public Sphere", *Theory, Culture and Society*, 24(2): 135-160.

Stemmann, Juan José Escobar (2006), "Middle East Salafism's Influence and Radicalization of Muslim Communities in Europe", *Middle East Review of International Affairs*, 10(3): 1-14.

Sunder Rajan, Rajeswari (2000), "Women between Community and State: Some Implications of the Uniform Civil Code Debates in India", *Social Text*, 18(4): 55-82.

Tibi, Bassam (1992), "Religious Fundamentalism and Ethnicity in the Crisis of the Nation-State in the Middle East: Superordinate Islamic and Pan-Arab Identities and Subordinate Ethnic and Sectarian Identities", Working Paper 5.4, International and Area Studies, University of California at Berkeley.

Tissot, Sylvie (2006), "Y a-t-il un 'Problème des Quartiers Sensibles'? Retour sur une catégorie d'action publique", *French Politics, Culture and Society*, 24(3): 42-57.

Wacquant, Loic (2008), "Urban Outcasts: A Comparative Sociology of Advanced Marginality", Cambridge: Polity Press.

Index

Index